Neither Bad Nor Mad

Forensic Focus 20

Neither Bad Nor Mad
The Competing Discourses of Psychiatry, Law and Politics
Deidre N. Greig

Jessica Kingsley Publishers
London and Philadelphia

The right of Deidre N. Greig to be identified as author of this work has been asserted by her in accordance with the Copyright, Designs and Patents Act 1998

First published in the United Kingdom in 2002
by Jessica Kingsley Publishers Ltd
116 Pentonville Road
London N1 9JB, England
and
325 Chestnut Street
Philadelphia, PA 19106, USA

www.jkp.com

Copyright © Deidre N. Greig

Library of Congress Cataloging in Publication Data
A CIP catalog record for this book is available from the Library of Congress

British Library Cataloguing in Publication Data
A CIP catalogue record for this book is available from the British Library

ISBN 1 84310 006 1

Printed and Bound in Great Britain by
Athenaeum Press, Gateshead, Tyne and Wear

For Alex

Raya, Kendra, Jarrod and Piertra

and in memory of Ngaio and Laurie

Contents

Acknowledgements

There have been many friends who have offered thoughtful criticism, for which I am most appreciative. In particular, I thank those who so generously undertook to read drafts or chapters: Irene Armstrong, John Dawes, Graham Fricke, Julian Gardner, Bill Glaser, Bill Lucas and Beth Wilson, all of whom made further suggestions. The occasional opportunities to share ideas with Leanne Craze have always been welcome, and her own substantial work on mentally disordered offenders in New South Wales remains a source of inspiration.

I owe a special debt of gratitude to Robert and Grace David, who were unfailingly helpful and cooperative in granting me access to their massive collection of documents obtained through a Freedom of Information request made after Garry's death. These materials were derived from a variety of sources: the Children's Welfare Department, the Children's Court, the Prisons and Youth Divisions of the Social Welfare Department, the Victoria Police, the Office of Corrections, the former Department of Community Welfare Services, and the Department of Health and Community Services. The reports accessed included some clinical assessments, documentation of prison incidents, court transcripts, police accounts, some classification summaries, movement listings, criminal history, management plans, some file notes and letters. Robert also made available the material on his brother's hard disk drive and approved the selection of poems from an extensive array of writings. Excerpts from the poems are reproduced with the kind permission of Robert David, who holds the copyright. Robyn Greensill and Sandra Neilson of Legal Aid Victoria were helpful with accessing many of the primary sources.

I also acknowledge the encouragement of Richard Gillespie and Warwick Anderson, who alerted me to various historical narratives and analyses of psychiatric issues, thereby encouraging the reshaping of a number of chapters in an interdisciplinary context.

As always, the errors and misinterpretations remain those of the author.

Author's Note

Whilst 'David' was Garry's preferred surname from approximately 1978 onwards, 'Webb' was that of his mother's de facto husband and frequently used in media reports. Throughout, I have followed the practice of referring to him as 'Garry David', or simply 'Garry' – the name used in many of the official files and documents.

Preface

*Let us pervert good sense and make thought play outside
the ordered category of resemblances.*

(Foucault 1997a, p.183)

Australia's penal history abounds with heroes, admired for their ability to tilt at authority figures and inspire incipient seeds of rebellion in the conforming majority. They are criminals, yet their legendary exploits are secretly applauded as a badge of courage and defiance in the face of seemingly insuperable odds. It is a symbolic celebration of the underdog; an expression of desire for an untrammelled freedom; a parody or inversion of the known order; an oblique criticism of the constraints with which we surround ourselves.

Madness confounds this vision. When the fluidity of madness is superimposed onto the notion of badness, it elicits an intuitive sense of fear among observers, because irrationality and unpredictability are now added to the volatility of the mix. There is a sharp reversal of judgment; a deep compounding of stigma: and the freewheeling spirit is doomed to extrusion.

Garry David entered this arena. In some respects he had the trappings of a hero, and he certainly sought to emulate this status by denouncing the heavy reprisals he attracted for his grandiose outbursts. His defiance was legendary, but suffused within the prison walls and destructively self-directed. He remained an enigma rather than the hero he craved to be, despite the justification he had to defy state authority in his later years. His death was a tragedy of his own making. So this is the story of an enigmatic person, who traversed an unstable professional terrain. In psychiatric terms he had a personality disorder and fell into that uncertain cleft separating criminality from insanity. The process of social ordering provoked an intense discourse between the law and psychiatry and succeeded in exposing the more sensitive areas of professional principles and knowledge. For the law, based as it is on notions of justice, the deprivation of liberty in the absence of a specific charge or evidence of mental illness is generally unsustainable. For psychiatry, there is a diversity of judgement about the appropriateness of civil commitment for the personality disordered, and the efficacy of being able to treat them. The ensuing struggle was about psychiatry's right to define its own knowledge boundaries and maintain an independence from the political will.

This narrative probes the intersecting points of a discourse pivotal to community beliefs about dangerousness, and exposes the non-rational aspects of society's need to expel those who possess a marked capacity to induce fear. It was a discourse, which gathered momentum – ultimately transcending the professional domain by tapping into the common-sense judgements of ordinary people, whose intuitive awareness and need for protection are as much a part of the Garry David story as are the attempts made by professionals to resolve myriad issues within their own frame of understanding.

The enigma of Garry David was that, unlike the heroes of the past, he remained peripheral, but was symbolically central to the enduring concerns of politicians, professionals and the public alike. At the time of attending Garry David's court hearings I was unaware that my interest would eventually culminate in the writing of this book. It gradually became apparent that the story required telling in a way consonant with the facts of the case and the struggle of those seeking a reasonable solution to quell community fears and promote the rehabilitation of a very disturbed individual. I really wanted to breathe life into this lengthy saga so absorbing of the time, skills and resources of senior bureaucrats and respected professionals in an experience many found to be intensely conflictual. Views about the subject varied from grudging admiration for some of his exploits to downright anger at the constant and flagrant manipulation. Although I have referred to Garry David in the text rather benignly as 'the master puppeteer', one psychologist recently told me of his resentment at having to deal with 'an emotional vandal'.

Whilst Garry David orchestrated many of the events, there were broader issues at stake in this story, especially the ethical and philosophical difficulties incurred by the practice of psychiatry in the courts and prisons. It would be hard to find a more salient example of the tenuousness of the line between criminality and mental illness – a problem undoubtedly to remain in the forefront of legal–psychiatric discourse. However even the use the term 'discourse', whilst convenient, is false if it is only intended to refer to some highly principled intellectual endeavour designed to arrive at truth within a given social space. This denies the ebb and flow of social influences, which have the power to alter outcomes. As this case attests, discourse is also about the choices made by individual professionals to define a problem in one way rather than another, a factor as much reflective of their personality and value systems as their background and training. For many of the issues raised, there were no right or wrong answers, simply different views about the way sanctions should be organised and the rationale for treatment of the distressed and non-conforming. Nonetheless the case became a source of angst for the way in which values were questioned, decisions disputed, and ethical dilemmas publicised, especially those pertaining to psychiatry's stance on psychopathy and dangerousness.

CHAPTER 1

Mad, Bad, and Dangerous to Know

Violence is not a politically neutral concept, it is entwined with the most
fundamental questions of state moral authority. (Ericson 1991, 233)

'That man is dangerous and should never be released.' With these words an experienced forensic psychiatrist with clinical responsibility for some of the most
fractious inmates in the gaols of the state of Victoria, Australia, pointed to a
seemingly docile and unassuming individual in the forensic section of the prison.
His observation was all the more surprising for another reason. Since the early
1980s psychiatrists had begun to distance themselves from expressing such
definite views about the future dangerousness of their clients, so these words raised
an intriguing question. What had convinced the psychiatrist to arrive at such an
explicit judgement about this one prisoner?

Further inquiry revealed that according to the scale of offenders this prisoner,
known as Garry David, was by no means the worst. In 1982 he had been convicted
of two counts of wounding with intent, one of shooting with intent and one each
of trespass and stealing a motor vehicle. Certainly the future did not augur well, for
he had been institutionalised since the age of five and had previously committed a
variety of offences – mostly car stealing, larceny and robberies. In personal terms
he presented as being articulate and cooperative, yet his years of confinement had
been marked by episodes of bizarre self-mutilation, aggression and chilling threats
to staff and the community at large. In short he could be described as a difficult, but
scarcely atypical, offender.

The recurring diagnosis in the files was that Garry David had a severe personality disorder. However this is not unusual in the general prison population. A significant proportion of prisoners comes within this category and self-mutilation is
not uncommon, often being a contagious response to an institutional environment.
The state of Victoria's Office of Corrections indicated that in one of the years of
Garry's imprisonment there were 115 separate incidents of self-mutilation and
attempted suicide involving 90 different Victorian prisoners, or about 4 per cent of
the prison population. Those with 'severe' personality disorder were estimated as
being between 20% and 25%, whilst 50% were regarded as having 'some degree'
of antisocial personality disorder. Currently this matter is being vigorously
debated in England with one media report claiming that 2000 to 5000 individuals
suffer from 'dangerous personality disorders' (*Daily Mail*, 27 July 1999).

Most of those with a demonstrable history of threats and violence, both in their criminal careers and within the prison system, can anticipate being released at the end of their sentence, admittedly with some community trepidation, but without the turmoil and debate so manifestly evident in this case. This prisoner's notoriety was further enhanced when cabinet ministers repeatedly referred to him as being *the* most dangerous person in the state and promised a fearful public in the state of Victoria that protective steps would be taken to ensure his continued custody. In this way, the government prepared the stage by launching a process leading to a series of complex, interlocking manoeuvres intended to achieve its stated objective of preventive detention. At the outset senior Ministers canvassed possible options presented by the criminal justice and mental health systems before enacting singular legislation, which would deflect responsibility for the final decision about Garry David's confinement to the Supreme Court, thereby distancing the Government itself from involvement in the proceedings.

The Garry David case became a cause célèbre both in terms of the cost and variety of associated court and tribunal hearings and the level of public debate it aroused. In a stark and personified way it focused on some of the historically unresolved issues confounding the medico-legal interaction, and it drew attention to the Government's willingness to intervene in areas of professional decision making. Admittedly there was general agreement amongst all concerned that Garry's behaviour in the prison system had been particularly challenging over many years, but this could scarcely justify detention beyond his release date in the absence of clear evidence of either criminality or mental illness. The benefit of resorting to special legislation lay in its appearance of overarching these two categories with a special hybrid one of 'dangerousness'. Whilst the title of the consequent Community Protection Act 1990 was broad in scope and therefore apolitical, the reality was very different, for this Act encompassed only the danger perceived to be intrinsic to the personality and behaviour of one named person. There was a patent irony in this legislative solution. Initially the state had placed Garry in an institution to protect *him*, but now the rhetoric had changed; it was his incarceration that was being required to protect the community *from him*. It was a risky step for any government to pursue. There is a fine line between preying on a community's sense of fear with the promise of protective action and that of creating a groundswell of sympathy for the perceived victim of an arbitrary exercise of political power.

The central themes anchoring the discourse between psychiatry, the law and politics in this case were those of *dangerousness* and *personality disorder*. In the interweaving of the events to follow, the questions were deceptively simple. *Was Garry David a danger to society, and did personality disorder constitute a mental illness?* Each had to be answered in a way compatible with psychiatric views, legal forms of analysis, community understandings, and in an atmosphere of political expectation. It was like throwing a stone into a millpond; the ever-widening ripples exposed dilemmas such as the duty of care in a forensic setting; diagnostic uncertainties; debates about treatment; political responsibilities; and the difficulties of translating clinical concepts into an acceptable legal format. Thus what might have remained within the realm of a recurrent internal border dispute between mental illness and personality disorder became subject to political intervention, lay opinions and contention about the direction of mental health policy. Many voices and many different understandings surfaced about where badness ends and where madness begins, but it was the ambiguous nature of the boundary and the inadvisability of governments meddling in areas of professional decision making which were strikingly documented in the accompanying discourses.

DANGEROUSNESS

The coalescence of the words 'mad, bad, and dangerous to know', so famously used by Lady Caroline Lamb about her first meeting with Lord Byron (quoted in Cecil 1939, p.85), conveys the disquiet attaching to behaviour perceived as being vaguely menacing and puzzling in its motivating force. Historically, dangerousness has always acted as a powerful metaphor to establish society's boundaries and justify the expulsion of those who do not appear to conform; and it is often reinforced by visual images, the most notable being the legendary Ship of Fools of mediaeval fame. In the Middle Ages, generalised fears were targeted at witches in wide-ranging accusations about their unnatural and evil exploits. The symbolic link between dangerousness and expulsion was reaffirmed later by its application to disparate groups, including vagabonds, lepers, the mentally ill, vagrants and the dissolute. Gradually, however, the need for differentiation grew and it was the newly recognised behavioural 'experts' who were allocated this task.

During the latter part of the nineteenth century, psychiatrists and psychologists became the holders of special knowledge about 'dangerous persons' and developed a number of explanatory models with quite diverse bases and a degree of slippage between madness and badness. One influential accounting schema, which came into vogue at the end of the nineteenth century, stemmed from the work of the Italian doctor, Cesare Lombroso (1913), who located the cause of crime as being innate to the individual and due to biological degeneration. His horrifying descriptions of ape-like stigmata provided the physical cues to identify such people, but at the same time reinforced a sense of helplessness about their inherently evil and irredeemable nature. This pioneering empirical study, with its detailed measurements of felons in an Italian prison, combined science and visual representation in the delineation of those with the seemingly undeniable quality of dangerousness. The presumed existence of such a criminal type had the advantage of crystallising a whole series of folk beliefs and imbuing them with scientific status. (See also Pick 1989 for a sophisticated analysis of the links between Lombroso's positivism, preventive detention, dangerousness, and the political landscape.) This transition from social exclusion, based on an undifferentiated fear of both the criminal and the madman, to the development of a 'scientific' mode of understanding and control has been graphically portrayed by the French philosopher and sociologist, Michel Foucault, in his exploration of the meaning, which dangerousness holds for both the law and psychiatry:

> The criminal designated as the enemy of all, whom it is in the interest of all to track down, falls outside the pact, disqualifies himself as a citizen and emerges, bearing within him as it were, a wild fragment of nature; he appears as a villain, a monster, a madman, perhaps, a sick and, before long, 'abnormal' individual. It is as such that, one day, he will belong to a scientific objectification and to the 'treatment' that is correlative to it... The power relation that underlies the exercise of punishment begins to be duplicated by an object relation in which are caught up not only the crime as a fact to be established according to common norms, but the criminal as an individual to be known according to specific criteria. (Foucault 1977b, pp.101–2)

In effect, the law gradually extended its ambit beyond an interest in the factual elements of the offence. In those circumstances defying rational explanation it sought an understanding of the personality and motivation of the offender, thereby gradually encouraging particular categories of dangerous persons to be devised on the basis of medical opinion. It was an important shift, transforming 'the power to punish' into one requiring an expert technology. In the first half of the twentieth century the emphasis on social defence strategies served to conflate penal and medical interests. The term 'dangerousness' began to gain a currency denied to 'madness' – that is, it inferred a specific quality, which could be readily appropriated to expel undesirable groups of people under the benign rubric of treatment, in order to protect society. The vulnerable were the mentally deficient, whose presumed dangerousness attracted either a eugenic response or prolonged incarceration (Watson 1994); habitual offenders and frequent sexual offenders referred to as sexual *psychopaths* or, in the current terminology, sexual *predators*.

The unwitting consequence was that moral elements of disapproval or rejection were barely disguised by this new knowledge, which largely went unquestioned in the legislation accompanying the identification of such undesirables. Medical expertise within the law was nonetheless enhanced and reconstituted as a legal justification for draconian outcomes. For instance, the formal category of psychopathy, based on immoral and criminal behaviour, could suffice for the indefinite confinement of those deemed to be dangerous persons and in some cases even lead to the death penalty, which is the ultimate form of social banishment. As Foucault further explains, this tenuous medical and legal knowledge embraced the misfits of society in a very compelling manner:

> In the course of the past century, penal law did not evolve from an ethic of freedom to a science of psychic determinism; rather, it enlarged, organized, and codified the suspicion and the locating of dangerous individuals, from the rare and monstrous figure of the monomaniac to the common everyday figure of the degenerate, of the pervert, of the constitutionally unbalanced, of the immature. (Foucault 1978, p.17)

The implication of this statement is that one could expect dangerous offenders to be located amongst the marginal groups in society, notably amongst those inspiring fear or disgust. This response was understandable in general community terms, but remarkable when it became the basis for criminological theory and began to be incorporated into penal policies designed to demarcate the dangerous individual, both physically, psychologically and morally. Thus, from the early part of the twentieth century the notion of dangerousness was reinforced in the courts through the contribution of the social and medical sciences, yet the fears, imagery and exclusionary mode of thinking which had dominated their research and their views were camouflaged. The courts were really building on shaky terrain, for if the mythical aspects of our belief systems are part of the general human experience, then they are likely to be resistant to the search for objectivity and, as the sociologist Norbert Elias (1991) has observed, some professional explanations may only possess a veneer of scientism. The issue of dangerousness would, therefore, appear to be charting a difficult course in the courtroom by seeking to merge emotion, fantasy and reason in an effort to arrive at some consensus. In this regard, the Garry David case provided an unusual opportunity to observe the blending of these elements through an analysis of the written files, courtroom exchanges and reported political comments, which formed part of the fabric woven by Parliament to achieve the exclusion of one member of society.

In spite of the difficulties associated with the concept of dangerousness, the search for some definable essence has persisted in the literature, although on closer examination it remains by and large illusory – provoking at least one writer to note that the only sensible comment to be made is that it is 'a dangerous concept' (Shaw 1973). An associated problem is the difficulty of separating facts and values. Thus what *ought* to be the relationship between the individual and society is intimately bound up with factual scientific constructions, a matter of acute significance for a specialty dedicating its clinical skills to an area of general moral condemnation (see Elias 1956). Ultimately, as Saleem Shah and many other writers have been forced to acknowledge, dangerousness simply 'lies in the eye of the beholder':

> Notions of 'dangerousness' are closely related to particular value systems, as
> well as philosophical, moral and ideological perspectives. Clearly the major
> values and sociopolitical process in a society will tend to determine what will
> be perceived, defined, and officially labeled as dangerous, and how condi-
> tions and behaviors so labeled will be handled. (Shah 1981, p.235)

If the sociopolitical process plays a part in defining just what a society considers to
be unacceptably dangerous behaviour, then it is important to understand the
values, which facilitate its translation into a powerful political weapon of
expulsion. One is led to ask why, in this instance, was Garry David chosen as the
epitome of the dangerous individual, and why was such an anomalous procedure
devised to achieve his social exclusion.

Some might wish to argue that the emphasis placed on dangerousness in this
study is retrograde and out of touch with recent developments in this area. It is true
that definitional difficulties and the weak outcomes of predictive studies have
encouraged its conversion into the more professionally acceptable notion of 'risk'.
The decade of the 1990s has seen risk assessment and risk management recognised as integral components of governance (Brown and Pratt 2000; Castel 1991;
O'Malley 1998; Rose 1998; Steadman *et al.* 1993). Risk also suggests a breadth,
fluidity and adaptiveness denied dangerousness. Yet this latter term has not, and
possibly will not, disappear. It retains a directness and an evocative quality which
are deeply entrenched in the public idiom and brings the law and psychiatry
together in a mutual task, which cannot override ordinary, common-sense perceptions. It is for this reason that I have chosen to focus on the term, for it was the one
used throughout the discourse created by Victoria's State Parliament and most
directly reflects the concerns of all those involved. No persons were asked to
estimate *the degree of risk* that Garry David posed to society. They were asked
whether he was *a danger* to that society, which is indeed a very different question.

Dangerousness retained a centrality in all the negotiations concerning Garry
David's future. This concept underpins legal–psychiatric dialogue, even though
each discipline approaches its task quite differently, and the law appears to have an
unrealistic expectation of what psychiatry is able to offer. Psychiatrists, too, experience difficulty in being uncomfortably constrained by legal convention, which
requires them to translate the moral issues of goodness/badness into a
health/illness referent. This is especially noticeable in relation to dangerousness,
where the clinical focus diverges and relates to symptomatology and
treatment/management, rather than to specific inferences about likely future
behaviour (see Foucault 1988(a), p.190; Shea 1993, chs. 6, 11). After all, dangerousness per se is not a special component of any clinical taxonomy, but it is a
central focus of legal criteria pertaining to most civil commitment procedures, for
which the courts and tribunals must elicit psychiatric views. The equivocation of

psychiatry and the pragmatism of the law became distinctive features of the ensuing discourse in the case.

COURTS, ASYLUMS AND PRISONS

Emerging dilemmas

So far, I have suggested that psychiatry and the law are uneasy bedfellows and this is particularly the case with formal assessments of dangerousness. The underlying question, then, is why a clinical profession has allowed itself to be drawn into providing answers, when it is known that a serious legal consequence such as preventive detention is the likely outcome. In this regard an historical perspective sheds light on psychiatry's developing liaison with the law.

It was in the first part of the nineteenth century that psychiatry emerged as a distinct branch of medicine, although it remained the Cinderella in the ranking of medical specialisations well in to the twentieth century. The struggle to be accepted on equal terms with other medical specialties was undoubtedly a factor contributing to its willingness to be aligned with the law from the 1840s onwards. Recognition of its expertise by an equally powerful discipline was a means of proclaiming that it did possess a special body of knowledge relevant to public decision making and, more importantly, that this knowledge concerned the dangerous offender (see Crawford 1994). Its place in the courts was formalised in 1843 with the introduction of the insanity defence, based on the M'Naghten Rules. These remain a landmark in the development of forensic psychiatry, because they set down the criteria required to establish culpability and thus separate badness from madness. They were formulated at the behest of Queen Victoria and emphasised the role of reason in controlling behaviour. On behalf of 14 of the 15 Judges, Tindal LCJ provided the answer, since known as the M'Naghten Rules, as follows:

> Every man is to be presumed to be sane, and to possess a sufficient degree of reason to be responsible for his crimes, until the contrary be proved to their satisfaction; and that to establish a defence on the ground of insanity, it must be clearly proved that, at the time of the committing of the act, the party accused was labouring under such a defect of reason, from disease of the mind, as not to know the nature and quality of the act he was doing; or, if he did know it, that he did not know he was doing what was wrong. ([1843] 10 Cl and Fin 200 at 210, 8 ER 718 at 722)

A secondary outcome was the way in which they clarified the role medical experts could expect to play in future trials. Although insanity is still held to be the ultimate issue for a jury decision, the opinions of those with professional knowledge about 'the mind' remain invaluable in interpreting the evidence.

Nonetheless in providing an expert opinion based on clinical experience, the psychiatrist is not immune from adversarial pressures and these are likely to impact on cases involving the higher range penalties, such as preventive detention or capital punishment. This latter circumstance is particularly likely to bring the law and psychiatry together in a common goal of extending the grounds for exculpation. As Roger Smith claims in his historical analysis, 'on many occasions the questions of insanity and of hanging were hopelessly confused and there was difficulty in separating out a description of behaviour from its consequences', thereby linking values with expert opinion (1981, p.25). This ethical quandary of being unable to separate values from clinical judgements is certainly exacerbated in such cases and suggests that the courtroom role may be influenced by adversarial persuasion, with evidence correspondingly tailored to a quest for a less punitive outcome.

However, the provision of expert opinion to the courts was only one aspect of the way forensic psychiatry developed. The second area of formal extension in the public sphere lay in its establishment of an institutional nexus. Initially, large-scale institutions were built very rapidly in many western societies from the 1840s onwards in the light of the prevailing belief that the mentally ill could be cared for humanely and, in most instances, cured. Doctors became asylum superintendents and proclaimed this rhetoric, which as Rothman (1971), Deutsch (1973), Scull (1993) and others have pointed out did not match the reality of overcrowding; nor could it deal with the chronicity of many psychiatric illnesses. Nevertheless, the message had been accepted by governments: the mentally ill were a proper medical responsibility and the main locus of care resided with the state institution. Psychiatry thus came of age and was both useful to and dependent upon the state. Broad civil commitment criteria encouraged the notion that the asylum was a refuge from the competitive pressures of an increasingly urban lifestyle, thereby resulting in an unusually broad mix of patients. However, the basic issue of separating mental illness from criminality remained unresolved and, in some instances, criminality itself was the trigger for using the mental institution as an enforced shelter.

In the first half of the nineteenth century, the Australian experience was markedly similar, except for the lack of initial infrastructure which necessitated confining the mentally ill in the gaols, often with prisoners as their carers. The unsatisfactory nature of this policy by default soon became evident and the rapid increase in population associated with the gold rush era of the 1850s provided the impetus and funding for a more permanent solution to the problem. As a consequence, large purpose-built institutions modelled on the imposing structures in the USA and England were established in most Australian states, enabling patients to be granted a respite in asylums in peaceful country surroundings. The links with the justice system did not entirely dissipate, for over the years there is evidence of

an interchangeable use of facilities dictated by expediency, rather than any conceptual differentiation of criminality and mental disorder (see Bostock 1968;
Brothers 1961; Craze 1993; Garton 1988; Lewis 1988). For example, the psychiatric facility of J Ward, which features in this study, was originally the Ararat
prison and remained designated as a 'temporary' ward of the Aradale Lunatic
Asylum for over 100 years until its dismantling in 1991 and use as a tourist facility.
It has now come full circle with its recent reopening as a prison pending the construction of a new 50-bed unit (*Ararat Advertiser*, 5 May 2001). The first asylum in
the state of Victoria – the Yarra Bend Lunatic Asylum – has since seen service as an
infectious diseases hospital, a women's prison and more recently a forensic
hospital has been built on part of the site.

   Gradually, during the next 150 years, the forensic patient became a separate
category of mentally ill persons and the appellation of 'criminal lunatic' or 'criminally insane' crept into popular currency, as if this indeed signified a special
category whose members could be doubly stigmatised. The coupling of criminality and insanity was undoubtedly something encouraged by the early legislation,
which was undifferentiated in its approach towards those perceived as being
potentially dangerous. Thus, in Australia, the first legal incursion into this area
came with the Dangerous Lunatics Act 1843 (NSW), after Governor Phillip had
been enjoined to 'take care and custody of the idiots and lunatics' and those 'too
dangerous to be abroad'. This Act became a rough system for managing the more
visible habitual criminals and the insane, and it was patterned on the English
Criminal Lunatics Act 1800. These early origins with their long history extending
back to the Elizabethan Poor Laws of 1601 linked vulnerability with the notion of
threat and, by implication, dangerousness. Later, the medical element crept in with
a system of thought expressly relating certain forms of *behaviour* to the need for
individual and community protection. The evocative combination of the words
hinted at an indubitable potential for extreme violence necessitating some form of
indefinite confinement.

   Despite verdicts of '*not guilty* on the grounds of insanity' in most Australian
jurisdictions, confusion reigned about the appropriate place of confinement and it
was not uncommon for the prison to be traditionally favoured, simply because
governments appeared too nervous to change the status quo in anything more than
name. The state of Victoria followed this pattern until the latter part of the 1990s,
so that those acquitted on the grounds of insanity were more usually held in the
prison for an indeterminate period, rather than in a psychiatric hospital. The legislative requirement was a Supreme Court order to be held in 'strict' then 'safe'
custody during the Governor's Pleasure, which meant that release was dependent
on Cabinet advice being conveyed to the Governor, thereby reflecting the political
nature of a process placed outside ordinary sentencing guidelines. (This situation
in Victoria has now been redressed with the implementation of the Crimes (Mental

Impairment and Unfitness to be Tried) Act 1997.) It was a practice according greater weight to presumed dangerousness and community fears than to the appropriateness of psychiatric or parole board decision making, and it cogently expressed a political reluctance to dismantle punitive goals in the face of a combination of insanity and offending.

This is not to claim that psychiatrists should be the sole arbiters of those exhibiting dangerous behaviour in the form of unprovoked violence. Almost 50 years ago the English literary critic, C.S. Lewis (1953) issued the then unheeded warning that courts seemed to be transferring their custodial power to psychiatrists in the guise of treatment with scant regard for any untoward consequences. He argued that this major shift in sentencing philosophy extends the parameters of sentencing discretion, wrongly eroding the fundamental legal concept of 'just deserts' by replacing the intrinsically moral element of punishment with a therapeutic milieu beyond the court's control. In his view a frankly retributive response must displace the expectation of cure, because it expresses a temporality which respects the individual's legal rights and is averse to any form of preventive containment. At the time Lewis's argument was disparaged and he had difficulty in publishing this article because of its challenge to the prevailing treatment ethos. It took several decades before civil libertarians were prepared to concede the merits of this type of argument and press for a more rigorous separation of criminal justice and mental health functions.

Criticisms of psychiatry's forensic role began to broaden with some writers advancing the general proposition that this discipline had no legitimate role in the court process, particularly at trial level (Menninger 1968; Stone 1984). Schiffer was one among many who wished to limit psychiatric evidence. He was quite explicit about proposed remedies: psychiatrists should confine their reports to diagnoses and assessments of treatability and avoid specifying appropriate sentences; they should reject dangerousness as a basis for imposing sentences of imprisonment; they should not increase the length of sentence for treatment reasons; and the proposed nature of treatment should be no more drastic than that merited by the seriousness of the offence (Schiffer 1976, p.340). Clearly, he regarded treatment and punishment as sometimes being indistinguishable, except perhaps for semantic niceties.

Similar reservations also began to surface in the literature about the criterion of dangerousness forming the basis of civil commitment, because it could virtually be a disguised form of coercion resulting in the indefinite deprivation of liberty in a psychiatric hospital. By the 1980s, the grounds for preventive detention, whether in the prison or mental health system, were becoming increasingly difficult to sustain, with the result that most western jurisdictions were cautious about exercising their powers, only doing so with an explicit legal rationale. Around the same time psychiatrists, already reeling from the multi-pronged although not cohesive attacks of so called anti-psychiatrists, began to resile from claims to special knowledge about dangerousness prediction in the face of empirical studies reporting little substantive evidence regarding their accuracy (see Floud and Young 1981; Monahan 1983; Monahan and Steadman 1983). Ennis and Litwack (1974) even made the startling claim that courtroom predictions have less chance of success than 'flipping a coin'. Although Lewis had not had the benefit of this material, his inference that courts might be abrogating their responsibility, whilst still achieving a seemingly benign form of indeterminate sentencing under dangerousness statutes, gathered credence. As a piece of legislation dependent on formally canvassing a broad range of psychiatric opinion about dangerousness at the behest of the Supreme Court, the Community Protection Act 1990 (Vic) flouted these developments and embroiled the profession in a difficult predicament, for it accorded 'dangerousness' a centrality which could not be ignored and directly challenged the profession's right to control its own knowledge boundaries.

If the external pressures influencing the medical role have problematic dimensions, then the internal prison ones are equally difficult, as Erving Goffman has so aptly portrayed in his pioneering work on the institutional relationship. His dramaturgical account of the interplay between staff and inmates highlights the moral gulf pertaining to professionals trained to define behaviour in 'a neutral, technical frame of reference', yet finding it difficult to reconcile this neutrality in the face of flagrant and offensive misconduct (Goffman 1961, p.365). In addition, their offers of treatment are frequently foiled by subtle rebuffs, as the inmate learns to construct a self-identity resilient to further psychological intrusion. Goffman holds that it is 'a false and difficult relationship' for both parties, even though bolstered by legal authority, and ultimately it encourages the medical task to be interpreted in terms of a service model (Goffman 1961, pp.368–70). This work is complemented by the Australian study of the psychiatrist and anthropologist Robert Barrett (1996), who uses ethnographic data to delineate the role institutional staff play in shaping the contextual frame of the diagnosis. An interplay was found to develop amongst the team members as various skills were melded to arrive at common ground. In his analysis of this team approach, Barrett draws attention to the interprofessional rivalries and the adjustments required in order to arrive at a consensual view of the person. Since Garry David had honed his social skills almost entirely within the institutional environment, I have chosen to identify the strategies he deployed in interacting with staff and prisoners in some detail in Chapter 2, because these were the precursors to encounters in other authoritative settings. There is a hint of theatrical interchange and it becomes clear that his non-compliance was a powerful weapon to magnify the differences among staff trying to balance professional standards with the reality of administrative pressures in a punishment/treatment complex.

Psychiatry's forensic role, both in the courts and prisons, exposes it to a number of dilemmas not normally faced by medical specialties, but the willingness with which it sought to enter the legal arena and offer understandings about dangerousness from the middle of the nineteenth century onwards must invite speculation. There are many possible interpretations, such as medical expansionism into the area of criminal deviance, or the need to promote the discipline's clinical expertise at a time of relatively ineffectual treatments. The dominant view in psychiatric writings focuses on medical beneficence as a means of ameliorating the harshness of the criminal justice system (Gunn *et al.* 1978). The rise of the 'therapeutic ideal', particularly within the custodial prison setting, together with the establishment of forensic psychiatry as a separate discipline, suggest that this view has been influential both for psychiatry and for the state's perception of the services it has to offer.

However, a very different perspective, rarely incorporated into histories of psychiatry, emphasises the disciplinary and regulatory aspects of the medical role. For example, Sim's (1990) study of the prison medical service in England documents the way in which biomedical techniques may coexist with punishment to provide a supplementary and very powerful means of control over fractious prisoners. This conclusion suggests that in seeking to practise within the forensic arena, psychiatrists were not recognising the conceptual and ethical minefield into which they had been lured – largely because the clinical focus of their medical training does not readily encompass broader philosophical and social issues (see Busfield 1986). I would argue that there has been an understandable reluctance to face problems, such as the reality of superimposing a treatment rationale onto a punitive foundation for an offender, and the difficulty of translating a clinical mode of discourse into one circumscribed by legally imposed rules. If the courts are about retribution and coercion of the miscreant, then there are subtle ways in which psychiatry can become inveigled in this process, as Sim has demonstrated and as this study seeks to investigate.

Forensic psychiatry's relationship with the state is problematic on two counts. Its technical competence and medical status do not imply an obligation-free relationship, and it cannot distance itself from broader community objectives of a frankly coercive nature. This is a perspective currently being amplified in the work of Nikolas Rose and Peter Miller (1992), who focus on the implications of governmentality for the professions. The authors draw attention to those activities of modern governments, which foster a variety of strategies to promote desirable forms of conduct. These intrude into many areas of expertise, including medicine, and can be studied through such mechanisms as the availability of funding, provision of personnel, application of pressure and the techniques employed (Rose and Miller 1992, p.177). Such elements were well documented in the Garry David case and assisted this analysis, but the approach I have chosen to take is based on a social realist model, rather than on a broader analysis of the way state power operates. Other writings in the area include Burchell, Gordon and Miller (1991), Rose (1996) and Rose (1999).

Of further relevance is the fact that Rose and Miller consider professional disciplines are being increasingly coopted to assist in the governmental task of identifying and containing risky persons, groups and risk situations. It is a role which is both *disciplinary* and *political*, and because the state is dependent on the technologies possessed by experts, the relationship is intrinsically symbiotic. There is a mutual interest in developing the definition of a problem in such a way as to satisfy both political and professional understandings. These are facets which all came to prominence in the negotiations surrounding Garry David.

PSYCHOPATHY, THE LAW AND AN UNCERTAIN KNOWLEDGE

It can be seen from this overview that the history of forensic psychiatry has been inextricably linked with the courts and institutions from the time it accepted the task of defusing the threat posed by those offenders deemed to be dangerous on account of their mental state. The personality disordered straddle an uncertain divide when, on the one hand, the law may seek to ascertain whether an antisocial personality disorder should remain within the psychiatric ambit of *mental disorder* or, on the other, whether it should be limited to the more restrictive notion of a certifiable *mental illness* in the meaning required by mental health legislation. In fact, the Mental Health Review Board stated the central question determining Garry David's status quite succinctly at the outset of his appeal hearing. *Does antisocial personality disorder constitute a mental illness within the meaning of the legislation?* Although both antisocial personality disorder and mental illness are part of the working knowledge of psychiatry, there has always been an elusivity about them and psychiatrists, primarily informed by their clinical constructs, cannot avoid taking cognisance of legal and commonsense views.

The idea that there are some people who seem immune to the moral precepts of society is grounded in the notion of psychopathy and can be traced to Pinel's early delineation of *'manie sans délire'* in 1806 (in Zilboorg and Henry 1941). This was followed by Prichard's 'moral insanity', which he considered to be:

> A morbid perversion of the natural feelings, affections, inclinations, temper, habits, moral dispositions, and natural impulses, without any remarkable disorder of the intellect or knowing and reasoning faculties, and particularly without any insane illusion or hallucination. (Prichard 1835, p.6)

Both Pinel and Prichard sought to explain that some people behave in criminal ways with an intellectual knowledge of right and wrong and yet, *for this very reason*, may be regarded as suffering from a form of mental disorder. It is an unpalatable position for the law to accommodate, since it suggests that the whole structure of criminal sanctions is ineffective, at least for some citizens, and this is a recurrent problem in the interaction of psychiatry and the law.

It was not until 1964 that Cleckley added more detail to the earlier broad description, especially in relation to the overlap between the morally deficient part of the psychopath's personality and criminality (Cleckley 1964). Such moral insensitivity was difficult to translate into the nomenclature of a clinical guide and the American Psychiatric Association's *Diagnostic and Statistical Manual of Mental Disorder III-R* opted for evidence of Conduct Disorder before the age of 15 years in conjunction with a continuing 'pattern of irresponsible and antisocial behaviour', as indicated by such factors as a poor work history, illegal acts, aggression, impulsivity, lying, recklessness, immature relationships and a lack of remorse (*DSM-III-R* 1987, p.342). This version has now been replaced by *DSM-IV* (1994) and DSM-IV-TR (2000), but is relied on here because of its relevance in the context of events. These criteria, couched in terms of a longitudinal view, require a psychosocial judgement about the quality of a person's lifestyle and the persistence of personality traits, rather than an assessment of mental state symptoms in the usual clinical sense.

The circularity of inferring some mental abnormality from evidence of a pattern of antisocial behaviour has been noted by a number of writers, including Dr John Ellard, a Sydney psychiatrist, who pithily contends:

> The concept of psychopathic disorder, or antisocial personality disorder, reaches the pinnacle of nonsense when it goes beyond a description of behaviour and becomes an explanatory principle. One still hears the circular argument: Why did this man do these things? Because he is a psychopath. How do you know that he is a psychopath? Look at what he has done. (Ellard 1991, p.42)

Ellard also maintains that the issues raised are primarily 'moral, legal, cultural, logical and then, after all that, psychiatric', adding that psychiatric categorisation is being used as a substitute for thought (Ellard 1991, p.43). Thus, even within a scientific context and despite a lengthy history, there is an enigmatic quality about psychopathy and the notion of antisocial personality disorder with which it is broadly aligned. Although the nosology of the latter is constantly being refined in the psychiatric manuals, there are still some unsatisfactory aspects in comparison with descriptions of the psychotic illnesses, which significantly disturb mental state functioning, including mood, perception or thought. The generality of the criteria contributes to uncertainty, thus making it difficult to distinguish between the normal and abnormal as the Victorian Branch of the Royal Australian and New Zealand College of Psychiatrists pointed out in a 1990 document tendered to the Mental Health Review Board:

The descriptions of the personality disorders found in most textbooks an
diagnostic manuals are so broad, that if they were to be construed as mental
illness we could face the absurd possibility that the majority of the population
are (sic) mentally ill. (*Some Comments on Personality Disorder, Mental Illness and
Involuntary Hospitalisation.* See Kiel 1992, p.181)

In 1987 'borderline personality disorder' was added to the list in the newly
published *DSM-III-R* and those with this disorder were described as being characterised by 'a pervasive pattern of instability of self-image, interpersonal relationships, and mood, beginning by early adulthood'. Such people appear to have a per-
sisting identity disturbance, find it difficult to sustain relationships and have a fear
of rejection. They are emotionally volatile and exhibit 'recurrent suicidal threats,
gestures, or behaviour and other self-mutilating behaviour', which may serve to
manipulate others or be the result of intense anger, or a sense of depersonalisation
arising during periods of extreme stress (*DSM-III-R* 1987, p.346). There is still
wariness about the use of this category, occasioned less by the criteria themselves,
than by the inexactitude of a term suggesting an ambiguous position somewhere
on the fringe of psychosis.

In view of all these difficulties, which have cast doubt on the validity of the
personality disorders as a proper category of psychiatric knowledge, it is pertinent
to ask why psychiatry chose to encompass them. One likely explanation is that in
moving beyond pathological behaviours and states of mind it may have been
following the lead of the developing discipline of psychology, which had elected
to focus on the stresses of everyday life as its primary referent (see Lunbeck 1994).
This was advantageous for two reasons: psychologists could not be viewed as challenging the medical orientation of psychiatry and, at the same time, their emphasis
on relationships and social adaptation proclaimed the relevance of their discipline
for dealing with ordinary problems, thereby establishing an expansive base for
subsequent therapeutic endeavours. In this way, psychology was shaping its
parameters in a distinctively broad, but parallel, direction to that of psychiatry.

Psychiatry's path was rather more hazardous, for in entering that indeterminate realm between normality and abnormality there were accompanying scientific, as well as sociopolitical implications. In terms of the former, the personality
disorders can never achieve the clarity and status of psychotic disorders owing to
the intrusion of value perspectives in the diagnosis. Of even greater consequence
was the fact that psychiatry began to stake a claim to expertise in managing the
misfits of society, and this provided an avenue for the politicians and law makers to
develop social defence strategies based on a medical understanding. Thus responsibility for this unfortunate group was deflected from the criminal justice system to
the mental health system simply by virtue of a deviation of *personality traits* from
some assumed norm, rather than from the presumption of any psychiatric illness

... as the policy makers were welcoming medical involvement ... ems, the cultural label of psychopathy captured the public ... ges extending beyond feckless irresponsibility to those of ... edator, in whom unimaginable dangers supposedly lurked. ... psychiatry was often trivialised with simplistic and lurid ... iopath, and subsequent professional attempts to restrict the expansiveness ... category by developing more stringent clinical criteria had little impact on the community judgements being made about those believed to be so flagrantly antisocial and amoral as to warrant some form of social exclusion.

The Garry David case is of particular interest because these elements of dangerousness, antisocial personality disorder, mental illness, mental disorder and the use of preventive detention coalesced to invoke an unusually intense discourse between the law and psychiatry and succeeded in exposing the more sensitive areas of professional principles and knowledge. Both professions experienced a mutual difficulty in grappling with the meaning of dangerousness in any definitive sense, and each was faced with problems engendered by the structure of their own discipline. For the law, based as it is on notions of justice, the deprivation of liberty in the absence of a specific charge or evidence of mental illness is generally unsustainable. For psychiatry, a variety of beliefs exists about the appropriateness of civil commitment for the personality disordered and the efficacy of treatment efforts.

THE SOCIOPOLITICAL BACKGROUND

The tensions in which the disciplines of psychiatry and the law were enmeshed in this case can be more fully comprehended against the sociopolitical background of the state of Victoria at that time. The decade of the 1980s was a particularly fertile one for changes affecting a broad range of disturbed offenders. By the time of Garry's expected release in February 1990, both disciplines were moving closer toward establishing principles for the care of mentally disordered offenders than ever before. The Labor Government of Victoria implemented a number of initiatives in line with its social justice strategy and established clearer guidelines for distinguishing between criminality and mental illness. After an extensive process of consultation with representatives of the legal and psychiatric professions, it enacted two important pieces of legislation proclaiming the paramountcy of the civil liberties and rights of both patients and prison inmates – the Mental Health Act 1986 and the Corrections Act 1986. The Intellectually Disabled Persons' Services Act 1986 (Vic) and the Guardianship and Administration Board Act 1986 (Vic) also affirmed these principles and extended the rights of mentally impaired persons.

The continuing work of the Law Reform Commission of Victoria and an all-party Parliamentary Social Development Committee aided the Government in

its reforming achievements. Many of the changes emanating as a result of this consultation later assumed particular relevance for decisions about the proper locus of
care and/or treatment for Garry David. For example, the treatment orientation of
the new Mental Health Act followed an emerging international trend of
emphasising 'the least restrictive environment' in relation to psychiatric care. The
primacy of this principle as one of the stated objects of this Act and related legislation was intended to foster the ethos of deinstitutionalisation by moving the
balance away from an institutional to a community model of care for the mentally
ill. The seriousness with which this philosophy was embraced was evident, when it
was even extended to those mentally disordered prisoners deemed to be security
patients, who might in certain circumstances be granted leave of absence from a
psychiatric facility (ss.51 and 52). In a related move the criteria for civil commitment were made more rigorous, so that detention in a psychiatric hospital could no
longer simply be on the grounds of the 'appearance' of mental illness and being in
need of 'care or treatment', as required by the earlier legislation (ss.42 (3) and 7(a)
and (b) Mental Health Act 1959). Section 8(1)(a) of the Mental Health Act 1986
added four additional elements to be also taken into account. Thus section 8(a)
required that, not only did the person 'appear to be mentally ill', but that:

(b)   the person's mental illness requires immediate treatment or care and
        that treatment or care can be obtained by admission to and detention
        in a psychiatric in-patient service; and

(c)   the person should be admitted and detained as an involuntary patient
        for that person's health or safety or for the protection of members of
        the public; and

(d)   the person has refused or is unable to consent to the necessary
        treatment or care for the mental illness; and

(e)   the person cannot receive adequate treatment or care for the mental
        illness in a manner less restrictive of that person's freedom of decision
        and action.

In essence, evidence had to be provided about the need for immediate treatment in
an institutional environment, and this treatment had to be both available and
necessary for 'health or safety reasons', or for 'protection of members of the
public'. Civil commitment could not be waived simply because a prospective
patient refused to consent to the treatment being offered.

   Whilst notions of *immediacy, availability and necessity* are always debatable in
relation to the personality disordered, it was the following section of the Act,
which compounded the confusion for all concerned and was later crucial to the
Garry David case. The legislation required that the section 8(1) criteria be considered in conjunction with section 8(2), which lists a number of specific behaviours,
philosophies, or conditions which, by themselves, do not constitute the appear-

ance of mental illness for the purposes of civil commitment. Subsection 8(2)(l) occasioned the greatest obstacle, for it stated that those with *an antisocial personality* cannot become involuntary patients of a psychiatric inpatient service by virtue of this ground alone. Had 'disorder' been added to these words, then Parliament's intention would have been indisputable: that is, the exclusion of those with the formal diagnosis of an antisocial personality disorder from civil commitment provisions. The omission of that one word, however, fostered an ambiguity, which encouraged caution in defining the legal boundaries of mental illness, casting doubts on the appropriateness of including the personality disordered within the ambit of public psychiatry. In turn, this meant that the position of those exhibiting patterns of criminality, in addition to a clinically recognised mental disorder, became inherently tenuous, thereby laying the groundwork for some form of interprofessional resolution which, in the Garry David case, provoked endless recrimination from all quarters.

The implementation of such radically different mental health legislation in 1986 was accompanied by the establishment of an Office of Psychiatric Services with a chief general manager, who would be a professional administrator with the power to appoint a psychiatrist as director. This was a reversal of the traditional hierarchical structure and placed the profession under the control of a health bureaucracy and, predictably, the Royal Australian and New Zealand College of Psychiatrists did not favour this change on the grounds that it would dilute medical autonomy. Nevertheless, the government was adamant that its plans for the regionalisation of services and mainstreaming of psychiatry within the framework of general medicine would be facilitated by the new style of corporate management. This major shift in orientation was very clearly signalled in an important policy document *New Directions for Psychiatric Services in Victoria* (1986), which rebuked the profession for its internal preoccupations taking precedence over the encouragement of client self-determination:

> We need to stop asking the question: 'Who owns the client?', which reflects
> the inflexibility of our current segmented service provision, and instead ask:
> 'How can clients determine service options for themselves?' (Health Depart-
> ment 1986, p.7)

A second major area of change provided for legal scrutiny of the process of involuntary detention. This was accomplished by the establishment of a Mental Health Review Board, whose president had to be a qualified lawyer appointed by the Governor in Council. Not only were there initial tensions within the hospital system in accommodating to the new requirement of justifying medical decisions to visiting tribunal members, but uncertainty was beginning to emerge about the future of institutional psychiatry in view of government support for the newly established community structures in mental health.

Parallel changes on the criminal justice front equally affected the place of the mentally disordered. The government rejected demands for activating Victoria's habitual offenders' legislation and even moved to the notion of fixed sentences for those who had been given natural life terms for homicide convictions, with the consequence that some 'lifers' were discharged almost immediately. The tenor of these two moves signalled the fact that indefinite confinement was no longer a viable sentencing option. The next step was to tackle the inequitable position of mentally disordered offenders, and in February 1987 the government gave a reference to the Law Reform Commission of Victoria requesting this body to examine the rules governing the use of mental state defences in the criminal courts. At the end of the following year, it established a Corrections Health Board, so that the mental health of prisoners would be recognised as the shared responsibility of two separate government departments – the Office of Corrections and the Office of Psychiatric Services. Thus, what had previously been an ad hoc forensic system awkwardly grafted on to a prison operation, now gained an explicit profile. There was an increase in staffing and, for the first time, incoming prisoners were subjected to a detailed screening system with classification and services based on indicators of vulnerability, including a history of past or current mental disorder.

The announcement at the end of the 1980s of the newly created position of Professor of Forensic Psychiatry, one which would rather unusually combine public service and academic responsibilities, further cemented the link between public psychiatry and government. The Victorian Labor Government's commitment to this area was thus confirmed and, at the same time, the new structure and increased resources implied a degree of centralised control far more apparent than previously. This restructuring promised a model of service delivery based on the integration of psychiatric services within the medical mainstream and the recognition that patients, even those in a prison setting, should have a degree of self-determination. The principles of social justice incorporated in the new Corrections Act 1986 proclaimed that every prisoner should have:

> s.47(d) The right to have access to reasonable medical care and treatment necessary for the preservation of health.

> (f) If intellectually disabled or mentally ill, the right to have reasonable access within the prison or, with the Governor's approval outside a prison, to such special care and treatment as the medical officer considers necessary or desirable in the circumstances.

These administrative and legislative changes acknowledged the need to separate criminality and mental illness, both on the pragmatic ground of providing the most appropriate service in accordance with the rights of each group, and on the conceptual one of separating punitive responses from treatment ones. However, the siting of the severely personality disordered within this binary structure was ambiguous. They could no longer readily access the psychiatric system because of the uncertain intent of the exclusionary clause of section 8 (2)(l) relating to those having 'an antisocial personality'. As will become evident in the Garry David case, this lack of clarity extended to the responsibilities of the therapeutic staff within the correctional system. An unforeseen consequence of the reforms is noted by Moynihan, who has argued that 'as it was being formulated in Victoria in 1989, reform of the legal system and reform of psychiatry were incompatible', because the boundaries of each system had been rationalised and tightened to make the residual capacity of each less accessible (Moynihan 1992, p.324). In effect, the personality disordered challenged the principles on which the new forensic structure had evolved. Disordered behaviour, which typically combines violence, flagrant breaches of prison regulations compounded by life-threatening self-abuse, evokes a control response, as well as a medical one – neither having primacy in itself – and this duality may thwart attempts to separate punishment and treatment as fundamentally different entities.

The spirit as well as the form of the legislative and administrative changes affecting forensic psychiatry in Victoria exacerbated the placement difficulties experienced by those with severe personality disorder. It was apparent that 'ware-housing' in the form of preventive detention in a prison would no longer be tolerated as a standard response; nor could it be masked as necessary treatment, when clinicians were unable to present a consensual position sufficient to satisfy the health mandate of the reforms. The principle of the least restrictive environ-ment permeated decision making in both the criminal justice and mental health spheres, so that confinement now became a move of last resort, and there was an increasing emphasis on Community Correction Orders and Community Treatment Orders, respectively. These developments did not augur well for the Government's determination to ensure that Garry David remained incarcerated; and they closed off any legitimate avenue to either system. Its task was not made any easier by the fact that the criminal justice and mental health reforms, which it had encouraged, were premised on the principle of civil liberties pertaining to the management of both prisoner and patient groups. For example, the former could exercise their right to refuse treatment for a mental or physical disorder whilst being held in the prison, but this right was overborne on transfer to the psychiatric system as a security patient. This distinction between competence in one sphere and presumed incompetence in another further complicated Garry's situation, for he could exploit it at will by drawing disproportionately on staffing resources and challenging the rationale of both systems. It is for this variety of reasons that decisions affecting the continued confinement of Garry David provoked a public outcry from many lawyers and psychiatrists. Had his release date not coincided with the far-reaching changes affecting the mentally disordered offender, then these debates would have been unlikely to be so visible and disturbing.

In the years immediately preceding Garry David's anticipated release, two large-scale massacres tested the more liberal notions of managing the mentally disordered and the separation of the 'mad' from the 'bad'. In August 1987 a young former soldier went on a 40-minute shooting spree in a Melbourne inner suburb one Sunday evening killing 7 people and injuring 19. Although at the later trial there was no suggestion that he had been mentally ill at the time, the public perception linked Julian Knight's violence to a lack of sanity. The second case was less equivocal. Frank Vitkovic, diagnosed as suffering from paranoid schizophrenia, shot and killed eight employees at the Australia Post building in the heart of the city prior to Christmas 1987. These random outbursts of violence, within the space of four months, increased the level of community apprehension about professionals' ability to identify and manage dangerous individuals, and the state's ability to contain them. In the public outcry to follow, one of the proposed solutions was a restriction on the use of automatic and semi-automatic weapons, but this law and order measure seemed punitive to the large number of law-abiding sporting shooters, who deflected the problem by insisting that a more appropriate response lay in increasing access to mental health services. The emerging criticisms of the policy of deinstitutionalisation were thus conflated with a fear of the mentally unstable roaming freely in the community and given a focus by these two highly publicised incidents, which, as Moynihan concludes: 'provided a spectre of such mythic proportions that any attempt to keep young people who threaten or are perceived as creating violence out of mental institutions could be recoded into narratives of mass murder and carnage' (1992, p.310).

This account of the broader sociopolitical setting indicates that the Government's unwillingness to grant Garry David freedom was incongruous with and radically compromised its own reform strategy. It explains why any dismantling of legal or psychiatric principles, even if only for one person, could not be regarded as inconsequential, because of its challenge to the dividing practice between badness and madness; the professional knowledge on which this is based; and the assignment of appropriate responsibility for care. The newly forged forensic structure, which had so carefully evolved over a decade with Government support, would also be in jeopardy. The contest between psychiatry, the law and the Government thus extended beyond the power of the state over one marginalised person and set at risk the coherence of the ideology on which legal and mental health initiatives had been predicated.

THE TAMING OF A MISCREANT: MICROPHYSICS OF POWER

The rich drama played out between legal, psychiatric and community beliefs about dangerous persons involved a number of other players including politicians, the police and Garry David himself. The sequence of this narrative is broadly chronological with each chapter tracing a different stage in the shaping of 'dangerousness' and 'antisocial personality disorder' into a series of multilayered public and professional discourses. It highlights the actions of the various participants and exposes the ethical and philosophical difficulties intrinsic to the practice of forensic psychiatry.

Chapter 2 follows Garry David's experiences in a maximum security prison, which became his training ground for testing the efficacy of strategies designed to maintain some control over a very harsh environment. The writer is well aware of the limitations inherent in identifying behavioural patterns from such extensive prison records. The process is selective and the more subtle aspects of record keeping in a public prison environment temper what are claimed as 'facts' (see Garfinkel 1984). In this instance there were particular internal constraints, because records were passing through a chain of dual accountability to the two funding Departments of Corrections and Health, and then to Parliament through the respective ministers. Institutional staff were unusually exposed to a heightened degree of surveillance and criticism, thereby indirectly contributing to a tendency to justify decisions and actions, or shroud the meaning from outside scrutiny by using coded forms of communication. At the same time, each record had to satisfy professional guidelines, whether these related to psychiatry, occupational therapy, social work or the custodial concerns of the prison officer, and justify the distinctiveness and contribution of each professional intervention. This facet of record keeping makes it a competitive process utilising either empirical knowledge about the personality or the custodial language of control and experience, in order to locate moral behaviour within an objective domain and arrive at an agreed set of management protocols. It is inevitable that different styles of personalities and practice become an integral component of the portrayal of prison incidents.

Frustration, anxiety, or the satisfaction associated with any one encounter with such a high-profile prisoner as Garry David, are related to the attempts to reconcile the goals of both safe custody and rehabilitation. The files are thus interpretative and reactive. It is for these reasons that I chose to search them thematically for a consistency of patterns, in order to avoid giving undue weight to individual incidents at times of residual tension within the prison. It is a chapter, too, in which I highlight the intensive efforts of the many staff who tried to assist this prisoner; document the moves between the prison and the psychiatric system; and question the feasibility of integrating therapeutic concerns with an essentially retributive sentence. As the chapter is about processes, perceptions and strategies, the identity of the institutional staff shaping the ongoing discourse is not revealed, except for some senior staff, whose evidence about past events formed an integral part of later Supreme Court evidence and were therefore in the public domain.

In Chapter 3 I take the case into a broader arena by recounting the various moves initiated by a Government anxious to ensure Garry's detention, and then trace the development of special legislation based on his potential dangerousness. Preventive detention threatened the new forensic structure, which had become more prone to bureaucratic direction and consequently more likely to be responsive to the political will. Here I detail the strategies initiated by the Government to persuade psychiatrists to incorporate antisocial personality disorder within the legal ambit of mental illness – a move rejected by a number of senior psychiatrists, as well as the Royal Australian and New Zealand College of Psychiatrists, primarily on the grounds of interference in internal matters.

Chapter 4 focuses on the diagnosis of antisocial personality disorder as a basis for explaining the referential frames constructed by law and psychiatry. These themes are explored more fully in the context of Garry David's appeal to the Mental Health Review Board, the tribunal charged with hearing reviews and appeals against involuntary detention. The task given this three-member Board was to assess, on the basis of wide-ranging evidence, whether personality disorder constituted a mental illness in the legal sense. The members had first to decide whether these words should be interpreted according to a common-sense understanding of 'madness', which in the ordinary view covers an undifferentiated range of inexplicable behaviours, or whether there should be reliance on expert interpretations, which typically focus on the specific disturbances of thought, mood and perception more usually associated with the psychotic illnesses. It was an important issue, already tested in the English courts, but not yet directly applied to the new legislation in Victoria. In this chapter, I identify the political ramifications, for it was undoubtedly favourable to the Government position to place reliance on a broad, common-sense view, rather than on the more restrictive expert one. Witnesses found their task daunting, despite the relative informality associated with natural justice principles. Here I pursue the underlying theme of translating professional perceptions about diagnosis and treatment into a legal format, in order to highlight the different modes of analysis utilised by those with medical training *vis-à-vis* those with legal training.

Next, I follow the variety of bridging manoeuvres set in train by the Government to find other solutions to 'the problem' of Garry David. Evidence is given about the developing friction between a number of public bodies, including the Law Institute of Victoria, the Law Reform Commission of Victoria and the Social Development Committee, as well as increasing vacillation about the legal status of a prisoner being held under the provisions of three Acts. Attempts to introduce more general dangerous offenders' legislation bear testimony to the Government's undiminished efforts to retain control of a situation largely of its own making.

Chapter 6 represents the formal culmination of events with a number of Supreme Court hearings based on the necessity for Garry to be preventively detained. Here I question the appropriateness of the legislation and highlight the deficiencies attaching to such a singular approach. There is indeed an uncanny resemblance between the Government's efforts to reduce Garry's status and a 'degradation ceremony' in Garfinkelian terms (Garfinkel 1956). Whether Garry was an apt subject for public denunciation had to depend, in large measure, on some consensus about the meaning of dangerousness, and on this point the views between the public and professional arenas diverged sharply. This chapter takes account of the minutiae of the courtroom interplay, because participants responded not only in an individual capacity, but also as representatives of their respective professions and organisations. Their responses and reactions reflect some of the more general difficulties of legal–psychiatric discourse, such as the way in which lawyers and psychiatrists struggle to interpret key concepts, particularly those of mental illness, antisocial personality disorder and treatment.

In the final chapters, I draw the material together by pursuing a number of themes, which were not directly related to the way the professional discourse was constructed, but were integral to the perception of dangerousness in this case. First, the voice of Garry David is introduced through his public statements, actions and writings, for he was both a participant and acute observer, who had to develop strategies to counter the media images of dangerousness. The media's role is briefly discussed and, finally, the legacy of Garry David is identified in relation to the subsequent changes affecting the place of the personality disordered in Victoria. The historical background of this legacy suggests that the issue should be viewed in broader terms and some parallels are observed. In particular, I make reference to a remarkably similar New South Wales case involving a Community Protection Act, which drew the attention of the High Court, effectively ending this form of singular legislation in Australia (*Kable v DPP for NSW* [1996] 138 ALR 577). Evidence from other jurisdictions suggests that the position of the personality disordered is likely to remain the subject of ongoing discourse between psychiatrists, lawyers and politicians seeking to find a resolution compatible with psychiatric and legal interests.

It will already be apparent from this overview that the Garry David case draws on theoretical perspectives ranging across the fields of sociology, criminology, political science, legal philosophy, ethnography and the history of the professions. Such an eclectic mix utilises a number of interdisciplinary perspectives, which are complementary rather than competitive or, as David Garland has argued, can be brought 'into conversation with one another' (Garland 1990, pp.14-15). The extraordinarily broad-ranging issues raised by this case demand flexibility, for they canvas the nature of legal–psychiatric discourse; measures of scientific knowledge; the exercise of disciplinary powers; notions of surveillance and resistance; therapy in a coercive environment; and various understandings about dangerousness, including their historical nexus with the criminal justice and mental health systems.

As with so much work in this field, it is hard to ignore the insightful contributions of Michel Foucault, especially his general allusion to the microphysics and techniques of power infiltrating the very fabric of carceral institutions in a constant interplay of tension (Foucault 1997b, pp.26 ff.). Garry David's interactions with and manipulation of the correctional process challenge Foucault's overview of the prison and court systems, and his depiction of the role of therapy in an institutional environment. The case calls for a more grounded exploration of the gaps, contradictions and silences emerging from the categorisation of criminally disordered behaviour and the treatment/punishment conflict inherent in medical and correctional modes of control. For example, the impression that individual prisoners are essentially powerless, admittedly expressed with less certainty by Foucault in his later Collège de France lectures, invites closer scrutiny of the nature of discipline and resistance (Foucault 1997b, pp.195 ff.) Even a cursory knowledge of Garry David's circumstances suggests that his was not a docile body to be coaxed, transformed and improved with the economy of therapeutic effort which Foucault requires (1997b, pp.137-8); but that the mechanics of the process were more subtle and far-reaching in their implications for the forensic endeavour. For discipline to be efficient, in Foucault's view, it must reduce the body as a political force, at the least cost and with maximum effect; but this was simply not happening – in fact. Garry seemed to possess an uncanny ability to enhance his political power, despite being publicly stripped of ordinary civil status with its inbuilt protections.

The more immediate institutional environment affecting Garry David also contributed to the political outcomes. As I will demonstrate from the prison files, his behavioural and legal challenges had their seeds in the discord and professional uncertainties he generated amongst the staff responsible for his institutional management. To their discomfort, he sought to alert senior politicians and advisers, including the Premier, the Ministers for Health and Corrections, and the Ombudsman, to seeming inequities in his care. In turn, they requested explanations about the apparent failure of psychiatrists and medical staff to propose a solution based on their special expertise. Thus, there was a history of Garry David transcending the correctional boundaries by exposing the clinical duty of care to political scrutiny. Over the period of his incarceration it became clear that, despite the efforts of all concerned, Garry remained an intractable problem for both psychiatry and the state. The way in which this intractability flourished, and the nuances of the interaction amongst those who came into direct contact with this

detainee in both legal and medical settings, reflect the tension which was precipi-
tated.

The Community Protection Act 1990 was the pivotal focus of the drama
because it provided the legislative framework to identify the dangerous elements
within Garry David's behaviour and personality. At the same time, the descriptions
given to the court of his self-mutilatory acts over such a lengthy period of incarceration linked his body to the ascription of dangerousness for two reasons. First,
they evoked fears about a capacity for personal violence suggestive of a flagrant
disregard of society's norms and set the scene for a variety of accounting systems,
in which there were formal attempts to sort out the differences between ordinary
common-sense judgements, which evoked fantasy images, from the 'expert' ones,
which supposedly did not. Second, they raised the disturbing fact that his body
seemed not to have been the locus of his punishment or treatment in the way anticipated by custodial authorities. Instead, it acted as the site of resistance, thereby
aiding a public perception about the inability of correctional authorities to manage
him. The notion of 'the body' has increasingly emerged as an analytical tool in
recent sociological writings in both a literal and metaphorical sense, and Foucault
certainly regards it as central to all discourse about the prison. It is his view, that if
the body cannot be disciplined within the most authoritative structure society can
devise, then the subtler, coercive powers used by society to control its members are
also placed at risk. It does, therefore, become part of the knowledge, power, surveillance, discipline and dangerousness matrix which, in this case, extended far
beyond the management of just one recalcitrant person. The *body* of Garry David
lent the debates a sense of immediacy, for they were about its positioning in the
institutional structures, just as the later habeas corpus applications tried to situate it
physically within the court process. There was also a sense of urgency to resolve
matters, given Garry's increasing debilitation, which enhanced an awareness of his
physical presence in the formal proceedings and highlighted the oppressive nature
of governmental actions.

History has shown us that the penetration of psychiatry into the legal process,
through the courts and the institutions, has allowed certain criminal behaviours to
be reconstituted within a framework of madness. It would be simplistic to argue
that this pathologising of crime has afforded a better understanding of the relationship between mental disorder and criminal behaviour, because the debates
have differed little over the entire period, except perhaps for changes in terminology, which ranged from the overtly moral connotations of 'manie sans délire',
'moral insanity' and 'moral defective' to the seemingly more objective 'psychopathy', 'sociopathy', followed by 'antisocial personality disorder' or 'dissocial personality disorder' (see Ellard 1989; Johnstone 1996; Watson 1994). Diagnoses
are still cautious and tentative; moral interpretations are difficult to exclude

entirely; and the delineation of psychopathy in terms of responsibility is as much a stumbling block as ever.

The legal focus on dangerousness in the Garry David case was disquieting for psychiatrists, in view of the message being conveyed by empirical studies. It encapsulated in a concentrated form the dilemmas intrinsic to psychiatry since its first self-conscious efforts to separate itself as a distinct branch of medicine in the middle of the nineteenth century. As Rosenberg reminds us, there has, as yet, been no real resolution for this forensic sub-specialty – only a reformulation of 'the continuing social dilemma created by the possibly insane criminal' (Rosenberg 1968, p.252).

The findings of more recent studies link violence and mental disorder in a more complex way than originally thought and posit a relationship between these two conditions in certain prescribed circumstances. The work currently being undertaken as part of the MacArthur Foundation's Violence Risk Assessment Study in refining these variables is enabling their predictive component to be better identified for clinical purposes (see Steadman *et al.* 2000).

CHAPTER 2

'A Macabre Dance
to His Well-Known Tune'
The Pathway of Resistance

The management of this prisoner has once more, as you know, become an issue, which threatens to create further dissonance between the Health Commission and the Office of Corrections. We are again taking the first steps of a macabre dance to his well-known tune and I fear that more damage will result to him and to us unless we improve on past performance. You are aware that one doctor has been caused to step aside from his job in the past as a result of conflicts, which were mostly about this prisoner, and we would not want such a poor result to be repeated ... Marcus Clarke in For the Term of His Natural Life makes the point that problems of this sort do not go away in real life as they do in a novel. Transferring the prisoner to J Ward or anywhere else does not close the book, it merely turns the page. (Memo, Coordinator of Forensic Services, 9 January 1985)

THE STAGE IS SET
Building an armoury of tactics

The decade from 1979 to 1989 was a testing period in the management of the recalcitrant prisoner, Garry David. He had just reached adulthood, but was physically small in stature and needed to find some means of survival within the threatening environment of the prison. A further complication was the presence of his father, Rupert, already well versed in the inmate hierarchy, and to whom the son posed a threat. Very soon, Garry began to secure his own notoriety. He was disruptive and self-mutilated in strange ways, attacking most sites of his body seemingly without fear of the consequences. Not only did he challenge the many professional staff, who tried to reduce his behavioural problems, but he also accomplished this in a manipulative and increasingly skilful manner.

It was during his time in Pentridge Prison, which was part of the central Melbourne prison complex with a population of some 1400 prisoners, that Garry David established a space enabling him to resist intrusions by both staff and other prisoners and establish a measure of personal autonomy. From the outset he was not subdued by prison discipline, despite spending a great deal of time in H

Division, colloquially referred to as the 'punishment' section of the gaol. Whilst surveillance is a technique of discipline and control, he revelled in this additional attention and used it for his own ends, thus instigating a bizarre dance of power, in which the staff's anticipation of the next move was often thwarted. In this chapter I document the techniques and strategies employed by both Garry himself and those professional staff involved in his care, situating these in the broader context of his overall institutional experience.

In the Garry David case the general problems associated with file gathering were exacerbated by the multiple forms of data accumulation, whereby clinical files, nursing notes and incident reports were augmented by reports to the Department of Health, Office of Corrections, the Classification Committee, the Adult Parole Board of Victoria and the Ombudsman. Inevitably, unwitting distortions arose as a result of the microscopic scrutiny of institutional life over such a lengthy period. Any reconstruction of events in these circumstances tends to focus on pathology and negative incidents, since they impact most directly on prison morale and discipline. Thus the type of material being recorded is largely beyond the actor's control and fundamentally different from that garnered about an ordinary person living in the community. In addition, it should be recognised that the process of surveillance and information gathering about Garry David might itself have been the catalyst for the occurrence of many of the recorded events. The selection and organisation of material for the purposes of interpretation, both here and in various judicial hearings, add yet another dimension and it is difficult to assess whether some reported incidents reflect the full meaning of the event for all concerned. Certainly, some facets of Garry's life did appear to gain folkloric status, and the factual components were difficult even for the courts to unravel later. For example, the general belief that Garry constituted a special danger to female therapists and police officers was questioned during various hearings of the Community Protection Act 1990.

Whilst the parallel collection of data was an administrative necessity and heightened surveillance, there was a further consequence of this splitting of different professional knowledges about one person. Incidents were documented from many perspectives and there were duplications and inefficiencies in the information-gathering process, as custodial and professional staff sought to justify their various actions in relation to this one prisoner. In this way, surveillance became as much a part of the network of relations between custodial and therapeutic staff working in the correctional system as it did between the prisoner and the system itself.

Garry David was born on 20 November 1954 to Rupert David, who was then 35 years old and had been intermittently in prison since 1936, and 19-year-old Elizabeth (Betty Joan, née Sinclair). Two years later, on 16 January 1957, Robert was born and occasionally the files allude to an older sister, Karen, whom neither of the boys appears to have known. This part of the family history is by no means clear. Garry always believed his father to be Rupert David and had an intermittent, ambivalent relationship with him. However, the files of the Family Welfare Division of the Department of Community Services occasionally allude to the possibility that Betty David was pregnant with Garry before she met Rupert, and that she married him within three days of this meeting. The natural child of their union would appear to have been Robert. A social worker's report of 17 February 1958 indicates that the mother 'has her first child with her, but David's son is in the care of his grandparents'.

Robert was the first to be placed in institutional care when, at the age of two years, he was made a ward of state after his mother had left him in the charge of another woman for a day and failed to return. Betty then spent some time interstate in the company of other men whom she used for financial support, since her husband was once more incarcerated. On 11 November 1960, Garry was also made a ward of state on the grounds that there were 'no visible means of support'. Although the mother was unreliable about visiting both boys, she appears to have been fonder of Garry than Robert. By 1960 she had begun a long-term de facto relationship with John Henry Webb, although some reports indicate that she was renting out the premises for daytime prostitution. Robert progressed through a number of children's institutions and had little contact with his brother. He was discharged from the care of the Family Welfare Division of the Social Welfare Department on 6 August 1973 to be apprenticed as a car body mechanic and was instructed to reside with his mother and Webb.

Garry's progress in the institutions, interspersed with periods of holiday leave with his mother, was rather more chequered. At the age of eight it is noted that he was largely left unsupervised whilst in his mother's care and given five shillings a day to buy food. He left school at 15 years and is reported to have been an indifferent student only reaching Year 10 level. It appears, however, that it was his early progression into delinquency, which interfered with his schooling. At 11 years he came under notice for school truancy and breaking into a number of neighbours' homes to steal money and jewellery. Until that time, he had only been in two children's homes, but a further spate of offending resulted in a transfer to the more secure facilities reserved for those 'committed', rather than 'admitted' for reasons of parental neglect by the Children's Court. By the age of 15 he was in a youth training centre, and at 18 years it is recorded that he had been convicted of 44 separate offences. These were mostly larcenies and the result of breaking into shops, offices and houses. Even though this number of recorded offences for a juvenile is indeed high, it included many multiple charges for separate events, augmented by associated breaches of parole and escaping from custody. There is no mention of violence in the official record, although at 17 he was charged with carrying an unlicensed firearm whilst under age.

Garry was transferred to an adult correctional institution before he reached 18, in order to serve the balance of his youth training centre sentence. From 10 January 1972 until 11 June 1993, he remained in custody apart from short spells of employment, when he worked for six weeks as a builder's labourer, seven months in a textile factory and two months as a zoo attendant. These alternated with bouts of unemployment, usually ending abruptly with further criminal activity and finally culminating in the serious charges of two counts of attempted murder and associated offences in 1980. Prior to this, Garry had managed to accumulate 46 further convictions, 3 breaches of parole and numerous breaches of prison regulations, with 9 of these attracting formal sanctions. Although most of the offences were property ones, there were now several involving being armed with an offensive weapon, carrying an unlicensed firearm, assaulting another prisoner and motor vehicle theft.

Soon after completion of one sentence, 27-year-old Garry shot the proprietor of a pizza shop in the seaside town of Rye just after midnight on 2 July 1980, in an attempt to ambush police and, in his own words, 'go out in a blaze of glory'. He had consumed some liquid from an infusion of the hallucinogenic datura lily, stolen two rifles with bullets and magazines, a torch, some loose change and a car from the zoo, and then driven to the Mornington Peninsula, just south of Melbourne. The police station was closed and in an effort to lure some officers to him he created a disturbance, with the consequence that two people were seriously injured. Garry appeared in the Supreme Court on 3 February 1982 charged with two counts of wounding with intent and shooting with intent to commit murder, one count of shooting at a policeman with intent to murder, and one count each of burglary and theft of a motor vehicle.

After only intermittent periods in the community during 1972, 1974, 1975 and 1979, Garry now faced a lengthy prison term and it appears that his confrontational responses became more entrenched from this time onwards. The trial itself was not without incident. He threatened to sack his counsel and to 'slash up'. On the second day of his appearance in the Supreme Court, he kicked a police officer and issued threats of violence to a wide range of people. Justice King was placed in the invidious position of bargaining with the accused over his possession of ballpoint pens, in order to avoid further delaying outbursts. As a senior prison officer wrote in his report to the Governor:

> Upon being returned to court once again, after threatening to refuse to dress, Webb tried to have a letter given to a Channel 10 reporter and to the police officer, whom he had shot. Refusal of permission to pass these letters, both by myself, and his Honour, after he had sought the Court's permission through his barrister, resulted in Webb becoming agitated and threatening from the dock to 'forget the coppers and go for the screws… I'll go for their eyes', he

said. Webb finished the day by refusing to stand for the adjournment of the
Court. (5 February 1982)

The Court was clearly nervous that Garry would disrupt the trial by carrying out
his self-mutilatory threats and advice was sought from the prison psychiatrist, who
was of the opinion that the risk was very real, given that he had an established
history of being able to conceal razor blades and other sharp objects and regurgi-
tate them at will. It was decided that the defendant should be X-rayed each day and
kept in a separate holding cell at the Court.

Two months after the trial, for which he received a 14-year sentence with a
12-year minimum term, the prisoner sent a self-justificatory account of his criminal
actions in the Rye shootings to the '60 Minutes' television programme, in which
he described them as being 'a direct result of a lifetime of struggle, deprivation,
hunger, brutality, harassment and victimisation by the police, government and
institutions of this country'. In grandiose vein, he warned of the 'very real danger'
of a further gun battle on his release:

> And my targets would be police, Government members, corrupt unionists,
> clergyman and anyone suspected of inhumanity. I would also be executioner
> of people suspected of cruelty to animals and also anyone involved in sexual
> offences against women and children. Also prison guards who will one day
> face justice at my hands ... I am going to get out of this prison in a matter of
> years. Who cares what happens to me? If I crawl into a hole and die no one
> will give a damn. But if I pick up a gun and start killing people, then people
> will care. (11 July 1982)

As one psychiatrist reminded his colleagues in writing, Garry's behaviour was
'stable and long-standing and, given his personality deficits, could be seen as quite
rational (for him) in the present circumstances. *Understandability* is the key concept
here; in a slightly different situation his behaviour could be seen as praiseworthy
and even heroic, for example, if he were a prisoner of conscience in a totalitarian
regime' (30 May 1983).

In custody, Garry's behavioural pattern was characterised by a barrage of
verbal and written threats to prison officers, psychiatrists, psychologists, occupational therapists, welfare and nursing staff, and reinforced by some physical
attacks. Furthermore, hunger strikes, cell barricades and damage to prison
property compounded the management of a very difficult detainee, who enjoyed
inciting rebellion in unstable prisoners, both by way of agitating about the regime
and by assisting them to plan their own suicide, including that by self-immolation.
By 1988, the problems associated with his management were worsening. He was
then located in G Division, often referred to as the 'psychiatric' section of the gaol
because of its complement of mentally disordered prisoners, but even within this

more flexible unit he immersed himself in cyclical bouts of disruptive behaviour, such as mutilations and threats to 'bronze up' the division with smeared faeces. Other incidents concerned persuading fellow prisoners to boycott programmes, playing the guitar loudly in group therapy and, during one memorable cooking class, eating live worms. It was all part of an escalating pattern, presaged by the Director of Forensic Psychiatry Services, Dr John Grigor, who had assumed responsibility for Garry's management in 1986:

> Garry has been 'top dog' within G Division, and has used this position with flair and imagination to the point that more vulnerable prisoners have been quite uncertain as to their proper course of action after 'counselling' ... Now that the population is even more vulnerable, due almost entirely to active psychosis, *there is concern as to the impact of an intelligent, very severe personality disorder on the well being of the psychosocial unit.* (24 February 1987)

Dr Grigor's concern was realistic, because the pattern of destabilisation within prison units continued. The following year, Garry pinned a notice on G Division's board inciting fellow prisoners to join the radical Prisoners' National Action group and riot. Disciplinary action was swift in the form of transfer to the harshest division of the gaol, despite Garry complaining that in a psychiatric division 'one ought to expect tolerance and not antagonism from prison officers'. The Governor, fearing further problems so close to Christmas, re-transferred him to the Special Purpose Unit, thereby providing him with further scope to influence vulnerable and intellectually disabled prisoners (30 December 1988). As the Supervisor of Classification reported to the Director of Prisons at this time, Garry was 'once more trying to assert himself as *king* of the inadequates'. This technique of denigrating the efforts of therapeutic staff in the prison was later transferred to mental health staff at J Ward and Mont Park. In one notable incident contributing to nurses' low morale and necessitating staff counselling, he persuaded a J Ward staff member to place a derogatory notice on the staff board likening psychiatrists to Hitler and J Ward to a concentration camp.

Garry enhanced his reputation in the prison environment and beyond with a dramatic flair for issuing threats, and many of these became public knowledge through two official documents leaked to the press (see Craze and Moynihan 1994). The first was a Bureau of Criminal Intelligence report, entitled 'Operation Thasm', which was part of a Victoria Police brief to document information about those persons seen to be posing a danger to members of the force. It covered Garry's written threats and included confidential material from the prison files to enphasise the frequency and extent of his self-mutilation. It also became the basis of an official video publicly dramatising likely incidents, such as the blowing up of petrol tankers in shopping malls and acts of violence at an inner city hospital. The second document, widely disseminated in the media, was the inflammatory 'Blueprint for Urban Warfare' (20 November 1987), which Garry claimed to have been a private document written at a psychologist's urging to counter his deeply entrenched anger. Here he listed in detail 49 chilling combat situations, but some sections diminished in force when a Supreme Court Judge later described them as falling into the category of 'comic book juvenility' and the 'distasteful, but essentially unlikely, imaginings of an unhealthy mind'. Justice Hedigan considered his other threats to be more serious, including:

> the poisoning of City water supplies, the bombing of Flinders Street Station and the Melbourne Cricket Ground on major sporting events, the bombing of major bridges and Zionist Centres, the execution of the Premier and Prime Minister, the desire to be Australia's worst civilian mass murderer, the bombing of St Vincent's Hospital, Melbourne, indiscriminate gunfire into a crowded public place, the pouring of inflammable liquids over crowds from high vantage points, the release of toxic poisons into public swimming pools, injection of AIDS contamination into milk cartons, the release of foot and mouth disease, bombing of crowded churches, universities, airports, major shopping retail outlets, Luna Park, TV studios, the indiscriminate shooting into crowds at Carols by Candlelight, freeways, bombing of airport facilities, the total devastation of the prison's office and re-creation of the Hoddle Street, Queen Street, Russell Street and Walsh Street massacres, with high death tolls in the same locations and on the same dates. (Hedigan J, *Second Hearing*, Judgment, 15 November 1991, pp.51–2)

Variants of these scenarios surfaced on many occasions and were embellished with graphic accounts of the suffering that would result from the torture and mutilation of his victims. In a letter of 30 October 1988, Garry pronounced his ambition 'to be the first in Australia to kill a Prime Minister or Premier. And it's my ambition to be Australia's worst mass murderer! I want to butcher, torture, and kill hundreds, and if possible, thousands!!!' By 21 February 1989 the Acting Supervisor of Classification reported Garry's plan 'to create havoc and murder upon his release' by bombing the Police Academy and Staff Training College, poisoning the water supply of Melbourne and 'killing anyone who looks at me [him] the wrong way'. Had this challenge not been written during a new climate of fear about the safety of members of the police force, there might not have been such a strong reaction, which reverberated around the various arms of government, guaranteeing a watchful preparedness on the part of authorities. The Victoria Police Force was unusually sensitive to criminal underworld activity and the risk posed to its members at this particular time for it had already suffered loss of life with the bombing of a car outside the Russell Street city operational headquarters in 1986, and the murder of two young constables on duty in Walsh Street, South Yarra, two years later. The Hoddle and Queen Street incidents, already noted, occurred in

1987. As Garry's release date approached, the Victoria Police took the unusual step of checking the prisoner's alleged contacts with criminal terrorist groups and sending its elite Special Operations Group to alert city hospitals about the need for increased security.

In addition to prison disruption and broad-ranging threats to the community, Garry employed a third strategy: self-mutilation. There was evidence that he had toyed with such ideas whilst in juvenile institutions and the early files refer to suicidal ideation, such as a preoccupation with gassing himself, swallowing marbles and holding his breath until lapsing into unconsciousness. In adult institutions, however, his performance was nothing short of spectacular, even when considered against an expected high level of violence within a security institution. In a period of 11 years there were at least 75 separate acts, including:

> drinking Brasso, swallowing razor blades, cutting off portions of both his right and left ears, cutting off his left nipple, cutting off the remainder of his right ear and his right nipple, severing the Achilles' tendons in his legs on a number of occasions, reopening wounds, cutting his scrotum and cutting off part of his penis, inserting staples and tin in his penis, cutting the heel of his left leg, swallowing wire, swallowing the contents of a nine volt battery, inserting fish bones into his left eye, hammering nails into his feet, obtaining blood from his arm, swallowing metal filings, broken glass and other objects, and innumerable occasions of slashing himself with sharp objects, including razor blades on his arms, chest, legs, feet, ankles, stomach and other parts of his body. (Hedigan J, *Second Hearing*, Judgment, 15 November 1991, p.51)

It was distressing for staff that treatment refusal, interference with dressings and the ripping out of sutures very frequently accompanied these excesses. Wounds were often contaminated with urine and faeces, and these substances then injected into body cavities impaled with pencils or ballpoint pens.

Such events were grotesque enough, but Garry was unusual in drawing attention to his mutilations by writing to the press, television stations and members of the Government. For example, in one of a series of letters to Pauline Toner, then Minister for Community Welfare Services, Garry pointed out that he was said to have cost the Government $300,000 in medical and hospital fees. His description of his actions conveyed sexual undertones and was a crude attempt at emotional blackmail with the intention of causing discomfiture and concern:

> Then [in] my most infamous act, I cut off my entire penis with a razor blade. According to my lawyers, psychos, and medical staff, it shocked the community. I have newspaper clippings with me now. It is not a pretty story. (19 May 1992)

In this same letter, he threatened to amputate what remained of his testicles, to lacerate one eye, cut off both eyelids, tongue and lips, extract the wire from his stomach, remove part of his intestines and also a section of leg muscles and tendons, unless he was moved from H Division, a unit renowned for its bleakness, isolation and loss of privileges, to the more liberal regime of G Division. His final dramatic threat was that should he survive he would expose his heart, and had instructed his mother and lawyers to inform the press of this event. In a sudden twist, he mentioned his achievements in poetry and music and deplored the brutality of H Division, expressing his wish to be transferred elsewhere. This letter typifies Garry's ability to shift suddenly from irrational outpourings to a more reasoned position, so that it was difficult to dismiss his threats entirely, despite the incongruity of their expression and the well-chosen images. His appeals were a curious compound of the primitive evoking abhorrence in the observer, oscillating with a demonstration of articulate reasonableness bolstered by a childlike belief in his own persuasiveness.

Garry's self-destructive behaviour was explained variously in the context of later court hearings, but it certainly enhanced his reputation within the macho, male environment of the prison system and guaranteed him an aura of inviolability. It was a symbolic expression of being beyond the reach of staff and inmates. As Dr Grigor graphically explained to a tribunal hearing:

> When he got to the point of slicing off his ears, his nipples and, ye Gods, his penis, that created in prison circles to this day an awe of Garry David, particularly in a very macho system... Senior prison officers have never seen anything like it and I think that he then achieved a status in the prison system which he knew that 'I've got you'. And in the very complex power struggles between prison officers and prisoners, Garry earned a reputation second to none of saying to prison officers 'Well, I can't bash you up physically. I can't do that because I'm not the biggest, toughest person...but you cannot touch me'. (*MHRB Statement of Reasons in GIPW*, 9 May 1990, p.10)

Through these three interlocking strategies, with their strong visual component of potential prison riots, terrorist strikes against the community and gross violation of the human body, Garry David challenged prison strategies of control. Whilst the flamboyance and grandiosity of his written statements generally created unease amongst senior staff rather than genuine fear in that environment, the misuse of his body was of a different order, because this violated a physical boundary and protected space, either his own or that of others. Over time it became a powerful weapon for, when all else failed, he could resort to the blackmail of further self-injury of an extreme kind, or hint at the unleashing of a primitive physical force with unforeseen consequences. Garry's wide-ranging tirade in a letter to Dr Grigor was blunt:

> What has happened to my body can happen to my enemies. Try to stop me, Dr Grigor. I dare you. But you can't. You can't certify me 'cos I'm not insane, even 'tho I worship Satan. (11 June 1989)

The autonomy displayed in this form of self-torture was as unsettling for the disciplinary responses of the custodial system as it was antithetical to therapeutic goals. If, as Foucault maintains, 'the body is involved in power relations; they invest it, mark it, train it, torture it, force it to carry out tasks, to perform ceremonies, to emit signs' (1977b, p.25), then the Garry David experience proved to be markedly different from this expectation of disciplinary control. Over a sustained period, Garry David was demonstrating that a recalcitrant prisoner could challenge the carceral process by flaunting his body as something to be mutilated at will, or used as a bargaining tool. He was not the 'knowable' and 'docile' recipient of panoptical attention in a Foucauldian sense, but was able to achieve considerable autonomy within the carceral system, at the same time generating an awareness of his potential dangerousness for the outside community. In such circumstances, it was scarcely surprising that his day-to-day management constituted an ongoing problem during more than a decade of incarceration, ultimately giving rise to some unusual therapeutic compromises.

VAN THERAPY AND INSTITUTIONAL MOBILITY

The ingredients for the authorities' experience of Garry during his incarceration were established early. He was manipulative, unpredictable and threatening. It was behaviour of a kind not unknown in a maximum security prison, but these elements were now being demonstrated at such an extreme level that they placed an onerous duty on all mental health professionals, as well as on custodial officers. Medical staff were in the invidious position of having to restrain his behavioural excesses chemically when physical ones had failed, and having to resort to certification in the absence of any apparent and sustained psychotic illness. Either action could incur criticism, as the following chain of events illustrates. On one evening in February 1985 Garry became highly agitated over a period of many hours, finally setting fire to his mattress. He was calmed with an injection of chlorpromazine and later appealed to the Ombudsman arguing that this constituted a legal assault. The subsequent inquiry canvassed, amongst other matters, the reasons for the medical staff's failure to certify the prisoner on this occasion (file note, 18 February 1985). It was seemingly a 'no-win' situation.

The staff's frustration is evident from the transcript of an important Health Department meeting held on 19 August, 1981 – nine years prior to Garry's release date – and attended by 11 medical personnel, one psychologist, the superintendent of the prison, a member of Community Welfare Services and the Ombudsman (*Notes on Meeting to Discuss Gary David (alias Webb)*). It was intended to provide a focus for the serious concerns being voiced about this prisoner and to emphasise the need for staff cooperation. The meeting's purpose was 'to agree [on] a policy of management which will result in the greatest benefit, or the least damage, to the prisoner and to the community'. Despite the equivocation implicit in the phrase 'or the least damage', it represented a clear intent to direct professional resources towards devising a management programme.

The problem was stated quite cogently at the outset as being either 'rehabilitation on the basis of putting right what is wrong, and not on the basis of a diagnosis of a disease (which does not exist), or of psychiatric responsibility (which has been ineffective)'. There was general agreement that rehabilitation would involve a minimal level of security and punishment, an operant conditioning programme, together with the expenditure of considerable time and effort by a wide range of professionals. In this way it was argued that there could be:

> avoidance of the garbage can kind of management that throws him into some allegedly beneficial receptacle when his behaviour becomes intolerable to some group. This is epitomised by certification which, far from being the therapeutic procedure it is supposed to be, has been harmful in this case and should be avoided at all costs, unless there should develop some new and treatable mental illness. (Meeting, 19 August 1981)

Yet, in the years to follow, there is little evidence to suggest that this 'garbage can kind of management' could be dissipated in the face of Garry's own techniques of survival and bouts of non-cooperation. Nine years later, the Director-General of Prisons, Peter Harmsworth, frankly admitted defeat to the all-party Social Development Committee in the following words:

> I must be candid and admit that the Office [of Corrections] could have done more. The point I make in defence is that obviously we are dealing with a lot of people in any one day who are coming up for release. On the whole we do a pretty good job in terms of welfare and community services picking up these people. However, we could have done more for Webb [David]. (SDC, *Evidence*, p.1167)

It is reasonable to question why such good intentions failed, despite the general willingness to utilise available resources. There was no doubt that the particular problems posed by Garry had been recognised at the earlier meeting, which had resulted from the Director-General of Community Welfare Services plea to the Health Commission 'to do something about him'. But, even then there were indications that it was the mixture of criminality coupled with bouts of frequent self-mutilation which led to uncertainty about the locus of management, as well as the authority to be held responsible. At the time, Dr TS of the Alcohol, Drug and Forensic Branch of the Mental Health Division, noted the dilemma for all concerned:

> The problem of diagnosis rests on the fact that his bizarre behaviour is such as to make it obvious to anybody that he must be a case for treatment, whereas he has persistently failed to show evidence of any mental illness. (Meeting, 19 August 1981)

He further suggested that the proper conclusion was that Garry had a 'borderline personality', which was neither a mental illness nor a personality disorder, and admitted that this conclusion might be seen 'as an example of building an imaginary fence and then sitting on it – a most inelegant position'! The unsatisfactory nature of the term 'borderline' had already been noted by the Psychiatrist Superintendent in written advice proffered to Garry's counsel, in which he referred to it as 'a state on the border of a psychosis…he may fluctuate between psychosis and non-psychosis' (8 July 1981). This was a matter about which Justice Fullagar later sought greater precision by questioning whether the adjective borderline positions itself on 'the border of normality or on the border of psychosis…or is it just there to confuse the unfortunate layman?' (Fullagar J, *First Hearing*, 6 August 1990).

From 1981 onwards were was little doubt that Garry sorely tested both the criminal justice and mental health systems, which are usually thought to operate under two quite distinct rationales: a retributive philosophy on the one hand and a treatment orientation on the other. Throughout his imprisonment he was frequently moved to an isolation cell when his behaviour became excessively disruptive and charged with breaches of regulations, although formal sanctions did not always ensue in view of their inflammatory nature. Even at the 1981 meeting, the prison Medical Superintendent highlighted the difficulty of trying to place Garry appropriately in the prison, for he was 'not mad…but untreatable and dangerous':

> His best behaviour inside the prison was when he was under some form of psychiatric care in G Division. Garry cannot be treated inside the prison system, and that accounts for the failure of the prison system to manage his problem.

It was a measure of last resort to transfer Garry to a psychiatric hospital. Between August 1976 and April 1984 he was certified on seven occasions by different doctors and treated as a voluntary patient at two institutions, from which he absconded. On the surface of it there was broad agreement during this period that he was at least transiently certifiable under the provisions of the 1959 Mental Health Act.

A history of Garry's hospital admissions at that time:

2 to 9 August 1976: Royal Park Psychiatric Hospital (involuntary). Certified by police surgeon after being found wandering around with a gun and threatening to kill his mother. Diagnosis of 'reactive depression' and 'personality disorder'. Absconded and made a voluntary patient on 4 August.

29 to 31 October 1978: Larundel Psychiatric Hospital (involuntary) – had been sniffing glue, drinking floor polish and injecting heroin once a week. The medical officer gave a diagnosis of 'classical psychopathic personality disorder' on the grounds of his life history and presenting mental state.

1 August to 6 September 1979: Aradale Hospital, J Ward. Certified s.52 from St Augustine's Ward at St Vincent's Hospital after self-mutilating, and threats to castrate himself and gouge his eyes out. Diagnosis of 'personality disorder (explosive type) and heroin abuse'.

10 January to 19 March 1980: Mont Park Mental Hospital. Certified s.52 with a diagnosis of 'antisocial sociopathic personality with poor prognosis'.

25 June to 27 June 1980: Lakeside Hospital, Ballarat. Referred as a voluntary patient after Mont Park had refused admission; absconded.

29 September to 7 November 1980: Aradale Hospital, J Ward. Certified from St Vincent's Hospital after threats of electrocution and an intention to shoot at Jews and police.

28 November 1980 to 15 January 1981: Aradale Hospital, J Ward. Certified on the grounds of refusing treatment for a festering self-inflicted wound.

10 December 1983 to 18 April 1984: Aradale Hospital, J Ward. Certified because of suicide risk. Diagnosis of 'personality disorder with predominantly sociopathic or asocial manifestation'.

In many respects, Garry's institutional career paralleled that of his father, Rupert, described in the files as a grossly institutionalised 'lovable rogue', who had been certified on a number of occasions during lengthy periods of imprisonment. He was first admitted to Kew Mental Hospital in 1945 and remained there until 1947, sometimes under restraint. In 1951 he returned for another 12 months, and there is reference in the prison files to admission to Kew Mental Hospital in 1960 for persecutory delusions of a psychotic type, which responded quickly to treatment with largactil, with a further certification to Mont Park Mental Hospital in 1980. Rupert's institutional career is perhaps best summarised in a prison officer's report:

> This prisoner is well known in the system due to his long record of imprisonment. This man is both erratic and mentally disturbed and completely institutionalised in every respect. At this stage it is doubtful as to whether he could cope with the normal problems of living when at liberty. Will probably continue to remain a burden to society in the future... Suggest he remains at Pentridge as a shelter in D Division Hospital (30 June 1981).

However, Garry's periods of hospitalisation were somewhat briefer than those of his father and began to be referred to, in colloquial vein, as 'van therapy' – that is, they were intended as a respite for prison personnel on those occasions of persistent treatment refusal for self-inflicted injuries. It was a pragmatic response, rather than one motivated by any reasonable expectation that psychiatric treatment was either necessary or possible. As the Chief Medical Officer (CMO) of the Mental Health Division, explained to the Director of Correctional Services:

> It is my opinion, and it is the opinion that I have held for a number of years in relation to Mr David and other prisoners of a similar type, that we can avoid the situations of escalation by responding rapidly to changing events. I have often spoken of what I term 'van therapy', namely avoiding a situation of mounting confrontation leading to a psychotic episode by physically moving the prisoner to a different location. I have always been willing to approve the transfer of patients from H Division to J Ward and I have found this to be a remarkably effective way of defusing such situations. I believe that such a policy in regard to Mr David could well be effective in reducing the strength and number of episodes of a traumatic nature in relation to him.

> I would envisage that, when he has been returned to Pentridge, should a confrontation be arising likely to lead to a psychotic episode, that he be promptly seen and, if there are sufficient grounds for certification, he should be immediately returned to J Ward. On the other hand, if it was found that his psychosis had substantially settled, he would again be returned to Pentridge. I appreciate that this process involves a considerable expenditure in man-hours and

trouble, but I am unable to think of any other solution more effective in this case. (28 February 1984)

The curious term 'van therapy' began to gain currency in medical and correctional circles, solely in relation to Garry David, and it was certainly not without a measure of control by the prisoner himself. By 1985, one psychiatrist openly conceded that 'he controls his own destiny by self-mutilation and manipulation of his gaolers'. He further contended that psychiatrists had employed strategies 'to protect ourselves from one another', thereby thwarting any plans for the long-term interest of the prisoner and the community at large:

> The strategies used can be summarised by the term 'van therapy' which has involved moving the problem from place to place at intervals, which have remained largely under the control of the prisoner, but never actually achieving anything therapeutic. Indeed, none has ever been forecast to my knowledge and certainly all that has been achieved has been deterioration. (Memo, 9 January 1985)

No further comments of this sort are contained in the files after the implementation of the Mental Health Act 1986 with its specific reference to the exclusion of those with 'an antisocial personality' and its emphasis on treatment, rather than custody for convenience. These two aspects were instrumental in fostering the growing belief that it would be unacceptable to certify Garry as an expedient short-term solution for an ongoing behavioural problem.

Whilst van therapy was used as a measure of last resort until 1985 to defuse escalating violence and counter the increasing loss of morale in the prison, Garry's frequent movement between institutions was a further factor adding to the general instability of his overall life experience. From early childhood he had not experienced a secure home environment and in the institutions was subjected to an inordinate number of moves, either at his own own request or as a direct consequence of his behaviour. These were interspersed with medical emergencies necessitating sudden shifts to the prison hospital or to St Augustine's Ward of St Vincent's Hospital in inner Melbourne with a security escort. For example, in 1981 there were 37 separate movements, ranging from the Pentridge Hospital, St Vincent's Hospital, H Division, police custody and D Division, with 32 in the following year. This pattern was sustained throughout his time in custody culminating in a remarkable total of almost 400 institutional movements.

The frequent relocations of this one prisoner entailed a number of consequences. In terms of Garry's relationship with other prisoners he acquired an increased visibility and special status, since he was both feared because of the unpredictability of his aggressive outbursts, and admired for his anti-authoritarian stance to the extent that many of his exploits were emulated. There was a duality in

Garry's self-presentation. He frequently chose to portray himself as a misunderstood folk hero aggrieved by the authorities' unnecessarily harsh treatment, but he also adopted a threatening stance towards the wider community. For example, he was often referred to as the founding member of the earless 'Van Gogh' club, which united discontented prisoners in common action. Even though his movements around the prison were triggered by medical or punitive reasons, the outcome was increased disturbance within the general prison community, for which there was no effective redress. Thus it appeared that this one prisoner was nullifying traditional correctional strategies, yet rendering innovative solutions risky when they diverged from existing regulations.

Second, Garry was able to acquire a great deal of knowledge about the way the two systems operated and reap the advantages of each. It was no doubt galling for mental health staff to be informed that he found prison preferable, because it provided opportunities lacking in the psychiatric system such as greater privacy and increased access to personal possessions. In vexatious vein Garry would then remind custodial staff about the benefits of psychiatric hospitals, where 'proper medical and psychiatric care is available'. On one occasion, with a piquant sense of irony, he challenged a psychiatrist to certify him on the grounds that 'his sanity' was at risk by confinement in H Division (letter, 9 June 1982).

It must be pointed out that some of Garry's concerns were realistic and appropriate, for his confinement experience had indeed been variable in terms of the degree of freedom of internal movement, the activities provided and the rigidity of the regime. Each Division within the prison was distinct and separate in its mode of operation. H Division was grim and forbidding with its cold, bluestone cells, restricted social contact, controlled movement and long periods of seclusion. In keeping with its punitive image, prisoners in H Division were highly regimented and governed by a regime of silence. They were moved around the prison singly and their small cells were bare, except for an iron bed. Originally sentenced by the courts to 'hard labour', this work consisted of breaking bluestone boulders into chips of road metal – a practice which continued into the 1960s until replaced, rather incongruously, by soft-toy making. On the other hand both the Special Purpose Unit (B Division) and G Division were characterised by the concessions each offered to prisoner movement and participation in a variety of activities with specially selected and skilled staff. Thus Garry could join occupational therapy groups, use a computer, keep birds and interact quite freely with other prisoners. These divisions had a more 'open' feel than the somewhat Dickensian J Ward at Ararat with its bluestone cells, inadequate facilities, lack of sanitation and isolated location.

Third, Garry's detailed knowledge of the way in which a maximum security institution functions allowed him to magnify differences in the philosophy and strategies designed for his management, so that at times there was an undeniable atmosphere of staff recriminations with blame being apportioned for failure to find constructive solutions. The stage on which he could generate tensions had widened, because his institutional mobility resulted in direct dealings with most of the psychiatrists, medical officers, psychologists, occupational therapists, nursing staff and welfare officers employed by the Office of Corrections. The files directly identify 18 psychiatrists, 8 medical officers, a large team of surgeons, 6 psychologists, 6 forensic nursing staff, 3 occupational therapists and 6 welfare staff as having had specific contact with Garry and some particular responsibility for his management during the period 1980 to 1990. In addition there was the staff of the Pentridge Hospital, St Augustine's Ward at St Vincent's Hospital and J Ward, Ararat. During the court and tribunal hearings in 1990, nine further psychiatrists were involved in giving evidence.

One of the consequences of this institutional mobility and contact with so many staff was his enhanced ability to avoid any long-term commitment to a therapeutic regime and, as many of the reports confirm, he delighted in playing off one staff member against another. At the same time, he was an acute observer of both the prison and mental health systems, often hinting that he might use information and evidence of dissension to his advantage. It is unlikely that the compounding effect of all these incidents over a ten-year period would not have had some impact on the views of those striving to express opinions about his dangerousness, especially in the formal knowledge confines of tribunal and court settings.

THERAPEUTIC PIROUETTES

Both Goffman (1961) and Foucault (1997b) rely on images of therapy being dispensed through the knowledge/power nexus to submissive recipients. Resistance may be generated, but it rarely assumes such interlocking and concurrent strategies as were initiated by Garry David. He constantly repudiated the way in which he was being made into 'a serviceable object' (Goffman 1961, pp.321–86), and indeed impugned medical ability by challenging the doctors' efficacy within the gaol, at least in their ability to provide services appropriate for a severely mentally disordered prisoner. In addition, he questioned the legitimacy of therapy in a custodial environment and drew attention to the fluctuating combination of treatment, advocacy and control on which it is premised. The interplay of the power component was akin to a game of anticipation and skill, for this prisoner patently possessed a remarkable ability to create serious staff divisions, reject the medical and psychiatric treatment being offered to him, and expose fundamental doubts about professional decision making.

Garry proceeded from an understanding that there was a duty of care to be provided by prison and therapeutic staff, who were ultimately responsible to the Ministers of Corrections and Health through their relevant departmental heads.

He was well aware that as a prisoner, but not as a psychiatric patient, he had the right to refuse this care, which would otherwise constitute an assault in law. This differentiation between the rights of prisoners and the rights of psychiatric patients allowed him many ingenious opportunities to exploit treatment and test the therapeutic relationship to advantage. This was accomplished in multifarious ways: he could make unreasonable demands, or simply not cooperate; he could bargain and even inject fear into the relationship; industrial unrest might be instigated; staff could be targetted with unpleasant and threatening allegations; and he could sometimes demand drugs of addiction. In essence, he was able to use his situation as a mentally disturbed prisoner to expose the inherent ambiguity of offering therapeutic services within the prison, as the following examples well illustrate.

First of all, Garry relayed the conflicting message that he required help, yet doubted the will and professional expertise of therapists to provide this. The naked challenge was ever present and dangled as a bait for inexperienced staff to test their skills. At times his appeals were patently childish and taunted staff with their apparent failure to meet basic professional obligations by using clinical objectivity as a shield against further involvement. In a letter to Dr John Grigor, about whom he was intermittently ambivalent, he complained:

> I cannot understand why you hate me so much and why you are against me. Doctor, with all the scars on my body, with all my sexual problems, and all my nightmares, life for me is a struggle. I want to change, but I need help... Please do not abandon me, Doctor, I'm worth saving. (18 January 1987)

He was masterly in finding direct and subtle ways to undermine the validity of the service model. He at once demanded treatment, yet could render it ineffective – a pattern, which became well honed. One early experience of the use of this tactic is described by the Acting CMO in a letter to J Ward's Superintendent:

> When asked to discuss his problems he said that he saw no point in wounds on his leg being sutured, nor in the open safety pin or razor blades in his stomach being removed, as he intended to kill himself even if he had to spread himself in little pieces... I pointed out to Mr David that we were bound to help him because of our opinions as to his condition. He became more distressed and ripped the dressings off the unsutured lacerations on his left arm and repeated that our efforts would be to no avail – that he would damage himself further and ultimately kill himself. (26 September 1980)

On this occasion, he was certified so that treatment could proceed in the absence of consent. However, at other times, doctors were forced to stand by helplessly for fear of being charged with assault should they override Garry's objections. Dr Grigor graphically detailed an early rejection of medical intervention as follows:

> Garry was adamant that without being allowed to be returned to 'G' Division he would not allow further dressings to occur on his legs and that ultimately this would necessitate amputation of some portions of his lower limbs… I formed a view that he was uncaring enough about his body to follow through with his established pattern of behaviour and, although I could smell his rotting wounds, I was unable to assess for myself, his current medical status. He did, however, look far from well. (24 February 1981)

Not only was Garry's behaviour offensive, but it derided medical training and authority by rejecting the basic principles of hygiene and healing, and by the deliberate defiling of wounds. At the same time, he dangled the tantalising hope of improvement as an incitement to further effort, but then nullified this with a spate of frenzied and unforeseen acts, often blaming those around him for their occurrence and failure to intercede. Therapeutic staff faced the humiliation of appearing ineffectual in front of prison officers and of being reduced to the role of passive observers, sometimes in life-threatening circumstances.

Second, Garry demanded instant attention, despite his knowledge of the acute lack of clinical resources in the prison. If this were not forthcoming, then property destruction resulted: setting fire to his cell, the erection of barricades and the self-violence of gross mutilation. Once again, it was blatant manipulation, but difficult to ignore when couched within a framework of medical or psychological need. Examples are innumerable, but the following note written from an isolation cell displays a provocative theatricality:

> wire pushed through vocal chords into throat and into back of spine at neck. Will have no treatment until I see K…, psychologist. My decision is irreversible. Wire is coated in faeces. Bad pain in back of spine and back [writing falters here]. Right arm almost paralysed…damaged throat. Wire pushed through vocal chords. Can't talk. Just barely… (24 February 1987)

He was taken to St Vincent's Hospital. On his return two days later, he set fire to his suicide blankets, and that same evening indicated that he *might* suspend further self-mutilation if the female psychiatric nurses were to visit him next day.

The third strategy was associated with this need for an immediate response and concerned Garry's ability to indulge in crude forms of therapeutic bargaining. Even treatment refusal became negotiable, when he suggested that staff members were taking him too seriously since he was prepared to accept treatment or a bath with 'a little bit of friendly force'. He inappropriately encouraged a female psychiatrist to try this approach (letter, 30 June 1982). The underlying message was that for psychiatry to operate within a prison environment, staff could not be blinded to elements of coercion and close bodily contact and had to accept the accompanying sexual innuendo. At other times, he capitalised on the fact that staff have a statutory duty to respond to medical need with threats that he was intending to cause self-injury. These were issued with dramatic flair, such as that to a female psychiatrist - 'I will remove a foot of my bowel; blood will flow' (13 September 1988). Such a possibility was not without precedent: on one occasion he had slashed his lower left arm after issuing a warning about staff refusal to give him an injection to relieve stomach pain and vomiting, even though the forensic nurse had informed him that a doctor's authority was required (incident report, 16 October 1985).

The fourth strategy preyed on the sense of fear, which Garry was able to inject into some therapeutic relationships, and there was evidence of its personal and industrial impact. In the period from 1987 onwards he appears to have been directly confrontational towards both prison and mental health staff in innumerable ways. For example, early that year, he cornered a chief prison officer and threatened him with meat hooks (27 November 1986); made threats to one female psychologist, whom he held hostage with a telephone cord wrapped around her neck whilst placing faeces in a pocket of her clothing (22 January 1987); and there was ongoing reference to release plans, which included shooting staff as they left the main gate at night (9 January 1987). After being moved from the greater freedom of G to H Division, Garry retaliated by locking an occupational therapist in a room with prisoners. Two female staff members consequently resigned. These incidents not unnaturally engendered a realistic apprehension of fear among the prison community and demeaned the role of the staff concerned.

Industrial discontent festered during the entire period of Garry's confinement and was compounded by the fact that many staff believed him to be inappropriately contained within the prison. As early as 1983 the nursing staff and the Victorian Prison Staff Association each proposed specific action to overcome the problem, a matter causing ministerial concern. The nurses were particularly appalled by the extent of Garry's self-injuries and threatened to withdraw their services. Later that year the Deputy Charge Nurse of the hospital requested a custodial escort to enable staff to continue performing their duties in G Division (12 October). In the ensuing years staff unrest did not abate, leading one medical practitioner to write to the Director-General of Corrections requesting a meeting with the Attorney-General 'to ensure that Garry David is not released from custody to cause damage to himself, health staff members, their families and the community in general' (13 May 1987). It was an unusual plea on behalf of professional staff inured to the strain of caring for troublesome prisoners and, in this instance, undoubtedly exacerbated by the prisoner's vivid descriptions of the mayhem and butchery he planned for two female psychologists and their families on his release.

Through these multifaceted threats to personal safety and professional reputations Garry orchestrated an unprecedented atmosphere of staff divisiveness.

Frictions were especially acute in relation to the position of female therapeutic staff, whom he cajoled with a portrayal of his very real needs, then later sought to humiliate by exposing their vulnerability to suggestive comments and their professional inadequacy in handling these. As early as 1982 his relationship with them had appeared to oscillate between extreme dependency and vitriolic rejection and the pattern continued throughout his confinement. This cruel vendetta typified in a letter to two psychologists conveyed the mixed message that they ought to help him, but were refusing to do so:

> To be honest, I am insanely and violently angry. I do not understand why you would abandon me, refuse me any psychological treatment… I am informing all Divisions that prisoners cannot trust you; you betray their trust and you will abandon them if they regress. (26 February 1989)

Garry's insistence on demanding the professional attentions of female staff prompted Dr Grigor to note, somewhat wryly, that 'nowhere else in psychiatry is it the patient who dictates the required sex of the therapist', adding that in his 23 years' experience as a medical practitioner and psychiatrist he found the letters written to these female staff members to be 'amongst the most objectionable, demeaning and vile' that he had ever encountered. He believed that individual therapeutic attention should be given by

> a very experienced male therapist of some seniority who might, just possibly, be able to work towards a breakthrough and interrupt a very predictable cycle of Mr David's which is, through a variety of strategies, to neutralise any female therapist, so that no effective therapy focused on his problems is possible. (24 March 1987)

However, there remained ongoing tension over this issue and some female staff clearly found their therapeutic role disquieting. In the words of one such psychiatrist:

> He then accused me of not caring or wanting to help him and also stated a lot of other people don't care or won't help him. Garry stated he would pay back those people by 'getting at their families'. Due to this man's history and his recent threats I feel that it would be better if I did not see his [him] again. (1 June 1989)

Soon afterwards, Dr Grigor indicated that he had instructed a female registrar not to continue seeing Garry on matters of psychiatric importance, because the prisoner has his own 'uncanny knack of vilifying people' in such a way as to cause marked distress. He added:

Garry has continued with his usual adroitness to play professional staff off against each other and has, as is his wont, been better at doing this with women professional staff than males. This has led to some fighting amongst professionals, no doubt to Garry's delight. (8 August 1989)

Other threats were perhaps more transparent in intent. For example, accusations were made in writing to the Director of Forensic Psychiatry Services himself that he was 'a careless, unfeeling, cold-hearted bastard' in comparison to the 'honest, hard-working and caring' occupational therapists (4 July 1988). A little earlier, however, Garry had pleaded with him to 'either help me or shoot me, or put the rope around my neck yourself' (2 May 1988). Whilst this histrionic tone may have diminished the seriousness of intent in this letter, the constant undercurrent of complaints and threats led to the open apportioning of blame, thereby focusing the attention of politicians and other authorities.

The fifth element in Garry's bargaining position centred on the use of drugs, which were used in his management. He is reported as 'requesting and demanding' high doses of valium, a sedative many staff considered likely to assist him in over-coming any lingering inhibition about self-mutilation, despite Garry arguing that it helped him to control his behavioural problems. An early report identified this medical dilemma and indicated that hospital staff would be negligent in acceding to such a request, although they might equally be considered negligent in refusing 'a treatment that would make the patient feel better about himself' (2 September 1981). It was indeed difficult to establish a firm policy about the use of drugs in this case, given the serious nature of his pattern of self-injury, and at least one doctor was censured for not observing the agreed protocol and allowing pethidine to be administered. It was as if Garry, quite early in his incarceration, had devised a therapeutic noose. Both the offering and withholding of drugs could lead to adverse consequences and allow further manipulation of his situation and the mocking of his custodians. This dilemma was the subject of a note at the time of one discharge from St Vincent's Hospital, when he was 'returned precipitately on a Sunday as untreatable, but paradoxically accompanied by amitriptyline pills'. There was some dispute about their efficacy, but a realisation that refusal of access to the tablets could also expose prison staff 'to the possible accusation of depriving him of treatment, which a hospital doctor presumably thought to be indicated' (medical advice to Governor, 16 July 1979).

Finally, the more general areas of treatment were exploited to the stage of trivialisation over the years. Whilst the prisoner refused to accept intervention for gross and life-threatening injuries, he insisted on medication in the absence of specific symptoms. Throughout his confinement, treatment became couched in terms of his legal rights. A staff meeting of 8 June 1982 affirmed his right to refuse treatment and the Health Commission approved a policy of acceptance of such refusals after self-mutilatory incidents. At this time, at least one doctor was casti-gated for not following the guidelines and allowing an opiate to be administered on the basis of telephoned instructions without direct examination by the doctor concerned. The incident occurred 'amid a stream of hostility, abuse and self-destruction, a second-hand complaint of pain, [which] resulted in his being given an addictive drug of questionable value to his condition'. It was evident, however, that this incident provided Garry with a new avenue by which to manip-ulate medical staff through complaints to the Victorian Ombudsman.

TREATMENT OR PUNISHMENT?

A policy struggle

An early statement by the Mental Health Department's CMO heralded the unusual nature of the difficulties accompanying Garry David's management in the prison system:

> As seen today, it would seem that there is no facility either in the prison system or the mental hospital system where he could be appropriately managed. The problems of management are dictated by him, and probably must always be so, regardless of the intensity of staff management. (11 December 1980)

Throughout Garry's confinement there is evidence of a growing sense of frustra-tion in the internal written reports and a level of frankness about the difficulty of maintaining objectivity. The word 'exasperated' was not infrequent, and even an early report described Garry as being 'a thorough nuisance, who is quite extraordi-narily good at manipulating matters' (7 September 1978). Over the years, it was painfully apparent that Garry was a problem that would not go away and, under-standably, one psychiatrist referred to him as a continuing 'irritant':

> His threatening behaviour to all staff who attempt to work with him thera-peutically continues unabated, and it is difficult to see any progress being made in attempting to assist him to behave in a more mature and appropriate manner. Although he professes to prefer female therapists, his most objec-tionable behaviour is usually restricted for female members of staff at many levels. His capacity to persuade other prisoners not to take medication, or not to comply with treatment, remains an irritant to all staff. (17 November 1986)

This reaction was to be expected with a prisoner engaged in a campaign of vilifica-tion jeopardising job security. Medical staff could unexpectedly be accused of a basic dereliction of their duty of care and, at one stage, Garry made formal threats to launch an investigation into their 'dismal' conduct towards prisoners (25 April 1988), and conducted a campaign against Dr Grigor threatening to 'tarnish his

[your] reputation or job' (13 May 1988). Around this time, and much to the chagrin of Pentridge staff, he mischievously issued a press statement under the dramatic heading: 'Lesbian Love Blossoms in Prison Psychologists' Love Scandal' (Melbourne *Truth* n.d.). These, and similar eruptions, enabled him to deflect personal responsibility for his own lack of progress and continued threats onto those working in the prison, and he did so in a very public way, as this letter to the anchor person of a nightly television news programme attests:

> People who work in this prison, such as psychiatrist Dr Grigor, certain nurses, occupational therapists and screws in the prison system have done nothing but hinder my chances to reform myself. In fact, they have on occasions, done their best to retard and destroy my rehabilitative and re-education goals. In fact some of them have tried to encourage me to become a 'raving psycho' by doing something similar to the Hoddle St, Queen St, etc. massacres. (15 July 1988 to 'Hinch at 7? or Hyprocrisy at 7?')

Constant criticism and unexpected vituperative attacks alternated with periods of cooperation, reasonableness and charm. Under such circumstances, it was scarcely surprising that staff found it difficult to maintain a coherent policy towards Garry David. Yet the need was imperative, as the Acting CMO of the Mental Health Division had recognised at the outset when he wrote to the Director General of the Department of Community Welfare Services establishing the guidelines to be followed. It is a considered letter, intended to clarify uncertainties about Garry David's status as either a prisoner or as a psychiatric patient and to lay the ground-work for his therapeutic management.

> Garry David was certified as Garry Ian Patrick Webb as a security patient on 24 September 1980, and was transferred from St Vincent's Hospital (where he had gone from Pentridge remand) on 29 September 1980. The following recommendations were made:
>
> (i)   Mr David has been occasionally, but not consistently, certifiable. During most of his contact with Mental Health and Community Welfare Services, his problem has been one of personality.
>
> (ii) Whether or not considered certifiable at any given time, one facet of his behaviour has been manipulation of his environment.
>
> (iii) Because of this manipulative element it is essential that he and all parties to his care, treatment or detention, clearly understand that:
>
> • when he acts psychotically he must be treated as psychotic in which case J Ward Ararat is the only suitable facility; and
>
> • when he is not acting psychotically he must be in the corrective system presumably in Pentridge;

• his desire to go to Mont Park mental hospital is not reasonable under the given circumstances. If he eventually shows long-term psychotic symptomatology, as sometimes happens in such cases, he must understand that J Ward is the only appropriate facility, but that given clear-cut and *long term* improvement Mont Park might become a possibility. This could only be so following an accomplished contract of acceptable behaviour in J Ward.

For such a scheme as outlined above to be effective it is essential that there be rapid transfer in either direction between the Mental Health Division and Community Welfare prison system as becomes appropriate under the 'contract'. The mechanism for transfer from Community Welfare Services to the Mental Health Division can be sufficiently rapid, but the procedure is, understandably, much more complex in the other direction. For the success of the proposed common course of action your good offices are requested in ensuring that decertification', when necessary, takes place with the greatest possible speed. (14 October 1980)

Whilst this plan did assist in clarifying Garry's status, the pattern of professional interactions within the prison continued to be affected in time-consuming and costly ways. There was abundant evidence of the diversion of scarce therapeutic resources, when psychiatrists were reminded of the need to be supportive of custodial and other staff seeking to express their 'natural anger and frustration' (14 October 1980). Thus skills were sometimes deployed laterally to assist colleagues and those outside the prison, such as the young women with whom Garry had a penchant for forming ongoing and sometimes disturbing, relationships by letter and telephone.

The fact that this prisoner did not abide by the accepted conventions of patient/therapist conduct had the propensity to generate one of two undesirable reactions from therapeutic staff. Either there was disproportionate energy and time invested in this one case; or there was a distancing from the excessive demands being made, especially when self-inflicted medical emergencies arose. An example of the latter comes from notations on the Office of Corrections' files indicating the difficulty of locating medical staff on one occasion, when Garry was suffering stomach pains from ingested wire (19 September 1985). Prison staff telephoned seven doctors to no avail, necessitating Garry's transfer to the security ward of St Vincent's Hospital. But in terms of the total number of professional interactions such incidents were few and understandable.

Psychiatric staff at Pentridge and J Ward were accustomed to disruptive actions and treatment refusal, yet rarely saw these in such a naked form in an ordinary medical setting. There were repeated scenarios of trips to St Vincent's Hospital, followed by immediate transfer back to the prison, treatment refusal, abuse of nursing staff and dressings being ripped off. Gradually St Vincent's and

Pentridge Hospitals began to express reluctance to be used as emergency backstops, in view of Garry's intolerable inpatient behaviour. For example, in one alarming hospital incident he became aggravated by a female prison officer, argued with a nursing sister, then barricaded the door, tied a noose to the curtain rail and refused to remove it until the doctor appeared (6 August 1989). In a further period of hospitalisation in the same month, he demanded the installation of a television set and, when refused, pulled out a drip feed tube, throwing the contents of his urine bottle at the prison officer escort. He was forcibly restrained and handcuffed to the bed. Although charged under prison regulations, this action only enhanced medical perceptions that he was an unsuitable candidate for the services of a general hospital and that it would be preferable to regard his behaviour as symptomatic of mental illness. Consequently, psychiatric staff members were asked to justify their refusal to certify him not only to politicians and administrators, but also to those in general and other specialist medical practices.

Even from the first days of Garry's confinement, he managed to affect staff morale, as the following letter from the Forensic Psychiatry Service Coordinator to the Governor encapsulates:

> Having arrived in H Division, he has again interfered with his wound and I have been requested to look at it. I have refused on the grounds that it has been seen by the appropriate doctor within the hour and no doubt could be seen again if required, and that he has refused to have it treated in any case. I would be prepared to see the man, even though not on call, if there was the slightest chance of it doing more good than harm, i.e. I know him only too well, am at a low to suggest something helpful, have no treatment to give him, and my presence would be an example of one of the things we are trying to avoid. That is to say it would 'reward' bad behaviour by giving him attention which, in his self-disgust, he probably feels he cannot obtain the other way. In this, incidentally, he is quite wrong, because he has received more attention and professional support than most prisoners in G Division. (16 September 1979)

There is a sense of demoralisation in the phrase 'I am at a low', when explaining the inefficacy of psychiatric and medical interventions to the custodial staff, and an awareness that Garry had managed to subvert treatment from a benevolent intervention to one which might be potentially iatrogenic – indicative of the vulnerability of psychiatric goals to transformation at the whim of a resisting prisoner and in face of the reality of custodial imperatives. Psychiatric staff had the power to order seclusion and physical restraint, but when Garry managed to cut his bindings with secreted razor blades, the only alternative was chemical control, which he then mocked as an ethical breach of their duty of care. In the summary of

available options succinctly outlined by the Forensic Services Coordinator, there
was an early recognition of the unpalatable choices involved for the practice of
psychiatry, and the pattern that was likely to continue:

> He behaves badly – and destructively – and at least makes people do things
> like transferring him backwards and forwards like a yo-yo… In theory, I have
> not the slightest doubt that he should be managed on a reward and punish-
> ment system, but there are many practical difficulties, not the least of which is
> that we cannot control the system e.g. he gets into St Vincent's, is sent back, is
> vociferously declared to be mad by people who refuse to accept responsibility
> for his behaviour etc. We have the alternative course of continuing as we are –
> demonstrably unsuccessful and bad for all, including Garry. We also have a
> possibility of putting him into 'G' – but that would create an impossible situa-
> tion. Or we could certify him – that would solve *our* immediate problem, but
> is ethically questionable and possibly destructive in the long run. I can only
> suggest that we face the fact of our incapacity to cope with Garry and move
> cautiously. (31 July 1979)

The introduction of the Freedom of Information Act in 1980 created an additional
avenue of exploitation and Garry's request for access to his files raised uncertainty
about their potential impact. As the Deputy Director of the Mental Health Division
lamented:

> I have great difficulty with the question of prejudice to Garry David's mental
> health for several reasons. The first of these is that many distinguished fellows
> of the Royal Australian and New Zealand College of Psychiatrists have failed
> to agree on whether he is mad or not anyway. More practically, I am sure that
> if he is presented with a large treatise about himself he will find plenty in it on
> which to work himself up to another probable round of self mutilation, or
> possibly of attacks of a legal or physical nature against some of the authors of
> the comments. On the other hand, I stick to my suggestion that not to reveal
> them might also be prejudicial to his mental health on the grounds that he
> will become worked up about that and possibly will take to self mutilation in
> revenge for the refusal … [it is] the horn of this dilemma on which we sit. (25
> July 1986)

In summary, the prison was the training ground for Garry to develop complex
strategies, which were self-defeating in a rehabilitative sense, but accounted for
many unexpected victories in terms of enhancing his autonomy and reputation for
physical violence. He demonstrated an unusual capacity for controlling his environment, even in those areas of the gaol, where staff–prisoner contact is restricted
for disciplinary reasons. He effectively limited the options available for his man-

agement; ensured that the therapeutic power could neither be wielded continuously, economically, nor effectively; confused the presumed dichotomy between treatment and punishment; and drew attention to the coercive elements of each. His next step was ensuring that medical techniques and disciplinary strategies came under outside scrutiny, thereby inciting further institutional tensions and vacillation in his day-to-day management.

POLITICAL SURVEILLANCE

From 1981 onwards there is evidence that the psychiatric management of Garry David was capturing the attention of the Ombudsman, the Premier, and the Chairman of the Health Commission. Garry's own letters were persuasive enough for the Ombudsman to seek explanations from the Directors of the Health Commission and of Prisons, and to express disquiet about the apparent lack of treatment being offered. At one stage, it was suggested that some of the difficulties might be defused if a special committee were to be appointed to manage this one prisoner. However, there was marked resistance from medical staff to such a measure and one psychiatrist pointed out that Garry was a classified prisoner and, as such, the ultimate responsibility for his management rested with the custodial officers rather than medical staff (30 May 1983). In the extensive correspondence generated throughout 1982 and 1983 the Forensic Psychiatry Service Coordinator reported to the Health Commissioner that an internal transfer from the psychiatric division to the punishment division had occurred because of Garry's disruptive behaviour, which in turn had incurred 'a degree of acrimony among the staff' regarding his appropriate management (14 December 1983). He considered the transfer to have triggered a sudden and dramatic escalation in self-destructive behaviours and treatment refusal, culminating in the establishment of a 'death watch'. During this period of considerable turmoil the medical officer of the prison agreed to take Garry into the hospital over the weekend, albeit reluctantly, should the situation 'become unmanageable'. It is clear from this report that Garry had become neither welcome in the prison, nor in the general and mental hospital systems and that, on occasions, decisions were politically influenced:

> Later, he removed the sutures from his abdominal wound, by then healed, and mounting excitement led to increasingly powerful influences being brought to bear. This resulted, on the following day, in his precipitate transfer to J Ward under Section 52 of the Mental Health Act... There are suggestions that he may not be considered certifiable in Ararat and it is even rumoured that his return to Pentridge might not be acceptable either. If both these threatening reports proved to be true it would seem that Mr David will have a fair chance of pitting Department of Community Welfare Services and Health

Commission staff at nearly all levels against one another. (14 December 1983)

A further letter of explanation about the same incident is a bitter reflection on the situation facing the prison doctors working with Garry David. Decisions appearing to be good in themselves, as the Coordinator noted, could adversely affect his management and 'authority is placed in the position of backing down or else advancing the confrontation another step', both decisions being 'inevitably wrong and some sort of disaster inescapable' (19 January 1984). From a psychiatric standpoint, the Coordinator maintained that certification was 'the only escape route possible' in response to the Minister for Health's expectation that there would be psychiatric intervention. 'The final twist', he wrote, 'lies in the complaint then made to the Minister for Health that the doctors had failed in their duty by not solving a problem which had been caused by management decisions, which we had advised against' (19 January 1984). This is one of the first hints of ministerial pressure seeking to influence professional decision making in the David case and is a frank allusion to the internal dissension generated. Even the choice of the word 'twist' suggests the metaphor of a knife blade being turned by some powerful force.

Over the years Garry's complaints about medical staff and his treatment intensified and were more effectively directed. On one occasion, he informed the Ombudsman that neglect of his medical needs was the trigger for 'sliding downhill again' after a very successful year. For further leverage he added that he was writing to his lawyers to instruct them about disposal of his property, should he 'die in the near future from [my] mutilations either by accident or design. It seems a shame that I am reverting back to my old ways, but I see no alternative' (1 November 1984). In this instance, the Ombudsman sought an explanation for the prisoner being unable to see a doctor 'other than the one he found to be unhelpful' issuing a mild rebuke to medical staff:

> I readily appreciate that the system would become unworkable if all prisoners sought to see the doctor of their choice. However, given the history of Mr David, it seems possible that he may not have been dealt with in an appropriate manner. (9 November 1984)

For his part, the Chairman of the Health Commission of Victoria reported that the prison Medical Officer (MO) had now 'decided that he should exclusively manage the prisoner's medical needs for the foreseeable future...[and] believes the best way to assist him is to return to the situation where he is the practitioner who administers medical care' (3 December 1984). It was just a matter of a few weeks before Garry found grounds for further complaint and this time he targetted the Crimes Compensation Tribunal as well as the Ombudsman. He alleged that whilst in H Division, he had been forcibly given an injection of largactil by a medical officer on the telephoned instructions of a duty doctor. He admitted that he had been disruptive, but claimed that the use of drugs to sedate quiet was illegal – 'nothing less than behaviour modification or mind control', and had told the medical officer that 'it was illegal to force drugs on me unless I am certified insane, or unless [I am] unconscious and it is necessary to administer that drug to save life or prevent serious injury' (28 December 1984).

In addition to seeking compensation for what he termed an 'assault' on his body, Garry indicated that he would draw the matter to the attention of the Prisoners' Action Group for publicity purposes, and rather illogically warned that he would 'continue to mutilate himself as a protest against such practices'. Once more medical staff members were placed in the uncomfortable position of having to justify their actions or inaction to the prison governor, as well as to the correctional and health authorities. The tables had turned. Surveillance had been deflected both from and by the prisoner, with clinical procedures being closely scrutinised from multiple directions by colleagues, the prison administration and the Governor, who found himself explaining medical decision-making to head office:

> As I am not qualified to comment on, nor criticise, any action taken by a Doctor in relation to treating a patient, I can only be guided by the information that I received from the Medical Superintendent and he believes that the matter was handled in the correct manner.

Some further hint of medical frustration is contained in this same letter:

> I was also informed by Dr... that Garry David received 100 milligrams of largactil and not 150 milligrams as stated by the prisoner. When asked about any adverse reaction to the medication that Garry David may have, as alleged in his complaint to the Ombudsman, Dr... advised that the only effect it has on the prisoner is to put him to sleep quicker than he [David] would like. (25 March 1985)

Political pressure in this case was building in the form of an insistence that Garry's bizarre behaviours placed him in the category of madness, despite the uncertainty of medical views. Staff members were criticised for their failure to act according to the prevailing expectations, and there was a discreet warning issued in a memo of 9 January 1985 from the Forensic Psychiatry Services Coordinator to the Acting Director of the Mental Health Division:

> You may be aware that there has been criticism of the conduct of psychiatrists in this case in the past, apparently by the Minister of Community Welfare Services. This time it is claimed that the Premier has become involved by means of personal communication. Whether or not this is so, the Director of

Prisons is certainly involved and requiring the transfer of the prisoner out of
Pentridge.

The interest of senior politicians did not wane and a file note indicates that the
Premier's department contacted the newly appointed Director of Forensic Psychi-
atry Services to discuss in detail the Premier's direct criticisms regarding Garry
David's management (21 March 1985).

In view of the fact that politicians, public servants and some members of the
legal and medical professions were expressing the view that Garry was 'mad'
rather than 'bad', the general medical response that he was *not psychotic* appeared to
be mere obduracy. Early in the period of Garry's incarceration the Coordinator
had quite reasonably pointed out that little could be gained by directing either
blame or responsibility to the psychiatric staff, for the real stumbling block was
Garry himself:

> The truth of the matter is that he does not want help and would not like it if he
> got it, because it would involve his learning acceptable methods of reaction
> instead of his present unpleasantly effective ones. (8 November 1978)

Several years later the response of the Health Commission Chairman to the
Ombudsman reflected a similar judgement, when he noted that 'nothing is served
by acceding to the facile diversion of responsibility to the psychiatric staff of a
problem, which is truly that of a deprived man in conflict with the community' (21
May 1981). A later chairman was not quite so sanguine in his assessment about the
building political pressure, which he considered to demonstrate a misunderstanding of 'psychiatrists' competency 'to give a diagnostic opinion on "madness", even
though they are accepted as sufficiently able to undertake management' (19
January 1984).

The files amply testify to the uncertainties and allocation of blame surrounding the care of Garry, who had succeeded in exposing both the historical ambiguities embedded in the practice of prison psychiatry, as well as the appropriate
administrative locus for the severely personality disordered. In an early detailed
psychiatric report to the medical superintendent of Pentridge Hospital an opinion
was expressed that 'psychiatry has virtually nothing to offer him', and this was a
recurrent view despite being at variance with that of politicians and senior administrators (30 March 1983). In 1989, when the prisoner was nearing release, a psychiatric report reaffirmed the position that 'there is little that psychiatry can offer
directly to Garry' and that he could be regarded 'as having graduated from forensic
psychiatry' so that his positive attributes, rather than deficits, should be the focus
of attention (23 April 1989). This opinion was later qualified as having been
intended to reflect the lack of forensic resources, rather being a reference to any
inadequacy of general psychiatry. It was incidents of this kind that illustrate the

difficulty of developing a sustained policy in relation to the management and care of Garry, whose allocation to the space of badness or madness was less a matter of professional knowledge than administrative expediency.

A PAUCITY OF OPTIONS

Garry's adroitness in managing many aspects of his confinement with intersecting strategies ultimately restricted his placement choices. Since certification as a security patient no longer appeared to be a viable option for those with antisocial personality disorders under the new legislation, Garry had to be managed within the confines of the prison and ordinary hospital systems. It was his impending release in 1990 which revived hope of once again using a mental health route. The issue had crystallised at this stage in both government circles and in the public mind as being the danger constituted by one person, whose behaviour was puzzling, even for experts. However, for the government itself to initiate direct action would have been *ultra vires* in the criminal law sense. At the time, legal powers for those deemed to be dangerous were restricted to certain prescribed circumstances, such as bail applications, sentencing and parole supervision, and Cabinet's only room for direct intervention lay in consideration of the possible release of Governor's Pleasure acquittees, which bore no relevance to this case.

It was not since the days of Robert Peter Tait, almost 30 years previously, that there had been such political determination to extend a government's role and override the views of lawyers and psychiatrists. (*Tait v The Queen* [1963] VR 647; see also C. Burns 1962). This case had been a landmark one for a public struggle between the government and psychiatry over the boundaries of mental illness. It was sparked by a belief in Tait's 'dangerousness', and the Premier declared that hanging was called for, in order 'to protect the community from any further atrocious criminal acts by this man' (Burns, p.141). The battle lines were drawn with those opposing capital punishment on one side pitting themselves against the state power to hang a person, who had failed the M'Naghten test. Ultimately the hand of the Government was stayed and Tait was certified with his papers marked 'never to be released'.

Garry David's circumstances differed in a major respect from those of Tait, who had aroused the ire of the Liberal Premier of the day. Garry had paid his debt to society, and because there was no residual holding power within the criminal justice system, diversion through the mental health route appealed as a safer political path for the incumbent Labor Government to pursue. After all, Garry had been certified on seven previous occasions and his behaviour had become increasingly erratic throughout the latter part of the 1980s. However, to proceed down the mental health pathway ignored three factors: the emerging policy regarding the management of Garry David during a decade of his confinement; the restrictions contained within the Mental Health Act 1986; and the differing opinion of psychiatrists about the responsible agency for those with personality disorders – something encouraged by the ambiguity of subsection 8(2)(l) of the Act, with its reference to the exclusion from civil commitment of those having 'an antisocial personality', rather than 'an antisocial personality *disorder*'. It is the first of these factors which is most relevant for consideration here, because it was Garry's long interaction with so many practitioners in the health system, and his developing reputation for violent outbursts, which rendered it difficult for expert witnesses to respond objectively during the many inquiries into his dangerousness.

Garry's multipronged attack on the professional reputations and abilities of psychiatrists throughout the 1980s and intermittent political pressures encouraged disagreements about his status as a psychiatric patient. At least one senior psychiatrist realised at the outset that decisions made about the prisoner, 'are not a medical responsibility' (10 July 1978), but the Consultant Psychiatrist to Pentridge Prison, Dr Allen Bartholomew, rebutted this conclusion on the grounds that a gross personality disorder, at times achieving the status of a psychosis, *is* sufficient reason for an attendance order to a psychiatric clinic for parolees. Nonetheless, for the next few years, the policy remained contentious and uncertain. It was repeatedly affirmed that psychiatrists rarely disagreed that Garry David was suffering from a severe personality disorder, but they differed in their views about the efficacy of active treatment *vis-à-vis* a careful management routine focused on behavioural change. Even the repeated certifications led to accusations of psychiatric staff being unable to deal constructively with a damaged personality. In 1984 Dr Grigor noted that it is 'the view of Community Welfare Services that if a person has been certified as insane, therefore he should remain within that category' – a comment undoubtedly based on that department's evident reluctance for Garry to return to the prison from J Ward (10 April 1984). Interdepartmental tension at this time was indeed palpable.

The handwritten notes of one senior psychiatrist at a case presentation held on 10 April 1981 encapsulate the problematic nature of the options available to psychiatrists, and the sense of entrapment Garry had created:

I have some questions:

(i)   *In the patient*:

    (a)   Must there be a diagnosis?

    (b)   In relation to recommendations – (i) is he mad?; (ii) if he *is* mad, does he remain so?; (iii) if he is mad, can he refuse treatment?; (iv) if he is *not* mad, can he refuse treatment?; (v) if he refuses treatment, is it negligent to accept that refusal?; (vi) if he accepts, should he receive tranquillising drugs?

(c) We know he is dangerous. Is it reasonable to expect nurses to care for him? Should prison officers care for him? Is it reasonable to have a rota system – prison *and* hospital (including St Vincent's)?

(ii) *In the prison*: All are agreed he is manipulating. (i) Should we accept this for peace?; (ii) Would we get peace?; (iii) If we refuse, will he escalate, and *when* do we acquiesce?

(iii) If we accept manipulation, is it significant that others will copy?

(iv) He has threatened to kill. He has made a serious attempt *and* he says he will do it again. Is this significant?

(v) What is the prognosis?

(vi) Can management affect it?

(Dr Allen Bartholomew, a former Consultant Psychiatrist of HM Pentridge, kindly gave permission to use these informal jottings in order to illustrate the complexities of the decision-making processes for professional staff. It is emphasised that these are spontaneous, personal jottings and have no formal status.)

These notes cogently express the dilemmas facing medical staff working in a prison environment: they had to balance their duty of care within the constraints imposed by the prisoner; meet their legal obligations; and uphold the needs and rights of other inmates. Had Garry suffered one of the major psychiatric disorders, his treatment and the allocation of resources would not have been a matter of dispute. But the personality disorders are essentially behavioural in their manifestation and invite moral condemnation, thus falling within that uncertain cleft between criminality and mental illness, so that discourse tends to vacillate between the two forms of explanation. Once dangerousness is added to the mix, objectivity diminishes, for such an implied threat invites repression, despite an incomplete comprehension on the part of the community and mental health profession of the actual reality of the danger posed.

During his lengthy term in an adult prison, Garry David delighted in his dangerous persona and used it to taunt staff by revealing the inadequacies of the institutional system. He demonstrated that the naked power of the prison with its rigid rules and punishments for disciplinary infractions could be rendered as ineffectual and unsustainable as therapeutic power, which he ensured was wielded neither discreetly, economically, nor rationally in the Foucauldian sense (1977b, pp.304 ff.). He had been observed, classified, examined, reclassified, transferred briefly to psychiatric settings, and his every action had been minutely scrutinised on a daily basis for more than ten years. Yet, to the frustration of all, this expert scrutiny was frequently deleterious in its effect on the recalcitrant prisoner and was dysfunctional for many staff by inciting professional doubts and a lowering of morale.

First, Garry drew attention to the divisions of opinion within psychiatric practice and highlighted legal injustices in his situation, whilst at the same time avoiding personal responsibility by implicating 'the system' in what he termed his 'mismanagement'. Although his diagnosis of severe personality disorder was never in doubt, it was recognised that this inmate was distinctive because of the severity and intensity of his symptoms, coupled with his practised ability to display these in a confrontational and often articulate way. Consequently, staff members found themselves in the position of using the process of certification as a matter of expediency at stressful times, rather than as a professional declaration of his 'madness'.

Second, he achieved a visibility, even in areas of close control that enhanced his reputation and provoked intense scrutiny of staff actions. By this means, he became adept at deflecting surveillance back on to the surveillers and also cast doubt on the efficacy of disciplinary mechanisms in a closed setting. Third, he exposed the incompatibility of treatment and punishment and, at the same time, strained the human and economic resources of the institution. Many of these strategies had multiple outcomes, which made them very difficult to counter effectively.

The Garry David case is a rare demonstration of the way in which power is diffused throughout the prison and its wider environs, as well as the multiplicities of its effects. It was not a one-sided contest, with Garry fending off intrusions into his ability to control his personal space of mind and body. Staff members too were moved to protect their professional integrity and safety and were active participants. The written reports document frustration, helplessness, wry humour and a sense of being held to ransom, as the struggle to gain a proper psychiatric perspective gained momentum. This struggle had pragmatic as well as professional dimensions, for power oscillated between inmate and staff and, in this respect there is a striking similarity with the findings of Goffman (1961) and Comaroff (1982, 1985), who both analyse the way in which resistance and acquiescence are perpetually in a state of flux (see also Rhodes 1991). The prison, the most coercive setting which society can legally devise, sharpened an interplay which did not mesh with the usual social control dynamic of the indisputable primacy of professional power. The dysfunctional body and mind of Garry David challenged the ideal of medical benevolence and raised doubts about the reality of a psychiatric frame of reference remaining uncontaminated by custodial objectives. In this way, his social and psychiatric marginality became the focus of the prevailing tensions between psychiatry and the law.

As Marcel Détienne contends, we can only understand society's symbolic values by mapping out its transgressions and deviants (Détienne 1979, p.ix; see also Stallybrass and White 1986). The significance of Garry's intransigence flowed well beyond the institution. He stirred community fears about a being capable of committing such an extreme degree of violence and bodily disfigurement with impunity. It was powerful imagery, disturbing in the context of the ordinary understanding of rules and values. His role as a transgressor achieved an importance surpassing his status as a mentally disordered prisoner, and he challenged the way in which society manages its fears of those who straddle the uncertain terrain of criminality and insanity. It became imperative for the Victorian Labor Government to find an acceptable political solution, even if it meant the state seeking to redefine the boundary between criminality and mental illness. It is the gathering of these forces and their increasing momentum, culminating in the implementation of special 'one-person' legislation in April 1990, which became the next step in the Garry David story.

CHAPTER 3

A Flurry of Activity

The Political Reaction to a Dangerous Person

I expect to be freed in February 1990, and I bloody well better be. To keep me in jail would be a declaration of war. And I will, as all prisoners of war must, attempt to escape and I will give no mercy to my enemies. (*Sun*, 11 December 1989)

This is an unhappy man caught in a deadly trap, but no amount of sympathy for him can disguise the facts that his reactions to offers of medical help are manipulations, aimed, in his own words, at getting attention. His destructive behaviour will not be reduced, but increased by timidity in allowing him to dictate events in the medical sense, while the community demands increasing restrictions on his liberty. (Health Department, 8 June 1982)

If I find a man to whom it literally makes no difference whether he kicks a pebble or kills his family, since either would be an antidote to ennui or inactivity, I shall not be disposed ... to attribute to him merely a different code of morality to my own or that of most men, or declare that we disagree on essentials, but shall begin to speak of insanity... I shall be inclined to consider him mad, as a man who thinks he is Napoleon is mad. (Berlin 1967, p.27)

PSYCHIATRIC PATIENT OR PRISONER?

Over the final decade of Garry David's imprisonment the gulf between the psychiatric and lay view of his condition became more pronounced, with those outside the profession finding it easier to explain his bizarre behaviour within a self-evident paradigm of mental illness. Jottings on a file written by a senior health administrator encapsulate the dichotomy between the 'lay' and 'expert' view and foreshadow the more formal exploration of these differences during various proceedings throughout 1990:

> Dr TS's vivid description helps me to understand that Mr David is merely a mixed-up, somewhat confused young man – and not a nut-case as I'm tempted to conclude in a display of layman ignorance. (14 December 1983)

At the time this was written, the interplay between the Department of Health and Community Welfare Services had intensified and the Minister for Health felt compelled to explain the approach being taken by his staff. It was an unusual ministerial letter, undoubtedly constructed from departmental briefing notes, and succinctly outlined the dilemmas being experienced. At the outset Tom Roper, the Minister for Health, referred back to the earlier conference of 1981, at which the general conclusion had been related that no one could define any *treatable* medical condition of the prisoner and self-mutilation alone was not evidence of a psychiatric illness. The impasse was still evident three years later, when the Department of Health claimed that certification was no longer appropriate and the Victorian Prison Staff Association began threatening industrial action unless 'something was done'. As the Minister wryly pointed out: 'This phrase has been heard many times in this case, the *something* often remaining unspecified, but the *done* always referring to somebody else, and in some other place, preferably far away!' However, he did concede that Garry's behaviour evoked such abhorrence amongst medical and lay observers alike that it was liable to be interpreted as non-rational. He believed too that the use of diagnostic labels such as those in the American Psychiatric Association's *Diagnostic and Statistical Manual* reinforces this view. Finally, he added an indirect but sympathetic reference to the expectations placed on psychiatrists, when he admitted that there had been 'an increasing tendency to *insist upon* psychiatric interventions' (18 January 1984).

Throughout the period of Garry's incarceration psychiatrists were well aware of the prevailing belief that their discipline held the answer, yet in reality they could offer little of lasting therapeutic value. Even as early as 1980 a senior Victorian psychiatrist had presciently described the situation pertaining to Garry David:

> I still believe that a Judge would say that any reasonable minded citizen would say that this man's gross behaviour demonstrated mental illness. However, from the psychiatrist's point of view it would be difficult at this stage to sustain such an argument in the light of professional knowledge. (11 December 1980)

A decade later, a senior Victorian Judge confirmed this opinion of the 'reasonable minded citizen' and deflected the problem back to psychiatry in no uncertain manner:

> I also have a great deal of difficulty coming to terms with the concept that if somebody cuts his ears off and slices part of his penis off and tries to burn himself with petrol and wants to shoot people, he is not mentally ill. It causes this problem about my perception of what is normal and what is not and I have said on occasions that it seems to me that any definition of the role of psychiatric medicine which seems to exclude this extraordinary section of

significant mental disturbance is itself crazy. (Vincent J, Social Development Committee, *Evidence*, 19 October 1989, p.795).

This comment was widely disseminated and given added weight because Justice Vincent was both an experienced Supreme Court Judge and Chairman of the Adult Parole Board. It accorded with popular opinion and suggested that psychiatrists were either being obstructive or misguided. The resonance of the imagery used by the Judge was difficult for members of that profession to counter effectively, especially as the method of constructing diagnostic boundaries is not widely understood outside clinical circles. It was also an image, which aided the Government's resolve to defuse the mounting disquiet about Garry's imminent release from custody. Not only was the Judge's conclusion widely quoted in the press by Ministers, but it was later to be used as a weapon to disparage psychiatry for its apparent lack of cooperation.

There were some significant developments in mid 1989. The Adult Parole Board of Victoria, which had rejected Garry's earlier parole applications after expiry of the minimum term, became increasingly concerned about the likelihood of his unsupervised freedom. However, the Chairman was reassured when Dr John Grigor, the Director of Forensic Services, informed him that he was revising his opinion about Garry *not* being mentally ill and might be prepared to certify him towards the end of his sentence. In a related move on 14 June 1989, the Government gave its all-party Parliamentary Social Development Committee (SDC) a reference to conduct 'An Inquiry into Mental Disturbance and Community Safety: Strategies to Deal with Persons with Severe Personality Disorder who Pose a Threat to Public Safety'. This body was empowered to receive both written and oral submissions and its report was intended to be apolitical. Although the terms of reference were broadly based, they encompassed existing legislation dealing with those 'people evidencing seriously disturbed behaviour associated with mental illness, intellectual disability, acquired brain damage or personality disorder', and recommendations were to be made about any necessary legislative changes to ensure the safety of the community. The exercise was patently well timed, since the report had to be finalised within six months. The terms of reference were broad, that is:

> To identify the dimensions, scope and impact on families and within the community of violent or criminal actions by people evidencing seriously disturbed behaviour associated with mental illness, intellectual disability, acquired brain damage or personality disorder;
>
> To examine existing legislation dealing with such people.
>
> To examine the role and relationships of agencies involved with both servicing the needs of behaviourally disturbed people and with providing protec-

tion and support to their families and the community, with particular reference to:

- the police, courts and correctional agencies;
- mental health services;
- disability services;
- community organisations;
- public and community housing;
- alcohol and drug services.

To make recommendations for action required to remedy any deficiencies or gaps in current policies, strategies and systems necessary to ensure the safety and well-being of individuals as well as the community in general, including recommendations on legislative change if required.

The Government now had a two-pronged strategy in place for detaining Garry David in a psychiatric service setting on completion of his sentence on 3 February 1990. The Director of Forensic Services *might* decide to certify him, or the Social Development Committee *might* recommend that personality disorder be considered a mental illness. Even so, the Office of Corrections was taking no chances and pressed ahead with a special release preparation programme in the latter part of 1989, its earlier attempts having been thwarted by Garry's episodic outbursts and internal prison transfers. However, progress stalled on account of the sensational media reporting which contributed to Garry's volatility throughout the remainder of 1989, necessitating frequent divisional moves.

In view of the prisoner's previous certifications and the fact that many experienced psychiatrists were employed by the Department of Health, the Government pursued a more direct path to achieve this option hoping that it would prove less controversial than continued custody in the prison. One of these was indeed novel. On 14 November 1989, four psychiatrists were invited to form a panel with a view to certifying Garry David. The panel's members were carefully selected and the result was a mix of senior Health Department personnel and a private forensic psychiatrist, all recognised for their extensive clinical experience. They were: Dr Carlyle Perera, Chief Psychiatrist of the Office of Psychiatric Services; Dr Peter Eisen, Acting Director of the Office of Psychiatric Services; Dr David Leonard, Director of Clinical Services at Royal Park Hospital; Dr Neville Parker, a consultant forensic psychiatrist in private practice. Not one member of this group had been directly involved in the management of Garry David, either within the prison or mental health services. The outcome of their examination at Pentridge Prison dealt the Government an unanticipated blow. Each psychiatrist concluded independently that the prisoner did not satisfy the legal requirements of section 8 of the Mental Health Act 1986 and therefore he could not be deemed mentally ill for the purposes of commitment, either as a civil or a security patient. For example, Dr Perera's evidence, later described by the Mental Health Review Board as being 'unequivocal', reported:

(a)   Mr David does not suffer from a psychiatric illness at the present time.

(b)   His past history would suggest that he suffers from a personality disorder with antisocial and borderline characteristics. I feel sure that he will not benefit from specific psychiatric treatment.

(c)   At the present time Mr David does not meet the criteria set down in section 16(2)(a) or section 8(1) of the Mental Health Act 1986; and as such cannot be recommended under the Act. (MHRB, *Statement of Reasons in GIPW*, 9 May 1990, p.24)

Dr Parker, who admitted that he had attended the meeting with a preconceived opinion that Garry David must be mentally ill in view of the frequency and severity of his reported mutilations, nonetheless concluded on closer examination that:

> I am unable to be party to his detention on psychiatric grounds and have no doubts whatever about the opinion that Garry David is not suffering, or has ever suffered, from a mental illness. (MHRB, *Statement of Reasons in GIPW*, 9 May 1990, p.24)

These excerpts from the reports illustrate the differing perceptions of the law and psychiatry about the meaning of insanity for commitment purposes. The more restrictive criteria of mental illness contained within the 1986 mental health legislation guaranteed that those with an antisocial personality disorder were even more ambiguously positioned in the mad–bad divide. From a psychiatric stance, it retained its classification within the broader coverage of a mental disorder, but there was some unease about the diagnostic inclusion of criminal-type behaviour, together with clinical reservations about treatment efficacy. As the Mental Health Review Board later observed:

> The fact that in psychiatry the preponderance of opinion is that a personality disorder is not a mental illness appears baffling to many people. The fact that psychiatrists see, classify, and attempt to treat people with personality disorders, adds to the confusion. (Kiel 1992, p.180)

The Christmas period was looming and 'the problem' of Garry had not been sorted out with any clarity. On 7 December 1989, the Victorian Government Solicitor sent a letter to the Director-General of Corrections offering advice about the possibility of amending sections of both the Corrections Act 1986 and the Mental

Health Act 1986 to allow proclamation of part of the prison as an approved psychiatric hospital and 'transfer of prisoner to that hospital', information which became available in the debates surrounding community protection legislation in the Victorian Legislative Assembly (10 April 1990). The curious phrase 'transfer of prisoner' without the use of the definite or indefinite article was undoubtedly intended to be an oblique reference to the prisoner, Garry David. To achieve the desired end would have required amendments to section 4(2) of the Corrections Act 1986 and sections 16, 47, 53 and 93 of the Mental Health Act 1986, in order to declare part or all of Pentridge's G Division to be a 'psychiatric in-patient service' in the formal legal sense.

There is no indication that the full consequences of this proposal had been assessed for their impact on mentally disordered prisoners, who form a significant group within the prison system and who would be profoundly affected. The proposed amendments implied only two possible choices. Either mentally disordered prisoners in the approved hospital section would have 'voluntary' status, which would entail, at least theoretically, the right to leave the prison unless detained and certified under the provisions of the Mental Health Act. However should the proposal mean that G Division receive only those already certified, then some prisoners requiring general therapeutic services might not meet the criteria of a certifiable mental illness under mental health legislation and thus be denied psychiatric services to the detriment of their behaviour in the institution. In either event, the administrative consequences of the proposal were far-reaching and awkward for the correctional staff, exacerbating the pressures imposed on them. For instance, responsibility for those prisoners deemed to be security patients would reside with the prison's Authorised Psychiatrist and with the Chief Psychiatrist at the Office of Forensic Psychiatry Services. This would diminish, or possibly negate, the Director-General of Corrections' authority in relation to this group, although custodial staff might be empowered to use the mental health provisions to apprehend those found 'absent without leave' whilst in the general prison, but outside the confines of G Division. In essence, the 'one-person' solution was remarkably ill considered on a number of grounds: it disregarded the carefully forged distinction between correctional and therapeutic functions and potentially disadvantaged the broader prison population in terms of psychiatric care. It was little more than a crude means of coercing psychiatrists to accept responsibility for those severely personality disordered, whom they had declared to be outside their legislative domain.

The nervousness within the Attorney-General's department was highlighted by the Government Solicitor's simultaneous letter to the Director of Public Prosecutions about possible recourse to the criminal law arising from Garry David's threats to kill (Hansard, 11 April 1990). Two pre-Christmas cabinet meetings canvassed possible moves and, immediately following the second of these meetings, the Melbourne *Sun* reported that 'the State Government is secretly working on special legislation to keep one of Victoria's most violent criminals in jail for life'. This article with the eye-catching headline 'Bid to Bar Gunman: Cabinet Plan to Block Prison Release for Life', gave as its source a 'Cabinet insider', who had offered information about the way the Government intended to find some breathing space for further decision making *(Sun,* 11 December 1989). Possible options included amendments to the Mental Health Act to provide for Garry David's certification and the introduction of a special regulation to expunge the automatic remissions of his 14-year sentence, thereby enabling him to be imprisoned for a further two years. Those involved in the discussions came from the highest administrative levels within criminal justice and mental health agencies. The article was blunt in its conclusion: 'Special legislation would involve finding a way to hold Webb until state Parliament resumes in March, when the Government would then have to get the Opposition support to change the Act' (*Sun,* 11 December 1989).

The Government was clearly desperate, for it had already used existing regulations to extend the release date by two weeks from 3 February to 17 February, the legality of this move being strongly disputed in advice obtained by the Mental Health Review Board. Sentencing information suggests that the earlier date was correct. The calculations were difficult, as the legislation at the time automatically allowed remissions for 'good behaviour' – clearly a euphemism in this case. The sentence commenced on 2 February 1982 and the total aggregate term was 14 years with a minimum non-parole period of 12 years. However, 561 days had to be deducted automatically, unless the Court had directed otherwise under section 16 of the Penalties and Sentences Act 1985; one-third was to be deducted automatically as remission for good behaviour under section 16 of the Corrections Act 1986 and Regulation 97 of the Corrections' Regulations; and 54 days were for a special remission of the D-G of Corrections under the Regulations of the Corrections Act. Also to be taken into account were 131 days to be added as lost remissions, plus 104 days for charges within the prison system making a total of 27 days discharge postponed. The complexity of these internal adjustments to the head sentence diminishes their force as an internal disciplinary mechanism for prison management purposes and has since been replaced by a 'truth in sentencing' model.

The thoroughness with which this mental health pathway was explored is apparent from a document prepared for departmental meetings and Cabinet discussions, and released by the Freedom of Information office. It is reproduced here because it clearly illustrates the complexity of the procedure and the interaction between the Office of Corrections and Office of Psychiatric Services in relation to a severely mentally disordered inmate (Figure 3.1).

MENTAL HEALTH OPTIONS

Prior to 3.2.90

VOLUNTARY

Section 56, Corrections Act 1986

- Voluntary Transfer i.e. the prisoner consents
- Requires consent of psychiatric hospital
- Order of transfer issued by Governer of prison, authorized by OOC
- Held as 'defacto' security patient
- Remains in custody of Director-General, OOC
- Prisoner, hospital, OOC can initiate return.

INVOLUNTARY

Section 16, Mental Health Act 1986

Director-General may make either of the following:

(3)(a) • hospital order to psychiatric in-patient service as involuntary patient

(3)(b) • restricted hospital order to psychiatric in-patient service as a security patient

- Must meet criteria in 16(1), (2), (4).

16(1) a) Person is lawfully imprisoned or detained in a prison or other places of confinement, and

b) appears to be mentally ill.

16(2) a) Director-General has received a certificate by a psychiatrist and is satisfied that:

i) person appears to be suffering from a mental illness that requires treatment AND

ii) treatment can be obtained by admission to and detention in a psychiatric in-patient service AND

iii) person should be admitted to and detained in a psychiatric in-patient service for her or his health or safety or for the protection of members of the public AND

b) the Director-General has received a report from the authorized psychiatrist of the psychiatric in-patient service to which it is proposed to admit the person which recommends that the transfer be made.

16(4) In determining whether to make a hospital order or restricted order, the Director-General must have regard to the public interest and all the circumstances of the case including the person's criminal record and psychiatric history.

• May be returned to prison by Chief Psychiatrist (s.45) or Mental Health Review Board (s.44).

MENTAL HEALTH OPTIONS

Post Sentence i.e. after 3.2.90

VOLUNTARY

Section 7, Mental Health Act 1986

• Voluntary patient – can leave at any time

• Authorized psychiatrist consent required

• May be detained for up to 6 hours if examination for S.12 admission is required

INVOLUNTARY

Section 12, Mental Health Act 1986

• Involuntary patient

• Must meet S.8 criteria

   • the person appears to be mentally ill AND

   • the person's mental illness requires immediate treatment or care and that treatment or care can be obtained by admission to and detention in a psychiatric in-patient service AND

- the person should be admitted and detained as an involuntary patient for that person's health or safety or for the protection of members of the public AND

- the person has refused or is unable to consent ot the necessary treatment or care for the mental illness AND

- the person cannot receive adequate treatment to care for the mental illness in a manner less restrictive of that person's freedom of decision or choice.

• Discharge (to freedom) may be authorized by authorized psychiatrist or Mental Health Board

Figure 3.1 Available mental health options. Source: Freedom of Information Office.

All these legislative possibilities emanated from the Office of the Attorney-General, but none could have been implemented until the start of the autumn session of Parliament early in the following year. In the meantime, the police commissioners were publicly expressing disquiet about their members' safety and referring to many of Garry's more alarming post-release threats. The Assistant Commissioner for Crime announced that the Victoria Police was considering applying to the Director of Public Prosecutions for possible court action (*Sun*, 16 and 21 December 1989). The timing was fortuitous given that police perception of the recent establishment of an external police complaints authority had been interpreted as a lack of confidence in the Force's own internal disciplinary mechanisms. It was therefore prudent for the Government to counter this view by demonstrating its support for police members and oppose Garry David's release. In April 1986 an independent Police Complaints' Authority had been established and was later replaced by Dr Barry Perry, who was appointed the Deputy Ombudsman (Police Complaints) in October 1988. Since that time there was growing malcontent amongst all levels of the Victoria Police, despite Perry's approach being more cautious than that of the previous body.

Two further developments emanated from police command. A Superintendent was appointed to negotiate with Pentridge authorities about Garry's alleged contacts with criminal terrorist groups such as the Ananda Marga sect and an organisation with the acronym WAR. The Special Operations Group took the unprecedented step of distributing photographs at the Royal Melbourne Hospital to warn staff of his imminent release. Whilst these particular fears proved to be unfounded, they point to Garry's skilful cultivation of his 'terrorist' image, and the entrenched police view of the danger he posed to their members and to the public entering well-known public buildings.

On 22 December 1989 Garry was charged in the Melbourne Magistrate's Court under section 20 of the Crimes Act 1958 that 'on 11 October 1989 he did without lawful excuse threaten to kill Steven Tatchell intending the threat to be carried out'. The information offered to the court was that Garry David had formed a relationship with Tatchell's former de facto wife, planned to marry her, and had threatened violence to prevent Tatchell having access to his own son. During his period of imprisonment Garry's use of threats had been a customary response to anger and frustration and the Mental Health Review Board documented 34 such incidents occurring between 1972 and 1989. Sometimes the threats were generalised, but very often they targetted specific persons such as staff, prisoners and public figures, including the Premier. In light of this response pattern it was remarkable that the threats made to another prisoner should be chosen as the basis for a legal holding action of such import.

Garry David was remanded in custody to appear again on 22 March, this date later being extended to 18 April 1990. Reports indicate that the police had considered laying further charges but were dissuaded from doing so by the Honourable Stephen Crabb, who in his dual role of Minister for Police and Emergency Services and Minister for Corrections understandably favoured a mental health option, which would diminish the economic burden on his own two departments (*Hansard*, 11 April 1990). Thus there was an element of pragmatism influencing the direction of political pressures in this case. Economic costs borne by particular government departments could not be ignored and the prison officers' and police unions sought appeasement. The message disseminated from the Minister was that the Office of Corrections had borne the primary burden for too long and was loath to continue shouldering the burden of further protracted custody.

The professional activity in the six weeks prior to Garry's release gave every appearance of being frenetic with the involvement of senior staff from the Health Department, the Attorney-General's Department, the Victoria Police and relevant Ministers, including the Premier. By early New Year, in the midst of the holiday period, it was clear that the Government was prepared to embark on innovative methods to achieve its desired goal. On the public holiday of 26 January 1990 the Attorney-General made an originating motion in the Supreme Court to define the meaning of 'appears to be mentally ill', which is central to the operation of section 8(1)(a) operation of the Mental Health Act 1986, but which had been purposefully left undefined to allow its interpretation as a matter of ongoing case law by the Mental Health Review Board. One week later, this matter was referred to the Full Supreme Court of Victoria for its consideration.

As a backstop measure the Government now turned to another of its statutory bodies, seeking some definitive solution to the impasse. It selected the Law Reform

Commission of Victoria, an advisory and research body which had been undertaking a report on *Mental Malfunction and Criminal Responsibility* (1990). The original terms of reference had been given on 28 February 1987 with the request that the commission 'examine, and make recommendations for the reform of the rules relating to insanity and automatism in the criminal law'. It was asked to focus on those suffering from some impairment of criminal responsibility owing to mental conditions in their progress through the courts and prisons. An interim report had already been produced and the final version was anticipated later in 1990. Without specific direction, it was unlikely that the Commission would have analysed any particular section of the Mental Health Act 1986, given that its terms of reference were focused on those provisions governing the use of fitness to plead and the insanity defence in the Crimes Act 1958 (ss.393 and 420). However, this additional request from the Attorney-General was more pointed. He now required a further and separate interim report regarding the extent of the powers under the current mental health legislation to detain those, who are both mentally ill and who pose a serious threat to the public. This was an evident reference to the ambiguity of section 8(2)(l) of the Act excluding the certification of those with 'an antisocial personality'. The Commission was asked to deal with this as an urgent and separate matter and its work would thus, rather strangely, either parallel or duplicate that of the parliamentary Social Development Committee. On any view, the Government's involvement was unusual, and signalled both pressure and the need for haste about the desired outcome. There was a concern to have the two bodies move in tandem on the issue of antisocial personality disorder, and in the original terms of reference the Social Development Committee had been enjoined to 'take account of the work of the Victorian Law Reform Commission' in their deliberations.

There was little doubt about the political agenda at this time in view of the way in which media reports set about clarifying the Government's intent. Many headlines were duly inflammatory such as 'Crabb's Vow on Psycho', which referred to the Minister for Police's announcement that 'everything will be done to keep him [Webb] from being released. But how we do that, we are not prepared to talk about at this stage' (*Sun*, 8 January 1990). Few would have recognised that Crabb was in a bind by virtue of his two portfolios straddling the areas of corrections and policing, and his consequent need to placate the members of two very separate government authorities. This duality had arisen as part of the tendency of governments to merge ministerial responsibilities into 'mega-departments' with the apparent assumption that there are common interests and few significant differences. It is then inevitable that Cabinet representation highlights this commonality at the expense of any variations in goals and strategies. In this particular instance, the Victoria Police and the Office of Corrections did diverge in their perspective about the problem that Garry presented, although each favoured the

Minister minimising the involvement of their respective departments. As a powerful Cabinet member it was thus incumbent on Crabb to deflect the matter to the mental health field rather than have it fester as a criminal justice issue.

The Government initiatives in trying to achieve this goal can only be viewed as extraordinary in nature and hastily conceived. In the space of six months, it had arranged the empanelling of four senior psychiatrists with a view to having Garry certified; commissioned reports from both the Social Development Committee and the Law Reform Commission of Victoria; made a request to the Supreme Court for a declaration about the meaning of mental illness for the purposes of certification; and conducted many meetings at both senior administrative and Cabinet levels to canvass extant and potential legal options, including the innovative step of expunging Garry's automatic remissions of sentence and declaring part of the prison to be a dual correctional and psychiatric facility.

CERTIFICATION

On 9 January 1990, despite no outward escalation in his behaviour, Garry's status suddenly changed from that of being a prisoner to a security patient. Dr John Grigor, the psychiatrist with the overall responsibility for his care since 1985, certified him as 'appearing to be mentally ill' under section 16 of the Mental Health Act 1986 and he was swiftly moved to J Ward at Ararat, some three hours' drive from Melbourne. Under the Act the Director-General of Corrections had the power to transfer any prisoner appearing to be mentally ill, provided that a psychiatrist was prepared to issue the requisite certificate and indicate that treatment was both necessary and available in a psychiatric in-patient service. At the time, Ararat was being used for floridly disturbed prisoners, as well as some severely mentally ill patients with Governor's Pleasure status – either owing to their inability to plead, or acquittal on the grounds of insanity. In addition, it housed a few long-term patients considered unsuitable for an ordinary psychiatric facility.

The reversal of Dr Grigor's view had been presaged some six months previously, when he admitted having received encouragement from his detailed discussions with Professor John Gunn of London's Maudsley Hospital about the difficulties presented by personality disordered prisoners (MHRB, 19 February 1990). That he should have sought professional support in this way was understandable, for in 1989 forensic psychiatry could only be regarded as a fledgling discipline in Victoria, yet to attract its first formal academic appointee to a newly created chair at Monash University. Those pursuing this career path were few and there had been no separate form of specialist training apart from the collegiate activities of the small Forensic Section of the Royal Australian and New Zealand College of Psychiatrists. Forensic psychiatry's standing did not match that of the USA and the UK, where it had been a well-recognised specialty for some time. As Dr Grigor commented somewhat facetiously to the Mental Health Review Board, 'It is only relatively recently that we've actually started to acquire these unusual beasts called forensic psychiatrists' (MHRB, 19 February 1990). Not unnaturally, at a time when practitioners were moving cautiously in their interpretation of the Mental Health Act, and enhancing their sense of collective identity, Garry David's sharp exposure of treatment obligations to the recalcitrant disturbed prisoner in a custodial setting tested the emergent discipline in Victoria.

In the same Mental Health Review Board hearing, Dr Grigor admitted that his own 'views about the possible use of the Mental Health Act were evolving', but nonetheless the suddenness of his action in certifying Garry was surprising for two quite separate reasons. First, some months previously, he had argued confidently and strenuously before the Mental Health Review Board about the necessity for DWP, a chronic schizophrenic, to be retained at J Ward for psychiatric treatment (MHRB, 10 May 1989). The Board accepted that, although this patient was suffering from a mental illness requiring treatment and posed a threat to the public, the requisite treatment was currently unavailable owing to inadequate staffing levels and the absence of a written, individualised treatment plan (Kiel 1992, pp.208–29). The issue was a sensitive one but, in arriving at its decision, the Board took into account Parliament's intention that 'persons who are mentally ill receive the best possible care and treatment in the least restrictive environment enabling the care and treatment to be effectively given' (section 4(2)(a)), and also considered a number of international human rights' instruments. For example, paragraphs 5 and 6 of the Declaration on the Rights of Disabled Persons (UN 1975), which Australia has ratified, focus on self-reliance and the right to treatment. These, and other documents, encouraged the Board to take the view that treatment must be 'sufficient' in terms of its provision under the Mental Health Act 1986.

Accordingly, the Mental Health Review Board ordered the transfer of DWP back to Pentridge. Even though this preference for a prison *vis-à-vis* a mental health facility for a seriously mentally ill person was occasioned by J Ward's lack of resources, it was also a judgment about the inadequacy of therapeutic levels and indicative of the Board's resolve to make decisions in the best interests of the patient, rather than simply ratify existing psychiatric practice. The carefully worded statement reflected the Board's dilemma, but was nonetheless an indictment of J Ward's inability to meet the needs of a seriously ill forensic patient and a bitter blow indeed for the Office of Psychiatric Services in the light of their treatment mandate:

> We accept that the treatment available to him in prison may be no better or even worse than that available to him at J Ward, but the Act does not require us to contrast the treatment available in a psychiatric in-patient service with that available in a prison. We have no desire to cause harm to Mr DWP, nor to

cause him to become an unwilling victim in a test case. However, we cannot
sanction a state of affairs which has caused him to receive inadequate treatment by ignoring this matter or by pretending that the treatment afforded to
him is better than it is. (Kiel 1992, p.229)

The significance of this case should not be underestimated in terms of its relevance
for the later Garry David hearing. For the first time, only 18 months after it was
established to protect patients' rights, the Mental Health Review Board was
flexing its muscle about the provision of necessary treatment. The DWP case was
argued against a background of American class actions, which determined that
treatment must meet certain standards, as well as the English *Bolam* test defining
the nature of the duty of care to a patient. In *Rouse v Cameron* ([1966] 373F 2d
451), the Washington Court of Appeals had upheld the principle that 'the purpose
of involuntary hospitalization is treatment not punishment', and although psychiatric care need not make a demonstrable improvement, there must be 'a *bone fide*
effort' involved and 'adequate' treatment provision (at p.456). The *Bolam* test,
which has been generally followed in the UK and Australia, was formulated by
McNair, J. as follows: 'The test is the standard of the ordinary skilled man exercising and professing to have that special skill. A man need not possess the highest
expert skill; it is well established law that it is sufficient if he exercises the ordinary
skill of an ordinary competent man, exercising that particular act' (p.589). From
these guiding decisions, the Board came to the conclusion that:

> In this case, the standard is that expected of a qualified psychiatrist for it is the
> authorised psychiatrist who is given the power under section 16(6), to give
> consent to treatment for mental illness when a security patient is not capable
> of consenting to that treatment and it is, on the evidence before us, the psychi-
> atrist who heads and coordinates the treatment team. (Kiel 1992, p.225)

This outcome was bound to cause dissension within psychiatric services and raised
doubts about the continued viability of J Ward, the level of staff morale and the
role of the Board in conducting an inquiry into the actual provision of psychiatric
treatment. The case went on appeal to the Administrative Appeals Tribunal (*Dr
Grigor and the Chief General Manager of the Department of Health v Mental Health Review
Board and Mr DWP*, 5 September 1989) and it was held that it is *not* a Tribunal's
task to determine the detailed nature or appropriateness of the treatment in a particular case; rather it should be concerned merely to identify the treatment to the
extent of determining whether it is available. This ruling did not make the Board's
task any easier in the Garry David case, when it was faced with a variety of
opinions about possible treatments and their efficacy for the personality disorders.

Thus, in certifying Garry David, Dr Grigor would have recognised that similar
ground would be revisited and he would once again play a central role in an

important case. However, he could not ignore the fact that the notoriety of the appellant guaranteed that the task facing the Board was potentially more difficult and unpopular than in the earlier case and any granting of an appeal might lead to a significant backlash against the Board itself. There was even more at stake with Garry David, because of the complex and diverse nature of psychiatric judgments surrounding the personality disorders, and the fact that a decision would have to be made in a climate sensitive to political and community interest.

Second, the certification decision needs to be assessed in the light of the policy which had evolved within Dr Grigor's department over many years, and with which he had evidently concurred. Garry David had not been in the mental health system since his last admission to J Ward in April 1984, despite periods of disruptive and self-mutilating behaviour in the gaol. The implementation of the 1986 legislation was undoubtedly influential in the reluctance to resort to 'van therapy' from this period onwards. In addition, arguments put forward by the Minister for Health to the Minister for Corrections in 1983 and 1984 for the latter to accept responsibility for this prisoner, in the clear absence of any medical necessity, had also been persuasive. Psychiatrists had begun to re-evaluate their forensic role and had developed firmer policies based on the feasibility of treatment. For example, Dr TS analysed the chain of events leading to one of Garry's certifications, when the minister had, in that instance, 'insisted' on psychiatric intervention, and the actual 'surrender' to the prisoner had been effected by psychiatrists (19 January 1984). The use of a warlike metaphor graphically depicts the sense of siege erupting long before Garry's release date. This letter also emphasised Dr TS's belief in the inefficacy of certification as a solution and from this time onwards there was an understood reluctance to rely on its use. It appeared that it had simply served to foster conflict between the correctional and medical staff, and Garry's presence in a treatment setting disturbed the other patients.

Probably the clearest indication of this shift in policy was contained in Dr TS's memo to Dr Grigor, when the latter became the Acting Director of the Mental Health Division of the Health Department on 9 January 1985. This detailed past failures and ministerial involvement in a proposed future plan. It contained a grim reminder that there had been adverse criticism of psychiatrists previously responding to political pressure 'to get them to do what is necessary', but no firm psychiatric diagnosis seemed to have ever been possible, except for 'the comforting label of personality disorder'. This latter comment suggests an ambivalence about the legitimate place of personality disorder in the clinical manuals, particularly in view of the number of prisoners attracting this label without requiring any particular psychiatric intervention. In the future, Dr TS maintained, there should not be further recourse to short periods of respite in a psychiatric setting *in the absence of mental illness*, and it should be recognised that 'past attempts to treat him [Garry] as a psychiatric patient have been harmful'. Whilst psychiatrists were instructed to cooperate with the Office of Corrections, they should no longer accept delegation of responsibility for Garry David by decisions 'taken with, or against, our advice'. Dr TS prophesied that the road ahead would be difficult with further self-mutilations and the likelihood of unintended lethal consequences.

This clear policy directive appears to have been in place from 1985 and was partly responsible for Garry embarking on a number of vendettas against psychiatrists and psychologists within the prison, since he was less able to initiate his own moves between the two systems. The Health Department resisted pressures to certify him, even though they occasionally had to justify their apparently obdurate stance to correctional and welfare staff. On 14 January 1987, the Acting Senior Welfare Officer wrote to the Governor with a formal request to note staff concerns. She drew attention to the fact that Garry was becoming increasingly agitated and making irrational demands, yet the welfare staff could not identify any alternative sources of assistance. As she stated, 'psychological and psychiatric services have advised they are unable to provide further support' and this would cause additional frustration to Garry, thereby increasing the vulnerability of the welfare staff.

In the light of this background, the certification of Garry by the Director of Forensic Services appeared to reverse the policy, which had guided the correctional services staff for some five years. It was all the more unexpected, given that Dr Grigor had been the major adviser about Garry's management during the period between 1985 and 1990, and he estimated having spent approximately 100 hours counselling him during the preceding three and a half years (MHRB, *Statement of Reasons*, p.7). He was well aware that four colleagues, including the two most senior psychiatrists in his department, although acknowledging Garry's psychiatric disorder, had found him *not* to be mentally ill within the terms of the Mental Health Act 1986, and that the collegiate body shared a similar view. Dr Grigor examined Garry on 8 January 1990 and provided the Director-General of Corrections with the certificate on the following day. He was sufficiently concerned about the tenuousness of the grounds for this action that he informed the prisoner of his right of an immediate appeal. Even so, the certification appeared in a conservative morning newspaper with the headline: 'Psychiatrist Denies He Had Political Pressure' (*The Age*, 15 February 1990). Another article – 'State in Special Deal for Gunman: Madman Gets His Way on Cell Demands' – revealed details of the inducements which were offered to Garry should he agree to go to J Ward, including unlimited access to a word processor, an electric guitar, colour television, private shower and care by only female nursing staff (*The Age*, 14 January 1990). The division of opinion among psychiatrists at this time was typified by Dr Neville Parker's reported comments:

The fact that Garry was able to negotiate with prison authorities about what he wanted in Ararat before he was certified would clearly indicate his sanity. (*The Age*, 14 January 1990)

This same article also 'leaked' information that the Law Reform Commission interim report, due to go before Cabinet in February, would recommend amendments to the Mental Health Act 1986 to allow for the involuntary detention of those with antisocial personality disorders (see Williams 1990, pp.161–83). This was a matter of some difficulty for the Social Development Committee, since its brief was essentially similar and its hearings yet to be completed. It is not inconceivable that the information became public in order to suggest the type of approach consonant with the views of a body possessing recognised academic and legal expertise. On 5 February 1990, the Minister for Health requested the Committee to provide an interim report by 2 March about any legislative changes required to respond to those with 'a severe personality disorder and/or a mental illness, who present a danger to the community'. Once again, members understood that the Garry David situation was to be the focus of their work, although he was not specifically named. The deputy chairman of the Social Development Committee later used the parliamentary privilege to charge the Government with being both 'mischievous' and 'coy' for this oversight. He pointed out that no members were under any illusion as to the inquiry's real intent, and the Bill could be more honestly termed 'The Garry David Bill' (*Hansard*, 11 April 1990). The anxiety to find some resolution in the morass of legal and administrative manoeuvring was emphasised, when the Minister for Health later announced that she would be pleased to have any necessary draft amendments to the Mental Health Act included in the Committee's tabled report.

Garry lodged his appeal against his continued detention as a security patient at J Ward Ararat on 11 January 1990, and 12 days later there was an initial hearing to establish the procedures to be followed. The appellant had made it clear that he was prepared to remain as a voluntary patient in a psychiatric in-patient service following his release. It was a conciliatory offer causing the authorities some embarrassment, for Garry was publicly conceding that psychiatry *might* be able to help him and that *he* was prepared to cooperate. Also, by affirming his ability to act autonomously he was somewhat vexatiously abiding by the proper spirit of the 'rights' principles of legislation with a preference for 'the least restrictive environment'. In his view any programme offered to him would be negotiable, but should his proposition be officially rejected, the Government would be casting doubt on its commitment to its own mental health policies.

The Government was still not in a sufficiently secure position to ensure Garry David's detention. There had already been signs that the Mental Health Review Board would exercise an independent judgment, having rejected two early applications from the Victorian Solicitor-General for definitions of 'mentally ill' and 'mental illness' as appearing in sections 8, 15 and 16 of the Act. The first application asked the Board to exercise its power to reserve a question of law in the form of a special case for the opinion of the Supreme Court by seeking a construction of both 'mentally ill' and 'mental illness' as they appear in the Act. Should the application be declined, then the Board itself was asked to define these expressions.

If a judicial body of tribunal status was not acceding to applications from Victoria's highest ranking legal officer made on behalf of the Government, then doubt was also cast on the outcome of future legal proceedings in the Supreme Court. Should Garry's appeal be upheld, then his continued detention would be placed at risk, given that charges of threatening to kill ordinarily attract bail (*Hansard*, 10 April 1990). The Attorney-General is reported to have briefed his department that a conviction could not be guaranteed, because the provisions in the Act might not apply and the witnesses were likely to present as being unreliable (*Hansard*, 10 April 1990). The Acting Director-General of Corrections also warned that if a further warrant detaining Garry in custody were not issued on or prior to 22 March, he would be discharged as a security patient and the appropriate police personnel notified (19 January 1990). The uncertainties of the holding powers were becoming increasingly clear to the authorities concerned and a further stumbling block was posed by the Parliament's own Social Development Committee being unwilling to support the direction the Law Reform Commission was taking in regard to proposed legislative change. The fact that the Solicitor-General was so directly involved in negotiations with senior members of government departments highlights the sensitivity and importance attached to Garry David's continued custody. In the political point scoring of parliamentary debate, he was referred to by the opposition as 'the Premier's personal hatchet man and Mr Fix-it-man' who:

> has managed to drag in honest and sincere people from the Solicitor-General's office; they have been running around telling departmental officers what to do. They have been trying by any means to keep the person named in the Bill in custody, whether it is by criminal charges or by finding a psychiatrist to say he is mentally ill. There is no end to the exotic ways the government will try to do it behind the scenes if it can.

> Honourable members now know that the former Attorney-General apparently involved the Director of Public Prosecutions in the process and, in the course of doing so, clearly compromised the independence of the Director of Public Prosecution. How will he be able to determine honestly and independently whether the prosecution should proceed if he has been involved in determining whether the prosecution should be laid? How will he review his own decision? What was he doing with the Attorney-General? What was the

previous Attorney-General concerned about in the laying of criminal charges against the person named in the Bill? (*Hansard*, 10 April 1990)

A DISTASTEFUL TASK FOR PARLIAMENT

After 3 February 1990 Garry's status was decidedly unclear. His sentence had expired; he was remanded in custody pending a court hearing; and he was an appellant to the Mental Health Review Board. Section 50 of the Mental Health Act 1986 provides for the Director-General of Corrections to notify the Chief Psychiatrist when a sentence of imprisonment is due to expire in order to allow for the 'automatic discharge' of a security patient. However, as I have previously indicated, there was some confusion about the precise expiry date, and the Board's hearing was still in progress. A letter from the Director-General of Corrections to the Authorised Psychiatrist of J Ward, dated 13 February 1990, pointed out that Garry was being 'given the benefit of fourteen days' additional remission, which had for a time been denied him, but which were restored to him on the advice of the Solicitor-General'.

Despite this, Garry should have been discharged on either 3 or 17 February and returned to Pentridge to be held in custody pending his trial, then recertified under section 16 and conveyed back to J Ward. An amendment to Section 50 in the Mental Health (General Amendment) Act 1990 has rectified this anomaly and security patient status ceases on the granting of bail (section 17 (1)(a)). Whilst this might have constituted the correct procedure, it would have been unnecessarily cumbersome, and likely to have triggered understandable anger from the prisoner, fostering further instability in both systems. In addition, as the Attorney-General pointed out, it was conceivable that he may not have met the stricter criteria for involuntary detention of non-prisoners under the Mental Health Act (*Hansard*, 4 April 1990). This would not be the only occasion when legal complexities arose about Garry's formal status, allowing him the opportunity to exploit the issue should he so choose.

The next move was the culmination of all the activity surrounding Garry David's detention. On Tuesday 4 April 1990, prior to the Mental Health Review Board bringing down its finding, the Government introduced into Parliament a novel piece of legislation entitled the Community Protection Bill 1990, which would provide the framework for a formal and authoritative ascription of dangerousness. Colloquially referred to as a 'one-person Act', it was intended as a temporary measure with a 6-monthly review and sunset clause of 12 months. The stated purposes of the Bill were explicitly custodial:

(a) to provide for the safety of members of the public and the care or treatment and the management of Garry David, a person who has been convicted of attempted murder and other offences and is, or has been, in a psychiatric in-patient service; and

(b) to provide for proceedings to be instituted in the Supreme Court for an Order for the detention of Garry David.

In essence, a Supreme Court judge would be required to consider the evidence about the 'dangerousness' of this one person as a precursor to his exclusion from the general community. The 'proof' required to effect the transition was to be elicited from medical experts on the basis of their special knowledge. The court was empowered to arrange for an examination of Garry David 'by a legally qualified medical practitioner, psychiatrist or psychologist and may require a report covering such aspects as his mental and physical health, past and proposed care and treatment, an opinion about his dangerousness and the necessity for his continued detention'. It was decided, too, that Police and Parole Board reports would be made available to the court on request. The matters to which the court was to have regard were set out in section 15 as follows:

(a) the state of mental health of Garry David; and

(b) the state of physical health of Garry David; and

(c) any care or treatment undergone by Garry David whilst in detention; and

(d) any care or treatment proposed for Garry David; and

(e) the general behaviour of Garry David whilst in detention; and

(f) the opinion of the person making the report as to the likelihood of Garry David, if discharged, being a danger to any member of the public; and

(g) the opinion of the person making the report as to whether the continued detention of Garry David is necessary for the safety of any member of the public; and

(h) the opinion of the person making the report as to whether Garry David should be transferred to another psychiatric in-patient service, prison or institution of detention.

It was therefore being assumed that the scientific status of this knowledge would be sufficiently authoritative to validate political, police and community views. However, the ground rules established by this unique legislation to obtain relevant information posed a dilemma for the psychiatrists and psychologists subpoenaed to give evidence. Whilst their opinion about dangerousness would be the focal point of the legislation, empirical studies had for some time been disputing their ability to offer an informed view, apart from a history of past violence, which relates to the general knowledge domain as much as the expert one. Thus the very basis of the legislation was grounded in a legal fiction, which would make it distinctly difficult for those providing evidence.

In introducing this Bill concurrently with other modes of inquiry and reporting, Parliament was overshadowing the role of its statutory bodies and almost cavalierly disregarding the relevance of their work. The distinct advantage of a Community Protection Act from the Government's point of view lay in its *appearance* of judicial discretion. A Supreme Court judge would be required to decide whether Garry David's status should be that of a prisoner within the meaning of the Corrections Act 1986, or a psychiatric patient within that of the Mental Health Act 1986. Either choice was to be underpinned by the need for preventive detention, for the legislation provided that on a finding of serious risk to the safety of any member of the public or likelihood of an act of violence to another person 'the Supreme Court *may* order [my italics] that Garry David be placed in preventive detention' (ss.8 (1)(a) and (b)). Although judicial care would, of course, govern the choice of institution, Garry later undermined the distinction between a correctional and mental health facility by referring to himself as a 'psychiatric prisoner' – a phrase eagerly seized upon by the media for its evocative combination of dual attributes.

Since Garry David was due to appear before the Melbourne Magistrate's Court on 18 April, immediately after Easter, the Community Protection Bill was introduced into Parliament somewhat precipitately and debated in late-night sittings. The appearance of haste in both its drafting and presentation did not pass unnoticed and neither Garry nor his solicitors were informed about the timing of its introduction. The reaction from both sides of the house was similar. Misgivings were expressed about the necessity for legislation of this sort, and the Bill rankled with members of the Labor Party who had carefully shepherded the 1986 legislation heralding the rights of the mentally ill and intellectually disabled through Parliament to ensure that these would include detention in a psychiatric hospital, a prison and residence in the community. The principles formed the preamble to the various Acts and emphasised that there should be minimal interference with the liberty and dignity of mentally impaired persons. The mental health legislation, in particular, had been thoroughly debated over 10 days with each clause being subjected to intense scrutiny, resulting in 211 amendments (*Hansard*, 22 April 1986). Considering that many of the innovative proposals had only gained support after extensive consultation with the Royal Australian and New Zealand College of Psychiatrists, the Government may have been hesitant in directly intervening in the legislative definition of mental illness without ratification by a superior court. Certainly, at the time when the Community Protection Bill was introduced, there had been no tabling of the Law Reform Commission's report, which favoured a shift to encompass personality disorder.

Whilst the legislation was introduced on 4 April 1990 with the original intention of shepherding its passage through Parliament on the following day, the Opposition was alarmed by some of its implications and requested an adjournment to allow time for community consultation and party room debate, together with access to the Mental Health Review Board's transcript of evidence. Robert Maclellan, a shadow minister, complained:

> I anticipate what the government is signalling to the opposition parties is that Mr Garry David will win his review and that, for some reason known only to the Government or the Director of Public Prosecutions, he will not be prosecuted under the Crimes Act; and we are not to be given any assistance – or at least no assistance was offered in determining our parties' attitude in regard to the matter…it is a matter of brinkmanship; it is outrageous to expect a Bill such as this to be debated without an appropriate adjournment and without appropriate opportunity for the parties to inform themselves so that they may make informed decisions about the matter rather than relying solely upon press reports and the Minister's second-reading speech, which is notable for its lack of information. (4 April 1990)

He found himself at some disadvantage in the parliamentary debate in the absence of a definition of mental illness, and further argued that members of parliament were being asked to vote on a Bill based on the presumed dangerousness of one person in the absence of any hard evidence. As he saw it, their understanding was informed by only four factors: general knowledge filtering through the media, a brief outline contained in the Second Reading Speech, an awareness of the trauma caused by recent large-scale Melbourne massacres, and the attitude of the police. There was a certain awkwardness to the debate that followed. Members of parliament are accustomed to evaluating legislation for its general impact yet, in this instance, there was no broader applicability beyond the link between Garry David's mental state and his 'probable' dangerousness. It was inevitable that the Bill would have to specify the lesser standard of proof on the balance of probabilities rather than the ordinary criminal standard of beyond reasonable doubt, for future dangerousness can never be categorically proven. The sense of pressure accompanying the debate was unpalatable for some parliamentarians, and one member thought that it 'quite wrong' that the parliament was being rushed into a decision (*Hansard*, 4 April 1990). The Opposition suggested that 'the fatal crisis of time' could perhaps be remedied if the Government were to introduce an amendment to the Bail Act 1977, limiting the ability of a Supreme Court judge to grant bail in the case of those charged under sections 20 and 21 of the Crimes Act 1958. However, this suggestion would have entailed retrospective application to cover Garry David's circumstance. An interesting argument emerged that legislation based on dangerousness might be *sub judice* in view of the fact that Garry had already been charged with threats of violence, but legal advice quickly dispelled this possibility. Even so, the Government had placed itself in the position of disregarding convention by canvassing opinion about Garry's presumed dangerousness in a parliamentary forum, before any determination could be made in the Supreme Court.

The opposition Liberal party, although ideologically in favour of a law and order approach, was hard pressed to debate the Bill in the absence of other solutions and hence tended to rely on innuendo about the Government's motives for its introduction. It was suggested that it was 'more in the nature of a back-up to the opinion of Dr Grigor that the person named in the Bill is, in fact, mentally ill' (*Hansard*, 10 April 1990). Despite assurances to the contrary it appeared that, if the legislation could be implemented quickly enough, it would pre-empt any decision of the Mental Health Review Board and the findings of the Social Development Committee (*Hansard*, 10 April). Potentially, the incongruous position could then arise whereby the Mental Health Review Board might find Garry David not to be mentally ill, yet the Supreme Court could still have leeway to decide that he should be detained in a psychiatric in-patient service, thus placing psychiatrists in an invidious position.

There are particular problems with legislation of this type and these were noted in the context of parliamentary debate. Could it create the precedent for separate Acts naming individual persons, or would it simply be used to pave the way for broader provisions of preventive detention and 'scapegoat' Garry David in the process? Was its 12 months' sunset clause intended as a delaying tactic to facilitate the drafting of more general legislation? And should such legislation be applied at the time of sentencing, as happens in some other Australian states, or retrospectively? Many Parliamentarians and professionals were acutely aware that special legislation was simply playing into Garry's hands. As has been noted, Dr TS had earlier referred to the dissonance between the Health Commission and the Office of Corrections' staff, who seemed to be 'taking the first steps of a macabre dance to his well-known tune', and now the Government was enveloping itself in the same scenario. As Maclellan lamented:

> But maybe, just maybe, Parliament, the Social Development Committee, the Labor caucus, the Opposition and National Party party rooms and the media are dancing to his tune by granting this man the one gift we can give him – the one final gift that we can give to his obsessions or fantasies, a Bill aimed at him, an Act of Parliament, a special one for him. (*Hansard*, 10 April 1990)

In the eyes of some Parliamentary members, Garry David was holding the state to ransom, both in a general sense and by specific threats against those supposedly on his 'hit list'. As a consequence, many considered that the Government had been panicked into devising a solution resembling the English bills of attainder, notorious for their stark abrogation of common law principles. The dilemma for all members was painful, whatever their personal inclinations in the matter, and there was frequent reference to the Bill being 'pernicious', 'obnoxious', 'abhorrent' and a move of 'last resort'. One member alluded to the difficulty of finding a proper way of dealing with Garry David at this time, for he considered him to be 'not insane; he is an unreasonable but rational, a quite clever and devious person and Parliament cannot create retrospective criminal offences' (James Guest, *Hansard*, 11 April 1990).

THE WISH OF THE EXECUTIVE

Jim Kennan, the Attorney-General, who was formally responsible for introducing the Bill and steering it through Parliament, was a Queen's Counsel and well known for his civil libertarian views. He had only been in this portfolio for a week, the previous incumbent having been a non-lawyer, and undoubtedly his first major task was singularly distasteful, because the Act would empower him to apply *ex parte* for an interim order to the Supreme Court to place Garry David in detention, thus denying him ordinary civil rights (ss.4 (1) and (2)). Such an action, indicative of Parliament's wishes in this matter of preventive detention, would set in train a process altering the usual separation of the powers of the executive and the judiciary. Despite these legislative weaknesses, the Attorney-General delivered a carefully crafted speech to the Parliament, arguing that the legislation was insti-gated by a concern for community protection and should not be viewed as 'pre-empting the report of the Social Development Committee, or…compromising either the mental health system or the criminal justice system' (*Second Reading Speech, Hansard*, 4 April 1990). In later debate, he conceded it to be 'a holding operation' (*Hansard*, 10 April 1990).

Jeffrey Kennett, the leader of the Opposition, spoke of 'the politics of hypocrisy, or indecision, and of failure of the system', and declared it to be obvious that Garry David was not ready to leave an institutional setting, but that such extreme legislation compelling him to remain was both repugnant and unjust. He echoed the views of other members, who were dissatisfied with the lack of infor-mation provided and the necessity of having to form opinions from media reports about Garry's threats and self-mutilation, many of which appeared to have been systematically leaked from sources within the Office of Corrections (*Hansard*, 10 April 1990; also Geoffrey Connard, 11 April 1990).

Whilst Garry's custodial separation had encouraged rumours and exaggera-tion about his exploits and capacity for violence, and he himself had aided and abetted this view, there was disturbing evidence of unfavourable material being disseminated from internal sources, giving some credence to the prisoner's bitter complaints about his victimisation by the authorities. Peter Harmsworth, the

Director-General of Corrections, expressed some sympathy for this view in the evidence he gave to the Social Development Committee's Inquiry and later reported to Parliament:

> *Harmsworth*: I certainly believe there was the possibility of public servants communicating with the media. Some of the details given to the media were privy only to a dozen or so people. I was amazed when I read about it.
>
> *Maclellan*: What was it all for; was it part of an 'integrate Garry Webb into the community' program or, 'Let's make it an impossible' program?
>
> *Harmsworth*: I think the latter. (*Hansard*, 10 April 1990)

It was inevitable that the media campaign about Garry's unbounded violence should fuel fantasy images which were not easy to dispel, but it was disturbing when these infiltrated parliamentary debate. For example, the member whose electorate bounded Pentridge Prison made the startling pronouncement that:

> Not only has the man tried to kill once but also experts have said, if he is released, he will repeat that offence 20 or 30 times. That alone should be enough for anyone to say that the person is not fit to be in the community, as much as we would like everyone to be free. The man is sick, if he is capable of killing 20 or 30 people. (*Hansard*, 11 April 1990)

Haddon Storey was yet another Opposition member to draw attention to the fact that all major reports pertaining to the case had been suppressed, including the transcripts of evidence given to the Mental Health Review Board, together with reports prepared by psychiatrists, the Victoria Police and the Office of Corrections. This withholding of the abundant factual information, he argued, created the impression that only token debate was required, and that it could be based on knowledge in the public domain, which was largely impressionistic (*Hansard*, 11 April 1990). Although so little reliable information was forthcoming, parliamentary members of the Social Development Committee were able to assist the debate with information they had gathered during the hearings of the preceding months. However, on legal advice, the transcript of the Mental Health Review Board hearing had been withheld and their Research Officer was denied access to the hearings. This was not mere obstructionism on the Board's part. In the interests of privacy, section 35 of the Mental Health Act 1986 contains a secrecy provision restricting Board members, and any person present at a hearing, from divulging information to a third party, even though the Garry David appeal was one of its rare public hearings. The Board received advice from counsel that under section 35(1) they could not provide the Social Development Committee with a transcript or copies of the exhibits in the Garry David case. On 28 June 1990, the Committee passed a formal resolution, pursuant to its powers under the Parliamentary Committee Act 1968 to gain access, but the Board still considered that any such action on their part would be unlawful. In its *Annual Report* 1990 the MHRB noted the incongruity of section 35 denying a parliamentary committee, charged with inquiring into mental health legislation, access to relevant material from a duly constituted body administering that legislation (see p.18).

The restriction had immediate consequences in this case: the costs of the two closely related inquiries were compounded; there was a degree of overlap; and the Committee's information was restricted to verbal and written evidence, supplemented by the literature relating to personality disorder and preventive detention, thus rendering its information less rigorous than that tested by the Board's process of examination and cross-examination. As one member noted in Parliament, members were denied access to psychiatrists' reports as well as the Law Reform Commission's interim report, although its findings were reported in the media and its general position known. The only conclusion he could draw was that the Government had deliberately limited the evidence it wished to be made available (*Hansard*, 11 April 1990).

In the debates, Parliament did learn, however, that Garry was willing to become a voluntary patient, although all concerned realised that this 'offer' entailed the risk of legal discharge. There were two further problems. Victoria had no suitable therapeutic community for those with personality disorders and some holding mechanism would, paradoxically, have to accompany any proposed voluntary status. In this, Garry David touched a sensitive nerve by alluding to the conceptual and legal contradictions involved in the notion of enforced treatment in his instructions forwarded to the Attorney-General:

> Mr David is willing to voluntarily enter such a community on the understand-
> ing that the 'voluntariness' will have a degree of coercion. However, before he
> would agree to such, he would have to be satisfied that there was a fair mecha-
> nism by which the element of coercion would be removed. Mr David points
> out that he has consistently said that he would not be able to survive in the
> wider community, if released straight to it, and that he is certainly in need of
> rehabilitation. (9 April 1990)

Members on both sides of the house found sole-person legislation to be abhorrent and made emotive reference to the lapse of constitutional principles akin to the policies, which had prevailed in Nazi Germany, revolutionary France, apartheid South Africa, the imprisonment of dissidents in the Soviet Union, and various dictatorships in South America. In another rhetorical flourish, the Bill was referred to as 'the poisoned chalice' in both Houses (*Hansard*, 10 and 11 April 1990). This lapse into hyperbole may not have arisen if more facts had been available and if psychiatrists had been able to provide a clear direction. One Parliamentarian was clearly frustrated by what he termed the 'divergence of opinion' among psychiatrists in relation to the appropriate handling of serious personality disorders. He conceded that there were conceptual difficulties in trying to provide definitions of insanity, but nevertheless those available were mystifying by being 'broad and somewhat diverse, diffuse and even abstruse' (Dr Ronald Wells, *Hansard*, 10 April 1990). Even more pertinent, he considered, was the fact that psychiatrists appeared to have distanced themselves from the issue by developing an esoteric understanding of the meaning of insanity, which was out of touch with the ordinary community. What Dr Ronald Wells was putting very clearly to the Parliament was the substantive issue, which arose in Garry David's appeal to the Mental Health Review Board: that there is a dichotomy between the ordinary common-sense view of madness and expert opinion, as well as a gulf between the law and medicine. His view of the way psychiatrists seemingly distance themselves from ordinary community concerns echoed those of Justice Vincent and he told the House that:

> If one talks, as I have done, with senior police in my area, one finds a practical, pragmatic judgment by people who are not professional psychiatrists, but who deal with many offenders of all sorts, that the man concerned does not fit within the normal bounds of sanity. I wonder whether we are looking at a situation in which the experts have departed from the practical realm of normal living. (*Hansard*, 10 April 1990)

The Law Reform Commission's Report (No. 31) *The Concept of Mental Illness in the 'Mental Health Act' 1986* was finally tabled in the afternoon during the Legislative Council debate – a departure from normal practice occasioning some delay in its reception. The proceedings of the House continued, allowing members only a cursory scanning of the Report's contents, which pursued a different path altogether from the one that Parliament was debating. The crux of the arguments was a recommendation that a sub-clause be added to section 8 of the Mental Health Act 1986:

> Subsection 8(2)(l) does not prevent a person who is suffering only from an antisocial personality disorder from being considered to be mentally ill.

It was not until the next day that it was realised that the crucial words *disorder* and *only* had been omitted from the printed Draft Bill Mental Health (Amendment) Act 1986, thus distorting the intention of the proposed amendment. Given that there was such sensitivity about amending the Mental Health Act, together with resistance from the Australian and New Zealand College of Psychiatrists, opposition from the Law Institute of Victoria, and evidence of dissension within the Commission itself over the issue, this omission cannot be regarded as inadvertent and suggests some internal tampering. Nevertheless, it initially went unnoticed due to the Report's late tabling. The matter was an embarrassment to the Commissioner, who circulated a letter on 18 April to those who had received a copy of the Report, pointing out that the correct wording had been used in the text itself, so that the Commission's intentions still remained clear, although the crucial words omitted would be added to the draft amendment.

The debates on the Bill recognised the problems associated with accommodating Garry David in either the mental health or criminal justice system. Effectively, however, Parliamentarians were passing responsibility for the final outcome to psychiatrists, but within an unusual legal framework requiring regular review by the Supreme Court. Psychiatrists would be constrained by novel guidelines and presented with a new duty, and a Supreme Court judge would be given a message of direction from the Executive. As Joan Coxsedge cogently argued in the Upper House:

> When a person makes threats to kill others it is accepted that sanctions should be imposed by the State against that person. The question is: what sanctions should we apply? At least two competing approaches have been identified, the first through the mental health system and the second through the criminal justice system. To a certain extent the choice depends on whether one views the people concerned as mad or bad, and we need to consider the practical consequences that would flow from whatever choice we make.
>
> The mental health approach seems to have received more attention than its competitor and the rationale for it is based on an appeal to community attitudes. To the lay person, anyone who goes around making open threats to kill must be mad. Perhaps a less publicised reason is expediency: it is undoubtedly much quicker to certify someone than to go through a criminal trial. However, the problem is that the weight of professional opinion is opposed to this. The majority of Victorian psychiatrists do not believe the making of threats to kill necessarily and of itself constitutes mental illness. There is a strongly held view that, although some people who make threats to kill may be mentally ill, this will not always be the case.
>
> If prisons are not appropriate for Garry David and psychiatrists say he is not mad, maybe because he does not fit into a treatable category – or maybe they are passing the buck; I am not sure – it may be that we need something that is halfway between a prison and a psychiatric institution – some other place – but that place must be secure, because, of course, we have an absolute duty to protect the community. (*Hansard*, 11 April 1990)

In creating a framework for judicial decision making likely to lead to custody, Parliament was in the position of presuming Garry David was dangerous and, as one member noted, it made their deliberations akin to a trial (James Guest, *Hansard*, 11 April 1990). It was also presuming that a Supreme Court judge would be able to assess, from the evidence, including a possible rational account of events from Garry David himself, whether he was mad or bad, despite any lack of clear direction from psychiatrists. If the judge were to choose the psychiatric option, then the position of Garry David would still be anomalous, because the legislation specifically excluded clauses in the Mental Health Act, thereby curtailing the powers exercised by the Chief Psychiatrist and Mental Health Review Board in relation to ordinary psychiatric patients. Thus Garry would be severely restricted on a number of counts: in his use of appellate and review procedures, discharge as a security patient to a prison, transfer to another psychiatric in-patient service, leave of absence or special leave. Section 10(2) of the Bill stated: 'If Garry David is detained in a psychiatric in-patient service under an Order under this Act, he is deemed to be a security patient within the meaning of the Mental Health Act 1986 and to be in the custody of the authorized psychiatrist but sections 29, 30, 44, 45, 46, 49, 50, 51 and 52 of the Act do not apply to him.'

The Bill made a public statement, that whilst psychiatry could, or perhaps ought to, care for Garry David, it required the supervision of the Court to do so. Overall, this Bill can only be described as a crude mechanism for the preventive detention of one person. It effectively transferred control over Garry David from psychiatry to Parliament, then to the Supreme Court, and back to either a prison or a psychiatric inpatient service all at the Court's direction. Yet, the Court was restricted by its ordinary powers. Whilst it might express an opinion about a desirable custodial regime, it has no power to *direct* the administration to provide these services. This traditional division between judicial and administrative roles, in this case, meant that it could determine the location of Garry's custody, but it could not monitor his management in an ongoing manner.

On 11 April 1990, just prior to the Easter break, the Bill passed through the Legislative Council, with a vote of 36 in favour and 4 members dissenting. Although there had been general dissatisfaction about the need for haste and the subversion of common law principles, Parliamentary support was derived from a fear of the consequences should Garry David be released into the community. The Bill received Assent on 24 April, enabling the Attorney-General to make an originating motion under section 6 of the Community Protection Act 1990 for an order for preventive detention on 10 May. The appearance of urgency was inescapable, when Garry's lawyers had to request a photocopy of the unprinted legislation and time to read its provisions, before the application could proceed. The media was left in no doubt about the Act's purpose, and a conservative morning daily reported that:

> The State Government took a landmark legal step yesterday to throw away
> the key on Garry Webb, the man it says is too dangerous to be free. Webb, the
> first person in Victoria to become the exclusive subject of an Act of Parlia-
> ment, is now the target of court action designed to keep him in custody per-
> manently. (*The Age*, 11 May 1990)

The Community Protection Act came into being because the experts were unable
or unwilling to implement the direction the Government required. Their technical
knowledge did not match the demands being made on them. Disciplinary and
therapeutic strategies had been rendered ineffective by a prisoner who revelled in
the discomfiture caused by his bizarre acts of self-punishment, yet who could still
tantalise with the hope of reform. On the political front, the Act can only be
regarded as the unresolved culmination of six months' activity involving a number
of senior bureaucrats. The Government's attempts to enforce custody had taken
some strange turns and it was evident that considerable pressure had been placed
on the Solicitor-General, the Government Solicitor, the Office of Psychiatric
Services, the Victoria Police, the Social Development Committee and the Law
Reform Commission of Victoria to carve a way out of the impasse. Some of the
innovative solutions which emerged bore the hallmark of desperation and
disregard for the usual conventions. These included the abortive attempt to extend
Garry's release date by two weeks; the proposal to amend two Acts to enable part
of the prison to be proclaimed as a psychiatric hospital; the formal request to have
the meaning of 'mental illness' redefined; and the convening of a panel of four psychiatrists with the intention of effecting certification. All these separate actions to
manipulate the boundary between criminality and mental illness foundered and
became a matter of some embarrassment to a Government beleaguered on the issue
of Garry David. Its last resort was to create a public spectacle by seeking to expose
this man's depredations in an authoritative setting. Yet in this process of finding a
solution for just one person in a state of more than four million people, Parliament
seemed to be initiating changes in the roles of all concerned with little heed for the
consequences. On another front, it was now necessary for the Mental Health
Review Board to produce its finding about Garry David's continued status of that
of a security patient. This different mode of inquiry focused the spotlight on psychiatrists and the credibility of their profession was under review.

CHAPTER 4

Bad Or Mad?

The Credibility of Psychiatry

Professional opinion is divided – I've never known otherwise with this man.

Psychiatrists are split in their ranks about whether such a person should go to prison.

I notice that 'DSM-III-R' is next to the Holy Bible, but I don't regard it as Holy Writ quite frankly. ('DSM' is a psychiatric Bible it appears?) Well, I don't think it is. I think it tries to squeeze people into watertight categories and this is not possible.

I have always believed he was mentally ill, but only lately realised he was certifiable.

My own personal view is that there is more puff and blow in this man and his rhetoric than there possibly is in his real dangerousness.

I told him that we were on the borderlands of what is certifiability. I'd come to the view that he was certifiable, but that it was at the edge.

I became a verbal punching bag for him.

Garry David's capacity for splitting staff is legion. . . in all my dealings with him, as you would well appreciate, you can split every group of people right down the middle as to whether he is merely bad, or whether he has an illness.

I'm concerned that this matter has been very badly bungled.

A person can be mentally ill, but not suffer from a mental illness.

In my view David has an unstable self-image. At times he sees himself as a poet and a guitarist, and someone who is sensitive, a latterday Che Guevara; at other times he sees himself as a sort of Angel of Death who must wreak havoc.

(MHRB, *Appeal of GIPW*, February–March 1990).

PERSONALITY DISORDERS AND THE LAW

This plethora of psychiatric opinions offered during Garry David's appeal against his certification as a security patient illustrates the disparate views and uncertainties that had developed in his management, as well as the difficulty of separating the more restrictive notion of a certifiable *mental illness* from the broader psychiatric one of a *mental disorder*. Their frankness and the hints of hyperbole conveyed to Board members the long-standing sense of frustration which had been the experience of so many psychiatrists and others involved in this case of a severely personality-disordered prisoner, who was only occasionally certifiable.

If the personality disorders are the Achilles' heel of psychiatry, then they are also the bane of the law, which is premised on the view that criminal behaviour has three attributes: it must be *conscious*, *intentional* and *voluntary*. The adversarial process of the criminal courts requires psychopathic behaviour to be shaped to fit the parameters of badness, whereby actions are explained with reference to immorality coupled with a knowledge of wrongness; or that of madness with emphasis on long standing personality deficits, poor judgement, impulsivity and social deprivation. Legal history would suggest that this allocation is problematic because of the way in which public interest and a perception of dangerousness may shift the balance towards a criminal justice response. For example, Charles Rosenberg's *The Trial of the Assassin Guiteau* (1968) recounts an early case which was a testing ground for the relationship between immoral behaviour, delusions and criminal responsibility. In 1881 Charles John Guiteau assassinated the President, James Garfield, and this act aroused community fear and a political determination to have him dealt with by the criminal law, rather than excused by virtue of mental illness (Rosenberg 1968, pp.81–2). Of the many expert witnesses, those appearing for the prosecution drew attention to the immorality of Guiteau's actions, whilst the defence couched this same behaviour in terms of mental impairment. For example, the psychiatrist superintendent of New York's Utica asylum contended that he could 'see nothing but a life of moral obliquity, profound selfishness and disregard for the rights of others', whereas a defence psychiatrist focused on Guiteau's 'insane temperament or partial (moral) imbecility' of organic origin; a diagnosis given credence by the taxonomy then in favour (Rosenberg 1968, p.97).

The fact that psychiatric interpretations are a product of the way in which knowledge is organised at any one time was particularly evident in the Guiteau case. *'Manie sans délire'* and moral insanity had extended madness beyond the 'defect of reason' posed by the insanity defence, and explanations of neurological degeneration were beginning to gain medical currency (see Pick 1989). Cesare Lombroso's (1913) approach was related and very influential. He proposed that criminality could be linked to an atavistic reversion to more primitive behaviour. This broadening of the medical ambit of insanity was and still is difficult for the law to assimilate, because it diminishes responsibility and opens the way for the court's use of psychiatric terminology to mask immoral or frankly criminal behaviour. For example, the main prosecution psychiatrist insisted in the Guiteau case that kleptomania, dipsomania and pyromania were simply diagnostic neologisms for thieving, drunkenness and arson (Rosenberg 1968, p.195). In contrast, those witnesses appearing for the defence chose to pursue the notion of moral insanity, but were clearly nervous about where this 'progress' in scientific knowledge might be leading them, for allowing immorality, even if couched in terms of moral insanity, to be a criterion of criminal behaviour would ultimately weaken legal sanctions and make the psychiatrist an apologist for the offender. It is a dilemma which has been played out in innumerable cases where mental state defences are raised, because scientific evidence is not presented in a vacuum devoid of its impact on the operation of the law, the offender, or community interests. And it is a dilemma too which is exacerbated by the adversarial nature of a court system designed to sharpen divergences in expert testimony. In general, the law has resisted psychiatric persuasion and excluded psychopathy from the doctrine of criminal responsibility. A well-known exception is the period between 1954 and 1972, when the District of Columbia and New Hampshire adopted as their criterion of legal insanity the Durham test: that is, 'an accused is not criminally responsible if his unlawful conduct is a product of mental disease or of mental defect'. Colloquially known as 'the product test', it fell into disrepute because it tended to take the issue of criminal responsibility out of the hands of the jury and transfer it to expert opinion on the basis of simply linking behaviour with mental state (see Moore 1984, pp.220–32).

There is emerging evidence of a significant challenge from empirical studies identifying a marked degree of frontal lobe dysfunction. Robert Hare, who has devised the famed Psychopathy Checklist, has referred to this research area as the 'new phrenology', or 'sub-clinical form of thought disorder' (see Damasio 1994; Damasio, Damasio and Christen 1996; Hare 1993;) If this line of inquiry is fruitful then a 'disease of the mind' in the M'Naghten sense could be said to exist and impair cognition, as well as legal responsibility for behaviour. Knowledge claims are important in the construction of the medico-legal discourse and, in the David case, the DSM-III-R's inclusion of borderline personality disorder became the lever to steer emphasis away from antisocial personality, which had been specifi-cally excluded by the legislation, despite some shared attributes. In another direc-tional twist, Dr Grigor suggested that Garry might have suffered some 'soft brain damage', thereby raising the spectre of a biological explanation, the consequence of which would negate legal responsibility. This claim could not be pursued because Garry consistently refused permission to conduct the requisite tests.

And Guiteau? He was found guilty and a date set for the hanging; but some psychiatrists immediately pressured the government to commute the sentence on the grounds of his mental incapacity and therefore certifiability, which raises an altogether different legal facet of 'madness' (Rosenberg 1968, p.227). It was to no avail; and the prisoner was duly hanged on 30 June 1882.

A second more recent case to explore the relationship between psychopathy and criminal responsibility is the high-profile one of John Hinckley, who attempted to assassinate the US President in 1981. Once again, the insanity defence was raised with varying diagnoses ranging broadly across the schizophrenias to the personality disorders. Highly contradictory psychiatric evidence emerged as the defence highlighted the serious nature of Hinckley's abnormalities, and the prosecution struggled to suggest that the defendant was on the boundary of normality and abnormality, but not so impaired as to negate criminal responsibility. After a costly and lengthy trial he was acquitted, but promptly certified and confined to the maximum security institution in which he currently resides.

The reaction to the Hinckley verdict was swift and strong. Many newspaper headlines conveyed a sense of outrage that neither psychiatry nor the law could confirm Hinckley's guilt and each profession appeared to exonerate him, even though the public had been assailed by countless television replays of the attempted assassination. Typical banners were: 'Psychiatry Goes on Trial with Hinckley'; 'Hinckley Verdict Sure to Spark Row'; and 'A Maddening Use of Psychiatry'. The political response was also immediate: the Crime Control Act 1984 established guidelines for the provision of psychiatric evidence and emphasised that witnesses should leave the question of the 'ultimate issue', or responsibility of the accused, to the jury. Yet there was little understanding that the legal setting shapes the discourse and affects the way experts choose to offer their opinion to the court. The Washington DC court required the prosecution to bear the impossible burden of proving legal sanity, thereby leaving counsel with the only option of countering the defence's clinical accounts with variants of moral obliquity.

According to John Gunn of London's Maudsley Hospital, psychopathy has 'wavering confines', which will only firm when 'more is known about genetics, (and) psychopathology' (Gunn 1977, p.325). In the Hinckley case, these 'wavering confines' have led to what Stone considers to be confusion between two different types of discourse, one based on free will and the other on determinism. In his view, a theory of appropriate behaviour requires explanations in terms of the mind, intention and motivation as agency, whereas an organic interpretation postulates some direct neurological change, which excludes notions of morality based on free will and choice (Stone 1984, p.95). The difficulty for both the law and psychiatry is that the same behaviour may occur as a matter of choice at one time, or be occasioned by biological factors at another, and insufficient effort is expended in distinguishing between these elements. He concludes:

> Psychiatry has not yet found a unified discourse about organisms and persons. That is the giant iceberg against which the insanity defense inevitably is wrecked. Neither psychiatry nor law nor moral philosophy has found a sure way past this barrier. It does no good to pretend the barrier does not exist or

to ask the jury to deal with it. These are not questions for which common sense has an answer. (Stone 1984, p.96)

Although the concept of psychopathy has remained central to the difficulties impinging on a coherent discourse between the law and psychiatry, and the boundary separating badness and madness is yet to be clearly delineated, at least one jurisdiction has pursued a different path with the inclusion of the special category of psychopathy in its legislation. The 1959 and 1983 English Mental Health Acts provide a framework for the indeterminate detention of this group in security hospitals, but it has been a move accompanied by ongoing debate. The initial construction of a definition of psychopathy focused on three attributes: persistence of the disorder; aggression or seriously irresponsible conduct; and susceptibility to treatment. The 1959 English Mental Health Act defined psychopathy as follows: 'In this Act *psychopathic disorder* means a persistent disorder or disability of mind (whether or not including subnormality of intelligence) which results in abnormally aggressive or seriously irresponsible conduct on the part of the patient, and requires or is susceptible to medical treatment. (Mental disorder includes psychopathic disorder.)'

The first attribute requires a quantitative evaluation; the second a moral judgement; and the third acknowledges that treatment may not necessarily be successful. Of these three attributes, only that relating to the persistence of a pervasively dysfunctional pattern can provide a strong basis for psychiatric intervention (see Ramon 1986, pp.214–40). The English legislation must be viewed as pragmatic in its creation of an intermediate position on medical grounds. The advantage is that it relieves the strain on the prison and general hospital systems and ratifies psychiatry's role for a small number of aggressive and/or dangerous patients.

New Zealand legislation differs from that of other jurisdictions and avoids definitional pitfalls by including a disorder of volition in its Mental Health (Compulsory Assessment and Treatment) Act 1992. However, a reading of relevant cases appearing before its Mental Health Review Tribunal suggests that the word 'volition' equally suffers the definitional elasticity pertaining to the meaning of 'mental illness'. In *The Matter of AC* (SRT 52/94), the Tribunal noted that:

Given a too wide interpretation the legislative intent would clearly be defeated. However, the argument that no disorders of volition should be recognised as it would open the door to abuse is equally untenable. The legislature has deliberately included the phrase *disorder of volition* in the definition section. It must be given appropriate meaning, appropriate to the overall legislative intent. The preamble to the Act refers to psychiatric assessment and *treatment* and the consolidation of the law relating to the assessment and *treatment* of persons suffering from a mental disorder. Clearly Parliament did not intend that all so-called disorders of volition were to come within the parameters of the Act.

However, as Coid points out, there is still considerable ambivalence about the treatability of this group:

> Despite the concerns by would be reformers, compulsory admission of psychopaths is now uncommon outside of the British maximum security hospitals. To a large extent this reflects the therapeutic nihilism of clinicians towards personality disorder, and a negative attitude to providing such patients with psychiatric resources. (Coid 1989, pp.750–1)

Victoria did not have the legislative shelter of the English position and so a maelstrom of uncertainty on two fronts enveloped politicians, lawyers and psychiatrists. On the one hand, the competing claims to 'ownership' of the knowledge about antisocial personality disorder were tested and, on the other, the problematic nature of its treatability raised serious doubts about non-consensual medical interventions. These issues were very much to the fore when the Mental Health Review Board convened to hear Garry David's appeal lodged under section 29(1)(a) of the Mental Health Act 1986.

THE BOARD CONVENES

On 23 January 1990, just 11 days prior to Garry David's expected release date, the Board commenced a hearing of unprecedented length. This body is quasi-judicial with tribunal status, designed as part of the appeal and review procedure of the Mental Health Act 1986 and bound by the rules of natural justice. Its usual procedure is to meet on site at various psychiatric locations with the patient being present and having the right of representation.

At the time of the hearing Garry David was a security patient of the now defunct J Ward, then an antiquated facility for some 20 'criminally insane' – a mixed grouping of those either certified whilst in the criminal justice system or deemed to be exceedingly violent in the mental health system. In this sense, J Ward had long acted as a hybrid institution, although it was officially regarded as a psychiatric hospital within the framework of mental health services. The original bluestone building with its high walls and bars bore the cold, forbidding atmosphere of its nineteenth-century prison origins and J Ward remained designated as a maximum secure facility, despite being staffed by nurses rather than uniformed correctional officers. The site was some 200 km from Melbourne and consequently those infrequent appeals against involuntary confinement as a security patient were usually scheduled for a city location. In the current instance, Mont Park Psychiatric Hospital was chosen, because it also had a forensic unit classified as medium security, should Garry choose to exercise his right to be present. The setting was relatively informal and a large recreation area of a recently refurbished building was set aside for the purpose. Although Board hearings are usually closed (section 34), an exception was made in this case because of the heightened public interest.

This matter was determined at the first meeting as follows:

> In accordance with the powers vested in the Mental Health Review Board by section 34(2) of the Mental Health Act 1986 the Mental Health Review Board has determined that it is in the public interest that any person may publish or broadcast or cause to be published or broadcast a report of these proceedings provided that the report does not contain any particulars calculated to lead to the identification of the person in respect of whom proceedings have been brought or any other person concerned in the proceedings and pictures are not taken of the person in respect of whom proceedings have been brought or any other person concerned in the proceedings.

However, the Board itself departed from its customary policy of identifying witnesses only by initials in its report of this hearing, and used the full names. Since the proceedings were later published (Kiel 1992), and similar evidence was led in the Supreme Court hearing with many of the same witnesses appearing, it seemed unnecessary to disguise here those participating in the Board hearing, when the information was replicated in other sources, which are part of the public record.

Members of the press were warned about the necessity of exercising restraint in their reporting, in order to protect both the appellant and witnesses and it was ruled that the names of either party could not be published. Media interest quickly waned and one reporter who breached the undertaking was warned and ceased to appear on later days. Few members of the public attended consistently and those who did so had some professional knowledge about the case.

It was an unusual hearing, not so much in its rarity as an appeal to return to prison, but because of the complexity of the issues it would raise, the number of witnesses and the parties to be represented. Sixteen witnesses were called and several thousand pages of transcript with extensive supporting documentation were generated. Bryan Keon-Cohen, a noted barrister and executive member of the Victorian Council for Civil Liberties represented Garry David, and Chris Maxwell was in the unusual position of being appointed counsel to assist the Board itself. The Office of Corrections declined to take part in the proceedings. Initially, the Chief General Manager of the Health Department and the Attorney-General were represented by the Victorian Solicitor-General, Hartog Berkeley, who appeared with the barrister Michael Adams, thereby co-joining two very different government departments: one with a health mandate and the other with a law and order emphasis. He also appeared for Dr Margaret Tobin, the authorised psychiatrist of Aradale Hospital, of which J Ward was then a specialised section. It was this dual role of the Solicitor-General which was disconcerting because it implied that the Government had a special interest in the matter to the extent of being willing to overlook any potential conflict of interest between health and criminal justice issues. This situation can be contrasted with that of South Australia, where the Crown will not represent two government departments in legal proceedings of that state, although it will provide the requisite funding.

The Board's practice in 1990 was to sit in divisions of three with a chairperson who is a barrister and solicitor of not less than eight years' standing; a medical practitioner; and a person appointed to represent the views and opinions of members of the community. (Although the term 'Board' will be used throughout, the correct terminology should be 'this Division' of the Mental Health Review Board.) The hearing was conducted over 16 days during a 3-month period, including evidence taken at J Ward because of Garry's disinclination to come to Melbourne for the hearing.

An early application from the Solicitor-General signalled the government's plan to intervene in the Board's decision-making by involving higher courts in the interpretation of the meaning of mental illness. He produced what he termed 'a very rough draft' of the case, which he invited the Board to reserve for the opinion of the Supreme Court. Since this draft represented the legal perception of the state of psychiatric knowledge, especially in relation to personality disorder, it is a significant document and is reproduced in full.

> 1. There is no general understanding amongst psychiatrists carrying on practice in Australia as to what is meant by the expressions *mentally ill* and *mental illness.*
>
> 2. There is a substantial consensus amongst psychiatrists generally that psychoses and neuroses are psychiatric disorders.
>
> 3. There is no consensus amongst psychiatrists generally as to:
>
> > (a) the aetiology of many psychoses and neuroses;
> >
> > (b) whether a personality disorder constitutes a psychiatric disorder.
>
> 4. For the purpose of psychiatric learning and theory psychiatrists in Victoria may for practical purposes be divided amongst those who adhere to United States' views as to the nature and causes of psychiatric disorders and those who adhere to European views about such matters.
>
> 5. The psychiatric profession in Victoria is fairly evenly divided between the two schools of thought referred to in paragraph 4.

6. In respect of any particular set of symptoms of mental disorder the under-standing among psychiatrists may be:

(a) a general understanding that the symptoms indicate (or do not indicate) the existence of a psychiatric disorder;

(b) a general understanding by one of the schools of psychiatrists referred to in paragraph 4 that the symptoms indicate the existence of a psychiatric disorder and a general understanding amongst the other school of psychiatrists that the symptoms do not indicate the existence of a psychiatric disorder.

7. Whether or not a psychiatrist adheres to one of these schools of thought or the other, the views of the psychiatrist as to what behaviour is indicative of mental illness encompasses a much narrower range of behaviour than that which an ordinary sensible lay person would regard as indicative of mental illness.

8. The reasons for the determination of the Board in the Matter of KMC are annexed to and form part of this special case.

9. The question of law for the opinion of the Court is:

How should the Board construe the expressions *mentally ill* and *mental illness*, as they appear in sections 8, 15 and 16 of the Mental Health Act 1986?

(MHRB, 23 January 1990)

Whilst the Solicitor-General's move was generally viewed as a stalling mechanism designed to thwart a possible Board decision to discharge Garry David from his security status, it also hinted at the Government's preference for the matter to be in the hands of the Supreme Court, rather than left to the vagaries of a body with tribunal status. The Solicitor-General's 'rough draft' of the case being put forward was entirely premised on a perception of disarray within psychiatry's knowledge base. Although the main thrust of this document is clear, it is clumsily expressed and does not acknowledge that the term 'mental illness' is a legal artefact, which does not necessarily accord with the models of mental disorder constructed within psychiatry for clinical and research purposes.

The Government was, in effect, putting forward a public view that psychia-trists are seemingly unable to achieve a consensus about aetiological factors and those symptoms constituting a psychiatric disorder. In addition, it was contending that they appeared to have divided themselves into two schools of thought. His-torically, these have diverged between the categorical and atheoretical approach dominated by the classifications used in the American *DSM* and the dimensional paradigm implicit in the European psychoanalytic school. (For a discussion of the implications of these two schools of thought see Kerr and McClelland 1991.) In addition the Government believed them to have a much more conservative view about what constitutes mental illness than the 'ordinary sensible lay person'. This was a serious allegation, suggestive of a lack of internal agreement about the most basic parameters of psychiatric knowledge, and implying that this knowledge was largely irrelevant to serious community concerns.

The Attorney-General advanced the view that if this discipline were in such a seemingly inchoate state, then definitional matters should not be entrusted to the Board, whose members would take advice from psychiatrists. As the matter came within the public interest, it should be resolved by law. The significance of this professional intrusion can perhaps best be understood by hypothetically reversing the position and envisaging the reaction of lawyers should *psychiatrists* have been required to resolve basic legal uncertainties.

This application to define the meanings of 'mentally ill' and 'mental illness' is based on the recognition that psychiatry and the law approach problems differently, and that each has developed a self-contained system of thought, attitudes and images. Psychiatry's diagnostic procedures are a means of allocating significance to clinical symptoms and are delineated within a working framework, which is cautious, equivocal and tentative. Thus categories of mental disorder, whose constituent indicators overlap and blur in distinctiveness, do not necessarily form discrete entities – a clinical attribute too conveniently disregarded by lawyers in their quest for certitude in the courtroom. The search to express the meaning of behavioural variations remains an omnipresent part of the diagnostic art, even when some illnesses appear to be less disputatious in their display of textbook symptomatology. The clinical focus is on treatment, and the fact that aetiology is not readily understood, or is variously interpreted within different theoretical orientations, does not undermine the discipline itself, as the law may too readily tend to assume.

The most contentious of all the diagnoses centres around the personality disordered, who typically experience bouts of acute distress in addition to a chronic pattern of behavioural dysfunction. Despite the psychiatric manuals clarifying the diagnostic indicators with a checklist, there is often contention about the process, compounded further by a lack of cohesion regarding the parameters of psychiatric treatment. 'Treatment' in a legally defined sense may focus on the act of intervention per se, or it can move a step forward by actually specifying the range of interventions, which may be considered as coming within the ambit of psychiatry. The former approach was that taken by Lord Denning, when he proclaimed: '*Treatment* means, I think, the exercise of professional skill to remedy the disease or disability, or to lessen its ill effects or the pain and suffering which it occasions' (*Minister of Health v Royal Midland County's Homes for Incurable: Leamington Spa's General*

Committee 1954 1 All ER 1013 at 1020). The second approach is an all-encompassing view of treatment, such as that articulated by the Victorian Mental Health Review Board in the case of DWP, whose appeal hearing preceded that of Garry David's by 12 months:

> We believe that the word 'treatment', as used by section 16(2) of the Act, means the physical, psychological, social and environment interventions used by psychiatrists and other health professionals working on the treatment team in order to combat mental illness. We also accept that adequate diagnosis is an essential part of treatment for the efficacy of treatment is enhanced by proper diagnosis. (Kiel 1992, p.198)

This latter view requires a further judgment to be made about the appropriateness of including chronic conditions. The Mental Health Review Board clearly rejected the view that the chronically ill should be excluded from treatment within the meaning of the Mental Health Act 1986, and it later strongly argued that treatment must be interpreted as those interventions 'designed to alleviate chronic conditions, as well as treatment designed to cure or improve acute conditions' (Kiel 1992, *The Appeal of PT*, pp.34–9). Although this determination places decisions about particular treatments squarely within the psychiatric domain, it still leaves the parameters of that treatment unresolved and allows internal cross-currents to develop. This is scarcely surprising, for historical studies have repeatedly demonstrated that psychiatry has never been characterised by a unified system of practice, or as Pressman reminds us, it has remained 'a loose confederation of very different kinds of clinical orientations and occupational locations' (1998, p.363).

However, such open diversity is foreign to the way in which the law strives to arrive at some consensus about its central tenets. Legal reality is of a very different order. It has developed a closed communication network dependent on internal rulings, which are hard to challenge and do not readily admit other modes of establishing a perceptual framework, even about the same object. Through a specialised form of reasoning integrating the law with established facts and logic, it constructs the outside world and, in doing so, it relies on judgments of a dichotomous nature. An individual ultimately *is* or *is not* mentally ill in legal terms, and this decision can only be made by matching the person against a legally defined template. In this way, decision making is dependent on the introduction of arbitrary criteria, which are upheld in an essentially adversarial process. The law thus *enslaves* other discourses by moulding them to fit its cognitive mode of deciding issues of responsibility and moral accountability. Human agency is abstracted in a semantic process, which overshadows the different reality of psychiatry's experiential mode of understanding. The finer shades of this discipline's decision making, which actually encourage equivocation or changed opinions, can readily be devalued in legal discourse, rather than respected for their contribution to the veracity of clinical judgments. Instead the law imposes a method of scrutiny governed by rules of evidence, which insert a value ordering of the material or opinions being offered to the court by testing and transforming them to match a legal reality. This means that two different epistemological systems are operating and have to adjust to each other's mode of communication. This tension became apparent in the Garry David case, when one psychiatrist articulated his concerns to the counsel assisting the Board:

> Where I suspect our minds may not meet is that you are asking for a touch-stone which will lead – by an inductive thinking process for which doctors are wired up differently and do not have…we are deductive thinkers based loosely on the scientific method. So the way in which we approach mental illness, or the concept of it, I think, might be fundamentally different from what you are struggling to draw out of me. (MHRB, 20 February 1990)

Whilst the law has more strongly infiltrated psychiatry in recent decades, and the construction of the Mental Health Act 1986 bears testimony to this, the question still persists about the legitimate extent of its intrusion into areas of psychiatric judgment. As the Board's President bluntly put to a 1989 hearing: 'Do we accept the psychiatrist's view at face value?' (*The Appeal of DWP*, 10 May 1989). Dr John Ellard encapsulates the gulf rather differently by holding that the law focuses on 'things or categories', rather than 'processes and dimensions', and he believes this problem permeates the construction of mental health legislation:

> To put it simply, those who draft Mental Health Acts, wise though they may be, cannot be expected to provide definitions which probably do not exist and which no one else has been able to discover. There are many useful words which simplify and abbreviate communication, but which will not stand up to critical examination. In psychiatry such words are often applied to processes and dimensions, and mislead the unwary into believing that they refer to things or categories. (Ellard 1990, p.167)

As a consequence, misperceptions arise because of differences in the way each profession encapsulates the same object in trying to ascribe meaning in a consensual manner; and this is both a philosophical as well as a professional problem attaching to the production of meaning (see, for example, Foucault 1977a; White 1987).

The various legal processes utilised to determine Garry David's future were very different in orientation from customary court procedures, because they were premised on the tenability of freedom rather than the attribution of guilt. The Mental Health Review Board, which was the first testing ground for the issues raised, is part of the mental health network of services under the aegis of the then Department of Health and answerable on appeal to the Administrative Appeals

Tribunal (now the Victorian Civil and Administrative Tribunal), and, if necessary, the Supreme Court. As such, its task is quite different from that of the guilt-finding process of the criminal courts. In hearing appeals or reviews against detention it is enjoined to 'have regard primarily to the patient's current mental condition and consider the patient's medical and psychiatric history and social circumstances' (section 22(2)). Hearings are conducted according to the principles of natural justice and are consequently more flexible than those of the ordinary courts with a focus on the subjective experience of the appellant and professional opinions about the need for continued custody. The Board had far greater scope to present Garry David as an autonomous, interacting human being than did the Supreme Court, where the mode of discourse must construct the subject and establish the artefact of dangerousness to satisfy legal guidelines, rather than more broadly based experiential ones (see McBarnet 1983).

This general background further explains why the Solicitor-General chose to reserve key matters about the definition of mental illness for the Supreme Court's consideration. This course is open in the following circumstances:

(1) Where a question of law arises in proceedings before the Board, the Board, of its own motion or on the application of any party who is a party to the proceedings, may reserve the question in the form of a special case stated for the opinion of the Supreme Court.

(2) Where a question of law has been reserved for the opinion of the Supreme Court under sub-section (1), the Board cannot (a) determine the matter until the opinion of the Supreme Court has been given; or (b) proceed in a manner or make a determination that is inconsistent with the opinion of the Supreme Court on the question of law.

The advantage lay in situating the Garry David case firmly within the more usual confines of legal decision making and enhancing the likelihood of achieving a custodial outcome. This can be inferred from the explanation given to the Board that any delay incurred would not be 'a significant problem in this case for there is a real likelihood that Mr David will be detained for an indefinite time, either in gaol or in a psychiatric hospital' (23 January 1990). In spite of this thinly veiled warning emanating from the Attorney-General's office, the Mental Health Review Board declined to reserve both the question of law, and the related one for an opinion about the legal meaning of 'mentally ill' and 'mental illness' for a higher court ruling. Although it conceded that the construction of key words and phrases in the Mental Health Act 1986, such as 'treatment', 'health or safety', 'protection of members of the public', 'the public interest', and 'all the circumstances of the case', were indeed significant, it would deal with them in the context of the case itself, rather than separately at the outset, in order to avoid delay. In a strongly worded rebuke, Board members reminded the Attorney-General through his senior legal officer of their broad procedural powers and rejected the application on the grounds that it was unusual, unduly premature and might unjustly increase the time or cost involved in the exercise.

The Board's planning for the hearing reflected the significance of its task and the need to base decisions on as wide a variety of practitioners' opinions as possible. Eleven psychiatrists were called to give evidence, together with two general medical practitioners, two psychiatric nurses, and Garry David himself, who was expected to be accompanied by three nurses with a police escort available on stand-by. In financial terms it was an expensive exercise and consumed 7.2 per cent of the Board's expenditure for the 1989–90 financial year. In fact, the direct costs to the Board, excluding any component of the salaries of full-time members and administrative staff, were estimated to be $62,242.00, or 180 times greater than the average cost per case during that year (MHRB, *Annual Report* 1990).

Unexpected tension was introduced into the proceedings at the outset when the first psychiatric witness detailed the threats made to her personally in the preceding days. Garry had told her that he could obtain a weapon via links made through his computer modem and that the hospital vehicle escorting him to the hearing would be ambushed on its journey from Ararat. Security was immediately tightened with the consequence that Garry refused police transportation and attended only the first day's hearing at Mont Park and the final one at J Ward.

The Board's method of inquiry was two-pronged. First it focused on the massive collection of longitudinal data available from the general files of the Office of Corrections and the clinical and nursing notes. The other avenue of inquiry relied on current diagnostic opinions. There were some novel features about this appeal, because of the scale of the inquiry and the fact that it was structured to expose differences of opinion not ordinarily at issue in professional psychiatric forums. Those giving evidence varied in their direct knowledge of the appellant, with some basing their views solely on the clinical history provided from the files, and others drawing on their extensive interaction with the prisoner, including those times when he chose to attack their therapeutic ability and undermine their professional competence.

Psychiatry became particularly vulnerable when witnesses were required to defend different clinical views and styles of practice and provide evidence about seeming contradictions. Part of the strain they experienced resulted from operating in an alien legal environment. Because of their training, lawyers are inclined to piece together single elements of behaviour as if they form part of a jigsaw puzzle, whereas psychiatrists use overarching intuitive and experiential judgments to grasp the level of current and potential functioning of patients. The legal mode of analysis tended to isolate events within Garry David's clinical history, in order to assign them a cumulative meaning and significance. His violence, written threats and self-mutilatory episodes were dissected and over-shadowed their contextual reality. By comparison, the mental health task shapes such incidents into the totality of the person by taking a longitudinal approach. In this case, not all efforts were successful in the wake of Garry's demands, and ironically it was left to the Board to remind medical witnesses that acontextual judgments should possibly carry diminished weight when forming the basis of a diagnostic opinion.

It was apparent in the hearing that psychiatrists found it difficult to transpose a clinical approach into the more rigid confines and the precision required by legal analysis. Some opinions changed or were qualified, much to the confusion of the lawyers, who did their best to maintain an inquisitorial rather than adversarial stance, since no party bore any particular onus of proof. There were variations of emphasis within the personality disorders; differences of opinion about the desir-ability of voluntary or involuntary status for Garry; evidence of strained working relationships on his account; and the almost wistful hope of one psychiatrist that perhaps neuropsychological tests might shed some light on the reason for his gross behavioural disturbance, even though treatment was likely to be ineffective (see Kiel 1992, p.200). After admitting that his view and that of others regarding mental illness, was 'muddled', this psychiatrist lamented that 'the law brings a certain view about the precision of things which we would like to have in psychia-try – which we will perhaps [have] down the track…' (Dr John Grigor, 19 February 1991).

The surveillance that Garry David had been able to exercise within the confines of the prison began to broaden. Since the daily transcript of proceedings was couriered to him in order to facilitate instructions to counsel, he had at hand an immediate written record of the psychiatric judgments made about his past and likely future behaviour. The contradictions and diversity of opinion were thus exposed to a very unpredictable appellant – a matter undoubtedly disquieting for the many witnesses facing the rigours of cross-examination. As Dr Neville Parker wrote in the College journal: 'Most witnesses found that giving evidence before the Board was a harrowing experience and at times wondered just who was on trial' (1991, p.372).

The Board was also sensitive to the peculiar difficulties of its own position, as only a few months previously it had decided that a borderline personality disorder *was* a recognised mental illness, which *did* constitute grounds for involuntary con-finement (*Appeal of KMC*, 7 November 1989). There were many similarities in the facts of the two cases, and it was anticipated that the current appeal would reopen the earlier complex legal arguments about psychiatric decision making. An addi-tional factor in the context of the Garry David appeal was the likely influence of the political will on the views and actions of witnesses, and this undercurrent was all the more apparent because Victoria's Solicitor-General had chosen to handle the Government's case.

THE SENSIBLE ORDINARY PERSON AND THE EXPERT

Before the specific criteria of section 16 of the Mental Health Act 1986 could be considered, it was agreed that the central issues to be first established were:

- the definition of mental illness within its legal context; and
- the relationship between personality disorder and mental illness.

But in stripping a complex maze of diagnostic opinions and case history down to these two simple requirements, the Board recognised that it was engaging in a legal device to impose constancy on a dynamic and fluctuant situation. First, Garry's explosive behavioural pattern was well known, and the hearing itself could well be the catalyst for a spate of further disturbances arising in the recounting of past incidents and in the provision of a frank psychiatric history. Second, some regard had to be given to the fact that psychiatric knowledge is not static, but constantly being refined in the light of clinical experience and the influence of theoretical frames of reference.

Although the application from the Attorney-General had not been pursued, the Board had to reassess its previous decisions in the absence of explicit direction from the Mental Health Act 1986, which allows for intervention only if 'the person appears to be mentally ill' and other conditions are met. Since it is really not possible to arrive at decisions affecting the liberty of a person without some agreed definition, a Board has two options: it may either have recourse to a judicial determination, as has occurred in New South Wales; or it may develop its own operational guidelines on the basis of evolving case law. Inevitably, these are different modes of decision making: the former being more exclusionary, and the latter more adaptive, although some difficulties still arise, as noted by the Board's President:

> There are no simple answers for the Board when seeking to give practical meaning to the bare language chosen by the legislature. The case law also demonstrates the difficulties occasioned by seeking to gather and further analyse facts in a branch of medicine which has no simple diagnostic tests and in a field of welfare where there are strongly held opposing views about liberty and compulsory treatment. (Kiel 1992, Introduction)

The difficulty with having a judicial determination of key concepts from a higher court is that decisions tend to be narrower than those of a tribunal, which is allowed greater flexibility in its approach. For example, the New South Wales' Supreme Court has not been free to give the term 'mentally ill' its ordinary and natural meaning or its meaning at common law, but must view it in its legislative context. Because this interpretation depends on the M'Naghten notion of 'disease of the mind', congenital conditions and those due to aging have generally been excluded. As a consequence, the following conditions do not constitute a mental illness in that state: senile dementia (*RAP v AEP* [1982] 2 NSWLR 508), Down's Syndrome (*DW v JMW* [1983] 1 NSWLR 61, brain damage resulting from a stroke (*GNM v ER* [1983] 1 NSWLR 144), mental retardation (*GPG v ACF* [1983] 1 NSWLR 54), anorexia nervosa (*JAH v The Medical Superintendent of Rozelle Hospital* [unreported, 4 March 1986] and alcohol dependency (*CN v The Medical Superintendent of Rozelle Hospital* (unreported, 4 March 1986).

In the David hearing, the Board accepted the views of counsel that a dichotomous mode of delineating mental illness should be employed: that is, either it had to be what the experts declare it to be, or it should accord with the views of ordinary sensible lay people (see Lawton LJ in *W v L* [1974] QB 712 and Kirby, P. in *B v The Medical Superintendent of Macquarie Hospital* [1987] 10 NSWLR at 440). The precedent for this decision was contained in an English case, when Lord Justice Lawton argued that 'mental illness' are two words in ordinary English usage with no particular legal or medical significance and, therefore, should be given an ordinary, sensible interpretation:

> I ask myself what would the ordinary sensible person have said about the patient's condition in this case if he had been informed of his behaviour to the dogs, the cat and his wife? In my judgment such a person would have said: 'Well the fellow is obviously mentally ill.' If that be right, then, although the case may fall within the definition of 'psychopathic disorder' in s.4(4), it also falls within the classification of 'mental illness'.

The UK had similarly faced a lack of definition of 'mental illness' in both its 1959 and 1983 Mental Health Act (UK). In 1974 the position had been tested in a case concerning a 23-year-old possible psychopath, who had been compulsorily detained for acts of sadistic cruelty to animals and for endangering the life of his wife and unborn child. Lord Denning MR held the interpretation of 'mental illness' to be grounds for continued detention and should be construed by the experts, whilst Lawton LJ and Orr LJ opted for the ordinary person test.

The Victorian Parliament had eschewed introducing a definition of mental illness for the guidance of the Mental Health Review Board. This was partly because that contained in the previous 1959 Act had been singularly unhelpful in its vague and circular declaration that 'mental illness means suffering from a psychiatric or other illness which substantially impairs mental health'. The Minister for Health in the Second Reading Speech explained:

The Bill adopts neither a legal nor a medical paradigm. It takes the approach that the state of a person's mental health is a matter for clinical judgment and, accordingly, does not attempt to define either the causes or the nature of mental illness. (Mental Health Bill No. 1, *Hansard*, 30 May 1985)

This reflection of Parliament's confidence in psychiatry's ability to govern itself and determine its own knowledge boundaries was undermined not five years later in the debates accompanying the Community Protection Bill. There was an underlying perception that psychiatry had rejected the Government's encouragement to transform the issue of Garry's 'dangerousness' into a medical paradigm. Members of Parliament considered that they lacked professional guidance on the matter and were confused by the diversity and elusiveness of insanity definitions:

We are in a dilemma because the experts have not managed to give us clear-cut definitions. I acknowledge that it may not be possible to do so, but the fact is that we have to go one way or the other, either towards pursuit and the use of the Mental Health Act or towards the use of criminal law acts. (*Hansard*, 10 April 1990)

This left the Mental Health Review Board with the challenge, in the David case, of subjecting the current state of knowledge about mental illness and personality disorders to psychiatric and legal analysis whilst, at the same time, taking common-sense views into account. Its task was to shape the boundaries of personality disorder and mental illness for legal purposes. Once again, the significance of this task can best be appreciated from a role reversal. What if psychiatrists were to recast the boundaries of the law on the basis of some 'mentality' analysis?

In opting for neither a legal nor a medical paradigm, Parliament retained the key words 'mentally ill' and 'mental illness' in the legislation. These have a commonly understood meaning, rather than a specialised psychiatric one, although they may sometimes be used by practitioners in a general sense about patients perceived as being psychiatrically unwell. From the time of its inception, the Mental Health Review Board in Victoria was aware that definitional issues would be paramount in its construction of the workings of the Act and that both Australian and English law had already encountered some difficulty in translating 'madness' into a legal entity. It recognised too that uncertainty about shades of meaning in 'mentally ill', 'mental illness', 'disease of the mind', 'insanity', 'mental disorder' and 'lunatic' are of little assistance to diagnostic and treatment decisions. In an earlier 'Statement of Reasons' Board members had already noted:

It appears that by and large these judicial enquiries have been concerned with a person's mental capacity at the time of a particular event and whether that person should be considered to be legally responsible for his or her actions.

> Thus the courts in these cases have concentrated upon behaviour which may be regarded as a consequence of a person's mental illness, or other conditions which affect human behaviours such as intellectual disability, rather than the very fact of whether a person is mentally ill. (Kiel 1992, p.6)

In order to develop a definition of mental illness, the Board drew on an earlier case in which it had used a three-part test hitherto unchallenged in the Administrative Appeals Tribunal. In the case of KMC, which preceded Garry David's appeal, the Board had developed the AB test and decided that the phrase 'appears to be mentally ill' should have an expert, technical meaning. That is, Board members would have to be:

- satisfied that the person has recently exhibited symptoms usually associated with a recognised mental illness; and

- in determining what is a recognised mental illness the Board should consider both expert evidence and the widely recognised diagnostic manuals; and be

- satisfied that the symptoms which the person has recently exhibited are evidence of the fact that the person appears to have some recognised mental illness and are not solely indicative of any of the matters listed in section 8(2) or explicable by some reason other than the existence of a recognised mental illness.

At the time of its formulation Dr William Glaser, while accepting the usefulness of the test, pointed out that such a phenomenological approach to mental illness still occasions difficulties. Different observers may disagree about the presence or absence of particular symptoms which in themselves are not necessarily indicative of a mental illness, nor of a psychiatric abnormality per se, for there may be other perceptual or cultural explanations for these phenomena. He pointed out that they cannot just be assessed in isolation, but are part of a total clinical picture (Kiel 1992, pp.62–5). By inference, any judicial attempts to specify *which* symptoms constitute mental illness, although a customary legal method of ensuring uniformity in the application of legislation, are inappropriate in the case of psychiatric disorders, which do not allow for such precision in trying to grasp the totality of the person.

The 'expert' test favoured by the Board was subject to lengthy legal discussion because it was in the interests of lawyers representing the state to argue that the broader public definition of mental illness had more legitimacy and would encompass personality disorders. The Board had earlier maintained that 'the symptoms must be those which are usually associated with a mental illness known to psychiatry' (Kiel 1992, p.338) and that there should also be some demonstrable connection between the symptoms and the mental illness, which would then necessitate choosing among 'the competing views of psychiatrists as to the breadth of the words "mental illness"' (Kiel 1992, p.175). The Board members were well aware that, once again, they faced a task with which they had previously grappled:

> The most unsatisfactory part of the AB test is that psychiatrists do not always agree that a particular condition is a recognised mental illness. Dr PE informed the Board that in his assessment 60 per cent of psychiatrists in Australia would be of the opinion that a borderline personality disorder is a mental illness, whilst 40 per cent would say that it is not. (Kiel 1992, *Appeal of KMC*, p.341)

The Board found definitions of insanity to be problematic and all counsel struggled to clarify areas of agreement among the witnesses, many of whom resisted using the words 'mental illness' in preference to other ways of expressing their understanding. From the Board's comments, psychiatrists were patently claiming their dominion over the process of ascription:

> There was no neat understanding advanced by any one witness in this case which was readily accepted by all the others. However, expert witnesses stated that in psychiatry one looks for symptoms of disturbance in mental functioning when determining whether a person is mentally ill. Ascertaining and giving meaning to these symptoms is a highly sophisticated undertaking. (Kiel 1992, p.174)

These matters become very different when translated into the sphere of community understandings. From comments made throughout this case, it was evident that the general public draws on another perceptual mode and tends to assume mental illness from the demonstration of bizarre behaviour, especially when there is a paucity of information. The technique of arriving at such a judgment is not well understood, but its import cannot be dismissed in the light of the authoritative 1983 English *Brutus v Cozens* case, which opts for interpreting words in the way ordinary people would probably construe them (AC 854).

Dr Ellard pointed out that the sensible person test was vacuous, since 'the man in the street will generally regard anyone who is alien from himself as mad' (Kiel 1992, p.195). Board members heeded the warning on the grounds that the test lends itself to acontextual use and can be too readily linked to some medical explanation for unusual acts of violence. Notwithstanding these problems, they initially applied it in order to allay any untoward criticism about favouring the expert view. On this basis, members arrived at the conclusion that Garry David *would not* be regarded as mentally ill by the general public, if he only suffered from intermittent outbursts of violence without any clear thought disturbance or other mental state symptoms (Kiel 1992, p.175). In particular, the Board noted the evidence of Dr Peter Hearne, the Medical Superintendent of the prison hospital, that Garry's self-destructive actions in prison were not randomly capricious, nor were they produced by a mind incapable of understanding their consequences, but were 'actions directed to a purpose and therefore, logical, albeit in a way that the ordinary person may find extremely difficult to comprehend'. Whilst this point was persuasive, it perhaps underestimates the purposiveness and internal logic of certain delusional states, which do not exclude a diagnosis of mental illness. Although the Board considered that the expert test could provide a fuller contextual appreciation of the circumstances of Garry's violence, its approach to its task was admirably cautious in the prevailing political circumstances.

CRACKS APPEAR

Gradually, as the hearing continued, areas of disagreement and confusion became apparent, and these seriously impacted on beliefs about diagnosis and treatment/management. Whilst all witnesses concurred that Garry David had a personality disorder, there was some vacillation about its type: whether *borderline with antisocial traits; a mixed personality disorder with borderline, antisocial with other traits* (four witnesses); or *an antisocial personality disorder* (Kiel 1992, p.179). However, attempts to reach a resolution about the label were hampered by a different referential frame proposed by several psychiatrists, who claimed that 'personality disorder' is a descriptive term requiring a psychosocial judgment based on the longitudinal history, and therefore distinct from the concept of mental illness (Kiel 1992, p.179). That is, a person with a personality disorder may also suffer from a mental illness, and it may simply be a matter of semantics to determine whether certain behaviours are a manifestation of a personality type, the direct outcome of the mental illness, or conceivably the outcome of both. Yet this was precisely the sort of issue which the Board was endeavouring to resolve through its own internal rules of logic. Ultimately, it was to argue that if personality disorder is the label for a personality type, then it becomes a *description* rather than an *entity* causing behavioural malfunction.

There were some absurdities in the entire exercise, no matter how carefully each side tried to place the issues within its own conceptual framework. Lawyers were required to dissect each shade of meaning implied by the diagnostic labels, behaviours and treatment, in order to extract the intrinsic component guiding practitioners in their clinical decision making. For their part, psychiatrists found it difficult to make discriminations within the personality disorders. Not only does this group occupy a less secure position than the psychoses in the psychiatric taxonomy, but there is also the further problem of separating antisocial and borderline personality disorder. First, many psychiatrists regard the latter as a contentious diagnostic category based on insufficient research evidence. Second, each condition is distinguishable on different grounds. Antisocial personality disorder relies on behavioural criteria including criminality and lack of concern for others, whereas borderline personality disorder emphasises elements closer to the notion of mental malfunction, such as affective lability and identity disturbance, although it still purports to combine these with personality *traits*. It became clear during Garry David's appeal that the finely balanced choice between the personality disorders might be sufficient to tip the balance for some practitioners in deciding whether 'badness' or 'madness' prevailed.

However, beyond this basic choice within the personality disorders, psychiatrists had to make some judgment about their relationship to mental illness, and it was at this juncture that the sharpest discrepancies and inconclusiveness emerged. Five of those giving evidence declared Garry David to be mentally ill (Drs Grigor, Tobin, Holden, Eisen and Perera); two having previously held the view that he was *not* mentally ill (Drs Grigor and Perera), and a third believing that he did not *appear* to be mentally ill (Dr Eisen). Dr John Grigor, the certifying doctor, justified his own equivocation by saying that the matter is 'at the edge of our knowledge', a concession the Board reported as being 'fair' in reflecting the difficulty of characterising Garry's behaviour (Kiel 1992, p.188).

Even so, the changed opinions of three out of five psychiatrists regarding a matter of such centrality was puzzling to the Board, because Garry David's behaviour and mental state had remained relatively stable in the longitudinal sense. The fragmentation of opinion is most aptly demonstrated in this summary:

1. Garry David has a personality disorder alone and this *is not* a mental illness – psychiatrists *Drs Leonard, Ellard, Parker and Walton* and general practitioners, *Drs Hearne and Dixon*.

2. Garry David has a personality disorder and this *is* a mental illness, but he only appears to be suffering from a mental illness when he shows symptoms of a superadded disturbed mental functioning and *does not appear at present to be certifiable* – Dr Eisen.

3. Garry David has a personality disorder and this *is* a mental illness, but he is certifiable only when he exhibits such symptoms – currently *not certifiably mentally ill* – Dr Holden.

4. No opinion profered by *Professor Singh and Dr Szmukler*, but agreement that personality disorder alone *is not* a mental illness and such a person is only mentally ill if there are additional disturbances in mental functioning. The implication is that they considered him not to be mentally ill on the basis of their evidence.

5. Garry David has a personality disorder and this *is* a mental illness, so he should be regarded as *certifiable* – Drs Grigor, Perera and Tobin.

This truncated overview of lengthy and difficult evidence reduces the diagnostic opinions the Board was seeking to their very essence. Six psychiatrists and two general practitioners with considerable experience in dealing with forensic patients considered personality disorder not to be a mental illness, and five psychiatrists took the opposite view, although only three were prepared to argue that Garry David was currently certifiable. In striving to distinguish mental illness in its broad general sense from the legal construct of a certifiable mental illness, four psychiatrists relied on some additional disturbance in mental functioning overlaid on to the basic personality disturbance. Sometimes only relentless questioning exposed significant ambiguities such as Dr Perera's admission that he was using the terms 'mental illness' and 'psychiatric illness' interchangeably (Kiel 1992, p.189). As each psychiatrist sought to clarify diagnostic decisions with the precision required by lawyers, the discriminations emerging in the process of examination and cross-examination became increasingly convoluted. For example, whilst two psychiatrists shifted from 'antisocial personality disorder' to 'borderline personality disorder', which did not appear to exclude certifiability, another expressed his change of opinion in a more finely balanced way by moving from 'personality disorder with antisocial and borderline characteristics' to 'borderline personality disorder with antisocial features'.

No witness in this appeal hearing could have given evidence without some view of the suitability of one of the two possible outcomes: that is, the incarceration of Garry David albeit in a psychiatric hospital, versus freedom in the community. It is not surprising then that most psychiatrists seemed to view their position as being precarious, both in terms of professional reputation and the legal ramifications which the hearing held for this one patient. That psychiatrists and lawyers should differ in their perception of the medico-legal role is an inevitable concomitant of professional training and the nature of the skills each brings to the task. The evolving discourse illustrates the greater flexibility of clinical choices based on an assumption of beneficence and concern for an individual's welfare *vis-à-vis* legal choices, which cannot diverge from principles of parity and natural justice in seeking to balance community interests with those of the offender. Thus lawyers are constrained to act in accordance with well-tested principles, which *enclose* the major issues in a definitive way, at least until challenged in a higher jurisdiction.

The Board did not accept the diagnostic shifts at face value and concluded that the Chief Psychiatrist, Dr Perera, 'may too readily have changed his opinion about Mr David' in the light of the documented observations of Drs Grigor and Tobin about an apparent psychotic episode and a 'flight of ideas' (Kiel 1992, p.189). The Board concluded from the evidence that Dr Grigor's observation of the former did not match the technical description in the literature, and Dr Tobin's evidence about the 'flight of ideas' could conceivably be interpreted as symptomatic of prison fantasy life, given the lack of additional substantiation. In essence, the Board considered that a clinical judgment made by one psychiatrist, in a particular circumstance, was unsustained by clinical evidence and therefore simply unwarranted. The second observation, which caused Dr Perera to change his mind, had been Dr Tobin's following description of an episode she considered to have been 'psychotic':

> My overall impression was of a terrified, inadequate man in a completely disorganised state with formal thought disorder, paranoid ideation and an intensity of anger which was pathological. The whole picture was totally consistent with psychosis. (Kiel 1992, p.191)

Once again, the Board found it difficult to draw firm conclusions from a specific observation. Although at least two other witnesses supported Dr Tobin's view, another two arrived at different conclusions on the basis of the same evidence. The Board finally found in favour of Drs David Leonard and John Ellard:

> Especially when coupled with the different conclusions drawn by Dr Holden, who has witnessed what appear to be similar episodes of Mr David in a violently angry state, make us cautious about relying too heavily upon this episode. Dr Leonard stated that it becomes 'ludicrous and useless' to describe the obvious rage demonstrated by Mr David as psychotic when one looks at the circumstances in which this behaviour took place. Dr Ellard cautioned against describing this episode as psychotic because of his concern about the evidentiary basis of Dr Tobin's conclusion and his knowledge of Mr David's history of aggressive behaviour. Dr Ellard warned against drawing conclusions from Dr Tobin's description of 'paranoid ideation'. (Kiel 1992, p.191)

This rebuff to Dr Tobin and the Government was further emphasised by the Board's comment that it assumed she was describing Garry's persecutory delusions rather than 'paranoid ideation', and that his beliefs might have reasonable foundation in view of the sudden loss of civil liberties he had experienced, despite completion of a lengthy gaol term without the benefit of parole. In effect, the Board was highlighting the inappropriateness of basing psychiatric judgments on symptomatology, rather than on their contextual relevance (Kiel 1992, p.191). Some of Dr Tobin's other conclusions were disputed even more strongly, with the Board again exhibiting the independence it had shown in the case of DWP. For example, members considered that the intensity of the pathological anger she had noted was not in itself symptomatic of disturbed mental functioning, and the formal thought disorder was of little significance, for although there 'may' have been some 'transient loosening of associations…some of the conversation which she [Tobin] describes seems to be possessed of a greater degree of logic, than she was prepared to concede':

> For example, she mentioned Mr David equating nurses with 'pigs' and com-
> plaining about the total lack of rights of patients. For a man who has been
> institutionalised all of his life to regard nurses as being equivalent to 'pigs'
> does not seem far-fetched if that term is taken to mean police officers and
> prison warders. Some of Dr Holden's observations support this view. Simi-
> larly, it does not seem illogical for a patient in a maximum security facility,
> such as J Ward, to complain about the lack of rights of patients. Mr David
> made this complaint in a rational way when he gave evidence to the Board.
> (Kiel 1992, p.192)

This comment is significant in focusing on the difficulties that therapeutic staff experience in discharging their clinical duty of care for security patients who have come from the prison system; that is, Garry David may have been deliberately pro-vocative rather than thought disordered when he attributed the term 'pigs' to both prison, therapeutic and custodial staff. The Board found Dr Tobin to be disin-clined to situate Garry's symptoms within the context of protracted and confronta-tional custody and implied that there was a certain naivety in drawing conclusions from a single, angry incident. As the Board members pointed out, 'Mr David's prison history is full of episodes of violent and angry outbursts which have not been regarded as instances of psychotic behaviour' (Kiel 1992, p.192). They also drew attention to other examples interpreted by another psychiatrist as being manipulative rather than symptomatic of mental disturbance, although they did suggest a fleeting 'micropsychotic' episode. In fact, the Board concluded that 'if these *micropsychotic* episodes exist(ed) at all', they were too infrequent to constitute certifiability within the terms of the legislation. As with DWP, the Board was cau-tiously encroaching into the area of clinical decision making, in order to safeguard the 'best interests' of the appellant.

The Board's mode of legal inquiry, designed to bring certitude to contestable matters, actually enhanced the impression of dissonance amongst psychiatrists struggling to apply the semantic discriminations being elicited from them about fundamental working concepts. Thus one psychiatrist believed that a borderline personality disorder *must* be a mental illness because it is a 'mental disorder' in *DSM-III-R*, even though this does not match the meaning of mental illness in the terms required by the Act (Dr Holden, in Kiel 1992, p.190). Much to the conster-nation of counsel, Dr Eisen considered that 'being mentally ill' and '*appearing to be* mentally ill' were significantly different states. In his examination and report of 14 November 1989 he found that Garry David did not meet the criteria of 'appearing to be mentally ill' in section 8(1)(a) of the Mental Health Act 1986, because this would have required some additional mental disturbance beyond his personality disorder. However, as he believed that a personality disorder *is* a mental illness, he could declare Garry to be mentally ill, despite that additional element being absent.

These are all salient examples of the way in which the legal process was leading to quite strained reasoning about personality and behaviour. Some psychiatrists were finding themselves contradicting their peers, although these differences may not have arisen or been significant in a clinical mode of reasoning. It is not too simplistic to suggest that lawyers were in the invidious position of applying the rules of logic to unreasonable behaviour; that is, they were paradoxically attempting to reason about unreason. In a sharp counter-stratagem, Dr Grigor, whom the President of the Board noted was given to 'a colourful turn of language', began referring to diagnostic criteria as a 'shopping list' of symptoms, thereby trivialising the seriousness of the legal fraternity's search for an unwarranted finesse of detail. For example, when questioned about the precise indicators for antisocial and borderline personality disorders, he said that 'a shopping list of symptoms best encapsulated Garry David'. This phrase was Invariably raised at times, when lawyers appeared to be going on further 'fishing expeditions' (transcript, p.347). Although initially introduced as a light-hearted means of fending off overly close legal scrutiny of clinical criteria, likening these to 'a shopping list' may have appeared to Garry to trivialise his situation. Observation of the proceedings and reading of the transcript suggest that the hearing did occasionally succumb to academic point scoring, yet Garry David's freedom or custody nonetheless hinged on which interpretation of his motivation could be presented as the most professionally compelling.

Faced with this degree of divergence amongst senior Victoria psychiatrists, the Board admitted that the public could be genuinely confused about the profession's views, especially as in reality some of those with a personality disorder are accepted for treatment, despite the majority of practitioners not regarding this condition as a 'mental illness' (Kiel 1992, p.180). The next issue to be tested concerned the treatment of those with severe personality disorders, even though this matter was peripheral should the Board find in Garry David's favour. The witnesses agreed that there was little definitive literature about the treatment of personality disorders and this was reflected by the poor state of knowledge and skills. Most were pessimistic about the likelihood of achieving success in the David case, with Dr Eisen suggesting that even attempting psychotherapy with him would border on the 'heroic', and Professor Singh being of the view that 'the best outcome might be an improved rating of *poor* to *fair*' (Kiel 1992, p.180). But once again there were variants within similar positions, with some conceding that those presenting as voluntary patients had a greater chance of improvement than involuntary patients. Dr Grigor, who had travelled extensively on behalf of the World Psychiatric Association, was adamant that he had been unable to identify any programme dealing effectively with either security or involuntary patients, and Dr Leonard was equally emphatic (Kiel 1992, p.200). Nonetheless, when pressed, the former opted for an eclectic mix as being the most favourable way to proceed in this instance. This would encompass neurological testing, a behavioural programme, psychotherapy and a possible drug regime, but 'no one pretends that in ten years' time Garry David will still not have a severe personality disorder' (Kiel 1992, p.200). Dr Eisen supported individual psychotherapy on the basis of his extensive experience with treating personality-disordered patients – a position also accepted by Drs Perera and Tobin; whereas Professor Singh and Drs Leonard and Walton thought it unlikely that there would be any improvement in Garry's functioning unless he entered behaviour therapy voluntarily, which was scarcely a realistic option.

The sharpest division of opinion emerged with Dr Tim Holden's evidence, which unwittingly gave public confirmation to Dr Grigor's view of Garry's infinite capacity for splitting staff (MHRB, 16 February 1990). Holden, a recent appointee with direct clinical responsibility for this security patient and under Grigor's supervision, told the Board that he could see no use at all for a behaviour modification programme in the immediate circumstances and that he 'would play no part in any medico-legal aspects of detaining Mr David involuntarily, or in any coercive treatment regime' (Kiel 1992, pp.200–1). Questioning revealed that the Director of Forensic Services had recently been forced to resume responsibility for Garry at J Ward, thus further reducing the available psychiatric resources – an arrangement which the Board considered unsatisfactory for the following reasons:

> Dr Holden would remain as the psychiatrist on the spot responsible for Mr David's psychiatric care. The evidence was that Dr Holden attends J Ward on two days per week and that Dr Grigor has no regular attendance at J Ward. Therefore, whilst Dr Grigor may be seen as the psychiatrist having direct clinical responsibility for Mr David, Dr Holden is still the psychiatrist with whom Mr David has most contact. The difficulties occasioned by this complex line of authority were referred to by the acting Unit Manager, Mr van Velsen. (Kiel 1992, pp.210–12)

For some, the issue of certifiability extended beyond the clinical sphere and verged on the political, thus broadening the psychiatric role unacceptably. However, the matter could not be considered in isolation from a treatment regime and this in itself raised a vortex of questions. Even those supporting some form of psychotherapy were confused about who might be responsible for its implementation. Dr Tobin distanced herself by declaring that her role was essentially administrative rather than clinical, which seemed to surprise the Chief Psychiatrist, who apparently had been under a misapprehension about the immediate division of staff responsibilities. Uncertainty surfaced too in relation to the *necessity* or mere *desir-*

ability of a treatment programme. Those supporting one were nonetheless at a loss to know who should provide it, with Dr Eisen categorically denying the requisite experience of J Ward staff.

In order that the Board could compare and assess professional opinions, witnesses were asked to account for variations in views about diagnosis, treatment or management in front of their colleagues – a daunting experience, justifying Dr Parker's description in the College journal as being 'harrowing'. There were hints of a split between the majority view of the collegiate body, the Australian and New Zealand College of Psychiatrists and those of senior practitioners working within the Office of Psychiatric Services. For example, Dr Lester Walton, a private forensic psychiatrist and member of the Forensic Section of the College, as well as a part-time consultant to the Department of Health, told the Board that he did not consider Garry David to be mentally ill because borderline personality disorder is not a mental illness. He further contended that this view accorded with the College position and that of the overwhelming majority of practitioners (MHRB, 26 February 1990). This was an undoubted rebuke to Dr Grigor, who had been a past president of the professional body and with whom Walton had previously worked at Mont Park. The implication was that a few senior College members, such as Dr Grigor, were prepared to embark on a course of action at odds with the general position held by their colleagues. As one lawyer assisting the Tribunal said privately, 'Cracks in the College were rapidly appearing.' This was augmented by the very nature of an inquiry which could not entirely eschew adversarial elements and even at times exposed interpersonal differences. For example, in cross-examination by Mr Adams, Dr Walton was asked whether, in preparing his report, he was 'at pains to disagree with Dr Grigor' – an inference he quickly rejected. He did, however, intimate that he personally would not have issued a certificate on the basis of the information it contained and drew attention to the fact that Dr Tobin's opinion had been based on observations made in only one interview and she was at variance with the views of nursing staff (MHRB, 26 February 1990).

There was little doubt about an irreconcilable gulf between the professional opinions of Dr Walton and those of senior staff within the Office of Psychiatric Services, such as Drs Tobin and Grigor, especially when the latter unequivocally came to the conclusion that the proper course of action would be to return Garry to prison (MHRB, 26 February 1990). Dr Peter Hearne agreed with this position, but it was one promptly rejected by Dr Eisen, who described it as 'atrocious' in judgment and declared that a psychiatric environment was preferable for the development of social skills (MHRB, 26 February 1990). As Garry's counsel quickly pointed out to the Board, this was indicative of a serious rift in staff views. A number of doctors, including Drs Dixon and Holden and two nursing staff, together with the unit manager, had already disputed the efficacy of J Ward as a psychiatric environment for their client and this claim promptly drew the acerbic response from Dr Eisen that if the superiority of Pentridge had been communicated in any way to Garry himself, then staff should be challenged about this matter (MHRB, 16 February 1990).

The process of examination and cross-examination brought to the fore simmering divisions of opinion. In particular, the views of the general medical officers with no specialist psychiatric training, but who had shouldered the burden of ongoing care for Garry, were occasionally criticised. Ordinarily, this gulf in treatment approaches may not have surfaced in such a public way. In the pressure of the Tribunal hearing there was evidence of public sector psychiatrists drawing together, but evincing less willingness to accommodate the differing views of their ancillary workers by suggesting that these derived from a lack of expertise or training in psychiatry (see MHRB 1990, 16 February 1990).

It was apparent to the Board that nurses were frustrated, confused by their role and exhibited an underlying sense of resentment. Members reached the conclusion that 'the nursing staff at J Ward did [do] not appear to have enthusiastically embraced the prospect of treating Mr David' (Kiel 1992, p.202). A number of reasons were ascertained: they had to prevent acute and chronically ill patients in J Ward from becoming manipulated or distressed by Garry's behaviour; there was an absence of clear guidelines from the medical staff involved; and there was a general belief that the certification had been inappropriate and disruptive to other patients. Chris van Velsen, a psychiatric nurse and Acting Unit Manager of J Ward, was scathing about the impasse from his perspective: 'The problem, moreover, is the fact that we have *three psychiatrists*, with *three different philosophies*, prepared to offer *three different management plans*' [my italics] (Kiel 1992, p.202).

Van Velsen believed that Garry was prepared to trust Dr Holden, but not Drs Grigor and Tobin. The Charge Nurse, Mr Leslie, was more conciliatory and suggested that staff members were tending to accept Garry, although they would still prefer him to be at Pentridge in the absence of proper treatment (Kiel 1992, p.203). The nursing care documents tendered in evidence confirmed the lack of guidance and programme specificity, once again drawing trenchant criticism from the Board:

> No evidence was offered to the Board of a behavioural analysis of Mr David, a reasonably sophisticated identification of problems, the formulation of specific goals of therapy other than the most trite and generalised, or, most particularly, of the techniques to be used in achieving those goals. After the Board heard evidence from the nursing staff, a revised *Nursing Care Management Plan* was produced but it appeared to do no more than reverse the numerical order of the three 'levels of nursing care management'. (Kiel 1992, p.203)

The fact that Garry was in a suspended state pending the outcome of the hearing no doubt contributed to staff inability to implement a coherent programme and compounded the polarisation of views. It was relatively easy to compare unfavourably the marginality of his illness with the treatment needs of those other patients exhibiting florid symptomatology. In the light of disproportionate resource levels and increased staff surveillance occasioned by this one patient, who required four nurses for each 24-hour period, it was not surprising that significant internal tensions developed. As in the case of DWP, the Board concluded that J Ward was ill-equipped to deal with the problems Garry presented, but that this was neither a criticism of the various psychiatrists involved, nor of the medical and nursing staff in the light of Dr Grigor's concession that 'Mr David has had dozens of doctors and hundreds of hours of medical intervention without any marked improvement in his condition' (Kiel 1992, p.204). Nonetheless, the overall tenor of the Board's conclusion compounded the adverse comments already aired in the DWP case and contributed to the deepening sense of low morale at this hospital, thereby enhancing Garry's ability to capitalise on the situation.

POLITICAL INTEREST OR POLITICAL PRESSURE?

Although the question of dangerousness was peripheral to Garry David's appeal, it was understood to be the overriding issue for the Government, and hence psychiatric opinions were canvassed. Many of Garry David's threats, whilst laden with melodrama, were concerning, but the general view was that individuals rather than the community at large might be at risk. It was generally recognised in professional circles that the stress of release, coupled with Garry's general unpreparedness for community life, could be a contributory factor. Later the Premier, John Cain, seized on this qualified support from such an unexpected quarter, using it as incontrovertible justification for protective legislation. The message relayed to the public appeared under the heading: 'Doctors Agreed David was Dangerous: Cain'. In this article the Premier declared that ten psychiatrists supported this view in their evidence to the Mental Health Review Board, only differing on the question of his 'insanity'. As a consequence, he declared it to 'be irresponsible to allow Garry David out of gaol or out of custody to inflict on the community the kind of mayhem that Julian Knight did in Hoddle Street' (*The Age*, 10 April 1990).

Some of the most troubling issues arising in the Board hearing focused on the possibility that political expediency had acted as a contaminant of professional views or actions. It was clearly a sensitive matter for the Board to probe, since it could expose the less visible links between the administrative and executive arms of government and impact on the professional credibility of those making decisions about Garry. Garry's counsel, Bryan Keon-Cohen, raised the general question of 'collusion or political pressure' towards the end of the hearing on 27

February as being a matter of public interest, and sought leave to call the adviser to the Minister for Health and executive officers of the Office of Corrections. The Board's Chairman rejected this move in favour of recalling Drs Grigor and Eisen, but it was the next witness, Dr Neville Parker, a private psychiatrist and member of the November panel, who unexpectedly gave voice to the way the matter had been 'bungled', as he saw it, through political interventions.

The interest of all those in the room quickened, when it became clear that information, hitherto the subject of rumour and innuendo, was likely to be canvassed. Dr Parker, whose psychiatric experience spanned 34 years, admitted that he was unaware of the provisions of the Mental Health Act 1986. In this, he would not have been in an unusual position, as many private psychiatrists and general practitioners are rarely directly involved in certification procedures; but this admission did raise the issue about his panel selection for a task focused on the legislative difficulties pertaining to the meaning of mental illness. Parker's view was expressed casually and in a refreshingly frank manner, undoubtedly discomforting some of the public psychiatrists present. He considered that he had been selected because the Government thought he'd 'be an easy bloke to certify him', and because he had published strong views about keeping violent offenders incarcerated in psychiatric hospitals to protect the community. Tongue-in-cheek, he added: 'They realised I was a pretty right-wing sort of fellow and I'd be the most likely person to dob him [Garry] in. That's how I saw it, but maybe they thought I was a marvellous psychiatrist and very objective' (MHRB, 27 February 1990).

He explained that at the preliminary briefing, conducted by Dr Peter Eisen, of the Office of Psychiatric Services, he learned of the panel's political agenda:

> The gist of the discussion was that the Corrections service was wanting to get rid of this fellow, David, and the Department had been asked to certify him. We, as a group, did not have to do it, only one of us was sufficient for him to be certified. This was a means of handling a situation that was regarded as a very serious matter politically and it was important to have this bloke out of circulation before his prison term expired. (MHRB, 27 February 1990)

The fact that only *one* out of four psychiatrists was considered sufficient for the panel certification process to proceed conveyed to all the clear message that powerful political pressures had been arrayed against Garry David in an unprecedented fashion and that the Government was prepared to use psychiatry for its own ends.

Parker recalled being informed of the Corrections Department's attempts to persuade the Health Department to accept responsibility for Garry. This was described in terms of 'an ongoing battle between the Office of Corrections and the Office of Psychiatric Services with very senior political figures directly involved' (MHRB, 27 February 1990). As a consequence, he considered that the panel was facing the obvious dilemma that Garry David's presence in a psychiatric hospital would seriously impact on mental health services. As he explained he had, as a clinician, expected to find someone so grossly self-mutilating to be mentally ill, at least in a lay sense, and that there would be a delusional basis to allow for certification. However, on examination, all panel members found this view to be unsustainable:

> At the end of the discussion we had with him, there was a stunned silence and I expected that we'd have a debate about whether we thought this bloke was mentally ill or not. And we all looked at each other and said 'Well, there it is. There's no argument. It's so obvious. He hasn't got a mental illness.' There was no debate, no discussion whatever. (MHRB, 27 February 1990)

It was now up to the Solicitor-General, Hartog Berkeley, to regain ground in cross-examination and he sought to discredit this witness by focusing on an article he had recently published under the heading of 'Mad or Bad?: The Law Walks a Fine Line' (*Sunday Age*, 14 January 1990). Berkeley suggested that it had been misleading for Parker to describe himself as 'a leading forensic psychiatrist' and he should not have relied on material gleaned from his membership of the panel. In his defence, Dr Parker responded that he believed confidentiality had been limited because David's examination had taken place 'under the full glare of media publicity', although he had informally sought legal advice on this matter (MHRB, 27 February 1990). By this stage, the cross-examination was becoming very vigorous, which was unsettling for this psychiatrist and, in the circumstances, the Board President allowed him to proceed with his own account in an unhindered fashion. The ensuing information shed much light on the way in which some psychiatrists perceived their role to have been distorted by political imperatives. Parker reported being 'infuriated' by an anonymous document placed under his door in mid-January urging public discussion and immediate action. It was, in fact, a copy of a recently prepared report of the Law Reform Commission, due to go to Cabinet in the next two days, and contained recommendations about proposed changes to the Mental Health Act 1986 to allow 'antisocial personality disorder and any other personality disorder' to become part of the certification criteria. He viewed the report as part of 'a power struggle between the Victorian Law Reform Commission and the Social Development Committee' and was 'worried about the horrendous implications' of this latest solution to the Garry David problem (MHRB, 27 February 1990).

In the context of the interaction between psychiatry and law, Dr Parker's broad-ranging comments are enlightening. His stance had undeniably been influenced by resentment about perceived legal intrusions into the psychiatric domain. He particularly referred to Justice Vincent's oft-quoted statement suggesting that psychiatrists who exclude self-mutilators are themselves 'crazy' as evincing a 'confused understanding of what is mental illness', and believed that the Judge had 'missed the point completely' (MHRB, 27 February 1990). As a consequence he took it upon himself to counter this scathing criticism by disputing the Judge's lay approach with an authoritative psychiatric view of mental illness. Additionally, he wished to draw attention to the inadvisability of using the mental hospital system as a refuge for antisocial personality disorder, despite the political expediency of the current circumstance (MHRB, 27 February 1990).

Now that the political agenda had been made so explicit by Dr Parker, it was germane for the Board to pursue this matter further, and it did so on the final hearing day at J Ward in the presence of Garry himself. Dr Peter Eisen, whose role was administrative and involved advising the Minister for Health, told the Board that the Chief General Manager of the Health Department had been 'consistently deeply concerned' about the adverse effects of managing Garry David within psychiatric services, because antisocial personality disorder did not come within the requirements of the Mental Health Act 1986. On Eisen's first day in the position (9 October 1989) a meeting had been requested by the Assistant Police Commissioner regarding that Office's ability to provide management advice, and several Cabinet meetings were convened to discuss possible options. However, he asserted that such activity only equated with 'political concern' and not 'political pressure', although he had openly stated that it could appear as if 'an act of collusion may be undertaken' (MHRB, 2 March 1990).

When Dr Grigor was called for further cross-examination by Keon-Cohen on this matter, he was subjected to intense scrutiny about disparities in his view at various stages of Garry's confinement. The difficulties of Grigor's position as a public sector psychiatrist were exposed, when he admitted that by December 1989 he believed the Minister for Health to be opposed to Garry's transfer to the health care system, and he thought that Dr Eisen had found himself 'between a rock and a hard place'. He gave evidence that the phrase 'we're being asked to collude' was used by Dr Eisen at a forensic meeting attended by senior health staff working at head office and at the prison in the presence of the ministerial adviser on 15 December 1989. When pressed about its meaning, he said that he understood it to mean 'something about plotting and scheming in an underhand way' about Garry David, but he could not link the request to particular politicians and was only aware that it emanated from 'a higher governmental level'. He recalled the prison medical officer, Dr Peter Hearne, objecting to its intent and expressing deep philosophical objections to doctors being used to facilitate 'the wishes of government' (MHRB, 2 March 1990).

In the lively cross-examination to follow, no further clarification about the political pressures on public psychiatrists in this case was forthcoming. However, Dr Grigor did admit that, although he was aware of the political agenda involved in articles in the *Sun* newspaper, the discussions within Government, and the desire that Garry David should not be released, he believed that his decision to certify this prisoner had been made on medical grounds alone and was unpressured. He explicitly denied a conflict of duties as a Health Department officer, on the one hand, and as a qualified psychiatrist, on the other, but accepted the fact that he was 'unavoidably associated with the collusion':

> I was caught up in it and that was an enormous moral – I believed I was the only person who could legitimately certify Garry David with any degree of credibility in the Department. I would have looked with scorn on anyone else coming in and doing it as a political manoeuvre and yet the whole thing had been so overcome by events that I regretted that very much... It took me a long time to get to my views... I would have thought that someone else might have had a 'St. Paul conversion on the road to Damascus' if they had taken that path and, unless I had respect for their integrity, I would have doubted that they could have done it with integrity. (MHRB, 2 March 1990)

The inevitability of the events in which he was enmeshed surfaced in the following interchange:

Keon-Cohen: My earlier question was: were you not unavoidably part of the process described by Dr Eisen as an invitation to collude and I think your answer was 'yes'?

Grigor: Yes.

Keon-Cohen: It would follow, would it not, that equally, inevitably you would be seen as a part of that process?

Grigor: You are so right. Yes. Yes. (MHRB, 2 March 1990)

From a psychiatric stance, the Director of Forensic Services was fully aware that his decision to certify Garry was a minority one and likely to be misinterpreted by colleagues and others as succumbing to the building political scenario. The fact that he had, at the time concerned, counselled Garry to lodge an appeal suggests some ambivalence and hesitation regarding the repercussions which the certification would have on staff already sensitive to the Board's criticism of J Ward's inability to cater for a seriously disturbed patient. But in view of the unusual public nature of the certification, this action can also be seen as a declaration about the uncertainties surrounding clinical knowledge of the personality disorders, and it openly hinted at the embattled position in which he, as Director of Forensic Services, found himself.

In broader terms, the process of matching the wide spectrum of personality disorders with the legal concept of either insanity or mental illness has always been politically contentious at the sharper end of threatened community interest. It would be simplistic to argue that such decisions lie solely in the political domain. The personality disorders open up a broader area of clinical discretion than is usual. In the Garry David case there was an open invitation to emphasise the borderline components of his dysfunction, rather than the antisocial ones, given that most conceded Garry to be suffering from both conditions. The second area of contention relates to certification itself. Here, there are differences between the law and psychiatry. The former focuses on the coercive element of this action and the latter regards it as being purposeful, that is, as having the aim of providing treatment and/or relieving distress. In this context, there must be room for differing professional views about whether this latter goal is achievable and coercion thereby justifiable. Whilst not denying the contextual framework in which the decision was made and its fortuitous timing, it is opportunistic to reduce complex knowledge and interprofessional issues to a simple political agenda. The Mental Health Review Board understandably refused to embark on drawing any particular conclusions about this matter in their *Statement of Reasons*.

THE OUTCOME

On 2 March all members of the Board arrived early at J Ward Ararat in time for a full day's hearing of the evidence. There was an opportunity to see over the facility and mingle socially with the patients, including Garry, with no reporters present. Nursing staff were pleased to meet with Board members and senior staff of the Office of Psychiatric Services, since they were geographically isolated from other parts of the health service. Finally Garry had his 'time in court' and could present his own interpretation of both his behaviour and current circumstances, which he did competently and articulately, despite the strain of detailed cross-examination by Mr Adams. As the Board noted:

> If the ordinary sensible person was [sic] to look at Mr David's behaviour the conclusion would be inescapable that he was not mentally ill when he appeared before the Board on 2 March 1990. On that day he answered questions for nearly three hours. He was logical, coherent and calm. He offered explanations for his bizarre behaviour which were highly unusual, but which were understandable when one looks at the life which this man has led. The staggering contrast between his outrageous past behaviour and his presentation and explanations for his behaviour on 2 March 1990 would lead the ordinary sensible person to consider psychiatric explanations for...disturbances in mental functioning. (Kiel 1992, p.195)

There is some parity here with the comments made by a Supreme Court Judge in an earlier case in Victoria about the composed courtroom behaviour of a man deemed to be a psychopath, whose control did not fit with the usual image of 'madness'. In that instance, the comments from the bench were influential in denying the appellant the benefit of the lunacy jurisdiction of the Supreme Court, and many lawyers and psychiatrists became joined in a common struggle against an unusual governmental determination to enforce capital punishment (*Tait v The Queen* [1963] VR 647). Both Tait and David were deemed to be psychopathic but, paradoxically, in the former instance it was psychiatrists, rather than the ordinary sensible person, who were agitating for use of mental health options, thereby highlighting the fact that the legal boundary of mental illness is indeed malleable according to circumstance.

After 14 days of listening to a wealth of conflicting detail, the Board's task was to decide on the weight as well as the substance of all the material brought before it. Counsel was provided with a detailed list of questions in relation to the Mental Health Act 1986 and invited to weigh the credibility of each of the various witnesses. A decision was urgently required in the light of surrounding events: Garry might be granted bail; the Social Development Committee was due to table its first report; and the Supreme Court had yet to inquire into the meaning of mental illness. Nonetheless, the Board required two months to evaluate the evidence in a case with implications for its future decisions regarding the personality disordered.

In the late afternoon of 9 May 1990, the three Board members, counsel, some witnesses, press, members of the public and Garry David himself converged on the large recreation area in Ward M5 at Mont Park, which had been set aside for the hearing. The atmosphere was tense and the outcome could by no means be foreshadowed. Several boxes of copies of the 130-page *Statement of Reasons* were carried in. Proceedings were brief, lasting only 15 minutes.

The key issue was the definition of mental illness. Here the Board's decision was a brave one in view of the opinions of Drs Perera, Grigor and Tobin, three of the key staff of the Office of Psychiatric Services with responsibility for the functioning of J Ward. Using the expert standard, the Board found, for reasons previously discussed, that the evidence of these psychiatrists was likely to be flawed and thus on balance the weight of expert opinion was that Garry David could *not* be held to be mentally ill. The application of the ordinary sensible person test had also led the Board to arrive at the same result, even though it recognised that, whilst a different outcome would have been 'comforting' for many people, it would have medicalised Garry's behaviour and precluded 'further consideration of the factors which may have led this man to behave as he has for most of his life' – a comment indirectly critical of the inability of various state agencies to assist him. Personality disorder, the Board considered, was *not* to be regarded as a mental illness unless there was a demonstration, at more than a fleeting level, of some distinctive symptomatology over and above a reaction to confinement. In this case, it accepted that Garry's beliefs had been coloured by a hatred for authority figures developed over a lengthy period of incarceration. This same reasoning also applied to the legislation's exclusionary criteria, which specify that a finding of mental illness cannot be made on the grounds of particular political and philosophical beliefs/activities, or immoral or illegal conduct alone. The previous decision reached in the case of KMC was now insupportable and the test used in the case of AB was reformulated as follows:

> A person appears to be suffering from a mental illness if he/she has recently exhibited symptoms which indicate a disturbance of mental functioning which constitutes an identifiable syndrome or if it not be possible to ascribe the symptoms of such a disturbance of mental functioning to a classifiable syndrome, they are symptoms of a disturbance of thought, mood, volition, perception, orientation or memory which are present to such a degree as to be considered pathological. (Kiel 1992, pp.177-8)

This new test extended the pivotal notion of a person having 'the appearance' of mental illness in section 8(1)(a) of the Act to encompass particular elements of diagnostic significance, whilst recognising the clinical difficulties inherent in attaching a specific label. It was a non-legal, technical definition that was now being proposed. Then came the decision crucial to Garry's future:

> After considering the relevant criteria we are not satisfied that the continued detention of Mr David as a security patient is necessary. We do not believe that in the exercise of our discretion we should decline to order that Mr David be discharged as a security patient and returned to a prison. The formal order of the Board is that the appeal is upheld and that Mr David be discharged as a security patient and returned to a prison.

It was a dramatic moment. Garry's counsel was clearly relieved, but the immediate implications were not so obvious. Since the responsibility for him had been effectively handed back to the Office of Corrections, he could no longer be detained as a security patient at Mont Park, yet no correctional staff members were present to effect the transfer. Meanwhile, Michael Adams, counsel for both the Chief General Manager of the Health Department and the Attorney-General, appeared not to have fully anticipated such a result and quickly sought advice. In a matter of minutes he announced that an appeal would be lodged with the Administrative Appeals Tribunal. It was close to four o'clock in the afternoon, as all counsel prepared for a rushed trip to the city to appear in person before the Tribunal and argue the necessity for an interim stay order to halt the operation of the Board's decision.

Despite a three-month hearing of such detail and complexity, Garry David had still not achieved his wish to be discharged as a security patient and the stage was set for further legal argument at higher court levels. The Board's hearing had been careful and thorough. It had canvassed the meaning and parameters of treatment for those with severe personality disorders on the grounds of their desirability, necessity and availability; and it had tested the relationship of the personality disorders to mental illness. After searching inquiry, it had exposed the fragility of psychiatric diagnoses and decision making, but still upheld the validity of the experts' view of mental illness.

These outcomes were all positive. However, there were unresolved issues which had surfaced during the lengthy inquiry. It had become apparent that the psychiatrists' professional body was holding firm in its resistance to borderline personality disorder coming within the ambit of mental illness, and that this was not the view favoured by the bureaucratic structure within the Office of Psychiatric Services, which was possibly responding in part to political imperatives. As a consequence, the position of psychiatrists working within this centralised forensic unit became strained, because the professional and political aspects of their role were becoming overtly difficult to separate in a non-conflictual way. This explains many of the inconsistencies and contradictions arising in the context of the Board hearing, where the legal mode of inquiry sharpened differences of opinion.

It was now up to the Supreme Court to resolve the problem by ruling on Garry David's 'dangerousness' and allocating him to his proper space within the confines of criminality, mental illness, or the community. At the same time, the use of the law to detain one person would be at issue.

CHAPTER 5

A Malleable Boundary
and the Bridging Manoeuvres

The Law Reform Commission proposal is a thinly disguised introduction of preventive detention achieved by transferring the odium for that process to the mental health care system. The issue of preventive detention is indeed a controversial one and it does raise substantial civil liberties issues. These issues will not go away because of a piece of legislative sleight of hand.

(A New South Wales psychiatrist's response to
the Report of the Law Reform Commission of Victoria)

Psychiatrists have fought a long battle to decrease the lumping together of criminals and the mentally ill – so that the quality of life for those in our institutions could be improved with reductions in violence and the removal of locked doors from our institutions. The Law Reform Commission of Victoria's recommendations may well see the reversal of this long historical development.

(A Queensland psychiatrist's response to
the Report of the Law Reform Commission of Victoria)

I expect to be freed in February 1990, and I bloody well better be. To keep me in gaol would be a declaration of war. And I will, as all prisoners of war must, attempt to escape … and I will give no mercy to my enemies.

(Garry David – letter to the *Sun* 11 December 1989)

THROWING DOWN THE GAUNTLET

Opposition marshals

The transition from the Mental Health Review Board to the Supreme Court was not smooth and the Government seemed to be losing ground at each step. The various attempts to situate the problem squarely within the framework of psychiatry had stalled. The only supporter for such a proposal was the government's own Law Reform Commission of Victoria, which presented its Report on the matter to the Attorney-General on 19 February 1990 recommending 'that an anti-social personality disorder *may be* [my emphasis] considered to be a mental illness for the purposes of the Act' (later tabled as: Law Reform Commission of Victoria, *The Concept of Mental Illness in the 'Mental Health Act' 1986*, Report No. 31, April 1990). Whilst the language was cautious, the intention and timing were impeccable in view of the concurrent deliberations of the Mental Health Review Board and the Social Development Committee.

However, the document went a step further with the radical proposal that psychiatrists should be brought under the scrutiny of the Office of the Attorney-General when making decisions about patients with severe personality disorders. It was the Commission's view that a person having 'the *appearance* of normality brought about by treatment' need not be discharged, if the psychiatrist 'knows that the person's symptoms will reappear after release, because the person will not take medication or cannot cope without supervision' (Law Reform Commission, April 1990, p.15). The consequences of this suggestion would have been far-reaching indeed and suggest that the Commission was bent on moderating some of the newly gained provisions of the Mental Health Act 1986, at least for those deemed to have a severe antisocial personality disorder. Implementation of its proposals would have seriously jeopardised the principle of the least restrictive environment relating to civil commitment and eroded the authority of the Mental Health Review Board in a number of ways. As the Board must be assured that the person '*appears* to be mentally ill', the Commission was significantly departing from this standard by suggesting that a psychiatrist's intuitive judgment about a person's *likely* pattern of behaviour on release could be sufficient justification for continued confinement:

> Those decisions – particularly ones to release a person from detention, which are not subject to any review – could have a seriously adverse effect on other members of the public. That risk could be minimised if guidelines concerning the meaning and effect of the Act were drawn up for the instruction of the psychiatrists who make decisions in relation to the commitment, detention and release of the mentally ill under section 8. The Commission believes that step [sic] should be taken and that the guidelines should be settled authoritatively by the Solicitor-General. (LRC Report No. 31 1990, pp.15–16)

In effect, the report was arguing that in such cases clinical decision making should be constrained by political realities, for in determining the necessity for civil commitment psychiatrists would be in breach of Parliament's intention, if they chose to ignore the guidelines. In legislative terms it would follow that the Mental Health Act should be amended to allow for the detention of some of those with an antisocial personality disorder, and that pressure might need to be exerted on psychiatrists, through the office of the Attorney-General, to undertake the necessary action. The Commission's views were tantamount to a declaration of no confidence in psychiatrists' ability to act appropriately in relation to civil detention and, if implemented, would have the capacity to make professional decisions subject to political direction in some instances. Despite its explicit denial of interference, the Report's proposal was intrusive and constituted a legislative form of boundary shifting.

Some of the Commission's arguments illustrated the difficulty of constructing a meaningful dialogue between psychiatry and the law, for they capitalised on the lack of clarity between a mental *disorder* and a mental *illness*; the former being part of the broad range of conditions contained in the expert manuals and the latter referring to the legal criteria of the mental health legislation. The Commission chose, for its own purpose, to exploit this semantic gulf, which had bedevilled the Mental Health Review Board appeal. In so doing, its argument was legalistic and focused on community protection in preference to an explicit concern with mental health needs. It maintained that the Act should not be used to detain people, who were 'bad' rather than 'mad', but that the ambit of madness should be widened to include some of those sufficiently disturbed to indulge in criminal behaviours:

> [The Commission] is suggesting that the Act should apply to all people who are mentally ill. The Act should not arbitrarily exclude a particular group of mentally ill people merely because psychiatrists classify their underlying condition as a disorder rather than an illness; or because psychiatrists cannot successfully treat them; or because they create major problems for the mental health system. (LRC Report No. 31, 1990, pp.16–17)

There are a number of implications which flow from this statement. The legal notion of 'mental illness' is more closely approximating that of 'mental disorder', thereby encouraging forensic expansion and conferring more power on psychiatrists. But, somewhat paradoxically, the Commission's report can only be viewed as demeaning in its attitude toward professional practice, implying that psychiatrists had been misguidedly resisting legal and political direction with selective patient intake, thereby avoiding responsibility, at least as far as some untreatable and difficult patients were concerned, and occasionally lapsing into questionable clinical judgments. In particular, a subsection, provocatively titled 'Misunderstandings by Psychiatrists Concerning the Meaning and Effect of the Act', espoused the view that Parliament's intentions were not being properly interpreted and had sometimes led doctors to discharge mistakenly some not possessing 'the appearance' of mental illness, as required in section 8(1)(a) (LRC Report 1990, p.14). In this way, the fact that the personality disordered may have an 'appearance of normality' was underpinning the Commission's proposal for amended mental health legislation, yet in seeking to assert the will of the Government by choosing this focus, it was threatening to undermine psychiatric judgments about the nature of mental illness. Whilst the clash may have emanated from pragmatic considerations, including the Attorney-General's resolve to confront the psychiatric profession about its limiting interpretation of 'mental illness' and thus regain some ground within party ranks, it also reflects the competitive and sometimes uneasy alliance which the law has historically shared with psychiatry. For the Commission to encompass normality of appearance within a psychiatric frame of reference deflected the legal difficulty, which arose in both the Tait and David cases, of reconciling cognition and composure with a judgment about irrationality and diminished control.

The rapidly formulated response of the Victorian Branch of the Royal Australian and New Zealand College of Psychiatrists to this external interference in their professional domain was unequivocal. The members' opposition to any possible amendments to the Mental Health Act 1986 was forwarded to the Social Development Inquiry hearing and couched succinctly:

> The Royal Australian and New Zealand College of Psychiatrists is most strongly opposed to such an amendment which we would regard as being incompatible with the theory and practice of psychiatry today, with the moral principles of the Mental Health Act and with our society's standards for civil liberties. A number of practical consequences would flow from such an amendment, which would have detrimental effects on the treatment of mentally ill patients within the state. (8 February 1990)

This statement attracted widespread support from College members outside the state of Victoria. For example, Dr John Ellard wrote indicating that the New South Wales Branch was in agreement. In this letter he implied that such an inquiry would require more than the few weeks allocated by the Government because the issue encompassed problems of morality, politics and criminality, as well as the subject's liberty, the nature of psychiatric classification, the meaning of mental illness, the nature of personality disorder and the distinction between badness and madness (8 February 1990). Other senior members of the profession professed a similar view. For example, Dr William Lucas then of Adelaide, an experienced forensic psychiatrist, wrote:

> I believe that using mental health legislation to achieve the ends desired by the Law Reform Commission, and perhaps the Government, would be ill judged, detrimental to the civil liberties of some individuals, unacceptable and detrimental to psychiatric hospitals and probably would not provide substantial or long standing protection for the public in many or most cases. (7 February 1990)

It was in the context of the Social Development Committee hearing that the forces arraigned against the Law Reform Commission of Victoria began to coalesce and intensify. Those familiar with Garry's plight were aware of the imminent danger of the political will being imposed on a professional discipline. The College indicted the Commission's report on the grounds of its limited understanding of psychiatry leading to poorly substantiated arguments and ill-considered implications (RANZCP, 8 February 1990). It alleged that the Commissioners had failed to recognise the conceptual distinction between mental illness and personality disorders and the likelihood of considerable 'variability between clinicians' judgments' outside highly structured research settings (RANZCP, 8 February 1990). At this point, each body was talking past the other, for the Commission *had* recognised the distinction, but concluded that psychiatrists were remiss in sheltering behind a clinical notion of 'disorder', instead of facing the reality of their legal obligation to deal with 'mental illness'. A New South Wales psychiatrist, Dr William Barclay, irked by this territorial impasse, gave a blunt rejoinder:

> The argument used by the Law Reform Commission (to certify and detain persons with personality disorder alone) begs the basic question. It says we can't detain people with personality disorder in prisons because that would be unfair. It is acceptable to detain the mentally ill in mental hospitals. Let us call those who have personality disorder mentally ill and then what is unfair has become fair. (Submission to SDC, 13 February 1990)

The College also pointed out that Law Reform Commission members appeared to have lost sight of the 'moral force' of the basic principles underlying the Mental Health Act and were being governed by a mistaken belief that the psychiatric system was more 'humane' than imprisonment (RANZCP, 8 February 1990). This was a particularly deft criticism on two grounds. Some of the Commissioners were members of the legal profession and well known for their civil liberties' stance, and some had also been involved in the careful drafting of an Act designed to safeguard the rights of mentally ill persons. In particular, these were Dr David Neal, the Commissioner in Charge, and some of the part-time members: the Hon Justice Frank Vincent, also head of the Adult Parole Board of Victoria, Professor Louis Waller, a Professor of Law at Monash University and Mr Robert Richter, a noted Queen's Counsel and executive member of the Victorian Council for Civil Liberties. Other members included the Chairman, Mr David St L. Kelly (a lawyer), Ms Judy Dixon (Community Council Against Violence), Mr Alan Rassaby (a lawyer with Community Services Victoria), as well as Mr Gary Sullivan and Ms Jude Wallace (both lawyers with the Legal Aid Commission of Victoria). Ms Agnes Borsody and Mr John Van Groningen were the full-time research assistants. These Commission members now found themselves being reminded by an allied profession of the bases of that legislation: that is, its promise to prevent any unnecessary interference with the rights, dignity and self-respect of the mentally ill. Above all, the health mandate was to be the justification for treatment interventions, in order to avoid the psychiatric system becoming unduly custodial in orientation. The College therefore argued:

> If the protection of others is the interest to be served and a health interest is
> absent, then detention, if it is to occur, must occur outside the framework of
> the Mental Health Act. Otherwise it must be an abuse of such an Act.
> (RANZCP, 8 February 1990)

The tables were turned on the lawyers, for the strength of these arguments lay in
their libertarianism; that is, their proclamation of the need to protect the individual
from unwarranted interference by the state. The College reinforced its attack by
pointing out that deleterious consequences of a wide-ranging kind would flow
from widening the ambit of mental health services to incorporate 'badness', and
these would impact on both professions. For example, one might expect psychopaths to be absolved from criminal responsibility and to experience fewer
restraints on their behaviour; medical practitioners would be tempted to certify
more frequently to avoid liability for the potentially dangerous behaviour of
patients; and an increase in the proportion of personality disorders within psychiatric hospitals would result, thereby diminishing the resources available for the
treatment of mentally ill patients.

Reference was also made to the fact that the Commission had been proposing
that psychopathy be regarded as a 'mental impairment' rather than 'mental illness'
for the purposes of the insanity defence and, should this occur, the safeguards of
the Act would be weakened by allowing the inappropriate detention of the personality disordered in a psychiatric hospital (LRC Report 1990). The direct
outcome of this detention could be staff refusal to work with such a broad mix of
patients and a compromise of professional and ethical values of psychiatrists.
These were all compelling arguments, undoubtedly sharpened by the knowledge
that the future management or treatment of Garry David was at the heart of the
debate, and that experience with him in the prison, medical and mental health
systems had produced no lasting positive outcomes, but had generated internal
dissension and diminished scarce therapeutic resources.

There were minor variations of views amongst individual psychiatrists, who
responded to the Social Development Committee's invitation to give evidence, but
the overall consensus was that dangerous offenders should remain in the province
of the criminal justice system, in order to avoid a misuse of clinical services for
sociopolitical purposes. This response is likely also to have been influenced by
other factors, such as the ongoing critiques emanating from anti-psychiatrists over
the previous two decades, and by a conscious concern to implement the policy of
deinstitutionalisation, both of which demanded more restrictive psychiatric
admissions and a clearer treatment rationale.

The debate, by this stage, was becoming very public. Several open forums
were convened and Dr William Glaser took the opportunity to publish an article
provocatively titled 'Morality and Medicine' in the *Legal Service Bulletin*, which

attracted rejoinders from two members of the Law Reform Commission (Glaser 1990). He argued that whilst the Commission's proposals were 'superficially attractive', they were 'based on some very muddled thinking regarding the nature of "mental illness"' and a 'cavalier' approach to the legislative background. He reminded the Commission that the grounds for not certifying those with antisocial personality disorders were both social justice and medical ones, for badness cannot be medicalised as an illness: 'In our society, there are priests, police and judges. Psychiatrists do not want to usurp their roles, nor should the Law Reform Commission allow them to do so' (Glaser 1990, pp.115–16).

The irony of this comment was barely veiled, since it was lawyers, who had so recently been indicting psychiatry for its 'gatekeeper of social control' role and had, as a consequence, drafted Victoria's legislation to limit that profession's therapeutic mandate. In Glaser's view, the current debate was motivated by political exigency to reverse this policy. However, as I have already indicated, a simple legislative shift simply masked the complexity of the issues involved in achieving agreement about the conceptual and administrative separation of badness and madness. From the psychiatric standpoint, these issues encompassed professional principles, philosophical beliefs, economic implications, a variation in views about treatment efficacy, an awareness of staff relations and management constraints, the countering of criticisms of its role, and the immediacy of difficult experiences with one very severely personality-disordered prisoner.

The Commission was not eliciting much support from members of the legal profession, some of whom were as vociferous in their protests as had been the psychiatrists. Professional bodies, including the Human Rights Commission, the Law Institute of Victoria, the Legal Aid Commission of Victoria and the Victorian Council for Civil Liberties, rightly argued that dangerous offenders must be handled in a *general* way in order to avoid the law being compromised by the creation of special provisions to deal with one person. As Professor Arie Freiberg of the University of Melbourne's Criminology Department reminded the Social Development Committee:

> One lesson to be learned from legal history is that hard cases make bad law and there is a risk that a hasty or ill-conceived response to one particular case on the periphery of the current law can seriously disturb a larger and well-thought structure. (12 February 1990)

The solution to 'the problem' of Garry David, he argued, was intense surveillance within the existing preventive detention provisions of the criminal justice system, rather than the introduction of any extraordinary legal remedy. The Law Institute of Victoria, representing the professional interests of lawyers, was equally adamant about separating criminal justice from mental health concerns:

> If preventive detention of dangerous offenders is what is required then we should be explicit about it and not seek to camouflage this reality beneath a politically acceptable veneer of presumed psychiatric disturbance... In essence, the problem posed by the dangerous offender is not how to treat him/her, but rather how to protect the public against the consequences of his/her actions. The latter is properly the domain of the criminal justice system. The former is properly the domain of the mental health system. (22 February 1990)

Intraprofessional debates rarely become so public as that of the Law Institute's urging the Social Development Committee to ignore the Law Reform Commission's report, which they considered to be a 'profoundly disappointing document', 'bereft of careful, comparative analysis and providing a dispiriting, expedient and hasty response to a complex problem, which has vexed lawyers, psychiatrists and legislators for many decades' (22 February 1990).

Professor Robert Williams of Monash University was yet another jurist to have difficulty avoiding the conclusion that the Commission had not been motivated 'by a desire to achieve a particular result in a manner calculated to minimise public criticism' (*The Age*, 2 July 1990). In his evidence to the Social Development Committee, he described its report as 'a combination of bad psychiatry, bad law and bad logic' in the expectation of achieving 'an acceptable result' (21 February 1990). Although, he agreed that the Mental Health Act should not be used for the detention of Garry David, he departed from his colleagues' views by proposing special legislation with a sunset clause, because this would have the safeguard of higher court scrutiny and ensure a temporary holding power. This later came to pass but, in the short term the Government retained three potential lifelines: support from the Social Development Committee for a custodial approach; and a broadening of the meaning of 'mental illness' and 'appears to be mentally ill' through determinations of the Supreme Court or the Administrative Appeals Tribunal – either of which would override any unfavourable outcome from the Mental Health Review Board.

THREE SIGNIFICANT REBUFFS

The pressure on the Social Development Committee intensified from February onwards, despite the fact that the Mental Health Review Board had just commenced its hearings. The Government issued a formal request for an interim report by 2 March 1990 with accompanying recommendations regarding the detention of the severely personality disordered in safe custody at the expiration of a sentence should public safety appear to be compromised by any unacceptable risk. (The Inquiry into Mental Disturbance and Community Safety was initially convened on 14 June 1989 and produced four reports dated May 1990, March 1992, April 1992 and August 1992.) The tight deadline concerned the Committee and, when inviting urgent responses from psychiatrists, staff of the Office of Corrections, lawyers and academics, its research officer described the situation as one of 'crisis'.

Another problem facing the Committee was the fact that, although their reference was drafted in general terms, it was difficult for this focus to be maintained, when the Government's interest in its application to one person was so immediately transparent. The urgency of the matter was further apparent on 1 March 1990, less than one month later, when the Minister for Health issued an additional request for 'draft amendments or draft bills' to be included in the tabled report – 'amendments' undoubtedly referring to mental health legislation and 'draft bills' to criminal justice initiatives. This euphemistic phrasing was in essence a method of deferring the choice of Garry's location in the punishment/treatment complex to an all-parliamentary Committee. The date for the report was now extended slightly and it was unfortunate for the Government that its tabling was coincidental with the release of the Mental Health Review Board's finding that Garry David was *not* mentally ill, for this reinforced the same conclusion in a more general way by arguing that the involuntary admission criteria of the Mental Health Act 1986 should not be amended to include a person with an antisocial personality disorder alone (SDC *Interim Report*, May 1990, p.v). This position was strengthened in view of the two inquiries having been conducted quite independently.

Thus two influential groups, the Social Development Committee of Victoria and the Royal Australian and New Zealand College of Psychiatrists, were opposed to tinkering with the sensitive and well-considered provisions of the Mental Health Act in order to provide the foundation for preventive detention. Both considered the problem to be located squarely within the provisions of the Crimes Act 1958, which gave ample protection in the case of threats to kill or injure others. Where there was evidence of more generalised threats against the community, the Committee found the onus to reside with Parliament to clarify the provisions of this Act. In a multipronged attack, it resoundingly rejected the position taken by the Law Reform Commission of Victoria, and the only common ground between the two statutory bodies appeared to be their lack of support for preventive detention as a matter of principle. The Committee pointed out that no evidence had been offered for the view that psychiatrists sometimes discharged patients inappropriately. It directed a stinging rebuke to the Attorney-General's Department that 'without such an argument and without expertise in mental illness, there is no role for the Solicitor-General to develop such guidelines' (SDC *Interim Report* May 1990, p.v). The members argued that the Commission lacked an understanding about mental illness and juxtaposed this point against the more discriminating interpretations emerging from its own inquiry, which generally supported Dr Peter Eisen's view that one can *have* a mental illness without being mentally ill. They further argued that the Commission appeared to be conflating these two elements by implying that the condition was an enduring one, and the appearance of mental illness was not always evident. Such an opinion would more readily allow for continued certification in the absence of symptomatology – an action neither matching the spirit of the Act, nor the current psychiatric practice. If the Government had pinned its faith on the Law Reform Commission of Victoria being able to steer a course through the rocky waters of the bad–mad divide, then their hopes were ill founded. Criticisms of their proposals were overwhelmingly strong, with the general conclusion that political interest had resulted in arguments of expediency rather than logic, the demonstration of a poor knowledge of psychiatry, an implicit denigration of the profession with a disregard for civil liberties and their relevance to forensic practice.

In its *Interim Report* the Social Development Committee also explored management implications and made the innovative suggestion that a small group of severely disturbed offenders should be allowed to reach 'an individually negotiated agreement' in relation to their rehabilitation programme (May 1990, pp.94–5). This accorded with Garry's own view, although both parties understood that some coercive mechanism would still be required to cope with the occurrence of a possible breach. It was an awkward solution, because it presumed a degree of financial commitment on the part of the Government, not only to Garry David, but to other seriously personality-disordered offenders whom the Office of Psychiatric Services and the Office of Corrections estimated to number between 15 and 30. However, the advantage of such a move was avoidance of a polarised choice between changes in mental health and criminal justice legislation, both steps the Committee considered to be of such magnitude as to require informed public debate, which the government was undoubtedly seeking to avoid (SDC *Interim Report*, May 1990, p.x).

Although by May 1990 the Government had the safety net of the Community Protection Act in place, it still had to contend with the weight of professional opinion rejecting tactical measures designed to lock away one individual, especially when many of the arguments were often semantic in nature. The fact that the Attorney-General's Department funded the Law Reform Commission of Victoria, which was therefore part of the executive arm of government, seemed not entirely irrelevant to the exercise. There was even an embarrassing indication of internal dissension, when one of the Commissioners chose to distance himself publicly from the majority opinion. Gary Sullivan was reported in the Melbourne *Age* as saying:

> The Commission has not reached a consensus on the issues. It appears there
> has been work in progress which I am not familiar with. I would be very con-
> cerned if that sort of recommendation was being put to the Government ...
> While rejecting the draft bill, Mr Sullivan said the psychiatric profession had
> failed to deal with difficult cases of anti-social personality disorders, or psy-
> chopaths. (*The Age,* 13 January 1990)

The second avenue of hope for the Government of Victoria now lay in the
Attorney-General's application to the Full Court stating that it was in the public
interest to have a ruling on whether the definition of mental illness fell within the
expert or lay view. The import of these proceedings was not lost on the Court. At
the outset the Chief Justice, Sir John Young, inquired whether the
Solicitor-General was trying to obtain a Supreme Court ruling, which could then
be used in the Government's favour at the imminent Administrative Appeals
Tribunal hearing on the stay of execution of the Mental Health Review Board's
order (Supreme Court, 10 May 1990). He indicated that the current application
was unusual, given that mental health was not part of the jurisdiction of the
Attorney-General, and he pointed out that the expert interpretation developed by
the Mental Health Review Board had been used without dispute since 1988. The
clear message was that the application was opportune for the Government in its
current circumstances. Although the Solicitor-General, Hartog Berkeley, insisted
that the need for a declaratory judgment was an issue of law in general, rather than
tied to the facts of the Garry David case, the Court was not swayed. In less than two
hours, the three Justices, Young CJ, Crockett and Southwell, dismissed the originating motion and reminded the Attorney-General that he should not seek to
bypass ordinary court procedures with an untimely appeal to the Full Court in a
matter on which he had failed to express any prior interest. The Judges cited 'compelling' reasons for deciding 'not to entertain the application which, on any view,
is an unusual one'. As they pointed out, the Mental Health Review Board had
already formulated a working definition of mental illness, which had been unchallenged over two years, and a decision from the Supreme Court in this instance was
not linked to a specific case. Any person aggrieved by a Mental Health Review
Board decision would still have recourse to further legal procedures (unpublished,
my hearing notes). In effect, the Judges were reminding the Attorney-General that
there was no reason to short-circuit established procedure.

Although the Government had lost yet another round, it nonetheless pressed
on doggedly. The Attorney-General now proceeded with a second application for
an advisory opinion on the meaning of mental illness, which it hoped might
become binding on the Mental Health Review Board. On 6 July 1990, all counsel
assembled again before His Honour Judge Smith in the Administrative Appeals
Tribunal. Once again, the application failed for a similar reason: it was regarded as

being in the nature of an hypothetical case. As Judge Smith concluded on hearing the evidence:

> It has long been held that Courts (and, I would think, by parity of reasoning, Tribunals) will not give advisory opinions… I have concluded that there is no live issue now pending between the parties and that a determination of this Tribunal would amount to the giving of an advisory opinion… I consider that the Tribunal cannot and should not proceed and determine this application and that no directions should be given as sought by the Attorney General. (AAT Appeal Decision, 12 July 1990)

The Government's attempt to transpose its problem with Garry David from one of 'badness' and relocate it within the sphere of 'mental illness' had failed to convince two superior courts that there should be a renegotiation of the concepts of ownership and responsibility for a social dilemma in the way that Gusfield has suggested (1981, p.10), and its attempts had been unequivocally rejected. The ensuing conflict and struggle shed light on the techniques and interests of the parties involved: positions were polarised and a level of antipathy between the more independent Law Institute and a seemingly compliant Law Reform Commission was demonstrable.

LEGAL MOVES, AN UNCERTAIN STATUS AND CONSTITUTIONAL ISSUES

The period from May to September 1990 saw quite intense legal activity, and matters relating to Garry David were raised in either a tribunal or court on 37 separate days. Court sitting days concerning applications under the Community Protection Act 1990 totalled 80 days in less than 3 years, including 29 days, 13 days and 16 days, respectively, for each of the three major hearings. The case had achieved almost industry status, and it was rumoured that approximately 100 professionals were involved during that year in some aspect of either Garry's management, preparation of material for the courts, or the presentation of evidence. The reason for such concerted efforts was twofold: first, the groundwork had to be laid for unprecedented proceedings in the Supreme Court; second, the multiplicity of provisions pertaining to Garry set in train legal entanglements about his status as either a security patient, a prisoner, a detainee under an interim order for preventive detention, or a remandee – the legal consequences of each being quite distinct. Because of the interplay of ensuant proceedings, Garry's allocation to either 'badness' or 'madness' was becoming increasingly tenuous and expensive to resolve. It was around this time that financial estimates published by the Attorney-General's and the Health Departments were quoted as being in the region of $9 to $12 million dollars, with the costs of the Supreme Court alone amounting to approximately $5,000 an hour (*Sunday Herald*, 19 August 1990). These figures significantly increased in the following two years with the addition of further court hearings, the provision of legal aid, the capital costs of purpose-built facilities, high security arrangements, increased staffing levels, medical treatment, frequent hospitalisations and court and police escort duties.

On the afternoon of 10 May, the day following the handing down of the findings of the Mental Health Review Board, a most significant event took place with little prior warning. This was the reassembling of counsel in the Practice Court before a single Supreme Court Judge. Michael Adams, again appearing for the Attorney-General, made an originating motion *ex parte* under section 8 of the Community Protection Act 1990 for an Order for the preventive detention of Garry David (section 4(1)). It was remarkable that within the space of 24 hours there had been *four different types of legal hearing relevant to Garry's continued custody*: the determination of the Mental Health Review Board; the application to the Administrative Appeals Tribunal for a stay of this order; the application for a declaratory judgment about mental illness in the Full Court of the Supreme Court; and the originating motion for an Order for preventive detention in the Practice Court of the Supreme Court.

The Supreme Court could not do otherwise than grant the Attorney-General's application, which specified that Garry's present legal status must continue until the matter of preventive detention was determined; that is, in the interim, he would be regarded as either a prisoner being held under the provisions of the Corrections Act 1986, or as a security patient within the meaning of the Mental Health Act 1986, depending on his status at the time of the application. However, for the Court to make even this allocation was no simple task, since the Attorney-General's appeal against Garry's discharge as a security patient had yet to be heard. Consequently, he was ordered to remain at J Ward and his security status under section 16(3)(b) of the Mental Health Act continued, despite the Mental Health Review Board's determination that he was not mentally ill.

At this stage of proceedings, Garry David was being detained under *three* levels of custody:

(a) the custodial provisions of the Bail Act 1977 pending the hearing of the charge of threat to kill in the County Court;

(b) the Mental Health Act 1986 by virtue of the stay of the order to discharge him as a security patient;

(c) and the interim Order for custody under the Community Protection Act 1990.

As Michael Adams was later to admit in an aside to Justice Fullagar, all these 'building blocks' were necessary in case any should fall (*Attorney-General for the State of Victoria v Garry Ian David*, Supreme Court of Victoria, Fullagar J, hereafter called

'First Hearing', 31 May 1990) – a comment similar to the one he used in the Administrative Appeals Tribunal, when he told Judge Smith that it was 'not a matter of overkill, but just to protect the status quo' should bail be granted enabling Garry to be at large in the community. In this instance, Judge Smith reached the conclusion that the application was indeed 'a balancing one involving the weighing up of the various competing interests at stake' (*Attorney-General for the State of Victoria v Mental Health Review Board*, Administrative Appeals Tribunal, Smith J, 15 May 1990).

By mid-May the additional uncertainty relating to the pending criminal proceedings was overshadowing other more complex manoeuvres that were taking place. On 16 May 1990 Garry David was committed in the Melbourne Magistrate's Court on the threat to kill charge, with the case being heard in the County Court on 15 June. Garry pleaded guilty and received a 12-month sentence, with 6 months suspended and backdated to his official release date of 3 February 1990. He was immediately returned to J Ward as a security patient, and only on the following Monday was it belatedly realised that, with pre-sentence detention and remissions, his sentence had effectively expired ten days previously. Since Garry could no longer be regarded as a prisoner, his status as a security prisoner was rescinded (section 50(1) Mental Health Act 1986). A subsection also required the Director-General of Corrections to notify the Chief Psychiatrist when a sentence has expired, which was clearly impossible in this instance, given the tangle of intersecting legal provisions and confusion about dates.

One of the building blocks had been removed and another was about to fall. The stay order of the Administrative Appeals Tribunal had now become irrelevant and Garry was duly discharged by mutual consent on 19 June. Although the situation had been partly clarified, Garry had used this interim period to exploit his placement difficulties in a perverse fashion. He argued that, as the Mental Health Review Board had declared him not to be mentally ill, he now wished to be held in a prison. On instructions, Bryan Keon-Cohen presented four arguments to Justice Gobbo in a directions' hearing on 14 May 1990; that is, his client would experience a greater degree of liberty in prison, he could pursue more activities, he would not be subject to mandatory treatment and he did not wish to mix with mentally ill patients. In effect, the Court was in the unusual position of being offered a succinct comparison of the prison and mental health systems from someone with extensive experience in each. The matter was taken further. On 18 May, Garry's counsel appealed to the Supreme Court on the grounds that his client considered that he was neither mentally ill nor did he need treatment, and that he had found J Ward to be 'unsettling and distressing'. He then took the rare step of making a *habeas corpus* application asking for Garry to be brought before the Court so that it could direct him to be detained at Pentridge. At this point Justice Gobbo suggested that *habeas corpus* literally meant 'give me the body', not 'shift him', and consequently declined to interfere. Counsel then foreshadowed that the matter would proceed to the Full Court in order to challenge Judge Smith's ruling.

These events set in train an inexorable progression to a final determination of custody in Victoria's highest criminal jurisdiction, the Supreme Court of Victoria, with a further application to that Court to allow Garry to be held at Pentridge Prison, rather than J Ward, in order to be present at the hearing. Certain preliminary matters had to be sorted out before the Attorney-General's application under the Act could proceed, and these related to the validity of the legislation itself; Garry's status as either a security patient or a prisoner; and the gathering of medical and other evidence (Justice Gobbo, 14 May 1990; Justice Marks, 15 May 1990). These areas of uncertainty bore witness to the legislation's hasty construction and certain unforeseen lacunae in its mode of operation, which had already drawn harsh, public criticism from the retired Supreme Court Judge, Sir John Starke: 'It disturbs me when there is this precedent that Parliament can phase out where the rules of evidence don't bind a judge in deciding a case. That is contrary to basic principles of justice...it is a rather dangerous precedent' (*The Age*, 4 April 1990).

The growing support from community groups, and the singularity of the legislation, raised doubts about the instrument created by Parliament. At the outset, Justice Fullagar, an eminent Supreme Court Judge, expressed his misgivings about the hearing in which he was to become involved. It was not that he was inexperienced in the role of forensic psychiatrists and psychologists in the court, for the Court of Criminal Appeal had upheld his painstaking analysis of the limits of this type of evidence in a previous case (*R v Darrington and McGauley* [1980] ALR 124). In his role as trial judge Justice Fullagar had held that professional qualifications alone were not sufficient expertise to satisfy the court: an expert must also demonstrate special study or knowledge of the area concerned. By extrapolation one might assume, therefore, that in hearing the *Community Protection Act* 1990, which was so heavily dependent on the provision of expert views, this same Judge would be led to evaluate the evidence in a general way by regarding the final determination as residing with the Court itself. After all, as he was well aware, psychiatrists had for some time been proclaiming their lack of expertise regarding dangerous persons, and this was the central focus of the exercise. Fullagar's primary difficulty, however, in the immediate context, lay with the legislation itself, which he pronounced to be ambiguous. He informed the Court that the case would be unduly protracted and indicated that this should be noted by the Attorney-General, 'if he has any interest in the matter at all' (*First Hearing*, 18 June 1990).

The Judge's concern was well founded, when Garry's counsel intimated that it would take him two days to present arguments on due process and constitutional doctrines, in order to challenge the validity of the legislation. In this, he would be relying on the fundamental principles of the English criminal justice system enshrined in traditional rights and freedoms upheld by the Magna Carta, the Bill of Rights 1688 and the Act of Settlement 1701, as well as international covenants and treaties. These included:

- a right not to be subject to arbitrary arrest or detention;
- a right not to be subject to cruel or unusual punishment or treatment;
- a right to a fair hearing (due process); and
- a right to equality before the law, and to equal protection of the law, (Keon-Cohen 1993, p.69).

In his brief outline, Keon-Cohen, who supported a Bill of Rights and had long been an executive member of the Victorian Council for Civil Liberties, foreshadowed his argument that the Constitution Act (Vic) 1975 was predicated on these principles, which thereby limit the power of the Victorian Parliament to usurp them. This power, therefore, cannot be regarded as supreme and overarching and sections 4 and 5 of the Community Protection Act 1990 violate common law restraints. Garry David, he maintained, was being gaoled by executive decree, for the Attorney-General's decision to make an application to the Court entailed 'instant imprisonment' pending any later judicial determination (Keon-Cohen 1993, p.75). Here he pointed to the similarity with the maligned Acts of Attainder of the Middle Ages, which allowed the king to punish those perceived to be dangerous to his rule. Transposed to the current context, the Victorian Attorney-General, as an executive officer of the state, was assuming a judicial function not open to scrutiny. In support of these arguments, Keon-Cohen listed 15 English Acts of Parliament ranging from Magna Carta in 1215 to the Habeas Corpus Act 1856 56 Geo III C.C.; 9 United Nations' documents, 2 European declarations and 2 from the United States of America. This issue of attainder is dealt with in detail by the High Court of Australia in a recent case regarding the application of the War Crimes Amendment Act 1988 (Cth): *Polyukovich v the Commonwealth of Australia and Another* (1991) 172 CLR 501 F.C. 91/026.

Whilst the notion of instant imprisonment at the behest of the state might seem extreme in most modern administrations, section 5 of the Act did actually allow for this. Garry's status as a prisoner or security patient would continue with any interim order for preventive detention, but section 5(1)(c) went a step further to provide for his detention even *in the event of residence in the community* at the time of the Attorney-General's application. Thus: 'If, immediately before the application is made, Garry David is neither such a prisoner nor such a security patient, he is deemed by reason of this Act to be such a prisoner until the determination of the application, and must be detained in a prison or psychiatric in-patient service.' This overreach of power encompassing one individual was a measure of the Government's desperation to close all possible loopholes. In so doing, it was prepared to ignore legal safeguards, which ordinarily prevent arrest and imprisonment in the absence of a bail hearing.

Justice Fullagar warned Keon-Cohen that the pursuit of due process arguments would effectively incur a significant extra custodial period for his client, especially if a right of appeal were to move to the High Court. As a consequence, the constitutional arguments were held in abeyance. However, by the end of 1991, the Federal Government expressed concern that some aspects of the Garry David case might breach international obligations. The *International Covenant on Civil and Political Rights* was to become enforceable in Australia on 25 December 1991 and the Secretary of the Department of Premier and Cabinet, Peter Kirby, intimated that Victoria was unprepared for the fact that citizens' complaints about state or federal laws breaching this Covenant could be taken directly to the UN Human Rights Committee, and the Garry David case could conceivably become a source of international embarrassment (*The Age*, 11 December 1991; also Charlesworth 1991, pp.428–34). Since Garry was well accustomed to using all available legal remedies to redress his grievances, there was a real likelihood that he would enjoy taking his cause into the international arena on the grounds that the Community Protection Act was an abuse of civil rights constituting 'cruel and unusual punishment' tantamount to life imprisonment. Although there is no customary obligation for state legislation to be set aside in such circumstances, courts and administrations do have a clear duty to make decisions in accordance with Australia's international position. At the very least, therefore, some doubt was being cast over the constitutional validity of the Community Protection Act 1990, as well as its compliance with Australia's international obligations.

The pre-hearing period did not progress smoothly and many unforeseen problems arose. Given the marshalling of powerful legal and professional forces, it might have been assumed that Garry would be left with little ability to manipulate his circumstances, but his previous experience of resistance within the prison system added an unexpected edge in the various legal hearings, despite this period being marked by escalating threats, uncontrolled violence and serious self-mutilation. The novelty of being held under the provisions of the Community Protection Act 1990 encouraged him to explore his limited options and reverse his arguments somewhat erratically. If he could not be deemed to be a prisoner in the formal sense, then he claimed the right to reside at the Mont Park Psychiatric Hospital. The fact that the Government had passed the choice of a prison or psychiatric hospital to the court provided the opportunity for him to exploit the inherent weaknesses of any decision and highlight the strange nature of his circumstances, as well as professional doubts about where badness ends and madness begins. His situation carried with it an implicit bargaining power, because he was simultaneously holding out the hope of reformation under unusual conditions outside the ordinary experience of the Supreme Court, then toying with the inducements offered. However, as soon as his wishes were granted, he would mock the decision by testing the capacity of the institution to tolerate some extreme behavioural manifestation of his underlying disorder. He would also watch passively, as large sums of money were expended on refurbishing a security facility for his personal use, then refuse to be located there, giving vent to a mixture of reasonable argument and vitriolic abuse difficult to counter.

On 22 June 1990 preparations were made for him to be placed in detention at Mont Park Hospital's Ward M6, which housed approximately 20 security patients. The decision was difficult, entailing argument about his interim status and the desirability of prison vis-à-vis a psychiatric hospital. As it transpired, the Mont Park move proved to be an ill-fated one, resulting in disturbance to other patients, staff difficulties and a spectacular outburst of self-mutilation and property damage. On 13 July, the Chief Justice was approached to have the Mont Park Order varied and, as a consequence, Garry David returned once again to J Ward. It was recognised that this might well be an interim measure and on 25 July a meeting was convened with representatives from the Attorney-General's Department, the Victoria Police, the Department of Health and the Office of Corrections, regarding his future placement. Garry, with his inimitable contrariness, was now expressing a desire to return to Mont Park, but the health authorities opposed this because of the damage so recently caused and the accompanying assaults on police personnel, who had been required to effect the transfer. J Ward was now regarded as impractical, because of its distant location. Another suggested option was the barren cells of the old City Watchhouse, but this was also rejected on a number of grounds: they were barely suitable for short-term emergencies; the rostered duty police would experience difficulties; and, above, all it would constitute an unfair holding arrangement for Garry should the Court hearing be protracted as anticipated. Whilst prison was considered 'philosophically undesirable', it was nevertheless the best-equipped facility in the circumstances. The outcome of this meeting was the 3 August application by the Attorney-General before Mr Justice Crockett to vary the place of detention from J Ward to Pentridge to allow Garry to attend the Supreme Court proceedings.

Some of these pre-hearing difficulties derived from the cumbersome special legislation created for Garry's preventive detention, but others reflected the techniques and experience honed during a decade of imprisonment. In the first half of 1990 he confidently orchestrated his movement between facilities, increased his involvement with an ever-growing list of professionals, found innovative ways to draw attention to the inequities of his position and used to advantage the vacillation about his legal rights. It was as if the skills acquired in a closed institutional environment were ready to be transposed to the more formal and public structure of a superior court. The problem was that the Government had unwittingly created a vehicle by which Garry David could claim to have been victimised, and this lessened his willingness to evaluate himself morally and limit his actions. In effect, the legislation was the catalyst to exacerbate the most dysfunctional features of his personality disorder.

A RITUAL OF SHAMING

The purpose of the Community Protection Act 1990 was never in doubt. Garry David was named as its sole subject, and it set out the legal method to confirm his dangerousness and provide for his detention.

Another rare instance of 'personal' legislation is that of a law passed by the US Congress to allow the seizure of the late President Nixon's official papers (*Nixon v GSA* 97 [1976] S Ct 2777). In this instance, the Court accepted the unique circumstances and indicated that the attainder clause did not limit Congress from 'legislating for the universe' but noted that 'mere under-inclusiveness is not fatal for the validity of a law under equal protection ... even if the law disadvantages an individual'. Since then, the Supreme Court has required three elements to determine whether a law constitutes attainder, or the specific punishment of any one individual:

1. The burden imposed must be within the historical meaning of legislative punishment.

2. The law, viewed in terms of the type and severity of the burdens imposed, cannot reasonably be said to further non-punitive legislative purposes.

3. The legislative record evinces an...intent to punish.

If tested in the terms of this US requirement, the custodial intent of the Community Protection Act 1990 might not be seen to exclude rehabilitation and thus its unconstitutionality, on the grounds of attainder, could not necessarily be assured.

Section 7 of the Community Protection Act 1990 specifically stated that 'if in the opinion of the Supreme Court, it is necessary to do so, the Court may make an interim Order that Garry David be placed in preventive detention'. In section 8 a Supreme Court Judge was given the power to make an order for preventive detention on the basis of evidence placed before him. The fact that the preliminary skirmishing had failed to reach a satisfactory resolution led Parliament to frame the discourse by transforming a political problem into one dependent on medical expertise, whilst still retaining some semblance of judicial control. This observation is not a criticism of the judicial role in these proceedings, but a reflection of the unusual limitations to which various judges were subjected in the discharge of their obligations under the Act. Their task was bounded by the medical testimony required to establish 'proof' of dangerousness, and thus the legal mechanism for incarceration was triggered by the Court's evaluation of this expert knowledge. It was in this way that the authority of the Victorian Supreme Court was expected to add legitimacy to an unprecedented display of custodial power. The overt level of the discourse concealed the struggle experienced by many witnesses in meshing their professional obligations with their duty to the Court, an aspect explored more fully with reference to the transcripts of proceedings.

The importance of the Community Protection Act 1990 as the focal ritual of the discourse should not be underestimated. The express purpose of preventive detention was fundamentally at odds with the Government's legislative and administrative initiatives designed to enhance the rights of the mentally disordered offender, as has been earlier outlined. This Act also accorded strange powers to a Supreme Court Judge to oversee the collation of relevant material relating to Garry's personality and behaviour. Ordinary psychiatric decision making was, in this instance, to be subjected to the scrutiny of the court in a very public way and sifted for its value according to legal standards of judgment.

Suddenly, outsiders were defining the reality of 'the problem', which could only be dispelled by evidence of the likely absence of fear-inducing behaviour in some unknown future circumstance. Not surprisingly, this pragmatic, legislative solution to almost two decades of relative inaction in relation to habitual or dangerous offenders was surrounded by controversy, with lawyers and others expressing disquiet about its implications for civil liberties and its incompatibility with the tenor of legal principles. However from the political viewpoint, it was an unassailable mechanism to present 'the facts' persuasively to the wider community through press coverage of the ensuing court hearings.

Although all legislation is symbolic in expressing the values and behaviour acceptable to a given society in a precise and succinct form, that specifically designed for the control of a named person is indubitably so. It suggests that the behaviour of this one individual is so flagrantly outside ordinary moral boundaries that an extraordinary display of the state's punitive power is justified to reassert society's authority (see Durkheim 1964, orig. 1893; Foucault 1977b; Garland 1990; Mead 1918). Despite the care taken to present the inquiry in a mode of abstract, rational discourse, its basic intent could not be camouflaged. The government had established a unique legislative instrument steeped in the imagery and symbolism of exclusion, and sought to draw psychiatrists within its ambit. The Act bore witness to a power struggle in the territorial sense and, at the same time, exposed an infringement of legal principles together with ambiguities in psychiatric knowledge.

In many respects the framework of the legislation, with its emphasis on the public disclosure of a lifelong pattern of misbehaviour, fostered a technique of entrapment linking it to Harold Garfinkel's analysis of a status degradation ceremony. In this author's view, the ceremony is a public mechanism of denunciation by which a person's social identity is relocated to a lower level in the categorisation of social types, allowing a new identity to be created to replace the former one (Garfinkel 1956, pp.420–24). Shaming is an accepted part of a society's solidarity and, for Garfinkel, the more problematic issue should centre on the communication strategy facilitating the denunciation. It is then relevant to ask whether the degradation ceremony actually leads to a changed total identity and how a successful outcome can be determined (Garfinkel 1956, p.421). The application of this approach to the Garry David case raises questions about the appropriateness of the Victorian Government's response to his custody by overriding ordinary legal conventions and widening professional divisions of opinion. A successful degradation ceremony should strengthen the political hand and, therefore, one would expect its subject to be chosen with due care and act submissively in the face of an overwhelming display of power; otherwise the public message would be diluted and the meaning of the ritual questionable. In the Garry David case, however, there is strong evidence that the Government embarked on a course which did not have the required degree of certitude owing to its unstable foundation of 'dangerousness' and its subject's retaliatory tactics.

Initially, the Government gained the upper hand in what was an overtly sociopolitical exercise posing the stark choice between release or incarceration based on experts' identification of the possession of dangerous attributes. Not only was there little room for judicial manoeuvring, but the fact that this legislation had been enacted in the first place seemed to confirm its political necessity. It signalled the Government's belief in dangerous persons roaming abroad for whom ordinary court sanctions might be insufficient. If Garry fell into a limbo somewhere between badness and madness, then the creation of the bridging category of potential dangerousness shifted the argument by providing a point of demarcation, which seemingly justified action of a special kind, because of the ostensibly unique circumstances. The legislation had the advantage of being apolitical in its appeal to community protection. It was still a risky step to take and invoked community apprehension, but at the same time the creation of a special status category sought to *explain* that apprehension as being legitimate and medically based (see Moynihan 1992). This tactic could easily have rebounded, because there is a delicate balance in the Australian psyche between translating the definition of dangerousness into the public idiom and lauding a defiance of authority, as in the legendary exploits of such figures as Ned Kelly and William O'Malley. Nonetheless, in this instance, the Government appeared to be pinning its hopes on the legislation acting as a powerful tool to shape people's perceptions and behaviour in an ambiguous situation, for the process of governance is dependent on moulding opinions to achieve a certain outcome (see Edelman 1971). In this instance, the Government needed to arrive at some synthesis of expert and lay views and the evocative term 'dangerousness' tapped into community fears and professional knowledges to become the pivot for the multi-layered discourse to follow. It evinced a tacit understanding that societies need social defence strategies to control the unmanageable, and it also indicated that such persons are identifiable and can be made governable. Inevitably, however, a strategy of this sort is symbolic, decontextualised and condensed. This is unsurprising, for as Edelman has argued elsewhere:

> Both legal and psychiatric discourse deals with roles and metaphors rather than with complex human beings; for both highlight individual virtues and vices rather than the opportunities and frustrations that flow from social structure. (Edelman 1980, p.237)

In the context of the Government's strategy, it was advantageous that Garry David's social structure was a prison environment with a very different pattern of interaction and behaviour, and this would have been of less interest both to the Court and the public at large than his instigation of dramatic events whilst in custody. Thus the Act was an expedient and persuasive measure in the absence of other acceptable solutions, but nevertheless it is unlikely that the full consequences of the various protracted judicial hearings were anticipated. In essence, they led to uncertainties in the handling of the professional discourse and unforeseen difficulties in Garry's management on a day-to-day basis. Aspects such as political authority, knowledge of the individual and risk assessment became inextricably linked, and these will be recounted through the various events, strategies and attempts of professionals to maintain their independence in decision making.

POLITICAL STRATEGIES AND THE REACTION

During the next three years, the Government sought more lasting solutions to the problem of those perceived to be dangerous and pursued alternative models. Its first foray into more general dangerous offenders legislation began in mid-1990, but had embarrassing repercussions when the Attorney-General was castigated by Justice Fullagar for agreeing to present a public lecture on the matter during the hearing of the Community Protection Act and seeking to justify this action on the grounds of Garry's dangerousness. His unwise comments had been: 'Does anyone seriously argue that Garry David should be released? If the answer is no, then we have to do something before the legislation keeping him in jail expires in March' (*Herald-Sun*, 8 August 1990).

Justice Fullagar responded by pointing out that a Minister of the Government who had 'burdened the Supreme Court with having to decide the matter' had undermined his own legal action, and there was a possibility that his remarks constituted contempt of court by publicly pre-judging the issue of Garry's dangerousness. They may also have cemented Garry David's opinion about a high-level conspiracy to keep him behind bars (*First Hearing*, 7 August 1990). The matter was adjourned until an apology for the unguarded ministerial comments was forthcoming. The Attorney-General immediately responded by saying that he had intended only to facilitate discussion about the need for general preventive detention and his remarks were not in reference to Garry David.

Whilst the Attorney-General had not sought to undermine the authority of the Court, his aim of finding a more permanent solution to the issue of dangerous persons was clearly on the agenda. By the end of 1991, a draft of the Community Protection (Violent Offenders) Bill was released and this immediately invoked criticisms in the Second and Third Reports of the Social Development Committee's *Inquiry into Mental Disturbance and Community Safety*. The Committee considered that the matter came squarely within their terms of reference and recommended to the Victorian Government:

1. That the proposed Draft Community Protection (Violent Offenders) Bill not proceed;

2. That at the expiry of the present sunset clause, the Community Protection Act 1990 not be extended.

3. That no legislation for the preventive detention of violent offenders proceed, given the current unreliability of predicting dangerousness.

4. That the involuntary admission criteria of the Mental Health Act 1986 not be amended to include a person with a personality disorder alone; and that the Act not be used for the involuntary detention of a person with a personality disorder alone who is deemed to be a threat to the safety of the community. (SDC *Third Report*, April 1992, p.v).

For a Parliamentary Committee to display such opposition to a Government's position was unusual, if not unprecedented, and even more pronounced with chapter headings such as: 'The Draft Bill is Unnecessary'; 'The Draft Bill is Misconceived'; 'The Draft Bill is Counterproductive'; 'The Draft Bill Will Erode Human Rights'.

The Australian Institute of Criminology, based in Canberra, was alarmed by the implications of the Community Protection (Violent Offenders) Bill and took the unusual step of canvassing professional opinion with a hastily convened conference in Melbourne on 'Serious Violent Offenders: Sentencing, Psychiatry and Law Reform' in October 1991. Not unexpectedly, the tenor of the papers was highly critical of this form of legislation, both on civil libertarian grounds and because of the clinical implications. Those offenders deemed to be dangerous by virtue of their 'severe personality disorder' would, under this model, be subjected to either a negotiated post-sentence supervision arrangement or a community protection order for a three-year period, with the possibility of renewal. The onus for diagnosis and ultimately the selection of this pool of offenders would effectively pass to psychiatrists, thus transforming their clinical skills into ones of custodial intent. Whilst private practitioners would be unaffected by this legislation, those in the public sector might well be compromised by ministerial pressure exercised through correctional or mental health authorities. In addition, the framing of the legislation would pose special difficulties for the Adult Parole Board of Victoria, since this body would be responsible for overseeing the negotiated agreements – a fundamentally different task from their statutory one of intervening in an individual's lifestyle within fixed sentence parameters. The proposed extension of their role hinted at supervision by executive decree with a possible impact on the Board's traditional independence in decision making.

As had occurred with the earlier Law Reform Commission Report, resistance to this new Bill was immediate. Dr Michael Duke expressed the view of the Victorian Branch of the College that it was 'seriously flawed, impractical and unachievable'. He argued that the mentally ill were the rightful responsibility of psychiatrists, but that the severely personality disordered required an ability to predict dangerousness, and psychiatrists could only do so in the most general sense. In addition, they were hampered by the paucity of evidence about successful treatment programmes. He issued the challenge that: 'To coerce psychiatrists to act as jailers for the state, in a situation where they acknowledge their limitations, will bring the Government and the profession into conflict and disrepute' (*The Age*, 2 April 1992).

Two weeks later, the Government was warned that psychiatrists in public hospitals might withhold their services, or even resign, should the Bill become law (*The Age*, 17 April 1992). At this point, the Attorney-General, Jim Kennan, questioned their right to decide the issue, claiming that they had a vested interest in the matter. He then used an analogy which he raised on a number of other occasions to detract from the professional issues involved. It was a crude appeal to populism, drawing on the fear-inducing undercurrents created by a well-known film depicting a predatory psychopath, who also happened to be a psychiatrist. It served Kennan's purpose in a double-edged way: the image he was raising through various media interviews was that of a flesh-eating monster in the guise of an articulate, highly trained professional. The recurring question he posed was: 'Would the community agree with psychiatrists that Hannibal Lecter, the character who eats other humans in *The Silence of the Lambs*, should not be detained in a mental institution to protect the public?' (*The Age*, 17 April 1992).

This was little more than a ploy intended to highlight the intransigence of psychiatrists and suggest that they were sheltering behind a form of knowledge out of touch with the reality of community fears, even to the extent of placing public safety at risk in the most basic physical sense. The headlines confirmed the strength of the Government's resolve to override relevant professional support and the headlines became increasingly bizarre with one front-page report proclaiming 'State Needs a "Cannibal" Law – Kennan' (*Herald-Sun*, 30 April 1992). The dissonance between the fictional image of Lecter with its overtones of cannibalism and Garry David, whose dismemberment of human flesh was actually his own, was camouflaged by the vividness of the body image and language. The rhetoric nevertheless was reassuring: 'vicious criminals with personality disorders – like the film character Hannibal "the Cannibal" Lecter – will face indefinite jail terms' (*Herald-Sun*, 30 April 1992). The visceral quality of an intuitive repugnance to cannibalism was difficult to counter with more rational arguments, such as the unconstitutional aspects of the legislation and its flawed basis of dangerousness prediction (*The Age*, 15 May 1992). Kennan's allusion to *Silence of the Lambs* carried more weight than the oft-repeated comment of Dr Grigor that, in his view, Garry David persisted in making threats to ensure his continued incarceration and if he [Grigor] took him 'to the front door and told him to go, he would turn around and run back inside. He is a troubled, poor wet poop' (*Sunday Herald*, 15 April 1990). It was a skilful 'one-liner', at once conveying concern about Garry's plight and bemusement that others were treating the case more seriously than it merited.

The political spectre of cannibalism versus the psychiatric one of 'a poor wet poop' cast the debate in an unedifying light. However, not all psychiatrists were convinced of Dr Grigor's picturesque description, which was designed to put to rest connotations of dangerousness. For Dr Bill Orchard, a Melbourne private psychiatrist, the issues were simple: lawyers should not intrude on psychiatric territory; and personality disorder must be equated with psychosis, since the associated symptoms typically appear in a transient way. His rather confused letter, headed 'Garry David Law: Is Rest of World Out of Step?', is illustrative of some clinicians' lack of knowledge about forensic practice, particularly the realities of day-to-day management in the prison (*The Age*, 15 May 1992). Its force diminished by juxtaposition with a very reasonable one from Garry himself ('I Have No Program to which to Respond'), together with one from a senior school student ('Students are Right to Study this Man'). In his letter, Orchard charged forensic psychiatrists with abandoning 'traditional concepts of psychosis' because of their legalistic bent:

> Victorians should realise that the concept of madness was around long before psychiatrists existed. Mr Justice Vincent is correct in questioning the nous of forensic psychiatrists who pronounce Garry David sane. Some common sense, please! Can a person, who is so compulsively violent that he himself is concerned, and who cuts off his nipples and bits of his penis and eats them be sane? I would be very surprised if Garry David was not insane on an MMPI and Rorshach examination. Without knowing the clinical facts, I suggest that Garry David is on psychotropic medication in prison, which is not in keeping

with the diagnosis of personality disorder, for which there is no appropriate medication. The Government should go back to its mental health legislation and revise this. And the lawyers should keep out of medicine's territory!

It should be noted that a less exasperated letter by the same author appeared two weeks later, expressing a more reasonable view of the problem from his perspective – 'The Dilemma of the Briefly Psychotic' (*The Age*, 2 June 1992). Here he deplores the restrictive threshold of mental health legislation that depends on 'the appearance' of mental illness, which may be concealed by a 'mask of sanity'. He believed that 'the Government has to revise radically the Act, not compound the situation by passing a fascist-type law'.

At this stage, the campaign was beginning to bear a marked similarity with aspects of the earlier Tait case, in which the issue of the mental state of the prisoner was in doubt and the Government had sought to override the views of psychiatrists and lawyers in an arbitrary manner. Now, in 1992, there were 30 identifiable community and church groups, as well as professional organisations, opposed to broad dangerous offenders' legislation. Dr Don Thomson, a spokesman for the Australian Psychological Society, confirmed the views of his professional body and indicated that there might be a lack of psychologists complying with court requests to diagnose criminals with personality disorders as being potentially dangerous (*The Sunday Age*, 17 May 1992). Margaret Ray, a senior member of the Labor Party and Chairman of the Social Development Committee, threatened to organise a revolt in caucus and Cabinet to thwart the wishes of the Attorney-General, even though such an action would probably have resulted in her own political expulsion (*Progress Press*, 13 May 1992). On a practical level she pointed out that an Act of this nature must inevitably be discriminatory, because the Office of Corrections had identified 161 Pentridge prisoners as fulfilling the sentencing provisions of the draft Bill, 50 of whom could be detained indefinitely on the basis of their likely future actions. The highly variable estimates given of prisoners with severe personality disorders further reflect the ambiguity of the boundary between badness and madness. It is difficult terrain, which invokes administrative, staffing and economic consequences for the Department accepting management responsibility and it is therefore highly negotiable, even if, as in the current case, this negotiation is politically driven rather than professionally directed.

Although the focus of the political activity had broadened, Garry David was germane to the exercise and his continued detention remained an embarrassment to authorities. A large number of Victorian Certificate of Education students had chosen to study preventive detention as their first common assessment task for the subject Legal Studies because it raised controversial legal issues. Many took the initiative to write to Garry at Pentridge for his view of the events. Some of them requested visits, until the Office of Corrections finally issued a formal plea to desist because the 'unwarranted and uninvited attention' might lead to management problems for the prisoner (*The Age*, 30 April 1992). Garry David, however, was undeterred. He delighted in the interest from such an unexpected quarter and accommodatingly produced a kit with audiotapes and written material for purchase by schools at the cost of $40.

In this climate, the strength of opposition to the possible preventive detention of the severely personality disordered continued to mount. For example, a large advertisement was placed in the daily newspapers with signatories representing a variety of organisations; Parliament's own Scrutiny of Bills and Regulations Committee rushed through some unusually adverse comments; and a public forum, chaired by Sir Edward Woodward, Chancellor of the University of Melbourne and a former Supreme Court Judge, was convened to debate the proposals. Despite these moves, the legislation was passed by parliament on 13 May 1992.

This chapter has traced the external activity centering around Garry David prior to the implementation of the Community Protection Act and the Government's attempts to replace this particular piece of legislation with more general preventive detention provisions, even though it had a history of resisting the use of sentencing of this nature. It has detailed the interplay between politics, law and psychiatry through the responses of the Social Development Committee, the Law Institute of Victoria, the Law Reform Commission of Victoria, the Royal Australian and New Zealand College of Psychiatrists and those of individual lawyers, psychiatrists and politicians. Whilst the discourse was being shaped on the periphery as a prelude to the hearing of the Act, Garry was beginning to test his exceedingly limited options, in order to wrest a measure of autonomy in unusually restrictive circumstances. The next step was for the main players to come together under the aegis of the Supreme Court of Victoria. The spotlight was now cast directly onto Garry David and his deviations of personality and behaviour. Next, I chart the construction of this discourse about dangerousness and consider just how lawyers and psychiatrists shaped the problem given to them by the Government. A number of questions immediately come to mind.

- Can dangerousness be defined in a way compatible with the interests of the community, the law, government and psychiatry?

- Did this legislation constitute a status degradation ceremony in the sense of absolute state power pitted against one individual, or did its subject retain an ability to temper the outcome?

- To what extent did the Act provide a resolution for the problem which the government had defined?

These are important questions, for all governments have a responsibility to fulfil their duty of safeguarding the welfare of those unable to care for themselves and protecting the community from foreseeable dangers. The mentally disordered challenge the compatibility of these functions, as well as the administrative separation of mental illness and criminality, as will be seen in the following chapter.

CHAPTER 6

The Supreme Court

David versus Goliath

The combination of madness and alleged dangerousness perhaps poses the greatest challenge to sentencers since it is always possible that harsher measures of restraint will be imposed on the mentally disordered offender, who is alleged to be dangerous, than would be imposed on the serious offender who is considered to be 'normal'. Furthermore, there is always the danger that such restrictive measures will be imposed upon mentally disordered offenders without the benefit of the due process of law that, in theory at least, is emphasized in the sentencing of 'normal' offenders. (Verdun-Jones 1989, p.1)

In such a matter, it seems to me, there can be no precise rules. The court is expected to rule on the qualifications of an expert witness, relying partly on what the expert himself explains, and partly on what is assumed, though seldom expressed, namely that there exists a general framework of discourse in which it is possible for the court, the expert and all men according to their degrees of education, to understand each other. Ex hypothesi this does not extend to the interior scope of the subject which the expert professes. But it is assumed that the judge can sufficiently grasp the nature of the expert's field of knowledge, relate it to his own general knowledge, and thus decide whether the expert has sufficient experience of a particular matter to make his evidence admissible. The process involves an exercise of personal judgment on the part of the judge, for which authority provides little help. (Blackburn J. in *Milirrpum v Nabalco Pty Ltd* [1971] 17 FLR 141 at 160)

FRAMING A DISCOURSE OF DANGEROUSNESS

The Supreme Court of Victoria is an imposing grey Victorian structure oriented around a central dome. The older courtrooms with their dark timber panelling and red upholstery add to a sombre effect, undiminished by the soft greys, creams and blues of the ornate plaster ceilings. The central focus of the criminal courts is the elaborately carved canopy with its throne-like chair elevating the judge from the body of the court and from the long bar table below, at which sit robed counsel and instructing solicitors. The positioning of all participants is important in this ritualised setting. The defendant or appellant is physically removed, but clearly visible in the enclosed dock and members of the public must view proceedings from the safe distance of the upper gallery. It is a criminal jurisdiction with adversarial-type proceedings, which follow a clearly understood sequence governed by rules. Generally, evidence offered to the court must be factual; that is, within the witness's direct knowledge or observation of the events that have occurred, and it is tested by a process of cross-examination. Those cases dependent on a formal assessment of the accused's state of mind at the time of committing the act are relatively infrequent and handled differently, with expert witnesses being able to assist the jury's decision-making by drawing on inferences and hearsay in arriving at their professional observations. Should the charge or charges be proven to the jury's satisfaction, then it is the Judge's duty to pass sentence in accordance with established legal principles and within the parameters set by parliament.

These familiar elements of the legal process have been recounted because they are an inherent part of the protective fabric of the law, and yet they were challenged in a myriad of ways during Garry David's appearance in courtroom number 4 as the respondent to an application made under the Community Protection Act of 1990. Parliament had placed the court in an invidious position and ordinary methods of handling its criminal jurisdiction were difficult from the outset, because the central issue was not this man's criminality, but proof of his dangerousness. A unique legal framework for decision-making had to be devised and this did not sit well with the law's sense of predictability, continuity and justice in the application of its principles and rules.

It was evident that the Community Protection Act 1990 was not conceived as a general measure for preventive detention, but as the vehicle by which an administrative solution to a difficult person could be achieved. In this way the separation of powers was at issue and the executive was passing on to the judiciary a specific problem, whilst maintaining a semblance of objectivity and fairness. Its failure to have Garry securely relegated to the category of mental illness had led to the shift in emphasis from 'madness' to 'dangerousness', thus entailing the need for community protection. However, the use of the criminal justice pathway was politically motivated and distorted ordinary Supreme Court procedures to the extent that there were many judicial asides about the Government's abrogation of its responsibility, particularly in the early discussion stages with counsel. For example, Justice Fullagar was blunt about a task he considered to be strange and singularly distasteful:

> I think it is an order so as everyone can blame the court if anything goes wrong, so that no blame can attach to anyone except the Judge. (*First Hearing*, 1 June 1990)

And in the context of the hearing itself, he commented:

> The buck has been thrown by Parliament at this Court... The Court is in the position where the Government can say if the Judge locks him up, 'What a

wicked thing to do and deprive him of his liberty.' If the Judge lets him out
and he savages some people, they say 'It was the Court that did it.' Great bit of
bravery! (*First Hearing*, 18 June 1990)

This observation guaranteed media exposure and the headlines duly proclaimed:
'Buckpass on Webb: Judge' (*Sun*, 19 June 1990) and 'Parliament has Passed the
Buck on Garry Webb, Says Judge' (*The Age*, 19 June 1990).

Justice Hedigan, in the second application under the Act, was equally adamant
about the implied loss of judicial discretion and observed:

The Community Protection Act 1990 passes the duty of making a relevant
decision to the Supreme Court of Victoria. In many jurisdictions, but not all,
that task, in the absence of habitual offenders' legislation, is left to judicial
determination… (*Second Hearing*, Judgment, 15 November 1991, p.81)

At the outset, there was more than usual attention given to security arrangements, a
matter indicative of the Court's nervousness about the possibility of disruption.
Garry chose to be present and this caused Justice Fullagar some concern in case the
defendant's 'dangerousness' should put any member of the public at risk. He
instructed police to provide security at the Court's entrance and in the public
gallery. After several days, undoubtedly influenced by Garry's calm demeanour,
this ruling was relaxed, although security remained tight throughout as a visible
reminder of the nature of the problem with which the Court was dealing. Two
years later, fears that Garry would orchestrate some disturbance inimical to court
proceedings had evaporated and counsel successfully argued that, owing to the
civil rather than criminal nature of the proceedings, their client should sit in the
body of the court rather than the dock.

On a conceptual level the choice of 'dangerousness' as the focal point of the
entire exercise exposed the differing frameworks of the legal and medical professions. Psychiatry had long been trying to shed responsibility for predicting the
dangerousness of persons involved in court proceedings, and pointed to empirical
studies disclaiming any special expertise in this arena. Interestingly, the law exudes
far more confidence, as Justice Fullagar made clear at the outset when he noted, 'I
don't need anyone to tell me what dangerousness means in the statute.' He added
that although in his perception 'criminology and psychiatry use words technically', he had more pragmatic concerns than the concept of dangerousness prediction and was simply 'interested in what this man will do, if he gets out' (*First
Hearing*, 8 August 1990). This comment was possibly influenced by his previous
experience in the *R v Darrington and McGauley* case, briefly discussed in the
previous chapter.

Only one forensic psychiatrist with extensive court experience spanning more
than 30 years was prepared to offer an opinion with the degree of certainty desired

by the law, and his stance undoubtedly emanated from his long knowledge of and sympathy with the legal process. Dr Allen Bartholomew was well known to the Victorian courts and had learned to bridge the gulf between psychiatric concepts and legal requirements with an unusual degree of clarity. Since his arrival in Victoria in 1959, he had appeared in most cases involving mental state defences and was highly regarded by judges of the Supreme and County Courts for his ability to distil the essence of psychiatric notions into the requisite legal format. In the *R v Darrington and McGauley* case, for example, Justice Fullagar had accepted his opinion that a defence psychologist's testimony in the matter 'was not provided by study in the field of psychology or psychiatry' (*R v Darrington and McGauley* [1980] ALR 124 at 157). Now, 11 years later, in this newly forged terrain of dangerousness on which the Court was embarking, it was not unexpected that this same Judge should describe Dr Bartholomew as 'an impressive and reliable witness', and put much credence on this psychiatrist's reiteration of views given in press interviews that Garry was a seriously dangerous person – 'one of half a dozen of the most dangerous persons I have met' (*First Hearing*, 18 September, 1990 p.23). Bartholomew's view had been used earlier by the police in their campaign to extend Garry's incarceration. For example, the headline in the *Sun* (15 December 1990) warned: 'Don't Let Him Out: Expert Warns of Risk – *He Could Kill*', and this was reinforced the following day with the report that 'Webb is [was] one of the most dangerous men he had met during 27 years at the gaol' ('Police Plan Webb Charge', *Sun*, 16 December 1989). By any measure it was an unusually confident psychiatric assertion.

In Bartholomew's analysis of the role of the expert psychiatric witness, he has always maintained that psychiatry is too often seduced by the law to 'enlarge its sphere of influence' and provide evidence outside its area of knowledge (Bartholomew 1986). In his view, information should be given about a diagnosis and held to account by the material on which it is based, but there should not be the tame provision of answers to other 'unpsychiatric' questions, such as intent and future dangerousness (p.210). Yet, in reality, Dr Bartholomew's own role in criminal trial procedures, and as a witness under the Community Protection Act 1990, had led him down this very same path. His opinion was at odds with the more equivocal responses of other witnesses, whose responsibilities tended to focus on the treatment role, rather than the court one. For example, Dr John Grigor told the Judge:

> One cannot predict dangerousness and forensic events. He [Garry David] is more puff and blow, than substance. If his bluff is called, my clinical opinion is that in a situation of confrontation he would be dangerous, if he had antipathy to police or others. (*First Hearing*, 8 August 1990)

Later, he softened his remarks by explaining that:

> Garry retains such an appalling self-image that he is indeed evil beyond com-
> prehension, that when people respond positively to him he finds this very
> threatening, becomes so destructive in the relationship that eventually he
> frightens people, who have become revolted by him, and let him know this.
> (*Second Hearing*, Judgment, 15 November 1991, p.19)

Throughout the hearing expert witnesses displayed a dysjunction between recognising the warnings in the academic literature and their personal belief that clinical
skills *did* give psychiatrists an edge in the assessment of dangerousness. When
counsel for Garry later asked Dr Grigor whether 'any part of his training permitted
him to offer opinions about dangerousness that are different from those of
community members', he agreed that he could comment 'more intelligently' and
project his opinion 'more accurately than an ordinary member of the community'
(*First Hearing*, 8 August 1990). On further questioning, he justified this accuracy as
stemming from his knowledge of Garry's past history and agreed that there was
indeed a measure of 'common sense' in arriving at such a conclusion. Later, he
accepted the proposition that it is notoriously difficult for anyone to predict dangerousness, but maintained that 'psychiatrists have a greater understanding of the
likelihood of the prediction of dangerousness in the mentally ill' (*First Hearing*, 8
August 1990).

The concept of 'dangerousness' in these initial proceedings was foreign to
psychiatric thinking, for it posed a binary divide between the attribute of dangerousness and non-dangerousness without regard for the specific context. There was
a real possibility that once dangerousness had been proven to the Supreme Court's
satisfaction, it would become the benchmark and subsequent hearings would only
add to the cumulation of violent incidents and threats, thereby lessening the likelihood of analysing the construct itself. In this regard, the Act was deficient. It
offered little guidance about the weight to be given to previous findings, and in the
ensuing applications the Court found itself almost in the position of a court of
appeal with discretion to veer from the original finding severely limited. As Justice
Smith later noted: 'I cannot think of any other case where a court considers applications heard previously except the Court of Appeal. Family law may come across
this problem from time to time, where there is an ongoing battle over custody and
access' (*Third Hearing and Second Appeal*, 30 October 1992).

Although some of the psychiatric opinions had an emotive quality, undoubtedly stemming from previous difficult interactions with Garry, and most were
based on undeniable generalisations about his propensity for violence, the Court
accepted these views as providing the substance of section 8(1) of the Act; that is,
proof of Garry being 'a serious risk to the safety of any member of the public' and
being 'likely to commit any act of personal violence to another person'. To do

otherwise would have been to ignore psychiatric opinions offered in evidence and firmed by direct legal questioning. Throughout the various hearings there remained an ambiguity about the phrases used in section 8(1), which were termed the 'critical requirements', and this extended to the language and powers of the Act, particularly the meaning of such fundamental terms as 'preventive detention' and 'community protection'. These matters remained central to the arguments employed in all the applications placed before the Court. (There were nine Supreme Court Judges involved at some stage in applications relating to the Community Protection Act 1990 from 1990 to 1993. In chronological order, these were Justices Gobbo, Marks, Fullagar, Crockett, Young CJ, Hedigan, Harper, Tadgell and Smith.) In this first hearing into Garry's dangerousness under the Community Protection Act 1990, Justice Fullagar determined that the critical requirements of the legislation had been satisfied and he consequently ordered Garry to be detained for six months preventive detention in J Ward at Ararat (*First Hearing*, 18 September 1990).

The second hearing of the Act before Justice Hedigan, covered 12 days between 19 September and 15 November 1991, and was distinguished by detailed inquiry into the nature of the evidence needed to satisfy the concepts of 'serious risk', 'likely to commit', 'member of the public', 'act of personal violence', and 'another person'. Whilst counsel for the Attorney-General argued that the inculcation of fear in any member of the community would be sufficient to meet the requirements of the Act, Justice Hedigan rejected this view in favour of receiving evidence about the likelihood of *bodily violence*, otherwise Garry would always be seen as satisfying the criteria of dangerousness and Judges would simply be ratifying previous decisions in an ongoing process (*Second Hearing*, Judgment, 15 November 1991, p.90). Justice Hedigan also vigorously rejected a further argument advanced by Michael Adams that the mere diagnoses of borderline personality disorder or antisocial personality disorder were sufficient to establish the critical requirements:

Hedigan: If you are going to investigate his personality, then ipso facto is he dangerous?

Adams   Yes.

Hedigan: This makes the Act outrageous. The word 'serious' becomes irrelevant. (*Second Hearing*, 15 October 1991)

This comment was further reinforced with several references to the Act being a 'charade' if personality disorder and dangerousness were to be inextricably linked in this way (*Second Hearing*, 15 October 1991).

Not only was the method of investigation into personality attributes problematic, but related terms from the mental health field such as 'care', 'management', and 'treatment' were as capable of an everyday general meaning as a technical one, and there was no clear direction regarding the intent of Parliament, as the Mental Health Review Board had also discovered to be the case with regard to 'mental illness'. This highlighted the traditional difficulty that the law experiences in arriving at some precision about the meaning of behavioural abnormalities and mental state impairment. Each Judge faced the onerous task of charting new ground to assess Garry's propensity for violence and handle the seemingly boundless scope of relevant supporting material. Even the selection of a time frame for the collation of the documentation to be used as the primary source of evidence proved contentious, when Michael Adams suggested that Garry's *entire life in custody* should be appraised for evidence of violence and threats to others. If this were to occur, then Judges were being placed in the unenviable position of trying to distinguish between appropriate and inappropriate responses elicited within an institutional context of which they could not have direct knowledge.

Although 'dangerousness' plays a specific role in the administration of the law because of its close association with potential recidivism, it had never previously been accorded quite the same centrality as required by the Community Protection Act; nor was preventive detention legislation philosophically acceptable to Victorian sentencing policy. Indeed, whilst other states and the Northern Territory had measures in place to detain either dangerous or habitual offenders, similar Victorian legislation had been repealed in 1985, ensuring that the common law principle of proportionality remained paramount as a sentencing objective (see Campbell 1988; Borsody and Van Groningen 1990; Svensson 1993). Section 192 of the Social Welfare Act 1970 pertaining to habitual offenders was repealed in 1991. More general moves to incorporate preventive detention as an additional form of punishment have been effectively constrained by the High Court cases of *Veen No. 1* [1979] 143 CLR 458 and *Veen No. 2* [1988] CLR 465 F.C. 88/011; this second case suggesting that it might be appropriately integrated with other sentencing factors in certain cases. Any introduction of indefinite detention, therefore, represented a radical policy reversal, made all the more remarkable for its distinctive features, which were out of step even with the variable practices of other Australian jurisdictions. As Professor Richard Fox is at pains to point out:

> There is, in fact, remarkably little consistency between the States in the form of their indeterminate detention legislation, the criteria for invoking it, the procedural safeguards to be applied, whether the measure is an extension of or substitute for a conventional sentence, and what are the steps to be taken to effect the ultimate release of the offender. (Fox 1993, p.406)

Not only was the Community Protection Act singular in its application, but the judgment of dangerousness was to be applied retrospectively at a time when all other Australian habitual offender statutes imposed it as a surcharge on sentencing for a criminal offence, or offences. In addition, the standard of proof was on the lesser standard of the Supreme Court being satisfied 'on the balance of probabilities' (section 8). There is an interesting comparison here with the determination of bail applications, whereby a person found to be 'an unacceptable risk that ... would endanger the safety or welfare of members of the public' appears to be based on the criminal standard of proof, presumably because the law views the deprivation of liberty with gravity (section 4(2)(d)(l) Bail Act 1977 (Vic); see also discussion by Priest 1992).

The discourse of dangerousness framed by the Community Protection Act symbolised the most public process of excluding one person from ordinary participation in society ever devised in Victoria. The Supreme Court invested the exercise with a credibility and moral authority not otherwise achievable, so that dangerousness could act as a political 'condensation symbol' defusing contention and enhancing the appearance of consensus (Edelman 1988). As I have argued elsewhere:

> Once the law attaches the label [of dangerousness] to a person, it does so with authority and clarity. Competent, respected professionals combine to bring a judgment to bear on someone whose actions or utterances are considered threatening to society. The concept is reified in what is a symbolic exercise of political power, which can then later be invoked in times of fear or uncertainty. Government distances itself by passing the responsibility to a court to persuade us of the rationality and morality of the solution initially devised by Parliament. (Greig 1993, p.51)

CUSTODY BY EXECUTIVE DECREE AND THE CONSEQUENCES

Whilst tribunals such as the Mental Health Review Board are quasi-judicial in format, superior courts are very different in terms of their powers and decision-making procedures. In this instance, the custodial purpose of the Act was understood and the Court struggled to balance due process with some regard for the format pertaining to a criminal-type setting. It was an uncomfortable compromise which surfaced in occasional asides, such as the rhetorical question posed by Michael Adams to Justice Marks in an early directions hearing: 'Has your Honour drawn the short straw to deal with this application?' (15 May 1990); and Justice Fullagar's: 'All I can do is complain about the legislation' (*First Hearing*, 6 August 1990).

There were many competing elements in Community Protection Act hearings, which had to satisfy not only legal imperatives, but political, moral and professional ones as well (for analyses of the symbolic and moral interplay of social events see Moore and Myerhoff 1977; Turner 1990 and Wagner-Pacifici 1986).

The law provided the framework for organising the competing elements of the discourse and gave the illusion that it was an exercise within its ordinary parameters. However, on another view, it proved to be a costly and cumbersome legal charade, even though each Judge handled the matters with great sensitivity. At the political level there was some short-term success in enabling the Government to regain ground after a number of unexpectedly humiliating defeats over the custody of Garry David. Its expectation was that this new legislation would be outside the vagaries of the decision-making powers of less august bodies. Thus the Attorney-General was a party to the proceedings, almost in a prosecutorial capacity, paving the way for the defendant to be brought before the court and making available much of the documentary evidence on which the case would be based. This is a notable departure from criminal court hearings. In this instance, counsel for the Attorney-General approached Justice Gobbo on 14 May 1990 to allow him to make orders for Garry to be present for the hearing of the Act.

It can be argued that the role of the Supreme Court was superfluous and window-dressing, since the clinical and prison records were already the property of Government departments and the more formal imprimatur of external decision making was simply a political stratagem. As Williams has written, a more 'correct approach to the issue would have been to pass an Act giving the Minister power to detain David, and for that power to have been exercised on the responsibility of the Minister' without involving the Supreme Court at all (Williams 1990, p.177).

But there was an even more important consequence of the Attorney-General's power in this case, which was outside the customary legal framework. He was the only one able to initiate the order for preventive detention, and thereby take advantage of its immediate holding powers. He controlled the timing of each application, which meant that he could increase the period of detention by choosing to make an application immediately prior to the cessation of any one order. Garry would then be remanded in custody during the progress of sequential hearings, extending his incarceration beyond the limits specified within the legislation. As a consequence of this executive power, Garry was subjected to an additional 11 months in custody over a 17-month period and, as Fairall has commented, this amounted to 'a significant period of *pre-trial* detention on the basis of administrative action', unmotivated by any criminal charge (Fairall 1993, p.44). The dates concerned were: 10 June to 18 September 1990 during the hearing of the first application; 18 April to 15 November 1991 for the second application; and 18 March to 23 April 1991 prior to the passing of the amendments to the Act. The Social Development Committee noted that this untoward extension of custody might well constitute a breach of Article 9(4) of the UN International Covenant on Civil and Political Rights (SDC, *Second Report*, March 1992, p.163; *Third Report*, April 1992, p.77). Garry's liberty was even further jeopardised because the Act did not follow the usual sentencing guidelines of allowing a deduction for remand in custody.

Two further components of the Attorney-General's power marked his unusual hold over Garry David. Not only was he able to bring an action *ex parte*, but he could introduce amendments to the legislation in Parliament. On 16 April 1991, just nine days prior to the Act's expiry, a series of amendments was hastily introduced with the effect of extending the sunset clause from one to three years, and requiring future applications to be for a twelve-, rather than six-month period, thus reducing judicial flexibility even further. This legislative extension ignored the fact that many Parliamentarians had initially been persuaded to support the Act solely on the grounds of its 12 months' expiry date. It was a sleight of hand designed to guarantee custody in the absence of progress towards a more palatable solution.

There was a distinct incongruity about the way the Community Protection Act worked in practice. Although its purpose was to inquire into Garry David's 'dangerousness', some of the hallmarks of a criminal hearing were unavoidable despite the absence of charges. It was difficult to eschew adversarial elements entirely, although the Court did try to pursue an inquisitorial method, which is far more suited to an inquiry into personality. This element was acknowledged at the outset by Justice Fullagar, who considered that 'it may not be entirely right to treat it as an adversary proceeding' (*First Hearing*, 1 June 1990). Later he drew counsels' attention to the fact that the hearing 'partly resembles an inquiry, and partly a criminal trial' (*First Hearing*, 6 August 1990). Justice Hedigan too observed that 'the Court's role appears to be an uneasy blend of inquisition and the judicial process' and he repeatedly commented on the matter being 'an inquiry, and not adversarial' (*Second Hearing*, 15 October 1991).

The various Judges sought to play an amicus role, but were keenly aware that Garry's release, although not entirely excluded by the legislation, was a notional choice since little guidance was given about the role of their judicial discretion, which if exercised might well contravene Parliament's stated intention of legislation providing '*for the detention of* Garry David' [my italics]. (See also Page 1992; Wood 1990.) Section 8 of the Act stated that, should a Judge be satisfied on the balance of probabilities of Garry's dangerousness, 'the Supreme Court *may* order that Garry David be placed in preventive detention' [my italics]. Even release after a lengthy period of preventive detention was not within the Court's purview, for the Adult Parole Board of Victoria makes decisions about those deemed to be a danger to the community, and has the power to attach supervisory conditions to its orders. This legislation did not envisage the possibility of gradual or supervised release and the Court could only contemplate peremptory discharge, making the argument about Garry's likely dangerousness far more difficult to rebut in the absence of any monitoring agency. Justice Smith drew attention to the diminution of choice in his remarks that 'it is likely to be disastrous to simply release such a person into society without control and support, no matter what advances he may have made' (*Third Hearing and Second Appeal*, Judgment, 30 October 1992, p.68). Even though Garry David had been denied parole towards the end of his sentence, it can be argued that Parliament could have elected to draw on the experience and supervisory powers of the parole system in enacting this piece of legislation. The fact that it did not do so underscored an elaborate facade of custodial intent.

Justice Smith's use of the word 'advances' raised a further problematic area for the Court. The Act did not clarify the role of the authorities involved and as a consequence Garry was able to explore this loophole at an institutional level and in the Court itself. If one of the Act's stated purposes was to provide 'for the care or treatment and the management of Garry David' (section 1(a)), then a therapeutic programme was not excluded, in which case one might expect the legislation to confer responsibility on the authorities to provide for behavioural improvement. All Judges were unimpressed by the submission put forward by Michael Adams, that the authorities concerned had no obligation beyond an ordinary duty of care and any special rehabilitative scheme was superfluous in the light of Parliamentary plans for introducing broader powers of preventive detention to ensure Garry's containment. Justice Smith, after a 15-day hearing combining an application for a variation of the order, as well as the third application by the Attorney-General for preventive detention (17 September to 30 October 1992), rejected these arguments as making a mockery of the court process. In his Judgment, he pointed out:

> A cynic might say that the annual requirement is there to ease the collective community conscience, but this is to assert that the annual review is a charade. I do not believe that such a charade was intended and that what was envisaged was that appropriate action would be taken during any period in which Mr David was in preventive detention to give him every opportunity to rehabilitate himself and equip himself for life in the outside world. (*Third Hearing and Second Appeal*, Judgment, 30 October 1992, p.59)

INTERSECTION OF THE PENAL AND MEDICAL

If the procedures associated with the Community Protection Act 1990 were frankly penal, then it curiously envisaged the possibility of custody in a psychiatric inpatient service by posing a stark judicial choice between this type of facility and a prison – the third option of 'an other institution' with security status being non-existent. At various stages in psychiatric practice in Victoria, small units had been established, such as Toad Hall at Royal Park Psychiatric Hospital. However, these were dependent on the interest and expertise of particular staff and the early

1990s were not a period of long-term commitment to the treatment of those on the boundary of the criminal justice and mental health systems.

The Judges were hampered in their selection of facilities from the limited range available by the fact that, although they routinely use prison as a time-based sanction, they rarely have any detailed information about the way specific institutions operate and may know even less about small secure psychiatric units. In addition, their experience in the criminal courts does not encompass reviews of previous custodial decisions in any ongoing sense. This statement remains largely true, although the 1993 amendments to the *Sentencing Act* 1991 do provide for indefinite detention, which is reviewable at intervals. Justice Fullagar was acutely aware of facing 'an unhappy choice between J Ward on the one hand and, on the other, the prison surroundings of G Division, where the respondent would be subjected to prison discipline and being locked in his cell for nearly 16 hours of every day' (*First Hearing*, Judgment, 18 September 1990, p.35). Nevertheless, for the Supreme Court to be granted this power suggested to members of the public that they might expect some discriminating decision based on close judicial inquiry of the most appropriate penal or mental health facility for Garry David. Whilst the symbolism of the Act was clear, the conceptual confusion bedevilling the bad–mad divide, coupled with the lack of institutional choice, diminished its effect and ensured that it was a crude response to the containment of a 'dangerous' person.

Evidence taken about the implications of a treatment rationale versus a punitive regime mirrored the difficulty which practitioners experience in separating criminal justice and the mental health components of their role, both in a linguistic and symbolic sense. There were some interesting exchanges. Dr Grigor rebuked Garry's counsel for using the term 'cells' in relation to J Ward, because despite its prison origins it was currently gazetted as a hospital facility and therefore the correct term was 'rooms' (*First Hearing*, 8 August 1990). But as Dr Peter Hearne, the Medical Superintendent of the Forensic Health Service and Garry's general practitioner, pointed out, this semantic nicety was lost on Garry himself, who found the keys and bars of J Ward to be like a prison annexe, even though it lacked the razor wire of G Division (*First Hearing*, 8 August 1990). Dr Allen Bartholomew concurred, and explained to the Court that he considered that 'J Ward is a prison being run as a hospital; while G Division is more patently a prison' (*First Hearing*, 8 August 1990). It would seem that even those working in the system found the necessity for secure custody obscured the important distinction between correctional and health services, which forensic psychiatry had been striving to establish in response to the 1986 policy document *New Directions for Psychiatric Services in Victoria.*

Parliament aided this obscurity by ensuring that the judicial choice between a prison and psychiatric inatient service was unevenly weighted. As documented,

Garry David was given fewer rights than an ordinary security patient and the powers of both the Chief Psychiatrist and the Mental Health Review Board were explicitly curtailed. These restrictions not only reflected the Government's determination to maintain control over the conditions of Garry's custody, but also emphasised its lack of confidence in psychiatric authorities doing likewise. There was a supreme irony in the Court even having to consider a mental health disposition in view of the Mental Health Review Board's finding that Garry was not mentally ill, and neither needed detention as a security patient nor coerced treatment. Furthermore, Board members had pointed out that he was unamenable to existing treatment regimes and likely to impact negatively on other patients.

Numerous examples have been given to demonstrate the way in which the custodial imperative implicit in this 'one-person' legislation had led the Victorian Government to step outside the time-honoured safeguards of the Supreme Court process, thereby displaying a fundamental mistrust in a number of its administrative arms. The Act undermined the authority of both the Chief Psychiatrist and Mental Health Review Board; it ignored the expertise of the Adult Parole Board; it reduced judicial flexibility by effectively limiting the Court's discretion; it indirectly pressured an inquisitorial process, which became at times undeniably adversarial; and it created a procedure adding further confusion to the boundary between madness and criminality. It was a clumsy and politically inept approach to a potential problem posed by one person and disregarded the ramifications for staff in psychiatric and correctional facilities. Whilst Garry's difficulties had previously been contained within the existing regulations, the separation of the penal and medical was blurring and leading to uncertainty in role division.

Since the legislation was premised on a searching inquiry into Garry's behaviour, institutional staff members were nervous, frustrated and occasionally resentful that any acts or omissions on their part could later come under the public scrutiny of a superior court. In this regard, the powers to gather evidence provided by this legislation were broad indeed. Section 7 enabled the Court to 'receive or require the production' of medical, prison and police records, as well as a range of other documented material pertaining to Garry. The consequences of this power were fourfold: some of this evidence would be in the nature of hearsay; opinions would not always be tested; Garry's right to privacy regarding the minutiae of his daily life would be overturned; and daily interactions of staff with him would be subject to cross-examination.

A further unforeseen problem arose in relation to the normally confidential reports of the Parole Board. These were to be available to the Court and a special application was necessary to release them to counsel. Justice Marks initially sought to add to the range of available material and ordered what he termed an 'independent' psychiatric report to be prepared by Dr Bartholomew, whose dealings with Garry in the prison system had been extensive, and whose outspoken opinions had already generated publicity. The Judge required him to be given access to Health and Corrections records and to approach other psychiatrists, who were to be released from their duty of confidentiality. Garry's counsel was alarmed. It appeared that any semblance of psychiatric diagnoses and opinions being offered in an entirely neutral, scientific context was in doubt, given that the psychiatrist concerned had already publicly affirmed his view of Garry's dangerousness.

The information-gathering techniques necessitated by the Act demonstrated Parliament's fundamental misunderstanding of forensic psychiatry, which struggles to stand apart from the coercive practices of the courts. Psychiatric reports are dependent on the cooperation of the prisoner or patient and, in this instance, Garry initially maintained that he would not talk with Dr Bartholomew 'under any circumstances, and would not stay in the same room with him'. Such intransigence had not been foreseen and raised the possibility of contempt, although the judicial power to deal with this breach of legal process by imprisonment was clearly ineffectual in circumstances of indefinite confinement (*First Hearing*, 19 June 1990). Nevertheless, Parliament heeded the threat and avoided any future impasse by later amending the Act to grant the Supreme Court the right to 'order' a psychiatric or medical examination (24 April 1991). There were two further problems with this solution: a failure to recognise that patients cannot be forced to assist with a mental state examination, and the loss of privacy, which would be violated by the introduction of personal material in an open court hearing. Issues of competency to consent to treatment and confidentiality had been carefully considered by the Victoria Labor Government as part of its social justice strategy, and now the Community Protection Act was overriding these in its pursuit of a custodial objective without due consideration for the consequent impact on the appellant's therapeutic relationships. This matter was raised quite explicitly during the second hearing. Justice Hedigan granted an application from the Attorney-General for Dr Peter Hearne's prison medical files on Garry David to be surrendered, although Garry had not given consent. Whilst sympathetic to Hearne's position, the Judge considered that little was to be gained by postponing the inevitable – an acknowledgment that the discretionary role of the Court was indeed constrained.

These courtroom examples illustrate Parliament's heavy-handed and misguided attempt to use the legislation to coerce a medical discipline, which necessarily relies on voluntary cooperation and is governed by a code of ethics. The implication was that a 'scientific' rationale could be found for the use of preventive detention, if only the medical witnesses were to cooperate in the task of evidence gathering. It was not appreciated that in any ordinary criminal trial there is some benefit for the defendant to participate in psychiatric interviews which are not formally court ordered. In this instance, there was little incentive for Garry to accede to such orders. He was only too well aware of the plethora of extant material about his 'dangerousness', yet he was being placed in the strange position of having to provide clinical evidence of a possibly self-incriminatory nature with little guidance about what was required to demonstrate his 'non-dangerousness' to the Supreme Court's satisfaction. His right to call psychiatric evidence on his own behalf, or have counsel present during interviews, was not covered by the Act. It was as if the focus on dangerousness had eclipsed the ordinary rules regarding the admissibility of expert evidence.

There were other troubling consequences of the legislation for those giving testimony. In the trial process, expert psychiatric witnesses are forbidden from testifying about 'the ultimate issue', or the criminal responsibility of the accused, since this is the central component of jury decision making. But in this case there was no jury, and although the Judge had the final task of sieving medical evidence, the witnesses were being asked to testify directly about Garry's 'dangerousness', thereby bypassing the usual conventions of a criminal hearing. As many of these medical witnesses were involved in his ongoing management, their therapeutic relationship and personal sense of security were tested by the necessity of answering the question 'Is he dangerous?' in front of the appellant, knowing that the answer would instantly attract media headlines.

Confidentiality was further breached in a rather unanticipated way. In its hearing the Mental Health Review Board had been able to impose restrictions on reporting and the use of clinical and Parole Board documents, and these were available only to Board members and counsel. However, this level of confidentiality could not be maintained in an open court and exhibits such as those previously protected were publicly exposed. For example, since much of the material relating to Garry's dangerousness was based on his institutional history, Michael Adams was forced into the uncomfortable position of spending three days reading out loud the daily nursing, prison and medical notes in order to provide incontrovertible evidence of unpredictable violence. Because the hearing resembled an inquiry rather than a trial, a summary of Pentridge incidents from 9 April to 11 September was prepared and the daily nursing notes from 13 July 1990 to 18 December 1990 were read to the court. This was a demeaning procedure for the appellant. As *The Age* reported to a curious public, the behaviour being alleged was 'strange beyond the dreams of those of us who live on the outside' (7 August 1990). Not only did this method of presenting evidence reinforce Garry's distinctiveness, albeit in a prison context, but it was left to Garry, through his counsel, to draw attention to the fact that any relationship with certain staff would suffer should he be subsequently placed in their care.

Justice Fullagar commented on what he perceived as 'a kind of character assassination in public', which required him to weigh up Garry's character, propensities, 'intimate details of past conduct' and his mental condition in published reasons. He also noted the fact that the medical evidence was given in front of

Garry 'without any inquiry before the Court as to any possible adverse consequences to him of the adoption of this course' (*First Hearing*, Judgment, 18
September, p.4). Not all shared this view. A practising barrister argued at the time
that information about background material and criminal history is a customary
part of the court's usual mode of inquiry:

> No concern for privacy is expressed in such cases. Furthermore, it is hard to
> believe that David's privacy could be any more reduced, after the numerous
> medical reports, inquiries, Parliamentary discussion and involvement of psy-
> chiatrists into David's everyday existence. (Page 1992, p.87)

The notion that Garry David had become *an object* of legal processes was not a view
shared by the various Judges, who were sensitive to the lack of confidentiality in a
public mental state inquiry according Garry little control over the process, and so
obviously in disregard of the spirit of mental health legislation.

In summary, the Government had chosen to raise the stakes in its confrontation with Garry David, but its instrument strayed far from the traditional path of
legal safeguards and precedent and demonstrated a poor understanding of the role
of forensic psychiatry, in contradistinction to its encouragement of this discipline
through the provision of staffing, structure and resources. Doctors should not have
been placed in the position of giving evidence about the ultimate issue; nor should
they have been required to express an opinion in court based on a reading of the
files alone without the benefit of direct examination of the person concerned, as
indeed occurred in this case. There had already been some indication that lack of
personal examination had been partially responsible for the changed psychiatric
opinions during the evidence given to the Mental Health Review Board. Although
understandable clinically, such vacillation did little to enhance the practitioners'
credibility with lawyers pressing for certainty. Clinical and legal imperatives are
different, and to distort the former, in order to match the way a court requires its
evidence to be given, may ultimately broaden the gulf between psychiatry and the
law. Clinical judgments have an intuitive element and diagnoses are working categories subject to later refinement on the basis of additional information. The law,
however, in its courting of psychiatry seeks definitive views and its role is to elicit
these, even to the extent of sometimes according mental state symptoms more
substance than they may perhaps merit.

In the case of psychopathy there is an additional factor with which to
contend. Behaviour is not only disordered but also amoral, and psychiatric
expertise requires its recouching in terms of symptoms, rather than criminality (see
Stone 1984 and Wootton 1980). If Justice Fullagar complained that 'the buck' had
been passed to his Court by having to decide between custody and freedom, then
one might argue that the law has had a century-old history of passing the buck to
psychiatry to reconceptualise what are fundamentally moral dilemmas in scientific

clothing. This is a pervasive problem in the forensic arena, where it is difficult to disentangle ordinary reactions from a more dispassionate ordering of knowledge about reprehensible human behaviours.

The Community Protection Act 1990 served as a watershed for forensic practice, especially in the courts and prison, by exposing many of the clashes which envelop clinical and legal objectives. To the chagrin of all, it proved to be counter-productive in the way it opened up new challenges for its subject, whom the press now labelled 'a psychiatric prisoner', as if both psychiatry and the law had colluded in a form of entrapment. The reality was that Garry was able to expose the ambiguity about his proper place of custody, and it has already been demonstrated that he did so with a great deal of contrariness. As a consequence, his intractability led the Government to devise some strangely hybrid solutions, which illustrate the tenuous boundary between badness and madness and its negotiable quality

A 'PSYCHIATRIC PRISONER'

The government seemed initially willing to make political capital out of Garry's abysmal behaviour at Mont Park, when Michael Adams listed the cost of the damage – woodwork scored by a knife, broken furniture and a forced opening in the ceiling – as being $100,000. This figure given in Court on 31 July gained wide exposure, with the event itself being described as a 'rampage' and conflated with earlier fears expressed about the safety of toddlers in a nearby university kindergarten (*Sunday Sun*, 24 June 1990). This simple tactic confirmed the public view of Garry's dangerousness, despite Adams's later retraction on the grounds of misunderstanding his instructions and admitting that the immediate repairs only totalled $2000 with a further $1000 for security arrangements (*Sunday Sun*, 24 June 1990). Garry's guileless explanation that he was unable to cope with Ward M6, because it was a 'paradise' after J Ward, beggared credulity. He offered to make reparation by returning and being locked in permanent seclusion, knowing full well that this was antithetical to prevailing psychiatric policy. These arguments were vexatious and unpredictable, as were later ones giving detailed computer instructions to his solicitors about a preference for the harsher regime of H Division over the more liberal one of G Division. The Court refused the application, but nonetheless it was a significant embarrassment to authorities striving to mitigate the harshness of the holding powers of the Community Protection Act. Garry returned to J Ward on 19 September 1990 and remained there until his transfer to Pentridge on 18 December.

Garry's institutional defiance followed a similar pattern over the following three years. He was increasingly able to play on the responses of those around him and highlight the weaknesses of the legislation's holding power. The flaw of particular concern to the various Judges was its failure to clarify the responsibilities of prison officers and therapists, because this provided Garry with an unexpected bargaining position. He could effectively bring wide-ranging accusations regarding the ambiguity of staff roles and divisiveness about his management to the attention of the court and its wider audience. Justice Hedigan considered the crux of the problem to be the fact that Garry was 'neither prisoner nor patient' (*Second Hearing* 1991), a position affirmed by Dr Grigor, who complained that he was 'not his treating doctor now, but a guardian under the Community Protection Act; he is not technically a patient' (*First Hearing*, 8 August 1990).

The anomalous nature of Garry's position manifested itself in a number of ways. He was no ordinary prisoner and, in the absence of specific guidelines, his notoriety guaranteed him different treatment, yet custody proved to be a particularly bleak experience. When it emerged that he had only been given cleaning duties during the previous four years in H Division, and his movement outside his cell had been restricted to 'a mere two and a quarter hours a day', the Court noted that the issue of the physical conditions appropriate for a *non-prisoner* could not be ignored (*Second Hearing*, Judgment, 15 November 1991, pp.53–60). As a detainee under the Act, Garry was being given mixed messages within the confines of the gaol. Many prison staff were overtly supportive because of the injustice he was suffering, but there was a backlash from some prisoners fearful that he had single-handedly paved the way for more general preventive detention legislation (*Second Hearing*, Judgment, 15 November 1991), as can be gleaned from one prisoner's letter prisoner, published under the heading: 'Is My Name on the List of 50?' (John Dixon-Jenkins, *The Age*, 5 May 1992). The simmering discontent resulted in two unprovoked stabbing incidents, which Garry declined to report officially, despite the delays to the court process.

In a report detailing a series of incidents occurring in B Annexe since Garry's arrival, Chief Prison Officer, Karen Linstrom, provided Governor Howden with a thoughtful insight into staff reaction:

> Staff acknowledge the uniqueness of Garry's case, and have shown considerable tolerance, which reflects in the relatively few incident reports and disciplinary action being taken. However, consensus supports the view that the excessive time consumed in managing this one prisoner impacts negatively on the other forty prisoners classified to this division on a legitimate needs basis. Staff need time out. Prisoners need time out. Tensions are palpable at present and other irritations are developing into flame ups between other prisoners as a result of the unsettled environment. In the interests of good order and management of the division, staff are requesting alternative placement until the Division is stabilised. (*Second Hearing*, 29 August 1991)

Her evidence to Justice Hedigan was particularly compelling, when she pointed out the difficulties of Garry's presence in a prison under such unusual conditions. On the one hand he viewed cooperation on his part as representing an unwarranted demand, but on the other he was demanding disproportionate access to scarce resources. She considered that whilst staff appreciated the political sensitivities surrounding this prisoner, they sometimes found that efforts to control him were at the expense of the needs of 'legitimately classified prisoners'. 'Prison officers,' she told Justice Hedigan, 'always have to weigh up to themselves their responsibility to execute the law and look after a prisoner for whom they have no warrant.' The situation had become acute. Pentridge had only one psychologist for 900 prisoners and Garry's demands were creating a momentum staff could not satisfy (Second Hearing, 11 October 1991). Later evidence indicated that this difficulty transferred from the prison to the mental health system, when Mont Park had to roster an additional staff member and pay some staff overtime during the short period of Garry's stay.

In the months following the first preventive detention order, which involved a transfer from Pentridge to Ararat's J Ward, there was further volatility resulting in property damage and self-mutilation. This type of behaviour was now escalating and adding to the confusion about Garry's unique position. He taunted the Health Department by drawing attention to the unwarranted seclusion of an AIDS patient at J Ward; a matter he contended to be an abuse of human rights significant enough to be taken to the Human Rights Commission, together with other violations at this facility (20 November 1990). His explanation for his own spate of threats to patients and staff focused on two factors: lack of treatment and inappropriate placement. Justice Hedigan noted in his Judgment the extreme nature of the disruption, which had occurred. It included a spree of self-mutilation, property damage, terrorising a Maori patient with an improvised Ku Klux Klan hood, ripping bedsheets and escaping from his room on many occasions (later detailed in Second Hearing, Judgment, 15 November 1991, pp.15, 63). A serious industrial crisis towards the end of the year intensified the situation as psychiatric nurses, who had withdrawn their services, were suddenly replaced by volunteers from Melbourne. This gave Garry an unprecedented opportunity to test the management skills of senior forensic staff and draw his complaints more directly to their attention. The files of 13 December carry the notation that his 'behaviour was characterised by extreme anger regarding his perceived "false" imprisonment and stated determination to resort to "bad behavior" and make his degree of distress understood'.

His agitation further demoralised staff and distressed the patients, whose routine was already disturbed in the wake of the strike. He aggravated his wounds causing considerable blood loss; smashed a large amount of furniture; set fire to his cell; and worked his way through the chain mesh to the external part of the roof, where he assailed volunteer staff with stones. By removing approximately 25 bricks and slate from the exterior of the two and a half storey bluestone building and exposing the crumbling mortar, Garry guaranteed that this institution, gazetted as a 'temporary ward' of the Ararat Lunatic Asylum since 1887, no longer had security status and had to be precipitously closed: a feat successive administrations had been unable to achieve. On 17 December 1990 the case was back in the Supreme Court and the Attorney-General had little choice but to apply to Justice Crockett for a variation of the order and Garry was once again returned to Pentridge. In pragmatic terms, even the limited array of facilities deemed suitable for his detention under the Community Protection Act 1990 had dwindled at his own instigation.

The prison proved to be just as untenable for Garry's management as J Ward. His presence there generated a high degree of tension, which was compounded by serious incidents such as the swallowing of a radio antenna and kitchen knife, the construction of cell barricades, the inciting of prisoners to go on hunger strikes, the biting of a prison officer and threats of hostagetaking (Dr Bertha Johnson's evidence, *Second Hearing*, Judgment, 15 November 1991, pp.67–71). Some of this behaviour was traced to his despair about the legislative extension of the Community Protection Act beyond its initial sunset clause and, on 12 March 1991, he attempted to hang himself, later issuing threats of self-immolation. Despite the imminence of the next hearing, Garry continued to be violently obstructive and difficult to control, even in H Division. By the end of August he produced a document called 'Assault on Fort P', which threatened the security of Pentridge Prison by detailing plans to terrorise staff from the watchtowers, poison the officers' food and drink, blow holes in walls and plant stolen cars with timed explosives (*Second Hearing*, Judgment, 5 November 1991, p.67). Whilst these threats were grandiose and unlikely, an aura of terror developed about the possibility of their occurrence.

It was around this same time that an outburst of self-destructive behaviours requiring intermittent hospitalisation delayed the second hearing of the Community Protection Act and Michael Adams, on behalf of the Attorney-General, announced the Government's plans to establish a special secure unit within the rehabilitation complex at Aradale at an overall cost of four and a half million dollars, in order to provide greater scope for Garry's privacy and development of self-care skills. Its features would be distinctive, for it would straddle the prison/psychiatric hospital boundary with staff from both the Corrections Department and the Office of Psychiatric Services (*Second Hearing*, Judgment, 15 November 1991, p.68). This proposal further symbolised the confusion about Garry's proper allocation to the space of badness or madness. The Government intended to proclaim the new unit as a prison within the meaning of the Corrections Act 1986, even though it would be integrated with an existing psychiatric facility and sited within the hospital grounds. Thus it would have an unprecedented duality of status. This awkward hybrid proposal had first surfaced at the end of 1989 and had not then been welcomed by the Director-General of Prisons, who considered it to pose insuperable administrative difficulties. It was an innovative and expensive solution, requiring a high level of staffing to carry out both the implied custodial and treatment obligations. However, the fact that the Government was seriously prepared to consider an institution straddling the correctional and mental health systems emphasised a desperation to extricate itself from the complex web in which it had become enmeshed. Garry, however, was obdurate in rejecting this new development on the grounds of its punitiveness and its status as a 'one-man prison grafted on to a sole-person Act'. In a graphic comparison, he told Justice Hedigan that 'Aradale is to psychiatry what H [Division] is to Pentridge: solitary confinement' (*Second Hearing*, 29 May 1991), and later informed him that detention there would be akin to Hess's experience in Spandau Gaol, providing a legitimate entitlement to resist (*Second Hearing*, Judgment, 15 November 1991, p.59).

The moves and counter moves were becoming chesslike. Anticipating that the Attorney-General would apply to the Supreme Court to use the Aradale Forensic Centre, despite his resistance, Garry took advantage of the 1991 amendment to section 9(2)(2) of the Act allowing him to make his own application for a variation of any order made by Justice Hedigan. This section now stated: 'The Supreme Court, on the application of Garry David by summons, may vary or revoke an Order under section 8. An application under this section (a) may be made *ex parte*; and (b) must be heard by a Judge of the Supreme Court.' Regulation 204 of 1978 of the Victoria Supreme Court Regulations gives priority to any matter in which the Attorney-General is involved, as the Court thinks fit.

On 23 April 1992, Garry asked Justice Harper to consider Mont Park on two grounds: his behaviour following the second order for preventive detention had been markedly quiescent; and he had been denied the benefit of a proper rehabilitation programme (*First Appeal*, 4 June 1992). The Government clearly miscalculated when Michael Adams estimated that this matter would require only half a day of the Court's time for submissions. It became evident that if the Attorney-General was not concerned about Garry's situation, then the Court certainly was. The hearing lasted a week and, since Aradale had yet to be gazetted as a dual facility, Justice Harper decided to view both Mont Park and Pentridge with counsel, accompanied by Garry himself, who later expressed appreciation at this unusual opportunity of being in the company of a judge vested with decision-making powers relating to his future.

In Court, Michael Burt, the Acting Manager of the Forensic Health Service, and Ian Tozer, the Programme Manager, strongly argued against Garry's relocation to Mont Park. In justification, they cited the lack of a treatment programme for those with a primary diagnosis of personality disorder; Garry's excessive use of staff time; his ability to disturb other patients; and his preparedness to jeopardise security arrangements. In addition, both these senior administrative staff considered he would not cope well with other patients having 'leave' for medical appointments, to attend court and even football matches, which could range between 70 and 350 separate movements in any one month (*First Appeal,* 22 May 1992). These arguments had legitimacy, but they also shed light on a preference for Garry to be at the more remote Aradale than create further disruption at Mont Park.

In this hearing, an air of urgency was displayed when Garry's counsel told the Court that Cabinet had met during the past week to proclaim Aradale as a prison, despite the contrary advice it had received from the Director-General of Corrections, who believed it would be 'an encumbrance' on the Corrections Act 1986. Peter Harmsworth claimed that his responsibility would become confused and untenable if Garry were to be in his custody, yet technically a resident of a psychiatric inpatient service and freed from many of the restraints applying to an ordinary prisoner. He told the Court:

> Legal opinion shows we can't have a dual skill status arrangement, that in fact it [Aradale Forensic Unit] would have to be decommissioned as an institution and turned into a prison solely, and that would not be an outcome I could support. (*First Appeal,* 22 May 1992)

Michael Adams confirmed that the proclamation would go ahead if Garry should be sent there, and the Attorney-General intended applying for an order. The message was clear: Garry's newfound power to apply to the court for a variation in his placement was being overshadowed by the Government's plans and, despite the careful judicial attention it was receiving, the Attorney-General viewed the application as an awkward and ill-timed interim move, which would become irrelevant under new administrative arrangements.

In view of such discernible pressure from within senior levels of government, Justice Harper's decision of 4 June 1992 was all the more unexpected. He announced that his Judgment was 'not an attempt to prejudice the Attorney-General's pending application' and ordered Garry to be placed in preventive detention at Mont Park. Aradale, he considered, was an unsatisfactory solution for his treatment. His further comments were directed at a Government that had immersed itself in a morass of legal, psychiatric and civil liberties concerns. He characterised Pentridge as being 'just detention' (in the sense of *mere* detention) with the bureaucratic entanglement of prison regulations causing the detainee considerable frustration. In the circumstances, he indicated that he would expect rehabilitation to be given equal weight and accepted the view of a private psychologist, Tim Watson-Munro, that it should be 'consistent, structured and protracted'. Only Mont Park appeared to him to hold out some prospect of such a programme, but he warned Garry that he would have to curtail his manipulative and demanding behaviour and abide by the general rules of the institution. Counsel for the Attorney-General was dismayed at the decision and requested time to study the comments. However, Justice Harper remained adamant that the move should occur with 'all practicable speed and no disruption' and allowed one week for the transfer to be effected (*First Appeal*, 4 June 1992).

The decision was a mark of the Supreme Court's independence, as well as a reflection of the paucity of available choices; and it also conveyed an air of judicial optimism. There was little doubt that the duty of care would be difficult for Mont Park staff, in view of their recent experience with Garry David and the need to provide resources for a different kind of programme within the ambit of caring for a small group of severely disturbed patients. Much of the evidence about Garry's brief stay was detailed in the next hearing of the Community Protection Act. Dr Ruth Vine, the Authorised Psychiatrist of the forensic ward at Mont Park, pointed out that Garry was not a security patient in the formal sense and had no psychotic symptoms, so that treatment was neither appropriate nor enforceable as with other psychiatric patients. It was also revealed that the newly appointed Professor of Forensic Psychiatry was opposed to Garry's continued presence there (*Third Hearing and Second Appeal*, 22 September 1992). In this same hearing Dr Lester Walton, a private forensic psychiatrist, put forward his view that he believed Garry's stay at Ward M6 would inevitably be 'hazardous [since] it is apparent that there is still an ongoing serious conflict about how this man should be managed – and with his particular type of problems, that sort of conflict is a recipe for disaster'.

Walton's anticipation of trouble was borne out in only a matter of days, and on 23 June 1992 an application was made to Justice Tadgell for Garry to be returned to Pentridge. The Mont Park placement had lasted for only 14 days, 5 of which were spent at St. Vincent's Hospital for repair of self-inflicted injuries, which he professed to be the result of a refusal to provide him with a female primary care nurse. On the third day, Garry had requested a prison transfer following an altercation with a staff member formerly employed at J Ward. Judicial optimism, it seemed, had been an insufficient incentive for Garry to adapt to the controlled, but less restrictive, regime of a secure psychiatric facility.

This brief outline of events cannot do justice to the degree of trauma Garry perpetrated on his own body and the havoc created for staff and patients at Mont Park during his brief time there. He extended an abdominal wound to expose a large section of the bowel, and then taunted staff and police by throwing cups of blood and flesh over them whilst, at the same time, refusing treatment. In addition, he made explicit threats to staff, police and their families, prison officers and ambulance officers. There were innumerable incidents in which he disrupted ward management by activating the emergency alarm, stripping off clothes, refusing to eat, smashing equipment and threatening to take patients hostage. An experienced psychiatric nurse subsequently claimed compensation in the County Court for suffering from a severe bipolar disorder 'after discovering a near-unconscious David with a self-inflicted injury'. She further argued that the hospital had ignored her complaints about David's management' ('Garry David's Nurse Seeks Compensation', *The Age*, 12 August 1999). Moreover, 'She was horrified when she learned later that…Garry David would have gained sexual gratification from her presence', while he was disembowelling himself ('Compo Bid After Man Cut Himself', *Herald-Sun*, 12 August 1999).

Dr Walton's comment about 'ongoing serious conflict' relating to Garry's management did not pertain only to psychiatric settings. A lack of clarity also permeated his regime within the prison, and there were many attempts to establish a plan sufficiently robust to withstand his manoeuvring. Again, strongly differing views emerged about the requirements of the legislation and appropriateness of treatment within a prison. Although the intention was to equip him with some independent living skills, Dr Peter Eisen of the Office of Psychiatric Services pointed out that such a plan was scarcely 'treatment', but a form of management based on the gradual reduction of containment levels as a reward for good behaviour. It was not, he contended, 'a traditional proposal' and very difficult to implement within the confines of a gaol. There were a number of reasons for this, including the element of coercion involved in any programme implemented in these unusual circumstances; Garry's uncertain status; and the disruption of court appearances, interspersed with periods of hospitalisation; all of which combined to make his cooperation unlikely, to the extent that Justice Hedigan referred to the situation as being that of 'an irresistible force meeting an immovable object' (*Second Hearing*, 9 October 1991).

All Judges were at pains to comment on the matter of Garry's rehabilitation and noted inconsistencies in the 'carrot and stick' approach of behavioural management techniques. For example, individual plans considered appropriate by prison staff differed in detail from those produced by the mental health system and there was vacillation about what actually constituted a 'reward', since Garry tended to redefine this at whim. The most obvious anomaly occurred when, early in 1992, one three-tiered plan proposed that Aradale should be used as a threat if Garry were to breach prison regulations, yet some months later the Court was informed that it was part of the reward structure of the Government's treatment plans: a therapeutic contradiction undoubtedly savoured by the proposed recipient of these services. This draft management plan was provisionally implemented on 25 January 1992 and endorsed on the following 21 March. Garry was able to avoid being sent to Aradale because of his 'good' behaviour and then learned in court that this was still the Government's intention.

Therapeutic staff found themselves in the difficult position of having to justify therapeutic programmes to the Court and, in so doing, reduce them to behavioural management procedures. As Michael Adams noted, the failure of these experiments at Pentridge could not be regarded as anyone's fault (*Third Hearing and Second Appeal*, 12 October 1992). Even the earlier hearings drew Justice Hedigan's criticism that management plans were 'long on principle and short on specifics' and detailed contracts were equally found wanting (*Second Hearing*, Judgment, 15 November 1991, p.77). Little had changed by the following year, when Justice Harper noted that the proposed move to Mont Park was still 'short on specifics' with only vague release plans, and the major advantage amounting to more computer access and a less restrictive environment. This legal perception of the inadequacy of psychiatric provision for Garry David was a gentle warning that the Court regarded rehabilitation as a priority under preventive detention and expected greater effort to be expended. Witnesses told him that Mont Park had heeded previous judicial comments and identified ten levels of Garry's threatening and dangerous behaviour, to which they would respond as part of a behavioural management programme (*Third Hearing and Second Appeal*, 12 October 1992). Paradoxically however, as Justice Smith pointed out, psychiatric custody would have exposed Garry to more penalties under this plan than with the prison's simpler, three-tiered approach: a factor he decided was likely to generate conflict (Third Hearing and Second Appeal, Judgment, 30 October 1992). But he did find that Pentridge staff seemed to be marking time owing to a lack of direction surrounding the future use of Aradale. (Some months later, this same dilemma was revived, when Mont Park staff had to contemplate providing a special plan for Garry as a non-psychiatric patient situated in a hybrid institution within the hospital grounds.)

Whilst it was a simple matter for the Court to identify the different styles of management used in the prison and mental health services and attempt to inspire, rather than direct, some rationalisation of resources, Garry undermined each approach very effectively, diminishing staff morale in the process. For instance, at Mont Park, the patient's level of threats, barricading, damage to equipment and severe self-mutilation exceeded any of the anticipated levels of disturbance, rendering the planned use of a tiered management model irrelevant. At Pentridge, the proposed behavioural reward of transfer to the Aradale Forensic Unit was demonstrably unrealistic, owing to the escalating level of the prisoner's self-injury, which required the availability of emergency medical treatment, even leading to the suggestion that a helicopter would need to be on stand-by. The increasing impracticality of the Attorney-General's plans led to their abandonment and reversion to a more convenient city location. Changes of this sort were indicative of internal confusion, when subjected to the searching light of a Supreme Court inquiry.

Professional opinions about management strategies became increasingly divisive as time passed. Early in 1992, in response to the Court's direction, a more formal Management Committee had been established at Pentridge and in April one of its members, prison chaplain Norman Gray, documented some of the issues for discussion. His allegations were serious and conveyed his impression that Committee members showed scant regard for Garry's interests; were not fully supportive; and exhibited a reluctance to meet with him. Although the Chairman of the Committee explained the necessity of maintaining some distance from Garry's manipulative endeavours, it was clear that there was a professional gulf between Gray's broad welfare role and the position of those adhering to a behavioural management programme based on psychological principles.

Irene Haas, the Pentridge psychologist chairing the Committee, disputed Gray's interpretation of its function on the basis that the prisoner was responsible for his own behaviour, including release from Pentridge, and this factor should be regarded as integral to any programme (*Third Hearing and Second Appeal*, 25 September 1992). At this stage, the Court was told that an amount of $60,000 had been allocated over 12 months to cover the cost of obtaining the services of experts to give Garry the relevant skills training, with an additional $50,000 being required for security purposes. Once again, Garry used this dissension to avoid cooperating with *his* Management Committee, denigrating its highly structured approach as being 'rather childish' (*Third Hearing and Second Appeal*, 30 October 1992). As he explained, quite insightfully, to Justice Harper, he was the only prisoner in the gaol who could not express anger or frustration 'because it can, and will be, used against me [him] in Court'. He went a step further, casting his arguments in therapeutic terms, by suggesting that the levels of deprivations were designed to suppress normal and healthy emotions, in order to satisfy the authorities of the effectiveness and humanity of their management plan (*First Appeal*, 22 May 1992). In essence, Garry was arguing that the programme was repressive and calculated to serve professional interests, rather than his own needs.

Justice Hedigan took the opportunity to explore in some detail Garry's reasons for his non-cooperative stance. The appellant painted a picture of himself as a political hostage who, in a masochistic display, was forced to hold his own body to ransom. He particularly targeted the Community Protection Act as the source of his unwillingness or inability to cooperate, as the following summarised exchange exemplifies:

Judge [Hedigan]: Why don't you behave properly to get out?

Garry David: I would be betraying my principles if I did.

Judge: It is a principle that you would rather not cooperate because of the Act? But the Government is asking for nothing. Those administering it are requiring you to cooperate to re-enter society and they didn't pass the legislation.

Garry: If you do the crime, you do the time – the punishment for breaking the law. I cannot accept that there is no charge and no jury.

Judge: You may be paying a disproportionate price. You are only 37, and if you will not open the door, you have to take some responsibility yourself.

Garry: I thought the recent changes were to niggle at me and act as a backstop until the Community Protection Act was extended. I think it is a conspiracy what has been done to me.

Judge: I think that the Government is concerned by a long history of self-mutilation and threats by letters of violence. Does it seem strange that there should be concern by authorities?

Garry: Yes. Self-mutilation was holding myself as a hostage. As for the threats. I have also written a lot of non-violent thoughts. Everyone is concentrating on the negative aspects, none on the positive. That is a mistake, too. There should be both. (*Second Hearing*, 14 October 1991)

From the end of June to mid-October 1992, Justice Smith took evidence in relation to the dual application by the Attorney-General for an order for Garry to reside at Pentridge Prison, and an application for a further 12 months' extension of that previously made by Justice Hedigan. On 30 October 1992 the decision was handed down that Garry David was to be held in preventive detention for a period of 12 months at Pentridge Prison with the possibility of being moved on temporary leave to a Mont Park 'cottage', which would be gazetted as a prison under the Corrections Act 1986. Garry's indeterminate position in the mental health/criminal justice boundary was thus confirmed and, at the same time, it added to the symbolic confusion enveloping this case. The house situated in the grounds of Mont Park had most recently been used as temporary accommodation for the incoming professor of forensic psychiatry and his family. This new proposal envisaged the addition of certain security features to transform domestic accommodation into a dual prison/psychiatric hospital for a severely personality-disordered patient. As it transpired, the move was held in abeyance over the next six months, as Garry spent an increasing amount of time in both Pentridge and St Vincent's Hospitals due to the incomplete healing of his serious abdominal wound.

THE POLITICAL, LEGAL AND PSYCHIATRIC IMPASSE

This outline belies the complexity of moves and counter-moves and the increasing inability of the Government to foresee and control the events it had set in train with its framing of a discourse of dangerousness. The complexity of the legislative framework is most clearly illustrated by Justice Smith's description of the task ahead of him:

> There are before me three summonses filed by the Attorney-General on 23 June 1992, 30 July 1992 and 19 August 1992. The August summons seeks relief, which combines the relief sought in the two preceding summonses. That relief is the following:
>
> 1. An order pursuant to s.9(1)(b) of the Community Protection Act 1990 that the order of the Honourable Mr Justice Hedigan made 15 November 1991, as varied by the order of the Hono urable Mr Justice Harper made 4 June 1992 and further varied by the interim order of the Honourable Mr Justice Tadgell made 23 June 1992, be further varied by providing that the place of preventive detention pursuant to s.8(2) of the Act be Her Majesty's Prison, Pentridge.
>
> 2. Pursuant to s.9(1)(a) of the Community Protection Act 1990 that the order of the Honourable Mr Justice Hedigan made 15 November 1991 be extended for a period of 12 months. (*Third Hearing and Second Appeal*, Judgment, 30 October 1991, p.1)

Michael Adams' role in carrying out the Government's instructions was equally difficult, for he was faced with rapidly changing circumstances at the institutional end. At one stage, he reported that: 'Garry is bringing the system down and enjoying it. Staff are going in droves' (*Second Hearing*, 9 October 1991). In a significant aside to Justice Hedigan, he suggested that some of the responsibility for the legal frustrations associated with the Act had arisen because in this 'historical clash between law and psychiatry…psychiatrists are not prepared to meld their profession to deal with him'.

Garry's own metaphor, in response to Justice Harper's questions about the personal impact of the Community Protection Act 1990, was that he found it to be isolating and devastating, 'like being kept in a war zone' (*First Appeal*, 3 June 1992). It was a recurring simile used for effect and it inspired him to challenge, both directly and in subtle ways, whatever plans were produced, leading Adams to note wryly that: 'no matter what way the authorities move, there is a counterbalancing defeat of their activity' (*Third Hearing and Second Appeal*, 6 October 1992). As time wore on, Garry utilised other techniques: he became unpredictable by sacking or threatening to sack his lawyers; he sometimes refused to come to the Court; he seriously self-mutilated during the hearing period; and he refused to be strip-searched, despite having submitted on innumerable other occasions when being moved between Pentridge and the Court (*Third Hearing and Second Appeal*, 9 October 1992). This latter refusal was a skilful ploy to reinforce his rejection of prisoner status and, at the same time, guarantee an adjournment, which had otherwise been refused. In addition, it conveyed the message that *he* was being obstructed by the prison authorities from appearing in Court. The various judges were undeniably patient in encouraging his participation in the proceedings, but the delaying tactics of dismissing and reinstating counsel were becoming costly and disruptive in this third hearing. On learning that the Legal Aid Commission was prepared to make yet another solicitor available on Garry's request, Justice Smith commented that:

> It smacks somewhat of manipulation for manipulation's sake. However, it seems to me, that provided I can make it clear to him, there are some clear limits to this, because of the nature of the proceedings, I should give him one more opportunity, but no more. (*Third Hearing and Second Appeal*, 2 October 1992)

Although Garry became adept at introducing stalling techniques, he maintained a veneer of cooperation, which discouraged all Judges from proceeding in his absence. At one stage, the Court seriously considered appointing a guardian *ad litem* on the grounds of his disability, but this raised two issues. It was by no means clear whether he came into the formal category of disabled persons; and it would have been a dangerous path to pursue, should Garry perceive his role in the proceedings to be usurped. In this particular instance, Justice Smith decided to continue, because the prisoner had 'the capacity to clearly articulate his wishes' and was simply refusing to attend (*Third Hearing and Second Appeal*, 1 October 1992).

The discourse of dangerousness was thus played out through the intersection of many competing elements. The Government had demonstrated its preparedness to use extraordinary powers to deflect responsibility for a dangerous person to the courts and psychiatry, but a number of unforeseen and unsatisfactory outcomes had emerged. Although the Government's use of the Supreme Court had been intended as a way of providing an incontestable resolution to the problem of Garry David, it had placed the various judges in a difficult position, burdening them with an unprecedented task and untried legislative machinery. Counsel struggled to find a reasonable pathway through an awkward process and, as one counsel who had been 'sacked' and reinstated several times remarked to Justice Smith, 'I find myself in a labyrinth, where the lamps are few' (Ian McIvor, *Third Hearing and Second Appeal*, 1 October 1992). Systemically, the discourse magnified the ambiguity of the mad–bad divide and led to an unproductive oscillation between prison and mental health services in its quest to identify a suitable niche for Garry.

Just as therapeutic economy and efficiency had not marked his management in the prison, the Act was thoroughly *untherapeutic* in its consequences. It created a much larger testing ground for Garry to parry his manipulative skills, so that these even began to intrude into the Court's sphere. Many of these problems would not have arisen had the Government not disregarded convention by seeking to usurp the judicial role through parliamentary direction. In so doing, it confused correctional and medical aims and used a Supreme Court process for a remarkable display of power, which then became difficult to retract or even moderate.

If the Community Protection Act symbolised a status degradation ceremony in Garfinkelian terms, then it was a manifest failure, as the events of 1990 to 1992 have demonstrated. First, the ripple effects of Garry David's practised art of resistance were underestimated. Second, the discourse on dangerousness could not remain focused, but merged with broader issues, such as philosophical and legal principles, ethical considerations, the administration of the prison and mental health systems, professional claims to special knowledge and the place of the severely personality disordered in society. Third, Garry was not aptly chosen as the sole recipient of such an unprecedented piece of legislation. He could not be relocated definitively to a 'lower social identity', despite formal adjudications, because he had the uncanny ability of exposing the weaker aspects of the Government's motives and strategy and disputing the reconstruction of his behaviour and personality, often in professional terminology. He was an active participant, not a submissive detainee to be overborne by custodial powers. The techniques he employed were complex, innovative and insightful.

By 1993, Garry began to show a renewed determination to take his case beyond the State's jurisdiction. On 19 May 1993 he sought a further variation of the order, which was adjourned by Justice Smith, to allow argument about the lapsed constitutional issues surrounding the Community Protection Act 1990 with a view to proceeding to the High Court. A Queen's Counsel was accordingly briefed. But before matters could be taken further, Garry David died in St. Vincent's Hospital on 11 June 1992 from peritonitis – a consequence of persistent self-injury to his bowel area over the preceding two years. The Coroner's report found death to have occurred from (i) purulent peritonitis; (ii) partial dehiscence of small bowel anastomosis; and (iii) laparotomy for subacute small bowel obstruction (*Coroner's Report*, 11 August 1993).

Garry had learned from experience that a discourse of dangerousness must rely on extrapolating a significant number of violent incidents from a person's life history and equating these with the possession of an innate capacity for violent actions. It is a method focusing on the extremes and it devalues other qualities, such as compassion and social interests. For this reason, the discourse described here would fall into the same trap of plausibility, selectivity and compression without some account of Garry beyond that of a resistant subject or skilful protagonist. The final chapters therefore, will look at his persona, or the image he sought to portray through the media and his own efforts to influence professional and public opinion. It is not, nor can it be, a psychological profile, but it does seek to present a more global picture than that constructed by his struggles with the prison, psychiatric system and the courts. The media's response will be taken into account, together with the legacy of the Garry David case for handling those perceived to be dangerous, both in a number of Australian jurisdictions and in the light of recent overseas developments.

CHAPTER 7

The Social Audience
and a Master Puppeteer

Representations, Images and the Media

If I am to be incarcerated it will be for a crime that I have committed and if I am properly punished I will do the time for that... The state has caused me an injustice, these other people are the servants of the state who are, if you like, the mechanics of the injustice and so I will resist them. (Second Hearing, 15 November 1991)

The Tortured Soul

It's cold and dark within this lonely cell
And the pain I feel inside is so hard to tell
I'm so afraid, sometimes I could cry
I'm so lonely, sometimes I want to die.

I need to get outside, the walls are closing in
I need a place to hide, from the tortured soul within
I need to see the clouds, blue sky and sun again
I need to be free from the tortured soul within.

I've forgotten how long now, the years I've been inside
The time I've lost count, the day and nights have passed me by
But memories still haunt me, and the guards are there to taunt me
Sometimes I wonder, if there's a future left for me.

My name is written in blood upon the wall
In the twilight gloom I hear the voices call
They're calling out my name from deep within my brain
Drivin' me insane with their sadistic games.

And the tortured soul within is the tortured flesh without
And the world I'm living in is a world I can live without
And the sorrow in my heart is a nightmare in the dark
And the scream in my throat is the madman's laugh.[1]

(Garry David 1981)

[1] Excerpts from the poems are reproduced with the kind permission of Robert David, who holds the copyright.

GARRY DAVID'S SELF-REPRESENTATION

One of the compelling lessons of an early French case of parricide, which involved medico-legal interaction, was that we should be mindful of the centrality, which the perpetrator of violence retains amidst the weaving of discourses. In a surprisingly sophisticated memoir, the semi-literate peasant and murderer, Paul Rivière, wrote in 1835 that:

> I shall…tell how I resolved to commit this crime, what my thoughts were at the time, and what was my intention. I shall also say what went on in my mind after doing this deed, the life I led among people, and the places I was in after the crime up to my arrest and what were the resolutions I took…all I ask is that what I mean shall be understood, and I have written it all down as best I can. (Foucault 1975, p.270)

This document forms both an explanation and clinical material in its own right. It is an explanation which retains a solidity lacking in the expert constructions; that is, the lawyers showed themselves uncertain about the exact nature of the link between mental state and criminal responsibility; and the doctors presented divided opinions, even though they were all described in court as being 'equally trustworthy' (Foucault 1975, p.216). Fontana refers to the exercise as 'a surreptitious complicity' (in Foucault 1975, p.179) on the part of doctors and lawyers to coax the victim into explaining either his criminality or madness, or to elicit an admission about feigning madness, thereby suggesting the coexistence of rationality and insanity. In his view, the extent to which the perpetrator's explanations were accepted would be advantageous in defining the limits of medical discourse and providing answers to legal questions.

Castel points out (in Foucault 1975, pp.250) that Dr Bouchard, who had spent the most time observing Rivière, relied on reference to the ancient Greek notion of an imbalance of bodily fluids, and popular interpretations of disordered behaviour. The specialist, Dr Vastel, fared somewhat better, having been trained in the tradition of Pinel and Esquirol. Nonetheless he did not marshal this knowledge sufficiently well to challenge legal authority over Rivière, but vacillated between mental deficiency and intellectual incoherence, when monomania alone could have sufficed. The third report was in the form of a petition from a group of eminent Parisian doctors who had not seen the defendant, but utilised the dossier to assert their opinion that he should be kept in confinement in a lunatic asylum. In this respect, they were harnessing medical knowledge to assert an important new authority in the legal sphere. A clinical diagnosis could now open the way to shift confinement from the penal sphere to an institution for the dangerous madman, thus asserting a newfound medical power based on special knowledge about madness. In hindsight, it is clear to see that the theoretical knowledge about insanity at the time, particularly that relating to monomania, offered little guidance for the law. In nineteenth-century terms, Rivière suffered from 'monomania', or partial delusion, which would now be termed paranoia. The jury rejected the defence's plea to find extenuating circumstances, although they then somewhat inconsistently petitioned the king for mercy. In 1840, Rivière committed suicide whilst in prison.

The resemblance of the discourse in the Rivière case to that arising in the context of the Garry David one is apparent, for knowledge about personality disorders is inherently uncertain, and Garry's own version of events confounded the more objective expert interpretations. As a consequence, in the search for an intrinsic element of 'dangerousness', his account tended to be ignored and the less rational components of his written work were sometimes used selectively as proof of a violent propensity. Roger Smith's comments about Rivière carry some resonance, when he notes that 'the relations between social groups, knowledge and power, in the struggle to reduce Rivière to a problem of social management' were exposed (Smith 1981, p.2). Although there were many important side skirmishes in the David case, there was a common thread of interest amongst politicians, lawyers, psychiatrists, the police and the community in identifying an acceptable means of social management. This common theme also links the cases of Charles John Guiteau, Robert Peter Tait and John Hinckley Jr, since the perception of dangerousness and delineation of the offender as either 'bad' or 'mad, were at the heart of a recurrent dilemma.

Yet if the story of Garry David were to be recounted solely from the perspective of those swept within the professional/political discourse about dangerousness, it would be incomplete because his personality might be sharpened to the point of caricature through the cumulation of negative incidents, at the expense of more positive attributes. As I have previously argued, discrete outbursts of violence are prone to become markers of unacceptable risk or social danger, and the professional mode of reconstructing their significance may diminish the more positive qualities about the person, so that these pale into irrelevance or are annulled (see Greig 1993, pp.48–9). For this reason, it is important to gain a sense of Garry beyond the more selective portrayal of the politicians, clinicians, prison officers, police, lawyers, and media. After all, *his* was the voice which should rightfully be at the centre; yet it was constantly being reshaped to meet professional and political expectations. The fact that this voice lacked constancy aided the process, for his personality disorder made him subject to mood swings and erratic ideas, intense anger, poor impulse control and, most relevantly of all, an unstable self-image with an accompanying degree of unpredictability. In other words, his voice could be described as having a mercurial quality, which contrasted with the objective evidence of violent incidents. In similar vein to the Rivière case, Garry David provoked a sense of uncertainty among his observers: there was a contradiction between his monumental lack of self-control and his unusual ability to use language skilfully to tease the emotions of his audience and elicit a mixture of fear, abhorrence, understanding, respect or pity. The challenge he issued was whether this contradiction between unreason and reason could be captured within the context of professional responses, and many examples have already been given of the way in which Elias's 'fantasy knowledge' did infiltrate more reality-based forms (Elias 1991, pp.57–75).

Garry's self-portrayal as a victim of arbitrary state power gave him an unprecedented opportunity to exploit the label of dangerousness. He clearly revelled in this opportunity, viewing himself with some justification as an actor on a broader stage. His enigmatic quality, together with his well-honed manipulative skills deriving from the severe personality disorder, suggest that a search for consistent themes or behavioural patterns would be unwise. Nevertheless, some exploration of his written work – poems, short stories and songs – enhances the sense of his presence in events, as do his more studied presentations before the Mental Health Review Board and the Supreme Court. The value of incorporating Garry's mode of communication into this narrative lies in its counterbalancing of the clinical/legal views, which were constrained by the need to situate him within the fluid boundaries of 'dangerousness'. The use of this material is naturally selective from a quite large literary and artistic output, and from observations made during the course of a series of ongoing and complex events.

There were many aspects about Garry David which confounded the media stereotype of dangerousness so confidently reinforced by politicians. First, he was short, of slight build and almost effeminate in physique. The thin, shoulder-length hair and cloth headband covered the mutilation of his ears. Small, round, tinted glasses made him appear studious and older than his mid-thirties, as did his pale, drawn appearance suggestive of a prison pallor. A brown mock leather jacket, collarless shirt and flared pants harked back to the style of the 1970s, as if he were somehow fixed in a time warp. Over the period 1990 to 1993, his increasing physical debilitation became evident and those who saw him only at intervals expressed concern about his health and weight loss. Garry himself was well aware of his appearance being at odds with his reputation. In one interview with a journalist, he said:

> A lot of people have the impression that I'm some sort of two-headed monster. They have created a persona that has grown from a small ogre to something else. Frankenstein was a fictional character, created just like me.

And the more Frankenstein was mistreated, the worse he became. (*Who Weekly*, 4 May 1992)

The sketch from his personal art folder, purporting to be a self-portrait, depicts an unassuming figure with drooping shoulders: hesitant, sad, and reluctant to face the world (figure 7.1). There is a distinct lack of resemblance to fictional images of masculine aggression, so that the sketch rather disconcertingly mocks the conventional stereotype. The only suggestion of danger is in the movement of the hand into the shoulderbag, where a weapon may perhaps be concealed. Otherwise, we are presented with a picture of a person who is introspective, self-contained and retains a notable self-possession, with perhaps even a touch of slyness. The sharp nose, scratched out eyes and firm, downward turn of the mouth hint at the remoteness, yet shrewdness and determination of a person who has neither the desire nor aptitude to engage fully with others.

Figure 7.1 Garry David's self-portrait

Second, Garry lived a rich fantasy life which was difficult to distinguish from reality, yet often used as an excuse for some of his misbehaviour. For example, he maintained throughout his imprisonment that he was the father of twin girls, one of whom had died unexpectedly at the age of three years, following which his de facto wife had committed suicide. Images of contented domesticity with his family sometimes crept into the poems and outbursts of violence often accompanied the anniversary of their supposed deaths. Another part of Garry's life, which is inherently uncertain, concerns his allegations about his father using him for bizarre acts of sexual abuse during childhood, such as nailing him to a crucifix at some Great Ocean Road location. His relationship with his mother later came to be romanticised, although there were accounts of Garry threatening to kill her on a number of occasions, and once attacking her with a knife. A 1977 letter to her contains a skull and crossbones, a drawing of a bomb and the words 'Poison' and 'Death is Justice'. His grandfather, he maintained, was a foundation member of the Palestinian Liberation movement commanding large forces of anarchists, but in reality he was part of a well-known merchant family in Melbourne. Many of these claims are simply grandiose and many can be confidently discounted, such as the occasional references to his degrees in music and literature at the university, extensive studies in marine biology and being the recipient of prestigious overseas literary prizes and music contracts. As Margaret Hobbs, his parole officer, reported, the father also 'displays the same *pseudologica fantastica* as Garry, but with far less dramatic impact' (2 March 1992).

A third aspect, which seemed discordant with the label of being the most violent offender in Victoria, was the diversity of his interests, including an appreciation of music and composing, playing the guitar, writing, computer programming and graphics, leatherwork, sketching, phonetics, the care of birds and collecting articles on gardening and gourmet cooking. His writings are not totally self-absorbed, but depict a sensitivity to social issues such as homelessness, abortion and suicide. In his poems, there is a sense of humour and wonderment at the human condition, as well as philosophical questioning; and evidence of a special concern for the young and elderly. But there are also glimpses of a person who relishes cruelty and violence, who indulges in childish obscenities and fantasises about sexually sadistic and extreme acts. Many of the poems exude a fascination with death and there are occasional forebodings about his own death in captivity. Yet in the totality of his writings these violent themes are by no means the most dominant. Many of the songs and poems are joyous and seem not to have been written by a person incarcerated for most of his life. Others are insightful and often disturbing in their commentary on the stresses of suburban life or the workplace and expression of the innocence of childhood or the difficulties attaching to old age. The writings reveal a strong empathy in depicting the lives and inner torments of others, such as the vagrant, social outcasts, the hustler, the drug-addicted female prisoner, the prison warder and homeless teenagers. Longer narratives deal with the rigours of life in Saigon following the Vietnam conflict; conservation issues, especially the need to protect animals and birds; and there are recurrent themes of love, grief and abandonment, often presented allegorically.

In many of these works we see glimpses of pathos, wit and nostalgia for an ordinary existence lost in childhood and denied in the future, because 'I'm walking out of rhythm, I can't find the beat' ('Resignation', 29 December 1989). Observations are astute. The nice contrast between the working week of the pin-suited executive and his activities as 'the weekend cowboy' is well drawn. In all, it is a remarkable collection of writings, only a small proportion of which can be dismissed as melodramatic or sentimental outpourings, for much is a commentary on society in general, and the custodial system in particular, from a highly moral stance. The extent to which these poems and stories are reflective of either a deep or fleeting emotional experience, or the degree to which they were intended as literary devices to arouse the sympathy and interest of particular readers, must remain a matter of speculation.

Not unnaturally, some of the material relates to Garry's own situation of being 'wounded by a system with singular views' ('An Ice-cube in Hell', February 1987), and while there are lurid and angry descriptions about the behaviour of prison officers, whom he depicts as being unhappy pawns of the confinement process, many pieces reflect on his own despair about the deprivations, lack of caring and anonymity ('memorise your number, forget your name; each day and night, more of the same' – 'The Beast', 16 October 1992). Two are illustrative:

Guarding the Gates

I am just a number
I have no name, no human face,
time has eroded my resistance
despair has overcome my rage;

my eyes, like a mirror
reflect the agony of my soul,
and my heart struggles faintly,
ravaged by pain and cold.

I have added my contribution
to the graffiti on the wall.
Who knows the miseries
behind these unknown writers' scrawls?

Some are signed with initials
some end with just a curse
a few offer solace,
but most are short and terse.

I see bloody prints upon the bars
left by some unknown hand.
I wonder if he lived?
But I guess it makes

little difference to the damned.
And besides, the guards just do their duty,
and the job pays rather well,
but how much do you pay a man

to guard the gates of hell?

(1984)

A Deeper Darkness

If a sighted man lives
For too long in the darkness
Then so, too, will he be blinded.
He may see, but his vision will not register.

There will be no poetry, music,
Or action in his movements.
He will not sense or be strong
Enough to clasp the caring hand,

Reaching out to guide his direction,
His legs will stumble, his heart will falter,
And his soul will cease to be.
His life will have lost all forward momentum,

For him, there is no light
At the end of the tunnel...
Only a deeper darkness.

(24 October 1984)

But despair is only one of the emotions repeatedly, and sometimes self-pityingly, expressed. Many of the poems describe the prison as a battleground, with his own status as being akin to that of a warrior. One of the more interesting of these is headed 'Internal Conflicts':

My heart is a desolate place, barren,
Haunted only by dreams and memories,
Populated by faceless figures
In a featureless landscape.

Sometimes I venture hesitantly
Into the timeless corridors of my tortured past,
My feet drag in the windswept sands
Of the endless roads of agony,

Etched like acid into glass.
It takes courage to return to soliciting avenues,
Looking for an escape that will not require
A quick exit from this world.

It is daunting when one is forced to face
The uncivilised jungle of war-torn youth,
Entombed in the computer-tapes of the ravaged mind
Like a sarcophagus in a time-worn pyramid.

I am guided only by my desire to seek and destroy the skeletons
Who too often return to attack my future stability;
Who claw at the fragile web of my sanity
Their teeth bared, fangs dripping venom

And using my lips to utter their profanities.
Yes, I hesitate, unsure of my strengths, my steps unsteady,
But urged on by my relentless soul
Offering encouragement to my trembling heart.

I wish I had a weapon with which to fight these formless demons
Something similar to the razor
With which I fight the bloody battles
Of my unprotesting body.

But I am unarmed and forced into conflict
With only intangibles to use in my defence,
Like a swordless gladiator or a toothless tiger;
Freedom must, I suppose have its expense.

I do not like retreats, I consider it cowardly regardless of costs;
If one must fight, one must also accept any loss;
But surrender is unthinkable and it cannot be contemplated,
Though a warrior should never rush blindly into battle,

Again, a warrior should not hesitate, or he may falter.
I have shed blood on many occasions, wounding, but more often
Being wounded by my more skilful opponents;
Yet, I have stood my ground, fighting to retain the remnants

Of my life, to erect a foundation on which I can built a future.
I believe we each live our lives like jugglers or tight-rope walkers,
If we slip, we may fall, and if we fall we may never recover.
Sometimes we must tiptoe like ballet dancers,

We must go around the domestic problems
We so often seem to encounter
Still knowing that we will have to face them sooner or later.
And some, like me, have to struggle for our very existence.

We must be heroes in a cowardly world,
But we are more often than not like children.
Forced to wear the mantle of demi-gods by circumstances.
I ask only for life, life that is free of the curses of human-kind.

Perhaps I ask for too much.
Perhaps I have no right to ask or expect anything.
But I cannot accept my fate like a weakling;
I must fight and to hell with the consequences.

(January 1986)

This is one of his less-polished efforts, but it still exhibits moments of insight, although it does degenerate into a crude justification for his resistant stance. A more philosophical appraisal of his position is contained in 'Time Is an Ambush':

Time is an ambush;
it creeps up from behind,
and preys upon my living flesh
like a vulture, stealing sanity from the mind.

I must guard my eyes
from this monster,
though my vision is all that's left.
Already have I lost my dreams

and aspirations, as I gasp painfully
with each tortured breath.
Time is an ambush;
the coward at my back,

its Judas' kiss upon my cheek
to distract my defences, from
its secret sneak attack.
I run forward to escape,

dodge, twist and turn, pursued,
ducking the heavy-handed blow.
A narrow miss, but its pendulum swing
assures it will return.

Time is an ambush:
a methodic cold assassin,
the ageless blade extended –
death its only passion.

And time is an ambush;
a grave yet to be filled,
but why do I still cling to flesh
when the soul immortal,

long ages passed, is killed?

(November 1984)

These passages are sufficient to indicate that writing was an important medium of communication for Garry. He used samples of his work to conduct correspondence with some 30 people from a variety of backgrounds, the majority of whom were women, and he invited thoughtful responses to philosophical questions and a sharing of emotional experiences. This contact with people outside the prison was a significant part of his social interaction and all communications, including the poetry received in return, were dated and filed in separate categories on his computer. In many instances, Garry developed a thoughtful and sustained correspondence over a lengthy period with a range of correspondents.

In 1992 he took advantage of the opportunity to cultivate an admiring coterie of young people undertaking their final year Victorian Certificate of Education examinations by inviting them to view his anomalous situation and the prison experience through his eyes. He suggested that they submit written questions, which he answered carefully and at length. The most frequent student request was for an explanation about the inflammatory document, *Blueprint for Urban Warfare* (20 November 1987), which police had discovered under his cell mattress during a 1989 raid. It was subsequently leaked to the *Sun* and used as a significant weapon in the Government's determination that he should not be released. One of Garry's answers to a student question about the import of this document was as follows:

Question: Considering that you wrote these alleged assaults on your cell wall, if you are rehabilitated, as you and your lawyer requested, would you actually commit these offences?

Answer: No, I would never do any of the things I am alleged to have threatened. The simple truth is that I have never made these threats. Back in the mid eighties, I worked with a psychologist, who suggested that a good way for me to release aggression would be to write down my anger instead of reacting violently, as I used to do, when I was confronted with a situation I found stressful. Her idea was to release that aggression the same way that people release aggression by yelling, smashing plates, etc. The idea was to externalise my anger in a harmless way. It is something most people do but in somewhat different ways, such as watching violent or pornographic movies and so on. The idea was that, after I had written down these angry thoughts, I would at a later stage come back and examine those thoughts and the anger I had felt at the time. But there was never a time when those written thoughts were related to the reasons for whatever may have caused my anger. It was simply a way of releasing tension.

Other written responses to students' questions related to the breadth of his interests; his strong belief in civil liberties; and the problems he had encountered with the prison system over such a lengthy period. They were calculated to arouse sympathy about the injustice of his position and show an uncanny ability to communicate with young people. For instance, his introduction was casual, and frank:

First of all, allow me to say that you kids sure ask a hell of a lot of questions! And my replies are, in some cases, also long. I have tried to answer your questions with total honesty, and have done so perhaps with some embarrassment on my part.

Answers such as these were intended to paint a picture of his persona in a far more complete way than could be achieved within the more formal discourse of dangerousness, and can be viewed as a skilful and subtly exercised means of eliciting student support. He was constantly attuned to student reaction, as this comment depicts so well:

Some of you would feel sorry for me or have some sympathy for me. Let me assure you I do not want sympathy. And not because I am too proud to accept it either, I just do not have any sympathy for myself, so I do not want it from others. Some of you must think I should be kept locked up and never be allowed to see daylight again. And many of you don't know what to think. But when you read some of the poetry I have written you will be even more confused...

In closing, I would like to say that before you judge me, look carefully at the poetry, the songs and short stories I have written. They come from my heart. Keeping me in gaol is a death sentence. Do I deserve that? I have something to offer the community. My future is not only in my hands, it is also in yours. (8 March 1992)

Garry's mode of giving evidence to the Mental Health Review Board and the Supreme Court, both orally and in writing, illustrates a keen rhetorical ability. In the former instance, in particular, his response to extensive questioning was consistent and reasonable, even when justifying his most provocative actions. In fact, it was an assured performance, contrasting with the changed views and inconsistencies of some of the psychiatric evidence, and Board members could only commend it. They noted that an 'ordinary sensible person' would be unlikely to regard him as being mentally ill on the basis of his appearance and his 'logical, calm and coherent' answers. Despite some of his explanations being 'highly unusual', they still retained an air of plausibility in the context in which they occurred (MHRB, 9 May 1990).

This view was upheld by the various Supreme Court Judges, who found an internal logic to much of Garry's evidence, although it was often a strained rationalisation of extraordinary events, such as the barricading, assaults and self-mutilation at Mont Park. The 'voice' of Garry David in these serious forums was articulate and reasonable, starkly at odds with the factual evidence of his unrestrained forays into displays of violence. Each Judge attempted to reconcile these two disparate images. Justice Hedigan admitted that Garry's personality 'loomed like a shadow' before him during the second hearing of the Community Protection Act, and he took the opportunity to make his own observations after probing the more difficult areas directly with the appellant (*Second Hearing*, Judgment, 15 November, 1991, p.89). Garry's composure was once again imperturbable, but the Judge discerned what appeared to be a tendency to redefine events to minimise criticism, and he considered that this might have been part of 'his manipulative disposition' (*Second Hearing*, Judgment, 15 November 1991, p.72). He found him to be intelligent, gifted, self-absorbed and wilful, and his self-mutilation to be consonant with his:

determination, obstinacy, fixation on refusing to submit, obsession with adhering to what passes for a principle in his mind, beating the prison by doing to himself far worse things than it could do to him, attention-seeking, self-absorption and the desire to cause others to fear him and wonder at him. (*Second Hearing*, Judgment, 15 November 1991, p.95)

In keeping with the unprecedented nature of the proceedings, he concluded with a literary analogy, likening Garry David to a shipwrecked sailor, tantalising close to would-be rescuers:

> The arid summary presented earlier in these reasons hardly depicts the inhuman landscape of David's existence, walled-in, optimism blighted, imagination stilled, the dreary round of the gaol's monotony, cell-confined 16 hours daily. Yet he has been the self-destroyer, the author of his own tragedy. No one, not even the absent parents or the orphanage minders made him steal, shoot or hate anyone. Even now, as he clings like a shipwrecked mariner to the wreckage, some obscure principle forbids him to accept the hand that beckons him towards rescue and the open door… The book on Garry David has not been closed. There has been but another page turned. (*Second Hearing*, Judgment, 15 November 1991, p.95)

In several of the hearings Garry amplified his views by submitting written statements to the relevant judges. For example, in an 11-page letter to Justice Hedigan, he outlined the 32 conditions he would accept to accede to the Government's desire to move him to Aradale. It was a blatant attempt to blackmail the Court and authorities, and many of the demands were outrageous. His later 5000 word submission to Justice Smith was more logical and restrained. It tackled some contentious areas of jurisprudence, such as the pressure being placed on him to behave appropriately, when experts had already given evidence that his personality disorder rendered him, at least to some degree, less than responsible for his actions (*Third Hearing and Second Appeal*, 1992). It is noteworthy that, at the time concerned, Garry was due to appear before the prison Governor's Court on four disciplinary charges, but his request to call a forensic psychiatrist and a forensic psychologist to give evidence on his behalf had been refused although, as he wryly commented, such witnesses were deemed essential to the Attorney-General's handling of its own case.

There were other legal issues to which Garry drew attention in this carefully worded document. He wrote that he had been distressed to learn that one barrister appeared to be keeping a scoreboard of the outcome of each court action, even though he had not been charged and the issue at stake was his liberty. He noted, too, that the legislation inevitably focused on the negative aspects of his character at the expense of an interest in other attributes. In an attempt to redress this balance, he did at one stage call some fellow prisoners as witnesses, so that they might tell the Court of his acts of kindness. However, they were unimpressive and distinctly uncomfortable in the formal surrounds of the Supreme Court, in marked contrast with the more assured performances of expert witnesses. Nonetheless, in both Garry's written document and in calling prisoners on his own behalf he had taken the initiative to present quite trenchant criticisms to a Supreme Court Judge,

using the only means available to him to encroach into the discourse being orchestrated by lawyers and psychiatrists.

MEDIA IMAGES

The reasoned strategy which Garry struggled to sustain in the face of his bouts of
uncooperative behaviour was undermined by some of the media publicity. I
propose now to turn to those images, which crept into community consciousness
and served to enhance his reputation for bizarre behaviour, if not frank dangerousness. Following this, I shall move to a consideration of the way in which the media
typically constructs images about deviant behaviour. This is a powerful means of
supporting the prevailing political view and in the Garry David case there was
evidence of increasing media vacillation about his portrayal in the light of the
Victorian Government's clear intentions. There were few means at Garry's disposal
to correct inaccurate reporting, which emanated from a variety of sources and,
indeed, he seemed to have a vicarious sense of enjoyment about the way his reputation for dangerousness was being enhanced without any specific direction on his
part, and despite being locked away in maximum security facilities. For example,
on a number of occasions media personnel received threatening letters, purportedly signed by him but which, on closer inspection, were later revealed to be a
hoax. For example, the presenter of a morning breakfast programme received such
a letter during the hearing of the Community Protection Bill, and this was later
published in the *Sun*. Closer inspection revealed that the author claimed to have
written it in J Division (not J Ward); it was signed by 'Gary J. David', not 'Garry Ian
Patrick David'. Despite such dubious origins, these added to the folklore confirm-
ing the general view about his violence, particularly from the end of 1989 through
to the first half of 1990. However, the ease with which such mischievous material
could enter the public domain did begin to lead to uncertainty about the author-
ship of other widely reported documents.

Sometimes counsel unintentionally assisted a slanted portrayal of Garry by
indulging in extravagant imagery of an eminently quotable kind. In Supreme
Court hearings, Garry's counsel, Dyson Hore-Lacey, compared him to the shrewd
protagonist, McMurphy, who was finally overcome by the power of psychiatric
treatment in *One Flew Over the Cuckoo's Nest*. (In other circumstances, this simile
would have found favour with its recipient, who had often likened himself to the
main protagonist in this book.) Another lawyer recalled Gollum, the malevolent
creature of Tolkien's *The Hobbit*: 'as dark as darkness, except for two big round
pale eyes like telescopes in his thin face' (reported in *The Age*, 14 June 1993). A
senior prison officer referred to him as 'a tortured child, trapped inside a man's
body' (CPO Karen Linstrom, *Third Hearing and Second Appeal*, 1992). It is scarcely
surprising that reporters too were tempted by the hyperbole. Their writings fre-

quently hinted at a sinister, uncontrollable madman, and some of the more nebulous allusions produced powerful images for public consumption. For example, one journalist described Garry's life as an 'amalgam of Dickens, Kafka and the Marquis de Sade' (A. Attwood, *The Age*, 14 June 1993). Others found the contradictory messages Garry enjoyed disseminating to be unnerving. There was the victim and the perpetrator; the friend and the assailant; the sentimentalist and the anarchist; the freedom lover, intensely fearful of liberation; the outcast, needing, but rejecting friendship; the cooperative prisoner and recalcitrant detainee; and the quietly spoken person dramatically transformed by explosive outbursts of rage. His own disturbing painting on a wall at J Ward was released by the press and, more than any other image, compounded the sense of these contradictions (figure 7.2). As one reporter described the representation, it showed:

> A bearded and long-haired figure, gaunt and furious, more than two metres tall and dressed in colonial convict garb, lunging through a wall of blackness. He has burst his chains and in his right fist he wields what looks like a straight razor. Behind him are glimpses of sky and trees that seem to ask whether the figure is escaping to – or from – freedom. It is an ominous and disturbing work. (G. Tippet, *Sunday Age*, 20 June 1993)

Prior to Garry's expected release date, the press immersed the public in images of his self-mutilation and violence. It was an effective campaign, because a general belief about his dangerousness seeped into deep-rooted community fears and justified a need for concerted action. The spectre of the Hoddle and Queen Street massacres was steeped in the community consciousness. Garry's particular threat of making the earlier event 'seem like a picnic' was couched in words reviving visual memories and taunting the populace of a painful event, not long past. It represented a deliberate and hurtful reminder of death and injury inflicted without cause and insinuated that the power of unleashed violence wielded by one person on an unsuspecting community had yet to be restrained.

In the context of these resurgent fears, it was inevitable for the media to strip Garry to essentials and depict him in a stereotypical way as being an intrinsically dangerous human being. This depersonalisation enabled the dramatic accounts of his violence and self-mutilation to be reordered in terms of the status category of dangerousness. Dissenting views were rarely incorporated into the early headlines, which emphasised his capacity for irrational bouts of violence towards general and specific targets. These included:

'Big Alert on Kill Threats' (*Herald*, 1 November 1989)

'Prisoner's Mental State Under Scrutiny After Mass-Slaughter Threat' (*The Age*, 2 November 1989)

Figure 7.2 Portrait by Garry David painted on a wall of J Ward, Ararat
Source: Courtesy of Craig Sillitoe, *Sunday Age*, 20 June 1993

'Prisoner Vows He'll Go On Killing Spree' (*The Age*, 2 November 1989)

'I'll Go to War When I Get Out: Prisoner' (*Sun*, 6 November 1989)

'Danger Man' (*Sun*, 6 November 1989)

'Don't Set Him Free – Victim' (*Sun*, 7 November 1989)

'Free Me – Or Else: Gunman Vows to Get Revenge' (*Sun*, 14 December 1989)

'Don't Let Him Out: Prison Expert Warns of Risk' (*Sun*, 15 December 1989)

'Kill Threat Letter Leads to Probe' (*Sun*, 16 December 1989)

'Webb "Featured in Jail Assaults"' (*Sunday Sun*, 17 December 1989)

'Torture "Target" Living in Fear' (*Sun*, 20 December 1989)

'Kill Threat Jail Man Certified' (*Herald*, 10 January 1990)

'Prisoner "Set for Gun Battle"' (*Sun*, 17 February 1990)

'Prisoner "Issued Murder Threats": Board Told of Danger to Police' (*Sun*, 21 February 1990)

'Kill Threat Letter to DJ Lawyers' (*Sun*, 8 April 1990)

'Ex-con to Flee Webb Kill Threat' (*Sun*, 14 June 1990)

'"Target" Looks for Place to Hide' (*Herald*, 18 June, 1990)

The major photographic image appearing in newspapers and television was that of a helpless David being carried into the Supreme Court to face the attempted murder charges of 1980 (figure 7.3). He had, at the time, lacerated his tendons and was being carried by two police officers. In many respects, the selection of this image was appealing, for it conveyed a number of different messages. It confirmed Garry's readiness to self-injure, and perhaps even to attempt preying on the sympathy of the Court, yet in the face of extreme provocation the police were being even-handed in their duty of care, although their beliefs about this man's dangerousness and capacity to attack them were well known. In the context of containment, the photograph reassured the public that they had nothing to fear, since authorities had the matter under control.

A sensationalist style of reporting from the tabloid press continued unabated well into 1990 during the appeal to the Mental Health Review Board and until the commencement of the Supreme Court hearings. After this time the emphasis on Garry's innate violence gradually broadened to focus on the boundary between madness and badness, especially in the light of his capacity for *self*-violence. One of the most deliberately alienating and alarming reports was carried in an Adelaide weekend broadsheet, and replicated in the Sydney press, under the heading of 'Australia's Most **Unwanted Man'**, with the last two words appearing in heavy red block lettering and taking up the full page width. The accompanying article expressed disbelief about the psychiatric panel's refusal to certify Garry David, who appeared to a general public to be so obviously 'mad':

Figure 7.3 Garry David is carried by the police into the Supreme Court
Source: Photographer: John Krutop, courtesy of *The Age*, 4 July 1980

> All we know is that they refused to certify as insane an attempted murderer,
> compulsive self-mutilator, highly dangerous, unrehabilitated criminal, who
> had repeatedly threatened to massacre thousands of his fellow citizens.
> (*Adelaide Advertiser*, 19 May 1990)

In the light of this summation, it was not surprising that the report should claim
that psychiatry had been 'shoved aside by politics'. Its central and most influential
feature was the large site-map of Garry's self-inflicted injuries with directional
arrows to the relevant areas of his body – undoubtedly intended to capture the
imagination of a wide weekend reading public (Figure 7.4). The explicit visual
imagery conveyed an instant message of this man's readiness to destroy bodily
parts and endanger his own life. In view of his threats to members of the public and
others, the possibility of more general physical harm was implied to be
self-evident. Because this physical evidence about his 'dangerousness' appealed to
intuitive and sensually based knowledge, it also marked him as being definitively
different from ordinary members of society. But the site-map had another
function; its outline of the human body further depersonalised Garry by caricatur-
ing his behaviour and ensuring that bodily disfigurement became synonymous
with the mere invocation of his name.

A similar emphasis is evident in a contemporaneous Melbourne report,
entitled 'The Life and Violent Crimes of Garry Webb', purportedly based on 'a
highly confidential document, which concluded that he should remain incarcerated' (*Sunday Herald*, 26 May 1990). It relied on photocopies of a Bureau of
Criminal Intelligence document, graphically detailing the dates and list of Garry's
self-mutilations. At this same time, the *Herald-Sun* continued its campaign to ensure
Garry's containment with a report entitled 'Blueprint of Death: Webb's 49 Steps to
Bloody Terror: Bizarre Hitlist of Hate' (16 June 1990). It was the timing and
content of this article, which generated criticism from counsel on both sides
during the early part of the Community Protection Act 1990 hearing, because it
had been one of the documents marked as 'confidential' and 'privileged', when
tendered to the Mental Health Review Board. Its use at such a crucial time demonstrated disregard by the tabloid press of the issues in the case, and the Court considered the possibility that this report constituted contempt of both the Board and
its own authority. However, it was recognised that, whilst it might incite further
alarm in the community, the fact that there was no jury in the case would have
made it difficult to sustain such an action.

This was the first of many criticisms directed by the Court at the way the
written media were handling the case, such as choosing to report some of the
inflammatory comments of politicians, which occurred during the hearing. As
Michael Adams noted in his submission to Justice Fullagar, 'I think there is
agreement along the whole of the bar table that the treatment that some areas of

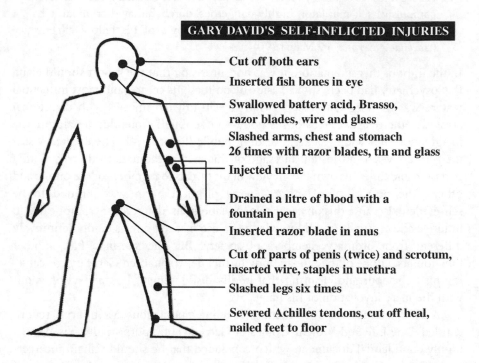

GARY DAVID'S SELF-INFLICTED INJURIES

- Cut off both ears
- Inserted fish bones in eye
- Swallowed battery acid, Brasso, razor blades, wire and glass
- Slashed arms, chest and stomach 26 times with razor blades, tin and glass
- Injected urine
- Drained a litre of blood with a fountain pen
- Inserted razor blade in anus
- Cut off parts of penis (twice) and scrotum, inserted wire, staples in urethra
- Slashed legs six times
- Severed Achilles tendons, cut off heal, nailed feet to floor

Figure 7.4 Body site map of Garry David's self-inflicted injuries
Source: Courtesy of the *Adelaide Advertiser*, 19 May 1990

the press have given Mr David has been absolutely outrageous – unfair, biased, and a disgrace to the journalistic profession' (*First Hearing*, 28 August 1990). The media interest was intense, intrusive and dehumanising throughout, in a number of respects. For example, in the Melbourne Magistrate's Court, Garry David had to endure more than a dozen artists staring at him for considerable periods of time before composing their sketches for the front page of the next edition. It was curious that the images varied so greatly and many seemed more evocative of the beliefs of the artist, rather than a simple representation of the physical persona of Garry David. In one sketch he is presented as a serious young man facing the Judge in a dignified and controlled way. Although fully aware of the gravity of his predicament, there is a hint of suppressed anger and frustration, but a resigned acceptance of the Court's authority (K. Joyce, *The Age*, 14 June 1990). The second sketch from a Supreme Court appearance is very different indeed (*The Age*, 7 August

1990). Here, the face is dark against a black background and has a surreal quality, demarcating this person from others (Figure 7.5). The features are gaunt, drawn and sharp, suggestive of an intense and brooding malevolence. The face has a haunting, sinister quality, heightened by the inscrutability of eyes hidden behind dark glasses. The strangeness and barely veiled threat in this visual image has to be regarded as a powerful medium of communication, creating a barrier to any attempts Garry David might initiate to evoke a more sympathetic response to his circumstances.

A second facet of the media response concerned the fact that most reporters consistently refused to use Garry's proper surname of 'David', rather than 'Webb', despite the courts and tribunals acceding to his wishes in this regard. A third asso-ciated, and alienating aspect of the mode of reporting, was the consistent practice

Figure 7.5 Sketch of Garry David in the Supreme Court
Source: Courtesy of John Spooner, *The Age,* 7 August 1990

of a centralised news source, the Australian Associated Press, referring to him inaccurately as the 'psychiatric prisoner Webb', thus moulding community beliefs that he possessed the dual attributes of madness and criminality, and hence by implication was to be doubly feared.

The media focus on Garry's violence did not lessen during 1990 to 1993, although the more conservative newspapers, such as the Melbourne *Age*, began to focus on other reporting avenues sympathetic to his situation, such as Government and police intransigence in dealing with him and the way in which civil rights violate preventive detention. Gradually, his image softened with a different style of headline:

- 'Sad Case of Hate and Fear' (*Sun*, 6 November 1989)
- 'Webb, A Scarred Legacy of '60s: Sex, Drugs and Abuse: One Man's Journey to Misery' (*Sun*, 14 June 1990)
- 'On the Cutting Edge of a Mad World' (*Australian* 2 July 1990)
- 'Public Enemy or a Public Victim?' (*The Age*, 8 April 1990)
- 'Trapped in a Web of Fear and Doubt' (*Herald*, 18 September 1990)
- 'Words From the Edge' (*Border Mail*, 8 October 1991)
- 'Portrait of a Tortured Soul' (*Herald-Sun*, 16 November 1991)

The next step was for reporters to seek Garry's own view about the proceedings, and he was quite inventive in finding ways to contact all forms of the media, despite the explicit prohibition of the Office of Corrections. Newspaper headings reflecting this more personal perspective included:

- 'Garry David Seeks Right of Reply' (*Sunday Age*, 15 July 1990),
- 'I am Not an Angel, But I am Also Not a Sinner' (*The Age*, 6 May 1991)
- 'Mutilation a Plea for Affection' (*The Age*, 8 October 1991)
- 'David Insists He is No Longer Violent' (*The Age*, 9 June 1992).

Garry's greatest media coup was to divert one of his telephone calls from Pentridge to a Melbourne talk back programme. This unexpected 15-minute interview was conducted while Victoria's Premier was waiting in an adjoining studio for his weekly radio session. When Premier Kennett became aware of the breach of prison regulations, he was angry and astonished, immediately issuing an order that all telephone privileges for prisoners at the gaol cease. The tables were turned when a Mont Park forensic patient used the same technique to claim an audience for his complaints about Garry's disruptive behaviour during the latter's brief stay there.

Although staff became increasingly vigilant, Garry breached security some weeks later by telephoning the same radio station – this time from the Mont Park Forensic Unit. The explanations he gave in these sessions were disturbing and difficult for the public to assimilate. He readily admitted to ongoing attempts to 'manipulate the system', but pleaded for rehabilitative support, which he claimed had been denied in any effective sense. In allowing this plea to go to air, the presenter was aware of a degree of manipulation and one radio critic later described the journalistic dilemma in the following terms:

> What we were hearing on radio was an argument pushed by a shrewd, but fundamentally disturbed man. As such, therefore, the act of putting him to air smacked as much of media exploitation of human pathos, as it did of a criminal/patient's bid for genuine social responsibility. As I write, I don't know which side of the fence to put David. All that is clear is the widening abyss of the man's suffering and, therefore, the unresolved difficulty relatively normal people must have interpreting his poignant utterances. (*The Age*, 16 July 1992)

DEVIANCE AND THE MEDIA'S ROLE

The changing attitudes of the media and attempts to relocate the issues within a broader framework of understanding are part of the way that social order issues are handled publicly. In this regard the media and the law share a similar function, since both individualise morality by creating narratives to enhance a sense of predictability and order (see Ericson, Baranek and Chan 1987, 1989, 1991). As Ericson himself has argued, they 'collectively constitute justice by turning accounts of what is into stories of what ought to be, fusing facts with normative commitments, values, beliefs and myths' (Ericson 1991, p.223). By focusing attention on the deviant person, the media simplifies the interpretation to be made and limits the range of actions considered appropriate. In this way, attention is deflected from structural issues of possible relevance, thereby legitimising political authority and supporting the activities of government

Initially, the Garry David case seemed to fit this formula very well and the Government was heartened by the obvious media support. The community was clearly faced with an exceptional flaunting of deviance and it was not unreasonable to expect a firm and authoritative stance to be taken. The press responded by seeking statements from the Premier and Cabinet Ministers. There was a plethora of reassuring headlines:

- 'Crabb's Vow on "Psycho"' (*Sun*, 8 January 1990)
- 'Bill a Must: Cain' (*Sun*, 10 April 1990)

- 'Cain Backs Bill to Stop Killer Release' (*Sun*, 10 April 1990 – a report to which Garry strongly objected, as he had not killed another person)

- 'Government Stands Firm: No Webb Release' (*Herald*, 10 May 1990)

- 'No Let-Up on Webb: State Vow' (*Herald-Sun*, 6 March 1991)

- 'State Moves to Keep Webb in Jail' (*The Age*, 6 March 1991).

Soon the assumption that the Government had the situation under control began to dissipate with questions surfacing about Garry's certification and the necessity of a one-man law, especially in view of the longstanding institutional failure to utilise an effective rehabilitative strategy. Media reports highlighted the ambiguity of the situation (see Manning 1987), with headlines critical of the regulatory mode of Government action, such as:

- 'Liberals Split on Jail Bill: Criminal Garry David Faces a Long Prison Stay' (*Herald*, 9 April 1990)

- 'ALP Group Opposes One-Man Law' (*The Age*, 10 April 1990)

- 'MP's Say State Should Let Garry Webb Go' (*The Age*, 31 May 1990)

- 'Outcry Over Law for One' (*Sun*, 5 April 1990)

- 'Justice "Denied" in Move on Prisoner' (*Sun*, 6 April 1990)

- 'Caution is Needed in One-Man Law' (*The Age*, 6 April 1990)

- 'Dangerous Offender Law is Last Option' (*The Age*, 25 July 1990).

The Government was not, at this stage, receiving the unqualified support of the media for its actions and the legal system was finding it difficult to carry out its tasks uncritically in view of the pressure to assist with proposed amendments to the Mental Health Act and the unusual structure created for Garry's preventive detention. A number of stumbling blocks had been encountered with the Law Institute of Victoria, some professors of law and individual barristers publicly criticising the Government's strategy and legislation. In addition, the Judges responsible for the hearings under the Community Protection Act had all expressed concern. More seriously still, the Federal Government had indicated that Victoria could possibly be in breach of international human rights obligations. Even the Government's intentions to broaden preventive detention had attracted influential legal critics.

In this climate of increasing doubt, media support was important to the Government in shoring up its official position in the eyes of the community. However, there were signs that journalists were increasingly sceptical about the necessity for governmental decisions of a singular kind and beginning to view its pursuit of Garry David as an unwarranted vendetta. The signs of a transformation in the style of reporting from the initial descriptions of bizarre behaviour and crude body maps began to recede to a more sympathetic portrayal of Garry's untenable position and the authorities' over-reaction. The stereotype of dangerousness, initially portrayed as self-evident, moderated in later articles, particularly in the light of society's power of banishment. By May 1992, one article bore the sub-title: 'Can Garry David Really Be the Most Dangerous Man in Australia?' (*Who Weekly*, 4 May 1992). In this he was referred to as 'a scapegoat' and the case likened to the over-zealousness of police and prosecutors in the much publicised 1980 Northern Territory case of Lindy Chamberlain, which rested on scientific evidence, much of which was compellingly dismantled in later hearings (see Bryson 1986). From 1991 onwards, Garry's image had a much more multifaceted presentation. He was viewed as having created 'a dilemma' for the Victorian Government, which 'had painted itself into a corner' with an unequivocal portrayal of one man's dangerousness, since this could only lead to moves for more broadly based indefinite sentencing in order to rationalise the original judgment (*The Age*, 14 May 1992).

In 1992 Garry made the cryptic comment: 'If they don't let me out this year, I think I will never get out. And, I will *not* stay locked up.' He was *not* to stay locked up. His prediction of his own death was borne out. The funeral, paid for by some senior members of the legal profession, academics, civil liberties groups, chaplains, doctors and politicians, brought together a diverse group of people, saddened by the loss of a gifted, but recalcitrant person, for whom society could find no lasting solution. There was a certain irony in the fact that contributions from many well-known people towards the cost of the funeral were channelled through a charity group and thereby became tax deductible. At the time Melbourne's conservative press resorted to emotive-style reporting of a life, which had finally ebbed in response to the frequent insults on his body:

> Garry David's funeral was his last rebellion. At exactly the moment his coffin sank through the floor to cremation, the strains of a heavy metal song, written specially for him could be heard: 'He's on the run/ He's somebody's son/ He's on the run/ He's got a gun'. (*The Age*, 22 June 1993)

The newspaper reports of Garry's death were low-key and there was sombre reflection about being observers to the increasing momentum of events which had engulfed such powerful professions as psychiatry, the law and politics. In many articles he was now accorded the dignity of the surname 'David' in place of 'Webb' – a minor victory, but one which seemed to be a symbolic expression of regret about so many of the facets of this case. There were other responses too, capturing that same sense of regret and ambivalence in being trapped with Garry in a struggle from which he could not be extricated, despite the best professional intentions. This is perhaps most clearly expressed in the words of Dr Peter Hearne to the Coroner:

> Throughout his time in prison Garry represented an enigma for those who were charged with his day to day care. It was almost beyond the ordinary comprehension even of those with custodial medical experience that a human being would be capable of performing self-mutilatory actions with the frequency and intensity performed over this time by this young man. Most regions of his body were involved at one time or another in a ceaseless war which he waged against those he perceived as powerful in his environment... Almost invariably...those who were charged with the task of caring for him would become tangled in the web of ambivalence he would weave rendering logical and compassionate care near impossible. (*Coronial Report*, 11 August 1993, p.2)

A psychiatrist, also involved in his care at Pentridge, adds another perspective to the impasse, which had evolved over a long period:

> What did Garry David want?... What would a man want who hated people, but who loved birds, who craved comfort but who avoided intimacy, who feared crowds, but wanted an audience? There is much to be gained in stating the obvious solution to his 'dangerousness': a comfortable home, hundreds of kilometres from nowhere, with an aviary and a radio-transmitter. If this sounds bizarre, then it is at least as pragmatic as the solution which the state seemed intent on imposing: incarceration by psychiatrists who did not want him as a patient, having treatment which he did not need for an illness he did not have. (Glaser 1994, pp.48–9)

His death should not be viewed as the end of the story, for there have been a number of developments designed to forestall any further Garry David sagas by reframing the boundary between badness and madness, and by articulating more clearly the responsibilities of both the Department of Corrections and Health in regard to the seriously personality disordered. The final chapter will explore the lessons of this case for both the Victoria context and other jurisdictions facing similar problems and provide some reasons for Garry David having been selected from amongst other personality disordered prisoners as having a dangerous propensity to wreak havoc on the community.

CHAPTER 8

The Prism of Dangerousness

And now the boy was being tried as a dangerous character against whom society must be protected.

'Just as dangerous a creature as yesterday's criminal', thought Nekhlyudov, listening to all that was going on. 'They are dangerous – but aren't we dangerous? ... I am a rake, a fornicator, a liar – and all of us, all those who know me for what I am, not only do not despise me but respect me. But even supposing this lad were more dangerous to society than anyone in this room, what in common sense ought to be done when he gets caught?' ...

'We rear not one but millions of such people, and then arrest one and imagine we have done something, protected ourselves, and nothing more can be required of us, now we have transported him from Moscow to Irkutsk.' (Tolstoy 1966, pp.165–6)

What, then is the role of the psychiatrist in penal matters? He is not an expert in responsibility, but an adviser on punishment; it is up to him to say whether the subject is 'dangerous', in what way one should be protected from him, how one should intervene to alter him, whether it would be better to try to force him into submission or to treat him. At the very beginning of its history, psychiatric expertise was called upon to formulate 'true' propositions as to the part that the liberty of the offender had played in the act he had committed; it is now called upon to suggest a prescription for what might be called his 'medico-judicial treatment'. (Foucault 1977b, p.22)

AN OVERVIEW

Garry David posed a fundamental paradox for the newly developed forensic structure of the state of Victoria. There was a marked contrast between the massive expenditure of time and effort to render him 'knowable' through the accumulation of prison files, clinical history, legal transcripts, incident reports, formal commissions of inquiry, parliamentary debate, media accounts and his own writings, and his uncanny ability to remain enigmatic by resisting the intensity of this examination, both subtly and directly. This combination of elusivity and a renowned unpredictability clouded by an aura of dangerousness enhanced the sense of drama surrounding the discourses designed to manage his exclusion. Although ostensibly rendered powerless by a web of unique legislation and legal moves, Garry still managed to provoke strong responses from observers, who were offered binary choices involving profound professional and policy implications: mental illness or personality disorder; treatment or punishment; a prison or an asylum; incarceration or release; dangerousness or non-dangerousness; criminality or mental illness. Whilst there is a certain artifice in highlighting these starkly opposed positions, it does assist in clarifying issues. Debates of this kind are not new, for the psychopath's position has historically been characterised by psychiatric and legal ambiguity. Neither were they dispassionate in this instance, since those closest to Garry had, over a period of years, been forced to reconcile their professional views with his needs and demanding behaviour, interspersed with moments of disarming charm and calculated attacks on their reputations.

Even this telling of the story is not immune from these considerations, for I had known Garry over many years. I was conscious of the difficulties he posed for the prison system, but was still unprepared for the reverberation of the political, legal and psychiatric reaction swirling around him at the time of his anticipated release. I also shared the growing sense of frustration about many aspects of this case: the closure of legal avenues of redress; the way in which ordinary civil rights had been disregarded and superseded by singular solutions; and the developing certainty that incarceration would be prolonged and eventually culminate in his custodial death. There was a dramatic irony about the struggle, which Garry had himself instigated, but which he could claim singled him out as being the unlucky victim of a political agenda, banishing him from the general community with images of dangerousness and persecution. In order to counteract proximity to these events, I have used a multiplicity of voices to augment the competing perspectives of this narrative, for to do otherwise would have encroached into the psychiatric domain with an unwarranted layer of interpretation. Even so, there is always a subjective element in searching for patterns and a degree of selectivity in identifying contrasting representations and policy shifts. For example, it is tempting to give undue weight to polarised views, yet this is the only way that the complex sequence of events begins to unfold in a meaningful sense, even though the author's perception adds a further layer to an already diverse mix of psychiatric, legal and political opinions. There is constant reinterpretation, too, for as Gusfield reminds us:

> The text we write is itself a stage in the process. What the reader does in the act of reading is still another. What is known, what is written, and what is conveyed are by no [means] the same. (Gusfield 1989, p.62; see also Maines 1993)

Garry David was chosen as the subject of this study for two reasons. Political and press statements had reinforced his burgeoning reputation as being Victoria's most dangerous person and consummated it in special legislation. It was an anomalous move since many prisoners exhibit similar characteristics of self-mutilation, aggression and personal threats, yet their actions remain concealed within the custodial system. Certainly his behaviour was particularly challenging, but this alone did not explain why the Government chose to embark on an unprecedented course of detention in the absence of either criminality or mental illness. This reaction begged further inquiry.

The second reason for choosing this prisoner as the focal point of analysis was because of my longstanding interest in the way in which the boundary between criminality and mental illness is drawn in practice, and three elements emerged to characterise the vexed attempts to separate these two states in the discourse, which followed. These were *ambiguity, contingency* and *negotiation*: ambiguity in terms of boundary uncertainty; contingency arising from the particular confluence of professional and sociopolitical circumstances at any one time; and negotiation as the process of clarifying 'ownership' of a problem, both legally and administratively. The use of 'dangerousness' as the bridge to facilitate movement between criminality and mental illness is problematic and poses very different legal and social consequences. Despite its essential lack of clarity, it alludes to a third state worthy of attention – that of the 'criminally insane', or 'psychiatric prisoner'. They are evocative words – 'a double whammy' – redolent of the idea that there exists among us a special group of people imbued with a volatile mix of criminality, mental disorder *and* dangerousness – their actions so beyond the bounds of ordinary comprehension that preventive detention, generally conceded to be a last resort measure, becomes an inviting solution. Its rationale is often couched in treatment terms, thus ignoring the empirical evidence dispelling its efficacy, especially in those extreme cases which have run the gamut of both the criminal justice and mental health systems.

By creating the legislative structure to isolate danger in any one individual, parliaments may actually be instituting socially dangerous procedures, which bypass the safety net of legal conventions. The justification for such new powers of detention can then shift from criminal justice controls to the civil bases of the mental health system, without the leavening effect of review processes and leave provisions. This gives rise to a form of double jeopardy whereby some persons are punished for criminal offences and then, on the basis of this same behaviour, treated in a psychiatric facility for their underlying trait of 'dangerousness'. Psychopaths were particularly disadvantaged by this type of legislation in the era of social defence strategies in many US states. The study by Linda Sleffel (1977) is particularly useful in pointing to the inconsistent use of this type of legislation and the way it can be used selectively with evidence of sharp variations between Canadian states. Such defence strategies typically introduced a separate status category of psychopathy, simply on the ground that proceedings were 'clearly, demonstrably or manifestly civil' and *ipso facto* beyond the provisions of any criminal code (Dershowitz 1973, p.1296). The fallacy of this circular reasoning is palpable, but it readily leads to the exclusion of the principles of proportionality, protection against cruel and unusual punishment, self-incrimination and the use of *ex post facto* laws (Dershowitz 1973, pp.1299–1300). The fact that the Government of Victoria chose to move beyond 'just deserts' to a strange form of selective incapacitation rendered it vulnerable to charges of neglecting these jurisprudential principles.

In the process of tracing the tangled web of events surrounding the construction of dangerousness as a form of professional knowledge, and its translation into policy conjoining civil and criminal elements, it became apparent that preventive detention is far more than just a specific legislative mechanism to guarantee continued custody. Perhaps because of the singular circumstances of this case, it had unanticipated effects on a broad range of people – from fellow prisoners, to carers, politicians, governmental advisers, the press and the judiciary. Its rationality as a legislative solution was exposed by the final folly of the proposal for secure containment in a mental health facility staffed by prison officers. If Garry could not be allocated with some certainty to either system, then the difficulty would scarcely be resolved by combining them. In essence, politicians were failing to recognise the distinctiveness and incompatibility of criminal justice and mental health provisions. They were placing at risk the autonomy of professional decision making by tampering with the ability of either psychiatry or the law to separate treatment/punishment issues and determine the proper location of a person with severe personality disorder. At the time, Dr William Glaser, a Melbourne psychiatrist, offered a particularly forthright evaluation:

> It is this deliberate attempt by the state to massively shift the power/knowledge balance in its favour which is the most frightening aspect of the Garry David saga. There is ample evidence that the relevant government departments were prepared to use extensive social and political influence in order not only to justify the use of powers not usually granted to government in a Western democracy but also to arbitrarily redefine the boundaries of scientific knowledge for purely political purposes. Psychiatry, often an ally of the state in this sort of endeavour, became in Garry David's case, one of the major casualties. (Glaser 1994, p.46)

Certainly the political pressures did generate a degree of rancour and division within the ranks of psychiatrists, not only in relation to the uncertainty of knowledge about the diagnosis, treatment and management of some with severe personality disorder, but also because of the political intrusions occasioned by public service appointees having replaced the traditional medical administration of the Office of Psychiatric Services. The forensic sphere now discovered that there were implications associated with the restructuring and significant expansion required by its *New Directions* policy (October 1986). From another perspective, however, Glaser's comments are perhaps too bleak. It was true that psychiatry was under siege and, in the short term its image was tarnished by having to reconcile competing professional and political demands; but, equally, there were some positive outcomes, such as the redefinition of its responsibility to create a niche for at least some persistent self-mutilators considered to be a danger to themselves, and legislative amendments, which currently offer more positive guidance about the clinical signs of mental illness and are supportive of the expert view.

On another ground too I would take issue with Glaser's views. His indictment of political interference suggests that the organisation of professional knowledge should be immune from outside influence, yet this study has shown that psychiatry's focus is on matters about which there are strongly held cultural beliefs. 'Dangerousness' and 'mental illness' come into this category, because they are linked with community fears. Whilst psychiatrists may utilise their clinical data and research in a more organised way than the ordinary person, knowledge about these states is not confined to their expertise alone. Community perceptions have an impact on what constitutes unreasonableness and, accordingly, professional knowledge cannot claim to be an unfettered power. It is tempered by ordinary understandings of human behaviour and, more particularly in the case of the law, by the need to moderate the state's power with attention to legal principles. One cannot therefore be entirely dismissive of the Government's attempts to 'redefine the boundaries of scientific knowledge for purely political purposes'. However, direct political intrusion into professional areas of decision making is yet another matter, and there are strong grounds for disputing the justification given for the various actions pertaining to Garry David. Nonetheless, governments do have a qualified part to play in creating the economic, social and therapeutic climate to deal effectively with the ungovernable, and to coopt the professions as allies in this goal. This is not a new role, but it is one being handled very differently in a neo-liberal environment with its various forms of managerialism and special concern with risk avoidance strategies (Greig 1997; Rose 1999). What went wrong in the Garry David case was twofold: the overly confronting nature of the political intrusion made it difficult to achieve any effective alliance; and the Government showed poor insight into the untoward forensic consequences of the path on which it had embarked. Essentially, it was trampling on well-established professional principles to defuse community fears already exacerbated by the published views of senior politicians.

The dilemmas in the Garry David case need to be situated against the historical and cultural components of redefining formal knowledge in forensic psychiatry, especially those cases evoking public and political concern about dangerous offenders. Brief reference has already been made to those involving Rivière, Guiteau, M'Naghten, Tait and Hinckley, which span different time frames and different continents. There is an enduring sense about a commonality of themes and as yet unresolved forensic issues. Probably one of the most compelling of these is the ambiguity deriving from the oscillation of violence in an otherwise articulate individual and its interpretation in a referential frame of 'madness' or 'badness'. In the Rivière case, for example, the nineteenth-century alienists were faced with the problem of accommodating the defendant's view within their own scientific reconstructions. The memoir was used as the tool to decide the question of Rivière's sanity or insanity but, as Fontana notes, the task given the defendant was a curious one, because it injected a new form of knowledge and challenged the distinction between these two conditions, even raising the possibility that madness could be feigned: 'If one is mad and pretends to be rational, and if one is rational and one pretends to be mad, what is one in reality?' (Fontana, in Foucault 1975, p.286)

The Looking Glass dilemma of who or 'what one is in reality, and the Rivière one of using reason to determine madness, were pivotal to the David case, as psychiatrists and lawyers struggled with the task of situating him within some clearly articulated format of dangerousness. It was a task rendered more difficult by the increased complexity of a psychiatric taxonomy, which had replaced the visual clarity of the 'wild beast' test on which the law had originally based its determination of criminal responsibility. Even in Victoria's Tait case, well over a century later, there was lingering evidence of the law's proclivity to rely on the outward loss of control as a sign of madness, when the Judge noted that Tait 'did not roll around as one would expect of a man who was not in full possession of his faculties' (Dean J. quoted in Burns 1962, p.130). In the David case, the subject's voice was a blend of rationality and irrationality, which was especially disquieting for the law to assimilate. Despite attempts to formalise him as the Other, or the epitome of the dangerous individual, the logic and rationality of some of his written responses were undeniable, but his behaviour was often locked in contradiction for which he could usually provide some tantalisingly ingenious explanation. For example, there was evidence that he invited concern and help, yet would repudiate this by indulging in extreme forms of human aberration, even disgusting staff ordinarily immune to such behaviour. Within the broader cultural setting, his publicised exploits made the threat of the psychopath real, because he represented the rational human being, who could seemingly flirt with madness, transgress its boundary at will and push the limits of the body and emotions. Garry's raw explanation was directed at the impotence of either system to help him:

> It is a form of shouting at someone. You call for attention, but no one listens. You call louder. You shout. Eventually you scream. But we cut longer and deeper.

> If the Government's going to put us in cages and allow us to be treated like criminals, society should not expect us to behave like men. (8 October 1992)

There were many theoretical perspectives interwoven throughout the narrative and they assisted in identifying Garry's place between the forensic structures of corrections and mental health, as well the nuances of the process designed to exclude him from society. Elias's blending of reason and fantasy; Garfinkel's focus on the symbolic role of status degradation; Goffman's analysis of the therapeutic interplay in total institutions; and Gusfield's views about the territorial struggle to define and 'own' a public problem were all elements in the construction of multiple discourses. Although primacy has been given to the way psychiatrists define their forensic role, the interaction between the many stakeholders involved in this exercise was also documented: that of other mental health professionals, politicians, the legal fraternity, Victoria Police, the community and, to a limited extent, Garry David himself. The way each player perceived the actions of others elucidated the hidden expectations within the medico-legal discourse and the accommodation process deployed in achieving a working partnership. There was a sense of drama in the complex sequence of events; and the exercise of knowledge and power was personified, thereby clarifying the reasons for variability in opinions about dangerousness, diagnostic emphases and management strategies.

Foucault's work on the intersection of law and psychiatry was a useful focus for some aspects of the Garry David case but, more particularly, it was his cognate analysis of the microphysics of power, which suggested the benefit of analysing the interconnection of these two disciplines with a variety of state instrumentalities. Garry's relations with treating staff and the custodial imperatives of a penal institution were core elements in considering the way in which knowledge and power are enmeshed in the processes of resistance and surveillance. These are central to Foucault's vision of disciplinary interplay within the prison, although he himself did not explain how power could be deflected or nullified, nor is there any clear sense of personal agency. As Peter Dews has pointed out, by assuming the voice of 'the controllers', Foucault inadvertently overestimates the effectiveness of disciplinary control (Dews 1987, pp.100 ff.). This, combined with a broad-brush approach to panoptical techniques, leaves the reader with the image that prisoners are the passive and malleable recipients of the ministrations of an array of penal authorities. Yet this study has shown that these same authorities *both created the form of Garry David's resistance and had to devise ways of countering* it in an ongoing process which never reached resolution in his lifetime. There were no winners in this saga. The futility of so many initiatives was exposed through the stratagems employed by this one prisoner. He foiled the discreet, economic and rational exercise of the power to punish, and was not 'homogenised' in the way Foucault suggests, for his violence was neither effaced, nor his revolt subdued (Foucault 1977b, pp.302–4). Even in the bleakest areas of the prison, Garry achieved a remarkable degree of autonomy and visibility, which enhanced his reputation for dangerousness and exposed the limitations of the therapeutic effort. Power was not exercised unilaterally through therapeutic interventions: it was subverted at each turn with destructive outcomes for subject and treaters alike. The process of intense examination magnified Garry's shortcomings, yet he was still an able observer and astute participant who could hold up a mirror to the practices of his captors ensuring that surveillance operated both bidirectionally and laterally. This sharply contrasts with David Armstrong's summary of the Foucauldian position: 'The prisoner in the panopticon and the patient at the end of the stethoscope both remain silent as the techniques of surveillance sweep over them' (see Armstrong 1987, pp.59–76). Garry's resistive tactics demonstrated that the power exercised in correctional and court settings might, in extreme instances, be characterised by arbitrariness, excessive cost, contradictions and inefficiencies. He contributed to these problems both in terms of the extraordinary expense involved and by amplifying the differences of opinion about therapeutic strategies.

In summary, if 'discipline is the unitary technique by which the body is reduced as a *political* force at the least cost and maximised as a useful force' (Foucault 1977b, p.221), then Garry David was a dispiriting experience for all involved. Whilst he may have been used politically as the embodiment of dangerousness, partly mad and partly bad, there was more at stake than the Government had envisaged. He also came to encapsulate the ambiguities inherent in psychopathy; the uncertainty of the knowledge on which this concept is based; and the difficulties of reconciling ordinary, moral judgments about culpability with the psychiatric mode of clinical appraisal. He challenged the Government to take action, and then derided their attempts to do so by flaunting 'his' special legislation as evidence of an unparalleled ability to withstand the disciplinary techniques of the penal system. In this respect, he highlighted two key aspects: the replacement of disciplinary strategies in the prison with ritual designed to bridge the gulf between badness and madness, and the use of his body as the visual focus of resistance. The shift from more concealed but still negotiable forms of control in a hidden environment to an overtly repressive strategy must be viewed as the state attempting to reassert its loss of authority over the mind and body of Garry David. However, the more visible this process became, the more vulnerable it was to misgivings, criticism and challenge.

The nuances of these subtle forms of resistance have many similarities with early prison studies, such as Goffman's analysis of the defensive strategies generated by the intrinsic management style of total institutions; and the work of Sykes and McCleery, who both focus on the role of subcultures within the prison and emphasise the impossibility of achieving complete control over prisoners, even in the most extreme conditions of maximum security (see Cloward *et al.* 1960; Goffman 1961; McCleery in Cressey 1961; Sykes 1958).

SOME KEY FACETS: A DEGRADATION RITUAL, THE BODY AND BOUNDARY TRANSGRESSION

In many ways, the discourse of dangerousness was the prism through which images of a 'dangerous' Garry David could be refracted. This prism was multifaceted and offered occasional flashes of insight, but any intrinsic clarity about the meaning of the danger was mired in deeper social and moral judgments. Psychiatry's technical understanding of the concept offered little guidance and opened the way for community fears to govern debate. It was not so much that Garry David represented an immediate danger which could be clearly foreseen, for his threats were grandiose and even outlandish, but that he triggered a diffuse anxiety about dangerous people in general, and this carried with it the accompanying perception that this fear would dissipate with his containment. Thus the term 'dangerousness' signals a self-fulfilling prophecy of incontrovertible evidence that a 'dangerous' propensity exists. This encourages its visualisation as a disembodied entity capable of gaining momentum only by its attachment to a person or a specific situation (see Shaw 1973, pp.269–71). Garry's disturbing threats of violence, chillingly resurrecting images of previous carnage on the streets of Melbourne and toying with the possibility of such a recurrence, encouraged this response.

The public do not always view 'madness' in a condemnatory fashion. For example, crowd reaction during a recent Melbourne incident, when a seemingly 'mad' person wielded a samurai sword and disrupted traffic at a major city intersection, was one of encouragement and laughter. In this incident, a large contingent of police created a safety barrier facilitating a response not dissimilar from that of the London onlookers, whose Sunday afternoon pasttime used to be the viewing of the chained lunatics in Bedlam. It is when the barrier separating the mad person is not secure that the laughter at and vicarious enjoyment of his or her antics changes to fear, because there is a glimmer of reason within the madness. Reason and unreason are tenuously balanced. Garry David could not simply be passed off as entirely 'mad', for he bridged this barrier with his intermittent demonstrations of reason. The balance then swung to fear, rather than derision, because reasoned violence might be limitless and premeditated and the fragility of the divide between madness and badness was no longer in doubt.

The effective delineation of Garry David in terms of dangerousness was facilitated by the many silences within the discourse. Two examples will suffice. First of all, the fact that at least some of the violence and disturbance attributed to his personality disorder could be linked to institutional behaviour, which operates by different norms and rules, was generally concealed by the hidden nature of the penal system. Second, the scapegoating aspect of the exercise was explained by the Government as a responsible reaction to an unusual situation of danger, rather than a response to more complex dimensions, including psychiatry's right to exclude the personality disordered from its client base, and escalating fears about the public incidence of violence. The Community Protection Act 1990 was the symbolic expression of this generalised fear. It provided the mechanism to isolate and exclude one person, who himself participated in the process of being viewed as the visible reminder of sudden and unanticipated outbursts of violence. By this means, Parliament gave a tangible presence to dangerousness, so that by the time of the Supreme Court hearings it had become the central focus of the dialogue between psychiatry and the law. At this point, the different ways in which lawyers and psychiatrists conceptualise their task began to surface.

In addition to political statements and singular legislation assuring the public that Garry David was *the* most dangerous person in Victoria, the Government invoked powerful imagery appealing to intuition and fantasy about his aberrations, so that the more moderate language of psychiatry was rendered an ineffectual counterbalance. The fact that this political tactic was unwittingly reinforced by psychiatrists and lawyers resorting to literary allusions, even in formal levels of the discourse, is illustrative of the sense of drama Garry managed to evoke, and the underlying fantasy terrain beneath the more reasoned appraisals. Folkloric images abounded with a portrayal of the primal, mythical quality inherent in his violence, and these were sustained by elements of exaggeration and distortion. There were psychiatrists' references to the 'Angel of Death', 'Che Guevara', 'For the Term of His Natural Life' and 'the macabre dance', to which it was claimed so many seemed to have been drawn; and lawyers alluded to some similarity with *One Flew Over the Cuckoo's Nest* and Tolkien's *The Hobbit*. The Attorney-General added yet another slant with public statements about Hannibal Lecter, thereby giving journalists the licence to insinuate that cannibalism could be added to the list of Garry's other depredations. Even Australian Associated Press reports of him as a 'psychiatric detainee' conjoined madness and badness in an alarming way. There was a sense that those participating in the discourse had been swept up by events whose outcome they could not control, and this is a vastly different experience from that of the usual medico-legal battles within the courtroom, which are structured by evidential rules. If the state had founded proceedings on a degradation ritual, then there was liberty to indulge in the sense of theatre in which Garry participated by likening his experience to that of Hess in Spandau.

The Community Protection Act was the lynchpin of the entire exercise. It placed Garry beyond the reach of ordinary legal processes and represented an authoritative means of excluding him from participation in ordinary life. I have concluded that there were no discernible positive outcomes, and it was little more than a cumbersome solution to a political dilemma, despite the judicial care taken with the issues raised. The format of the legislation proved to be ambiguous, inflexible, intrusive, judicially constraining and a breach of the ordinary principles applicable to the conduct of cases in the Supreme Court of Victoria. I have demonstrated the many inequities in its provisions, but the primary problem rested with Parliament having made its wishes clear in respect of a particular person, rather than *a class* of persons and, in so doing failing to separate the powers of the executive and judiciary. The Community Protection Act 1990 unashamedly established a structure under which preventive detention could be imposed upon completion of a sentence for previous offences and cloaked its provisions in rational discourse, even though it was apparent to most observers that the likelihood of threats being carried out in some unknown, future circumstance was speculative rather than scientific. The role of the Attorney-General was central throughout, and his actions resulted in lengthy periods of detention preceding each determination of dangerousness. Judges were offered little room to exercise discretion and each expressed frustration with the nature of the task, and with the Court's inability to control the administrative outcome.

The subsequent court hearings were intended to reach some resolution – to be a conciliatory drawing together of the expertise of psychiatry and the law, in conjunction with an affirmation of public knowledge about fear-inducing behaviour. The process of situating Garry definitively within this ambit depended on extrapolating violent prison incidents as significant markers of the underlying attribute of dangerousness and assuming their relevance for a wider sphere of social interaction. There are problems with such an *ex post facto* mode of analysis, especially when based on the civil legal standard of 'on the balance of probabilities'. First, the reconstruction of unacceptable violence in the terms demanded by the court depends on minimising its contextual relevance. Second, the cumulative approach discounts any lengthy periods of cooperation and quiescence, choosing instead to focus on what is a remarkably common form of prison behaviour. Furthermore, the ease with which the link between the behaviour and the total identity of the person can be made is persuasive, but offers no clear guidelines for rebuttal.

The Supreme Court was placed in the invidious position of having to frame its proceedings directly around the concept of dangerousness, which is more usually relegated to bail applications or sentencing dispositions. In these instances, the law may seek to include the views of experts, but it does not privilege them, and the ultimate decision remains entirely within the legal purview. In the David case, the balance shifted by making the part played by psychiatrists of a different order than elsewhere in the judicial system. An early aside by Justice Fullagar that 'Judges do not need experts to tell them what dangerousness means' (*First Hearing*, 8 August 1990) made plain the charade of a legislative mechanism requiring Supreme Court Judges to act as if they were involved in the task of amassing firm scientific data. A barrister privately expressed a similar view at the Mental Health Review Board hearing when he agreed that they were avoiding the issue of dangerousness, because it would encourage psychiatrists to venture down 'irrelevant' pathways of prediction difficulties and statistical inference, when lawyers 'know' what dangerousness means. He was, of course, implying that psychiatrists agonise uselessly over its meaning, whereas judges and magistrates have a sense of certitude. This example illustrates the disparity between the law's approach and that of psychiatry's to dangerousness and their mode of decision making in general. In assessing fear-inducing behaviour, the law resorts to a legal fiction that certainty can be achieved, whereas psychiatry becomes paralysed by understandable qualms.

In pragmatic terms, the Community Protection Act compounded the difficulties of managing Garry David within an institution. Other prisoners blamed him for opening up the sentencing crevice of preventive detention, and in the consequent prison backlash he was injured on several occasions. The difficulties of his environment were intensified with staff uncertain about their responsibilities in relation to this special detainee, who did not fit within the ordinary confines of correctional or mental health legislation. With the constancy of Court hearings, Garry was able to argue legitimately that management plans had not been fully implemented and, in this way, he deflected personal responsibility for his behavioural problems, thereby further impeding his release progress. The Court was sensitive to his position but, not unreasonably, required the demonstration of some cooperation to alter his status. In this, the Judges faced the disconcerting paradox that at times of high frustration levels Garry behaved well, yet when his requests were granted, such as in the move to Mont Park, his behaviour deteriorated sharply.

The inefficacy and injustice of sole-person legislation was highlighted by this Act, which exposed behaviours normally screened from public scrutiny and protected by the confidentiality of clinical record keeping. It enabled Garry to retaliate by challenging institutional structures and holding up their programmes and procedures for evaluation in an open court. At the same time, he could legitimately pursue the role of persecuted victim and expose the inequity of his position. In one of his most melodramatic yet despairing gestures he accused the Government of hypocrisy and offered to be hanged in preference to prolonged custody. It was an appeal designed to draw attention to his plight, but it can also be viewed as a logical extension of the penal course on which the state had embarked – that of annihilating him as an ordinary citizen with customary rights.

The ritual was as inhibiting for the Judges as for the respondent, but there was a sufficient veneer of due process to satisfy the Government that legal forms were actually being observed. The reality was different: the purpose of this ritual was to reduce Garry to the all-enveloping status of a dangerous person through a special ceremony outside the usual confines of criminality or mental illness. Whilst this mechanism contains obvious elements of exclusion and sacrifice, it also recognised that Parliament was conceding the possibility of reintegration through a mandatory review process. Although the initial six-months period suggested a degree of optimism, the extension to one year, then finally to three years, highlighted its tokenism. Judges were undaunted and took every opportunity to emphasise that the way was open for Garry to assume responsibility for his future. For example:

> The key to freedom is not far from his own hand. The maturity to understand that cooperation in the modes of behavioural assistance is not surrender but self-help lies at the moment beyond his perception but not beyond his intellect. The book on Garry David has not been closed. There has been but another page turned. (Hedigan J, *Second Hearing*, Judgment, 15 November 1991, p.95)

> This Court cannot open the door for him now, but it can hand him one of the keys. He must accept responsibility for its safe custody. If that key is lost, it will probably be some time before it is found again. (Harper J, *First Appeal*, Judgment, 4 June 1992, p.16)

Garry's repudiation of this judicial advice made the Government's position, in the light of the strategy it had pursued, increasingly untenable.

From a different perspective, it was surprising that Parliament demonstrated so little understanding of the way in which psychiatry can contribute to the court process, and so completely disregarded their poor predictive powers in the area of dangerousness. Either the Government misperceived the role of this discipline, or it chose the expedient path of couching dangerousness in the guise of illness, thereby enforcing cooperation, but also interfering in the psychiatric domain. The haste with which the Community Protection Act was implemented, and the hint of imminent battles looming over possible amendments to mental health legislation affecting the nexus between mental illness and personality disorder, stifled open debate and unfortunately no concerted protest from psychiatrists emerged over this matter of principle. This contrasted with the official psychiatric reaction to the draft Community Protection (Violent Offenders) Bill which, had it been implemented, would have extended the net of preventive detention (see Social Development Committee, *Second Report*, March 1992, pp.305–9).

The famous dictum that the expert should be 'on tap, not on top' was borne out by the Garry David experience and aptly suggests a more appropriate use of psychiatry by the courts. Experts are falsely restricted when compelled to give precise answers to questions which have neither diagnostic nor empirical clarity. They certainly can and should act in an advisory capacity, but their evidence cannot form the basis of a specific judgment about dangerousness. Scientific knowledge only partly informs such views; personal experience, direct encounters and intuition also play a mediatory role. It is time for the law to cease pretending that in areas such as dangerousness these subjective components are irrelevant. This is but one aspect of the legal tendency to reify psychiatric opinion in a way, which is unwarranted clinically. Whilst a disgruntled psychiatrist's comment to the President of the Mental Health Review Board, that placing the *DSM-III-R* next to the Bible was a misreflection of its unassailable or 'holy' status may have been a jocular aside, it did reflect his perception of the authority with which the law would prefer to regard his discipline.

In its quest for certainty and reliability of evidence, the law values the demonstration of inconsistencies as a method of establishing the veracity of any one account. For example, counsel at the Mental Health Review Board hearing formally weighted the 'credibility' of medical witnesses in this regard. It was a method both demeaning and rigorous and quite foreign to clinical exchanges. It evinced little awareness that psychiatry's approach to truth seeking is at variance with that of the law. In its clinical role, psychiatry may employ a range of diagnostic indicators to sift and assign clinical meaning. There is both selectivity and subjectivity about this process, since diagnoses are working instruments, capable of being modified by further observation or information. But the law, as controller of proceedings, devalues a method which allows for changed views and is unashamedly equivocal and tentative. In weighting the psychiatric evidence in this case, counsel had an opportunity to draw attention to the way in which a clinical opinion is formulated. Many of the expert witnesses offered general opinions based on a reading of the prison and clinical files alone, whilst others expressed views deriving from their management responsibility for Garry David. It is worth noting, that those who changed their opinions regarding the link between personality disorder and mental illness at the Board hearing did so on the basis of reading additional material in the files, rather than as a consequence of their clinical observation of Garry himself.

Because of the number of psychiatrists involved, the import of this distinction was sometimes insufficiently emphasised, although it was a factor contributing to the diversity of opinion. Generally, this aspect attracts little comment in the forensic sphere. The major exception is the case of *Barefoot v Estelle* [1983] (US), in which the hypothetical testimony of Dr Grigson, a Texan forensic psychiatrist, was challenged in an *amicus curiae* brief of the American Psychiatric Association on the grounds of being unethical. Yet it might be more appropriate for the law to regard evidence based on direct mental state examination as being qualitatively different from general clinical views formed on the basis of the history alone, especially as there is little differentiation in the ensuing legal consequences.

Whilst this study has demonstrated the extreme nature of Garry David's resistance, it is at the extremities that social processes can be more clearly articulated. His ability to violate physical, psychological and social boundaries carried with it the seeds of self-destruction, even though politicians and professionals attempted to find a means of rational curtailment. There is a parallel here with René Girard's argument that extreme characteristics attract destructive mechanisms, which must then be rationalised by political, moral and collective means (Girard 1986, p.19). It is an observation which matches Garry's confinement experience and the subsequent events. He refused to accept the ordinary conventions of the role of either prisoner or psychiatric patient. Custodial arrangements had a certain fragility and were contestable. Decisions made in relation to Garry were exceptional: sometimes disciplinary infractions were ignored to avoid escalating his violence or self-mutilatory behaviour; classification became a bargaining tool; transfer to psychiatric facilities served as a respite; and high security facilities were mocked by the patient's barricades and damage to the wall and roof. It was as if correctional interventions had been reduced to a ball game, with the ball constantly in play and Garry becoming increasingly adept at anticipating moves and demonstrating his skill with a certain degree of mockery and recklessness. This technique was later transferred to other more highly visible settings, much to the Government's chagrin.

Of considerable significance was the way in which Garry used his body as a weapon to control the reactions of others for more than a decade. Prisoners were in awe of his capacity to self-injure, and his mutilations were a constant reminder to staff of some possible remissness in their duty of care. His behaviour was self-expressive, rebellious and imaginative, extending well beyond governmental siting of the body as an object of either treatment or punishment. In this regard, he was able to demonstrate the inflexibility of an administrative system desperately striving to consign him to one of two categories. His body conveyed many different messages: allegations of staff neglect or assault; a plea for help; a medium for conveying sexual fantasies; a flirtation with death; mockery of the non-corporeality of modern punishment; the site of expensive medical repairs; the demoralisation of staff by rejecting emergency treatment; an object of revulsion and humiliation; a shield from interference by other prisoners; the lulling of staff into self-congratulation with periods of quiescence; and, above all, it was used as a threatening weapon. A written report by Dr Peter Hearne cogently summed up the situation from the medical perspective:

> The root of the enigma has been the vast problem of attempting to logically deal, using a medical model, with someone who appears to transcend all the usual rules of human self-protective behaviour by freely utilising his body as a bargaining tool in an apparently endless conflict with those who he sees as powerful in the prison – be they prison administrators, medical or nursing staff, psychologists or occupational therapists. (MHRB, *Statement of Reasons*, 9 May 1990, p.29)

But there was an even more fundamental struggle underlying the stratagem on which Garry David depended. Although his body was a powerful tool for expressing his desire for omnipotence, his reliance on 'victim' status was actually based on the reality of his own impotence. These were two incompatible and unresolved modes of presentation and help to explain why he was not elevated to some form of heroic martyrdom like other Australian folk heroes. His struggles with authority were diffuse, self-focused and idiosyncratic, rather than consistent and compelling in their social message.

There was a sense of incongruity in the linking of Garry's physical presence with the attribute of dangerousness, for he was small in stature, suffered constant bouts of pain from the ingestion of foreign objects and consequent internal scarring, and there was increasing evidence of his debilitation. Although his written and verbal threats against individuals and the community at large contributed to the perception of dangerousness, it was his readiness to inflict gross personal violence on his own body that visually focused a discourse oscillating between badness, madness and dangerousness. This link was reinforced by a senior Judge's widely reported comments, that he found it difficult not to deem somebody mentally ill if he 'cuts his ears off and slices part of his penis off and tries to burn himself with petrol and wants to shoot people' (Vincent, SDC, February 1990). In similar vein, the Attorney-General chose to appeal to the innate cultural fantasies surrounding violence and psychopathy, by linking *self*-violence with that of a predator lusting after the flesh of unsuspecting victims. Thus, it was both as a consequence of his own behaviour, and such well-publicised descriptions from those in authority, that Garry's body became the site through which the boundaries between criminality, personality disorder and mental illness blurred, and the discourse between psychiatry, the law and politics was generated.

Visceral imagery is powerful in its ability to convey both positive and negative messages for a society. The body classifies and divides people according to a perceived value, in order to place them in the social hierarchy. For example, adornments may be indicative of wealth and status; physical stigmata suggest a medical or other disorder; and scarification can be a rite of passage, or a sign of rebellion, depending on the form it takes. Self-mutilation is more confusing to interpret, partly because it is concealed as a medical issue, and also because there is no consensus about its aetiology. In the various legal hearings, no fewer than ten quite different, and equally plausible constructions were given for Garry's capacity in this regard. It is a problem particularly germane to custodial environments such as the prison, which rely on uniformity and the repression of individuality and use strict regimes and schedules to manage an errant population. Bodily scarring and the removal of body parts assume a special significance by providing a means of asserting autonomy and challenging the egalitarianism of the regime. They invert cultural values, but in the restricted custodial environment they also enhance a prisoner's status with their visible reminder of an ability to withstand pain and explore the limits of disfigurement: actions which if inflicted by the state would be tantamount to torture. Ironically, the prisoner's right to treatment embodied in section 47 of the Corrections Act 1986 (Vic) exists in conjunction with the retention of power to subject the body to injury.

These general observations were certainly applicable to Garry David. Just as his outrageous threats were a reminder that his mind could not be disciplined, his permanently scarred body became synonymous with an unparalleled ability to disregard customary boundaries and resist, whatever the personal cost. His physical body proclaimed his 'difference' and became the locus for the social message that he was prepared to invert ordinary societal values – in this case, those accorded to health, attractiveness and bodily perfection. There is a large anthropological literature on symbolic inversion and its functional reaffirmation of social structures. For example, Barbara Babcock (1978, p.14) defines it 'as an act of expressive behaviour which inverts, contradicts, abrogates, or in some fashion presents an alternative to commonly held cultural codes, values and norms be they linguistic, literary or artistic, religious, social and political' (see also Bakhtin 1968; Douglas 1966; Turner 1990).

Thus, whilst the grossness of Garry's self-injuries and his denial of the need to protect the human body were gestures signifying his individuality, they were also the markers of his social rejection. The publication of body site maps with arrows indicating the location of injuries confirmed this process by making him an object identifiable in terms of physical grotesqueness.

If one considers the arguments of Stallybrass and White, it is perhaps not unexpected that these elements were so much in evidence, for the authors view the extremes of high or low ordering in any of four major symbolic domains – the body, geographical space, psychic forms and the social order – as inviting 'a special and often powerful symbolic charge' in structuring the discourse (Stallybrass and White 1986, p.5). Garry's ordering in the social hierarchy could not possibly have been lower with its implicit connotations of badness, madness *and* dangerousness, but his ability to transgress physical and social boundaries was uncanny and likely to have been the trigger to provoke an unusual and extreme political responsiveness. It also led to point scoring between psychiatry and the law and examples of the courtroom banter suggest that this was a way of restoring an appearance of normality and engaging in a low-key form of territorial interplay. For example psychiatrists referring to the *Diagnostic and Statistical Manual* as 'a shopping list' of symptoms, or a 'cookbook of common wisdom', were using ordinary everyday language to demystify psychiatry and provoke amusement. At the same time, they were also disparaging the law's quest for certainty, which is so antithetical to psychiatry's experiential mode.

In this broader context of denigration the drama of the courtroom set the stage for the state to reassert its authority over the disposition of the body of Garry David and reinforce a sense of shared meanings about the danger it represented. Even the tactical and rare legal move of a *habeas corpus* application directed attention to the physical body of the appellant and heightened the sense of his presence in the courtroom. Although Garfinkel proposes that status degradation ceremonies are formal public events, it was Garry's defilement of his own body, which bore the hallmarks of a de facto degradation ceremony, particularly as it was immediately followed by official activity such as incident reports, medical explanations and inquiries by the respective government departments, often in direct response to ministerial requests. The prisoner's personal problems and the need to ensure his safety were widely acknowledged, but the frequency of the reporting inevitably condensed his profile to that of an unpredictable self-mutilator. Garry controlled the timing and severity of the mutilation, but he could not control the increasing degree of alienation which was its consequence, and thus his physical scarring, with its accompanying association of possible death, instigated a movement across the boundary from inclusion to exclusion. As Dr John Grigor explained: 'The slicing of his ears, his nipples and, ye Gods, his penis, [had] created in prison circles to this day an awe of Garry David' (MHRB, *Statement of Reasons*, 9 May 1990, p.10). Viewed in this light, the ritual of exclusion created by Parliament simply ratified a process commenced long before by Garry David himself.

The significance of this cycle of condemnation, scapegoating, exclusion and reintegration needs to be understood for the meaning this control mode holds for a society. There have been many quite distinct ideological approaches of the 'power to punish', including a Durkheimian emphasis on social solidarity and the bolstering of moral boundaries, Marxist interpretations of a class struggle based on the economic organisation of society and Foucault's depiction of disciplinary practice (see Garland 1990). Broadly speaking, sanctions reflect the value system of a society and communities have a sense of boundary separation between the included and the excluded. There are degrees of condemnation with sentencing mechanisms, such as parole and corrections' orders offering the possibility of reconciliation at the 'softer' end of the spectrum, whilst the physical, economic and social deprivations intrinsic to custody are a much harsher means of enforcing conformity.

However, the state's power in modelling its sanctions reaches an impasse in the face of a prisoner's explicit rejection, and this was the situation facing the Victoria government over Garry David. As a solution, the Community Protection Act 1990 fulfilled Gusfield's legislative criteria. It was at once *expressive, instrumental and symbolic* (Gusfield 1963, pp.167–8): expressive in the sense of harnessing the community's fears about dangerous behaviour; instrumental in its declared custodial intent; and symbolic in the organisation of 'the perceptions, attitudes, and feelings of observers' (see also Bourdieu 1977, p.117). Elements of drama and tragedy were heightened simply because the legislation was such an unexpected political reaction to the challenge of one, among many, personality-disordered prisoners. The possibility, which largely seems to have been overlooked, was that

Garry might regain the upper hand and come to be viewed as the heroic protagonist pitted against an uncaring state. Although we see some evidence of his
struggle to change the imbalance, he was unable to sustain such efforts sufficiently
to be assured of a more favourable outcome. Had his death not halted the process
of legislative detention, it was likely that the Victorian Government would have
had to suffer a similar rebuke from the High Court as did New South Wales in the
1996 *Kable* case. This case, together with other developments affecting the space
of those with severe antisocial personality disorder, will next be considered.

THE GARRY DAVID LEGACY

The legal maxim that 'hard cases make bad law' was borne out by the Victorian
Government's determination to enact 'one-person' legislation. The Garry David
case has acted as a warning that the preventive detention of those in that tenuous
space between criminality and mental illness must be applied cautiously and
appropriately. Whilst general preventive detention is now used sparingly in all
Australian jurisdictions to deal with extreme offenders, there is no future for
singular legislation. The arguments which were due to be put before the High
Court at the time of Garry's death have been vindicated. In a judgment of that
Court on 12 September 1996, a similar Community Protection Act in New South
Wales was deemed to be an invalid exercise of the power of that Parliament. Again,
the circumstances were similar. Gregory Wayne Kable had been found guilty of
the manslaughter of his wife following a bitter custody dispute which continued,
despite his imprisonment, leading him to write vitriolic letters to politicians and
other public figures in a bid to re-establish his family unit. His timing was inoppor-
tune in the light of a pending election, in which the Government's law and order
platform was paramount. There was considerable lobbying about the aptness of
this case for a specific legal remedy, and there were moves to seek support from
psychiatrists. When Kable's sentence was due to expire, the New South Wales Parliament passed legislation to detain him for six-monthly periods by order of the
Supreme Court, provided a Judge considered him likely to commit serious
violence on release. This legislation came into force on 6 December 1994, but its
implementation proved difficult owing to psychiatrists' reluctance to testify that
Kable fulfilled the criteria of dangerousness. Dr William Lucas, a private psychiatrist, provided information about the large boxes of material, colloquially referred
to as 'Kable kits', which were sent out to leading psychiatrists in a major effort to
find professionals willing to testify. Despite this strategy, only a few were prepared
to offer an opinion and the effect may have been to exclude many experienced psychiatrists from being called upon by the defence. Once again, the main body of
evidence revealed that there was no psychosis, but a personality disorder of
unspecified type which would not satisfy 'dangerousness' on the balance of proba-

bilities, the standard required by the legislation. Witnesses for the Attorney-General were reduced to concluding, in a fairly meaningless way, that Kable perhaps *could* be dangerous at some time in the future, since the Act did not specify any particular time frame.

Kable did, however, serve one period of preventive detention, before a second judge refused to commit him for a further term, and he was released in August the following year (see Fairall 1995; Waller 1997; Zdenkowski 1997). Notwithstanding the fact that the New South Wales Court of Appeal had previously upheld the validity of this law, Kable appealed to the High Court regarding the original decision, which had resulted in his detention (*Kable v DPP for NSW* [1996]). That Court found by a four to two majority that Parliaments could not require Courts to undertake functions incompatible with their judicial role, and that there were limits to the directions they may give to Supreme Courts, because these bodies also exercise a federal judicial power. Justices Toohey, Gaudron, McHugh and Gummow were in favour and Chief Justice Brennan dissented, together with Justice Dawson. Proceedings under the Community Protection Act 1994 (NSW) were deemed to be not 'judicial' and in breach of the doctrine of the separation of powers. This decision is a landmark one in the context of the struggle between the executive and judiciary which took place during Garry David's bid for freedom. The High Court has re-established the independence of Australian State Supreme Courts, protecting them from abolition or interference by the Parliament – an independence guaranteed by the Commonwealth Constitution, which by inference requires their continued existence. Consequently, State Parliaments are limited in their ability to interfere with Supreme Court jurisdiction. As Justice Gaudron argued:

> The integrity of the courts depends on their acting in accordance with the judicial process and, in no small measure, on the maintenance of public confidence in that process. Particularly is that so in relation to criminal proceedings which involve the most important of all judicial functions, namely, the determination of the guilt or innocence of persons accused of criminal offences. Public confidence cannot be maintained in the courts and their criminal processes if, as postulated by s. 5(1), the courts are required to deprive persons of their liberty, not on the basis that they have breached any law, but on the basis that an opinion is formed, by reference to material which may or may not be admissible in legal proceedings, that on the balance of probabilities, they may do so. (*Kable v DPP for NSW* [1996] p.615)

Essentially this means that State Parliaments cannot place the judiciary in the position of acting in a way incompatible with the exercise of Federal judicial powers, even in the exercise of its powers under state law. The High Court decision has thus sent a signal to State Governments to use their preventive detention powers with due caution, but many issues are still unresolved, including those of compliance with international obligations and the way in which the prediction of dangerousness may be utilised in the courts as a basis for community protection. As Zdenkowski makes abundantly clear, a Community Protection Act has its attractions for government, and New South Wales immediately began to explore innovative ways around Kable-type legislation in order to avoid future High Court challenges. For instance, a private member's Community Protection (Dangerous Offenders) Bill was mooted, which would make it a punishable offence for a classified dangerous offender to approach a specified person or persons on a special register of protected persons maintained by the Attorney-General. As Zdenkowski comments:

> The rationale behind the scheme is to avoid the legal and moral criticisms associated with preventive detention...[and] there is no constitutional impediment to the creation of such penalties, whatever their merits in terms of efficacy, cost, or humanity. (Zdenkowski 1997, p.48)

The Kable case is not the only one in which the High Court has had to consider the legitimacy of preventive detention as a sentencing principle and in Veen it faced the issue with evident caution (*Veen v R* (No. 1) [1979] and *Veen v R* (No. 2) [1988]; see also Fox 1988). Veen had killed on two separate occasions, eight years apart, in aggressive outbursts whilst under the influence of alcohol. In a High Court appeal his original sentence of life imprisonment was reduced on the ground that it should be proportionate to the offence, rather than warehousing for community protection. Veen's second High Court appeal invited reappraisal of this argument, for the New South Wales Supreme Court had again sentenced him to life imprisonment for a similar incident resulting in his victim's death. In this second decision, the arguments were finely balanced and the sentencing principle of proportionality reaffirmed in very cautious language with the Court leaving the way open for general preventive detention:

> It is one thing to say that the principle of proportionality precludes the imposition of a sentence extended beyond what is appropriate to the crime merely to protect society; it is another thing to say that the protection of society is not a material factor in fixing an appropriate sentence. The distinction in principle is clear between an extension merely by way of preventive detention, which is impermissible, and an exercise of the sentencing discretion having regard to the protection of society among other factors, which is permissible. (*Veen v R* (No 2) [1988] CLR 465 F.C. 88/01 at 227)

Another related development in Victoria involving preventive detention in the sentencing context, and one reliant on the expertise of psychiatrists, emanated from the law and order philosophy of the Liberal Government, which attained power in October 1992, mid-way through the third hearing of the Community Protection Act 1990. This emphasised the plight of the victim and paved the way for the introduction of general preventive detention provisions *at the time of* sentencing, rather than retrospectively. Section 18Q of the Sentencing (Amendment) Act 1993 rescinded the Community Protection Act 1990 in relation to Garry David, but made him subject to the three-yearly reviews of the indefinite sentencing provisions applicable to certain serious violent offenders (section 18H). This Act amends the Sentencing Act 1991 (Vic). 'Serious sexual offenders' and 'serious violent offenders' may now attract extended custodial sentences under broad provisions, which also cover 'serious offenders', who must be over 21 years and have been convicted of at least one of a range of specified offences, varying in their degree of gravity.

Despite the strong objections of the Scrutiny of Bills and Regulation Committee, this new legislation was rushed through Parliament in one hour on 13 May 1993. Thus, in the space of three years, mandatory court reviews of Garry David's 'dangerousness' had been extended from six months to three years in the absence of any further criminal convictions for violent offences. This was unacceptable to Garry's lawyers, who immediately briefed a Queen's Counsel with a view to taking the constitutional issues to the higher courts. This general legislation for preventive detention has, as yet, been used cautiously, indicating a judicial wariness about basing extensive incarceration on psychiatric history, rather than on criminal grounds. These comments pertain to the 1993 legislation, which can be directly linked with the need to find a more general solution to the problems posed by Garry David. The provisions have now been incorporated into the Sentencing and Other Acts (Amendment) Act 1997 (Vic). Currently, the courts have only granted three applications (for repeat rapists) since the inception of this legislation. A number of the DPP's applications have been rejected by the sentencing Judge on the grounds that indefinite sentencing must be reserved for exceptional cases, or it would otherwise act as a disincentive to rehabilitation.

As with the Community Protection Act 1990, there is a disturbing lack of clarity about these new amendments. The offender must be a *serious* danger to the community and the burden of proof relies on prosecution at a standard below that of the usual criminal onus; that is, a court needs to be satisfied 'to a high degree of probability' about the likely eventuality of this danger. In an early appeal against the imposition of a sentence of indefinite detention, Justice Winneke, the President of the Court of Appeal, commented that there were 'aspects of this legislation which are pretty unattractive to me'. He was particularly troubled by the phrase 'to a high degree of probability', because 'you can say this about every rapist that comes before the courts' (*Sunday Age,* 8 December 1996). The defendant's barrister raised the arguments, which had surfaced throughout the various hearings of the Community Protection Act 1990, that the judiciary were being asked to carry out a function more akin to an executive role and alien to the ordinary sentencing process.

The psychiatrist or psychologist is integral to the exercise of the judicial role, since indefinite sentencing depends on an assessment of the offender's character, past history, age, health or mental condition, which must be considered in conjunction with the exceptional nature and gravity of the offence, after allowing for any special circumstances (ss.18B(1)(a)(b)&(c)). Although there may be a 25-day adjournment to enable the convicted offender to respond to the application (section 18D), the criteria for proving *non*-dangerousness are as ill-defined as they were in the Community Protection Act, thus making indefinite sentencing a potentially powerful tool in the hands of the professions when ordinary correctional and therapeutic methods of control appear to have been ineffective. Politically, however, this form of selective incapacitation was a consequence of the Victoria Liberal Government's commitment to harsher punishments and lengthier sentences, which threaten to override the hard-won inclusion of the principle of proportionality made explicit in the objectives of the Sentencing Act 1991. This primary Act had been based on a decade of consolidating sentencing provisions, and incorporated the explicit recognition that 'in no circumstances should a sentence be increased beyond that which is justified on just deserts principles in order that one or more of the secondary aims are met' (*Sentencing Report of the Victorian Sentencing Committee*, December 1988, p.122). For example, section 1(d)(iv) proclaimed that offenders could only be punished to the extent justified by:

(A)   the nature and gravity of their offences; and

(B)   their culpability and degree of responsibility for their offences; and

(C)   the presence of any aggravating or mitigating factor concerning the offender and of any other relevant circumstance.

Once preventive detention is added to these objectives, the mental health professional is required to play a different role in the courtroom by moving beyond identifying mitigating psychological factors to predictions of dangerousness.

Recent changes in Victoria's mental health system have been low key in relation to the difficulties associated with the severely personality disordered who self-mutilate. The fact that they could be implemented so smoothly soon after Garry's death suggests that the personalisation of issues, and the pressing political need for a custodial decision in his case, had actually inhibited any effective resolution. Both his own personality and penchant for publicity, coupled with direct governmental intervention, promoted a divisiveness which ranged across professional boundaries, service goals, political philosophies and personal belief systems; the latter not uninfluenced by the fact that so many of those involved had been the target of Garry David's threats. Had there been an opportunity to deal with the issues more generally, then it is unlikely that so many difficulties would have been encountered.

There were a number of reasons why the problem of those with a severe personality disorder could later be cast in a different light. Of central importance was the guiding interest of the Federal Government in the mental health area. Although, historically, mental health has remained a state responsibility in Australia, it had become an urgent matter for the Commonwealth to ensure some parity, particularly since evidence suggested that individual consumers were being exposed to differential state practices regarding civil commitment. In April 1992 the *National Mental Health Policy and Plan* was endorsed by all Australian Ministers for Health and bolstered by the findings of a *Human Rights and Equal Opportunity Commission Report* (the 'Burdekin' Report 1993), and the Australian Health Ministers' *Advisory Council Report* (March 1995). As a result of this concerted inquiry, the Commonwealth provided financial incentives and a time-frame for State and Territory Governments to review their mental health services and legislation, in order to ensure consistency with the UN *Principles for the Protection of Persons with Mental Illness and for the Improvement of Mental Health Care* adopted by the UN Commission on Human Rights and ratified by the General Assembly in November 1991. Because of the Victorian Government's express concern with the rights of mentally ill persons, this state was well placed to confirm the policy direction of this document; and the key features of its approach were published in its *Mental Health Service – The Framework for Service Delivery* (April 1994). In this, the underlying principle of de-institutionalisation was paramount, but a new emphasis was given to the criteria for involuntary commitment in the context of international obligations and national mental health objectives. Of even more significance, in the light of the debacle surrounding Garry David, was the fact that clinicians were given the clear message that those 'suffering from a severe personality disorder, where the person's behaviour places themselves or others at risk of harm' were now to be regarded as part of the target group of mental health services, in tandem with those experiencing a serious mental illness (Mental Health Services, Psychiatric Services Division, April 1994, p.25). This was a major directional shift requiring the cooperation of psychiatrists, moving well beyond the simplistic, haunting Garry David debates of 'Is he in?' or 'Is he out?'

The next step was the convening of a working party of clinicians, staff and those from community settings to consider key matters in the proposed legislation, resulting in a widely circulated Discussion Paper, *Victoria's Mental Health Services: Proposed Amendments to the 'Mental Health Act' 1986* (August 1994). It was an important document which, proposed widening the ambit of involuntary commitment, yet managed to do so in a persuasive manner by reaffirming psychiatry's treatment mandate and incorporating the working definition of mental illness already developed by the Mental Health Review Board. Thus Recommendation 9 suggested inclusion of the following as a definition of mental illness:

> A person appears to be mentally ill if he or she has recently exhibited symptoms which indicate a disturbance of mental functioning which constitutes an identifiable syndrome or, if it is not possible to ascribe the symptoms of such a disturbance of mental functioning to a classifiable syndrome, they are symptoms of a disturbance of thought, mood, volition, perception, orientation or memory which are present to such a degree to be considered pathological. (p.31)

This definition favours the expert clinical view endorsed by the Board in a number of its decisions and was incorporated, in modified form, in section 8 of the ensuing amendments to the Mental Health Act 1986 to amplify the meaning of the phrase 'appears to be mentally ill'. Subject to the exclusionary provisions of subsection 2, which still prevent the commitment of those 'with an antisocial personality' on this basis alone, a person is to be regarded as being mentally ill 'if he or she has a mental illness, being a medical condition that is characterised by a significant disturbance of thought, mood, perception or memory' (section 8(1A)). Had this inclusion been available in 1990, the Attorney-General would not have found it necessary to overshadow the Board's role by applying to the Supreme Court for a ruling on the meaning of mental illness; nor would a duly constituted legal body have been placed in the disputatious position of having to advise on the proper boundary for psychiatric clients, as had been the Law Reform Commission's task.

Having reaffirmed the clinical, treating role of psychiatry, the Discussion Paper went a step further and Recommendation 10 proposed a working definition of personality disorder based on the diagnostic criteria in *DSM-1V* should be included in the Act as follows:

> A person appears to have a personality disorder where the person has an enduring pattern of inner experience and behaviour which:

(a)   is inflexible and pervasive across a broad range of personal and social situations; and

(b)   deviates markedly from the expectations of the person's culture and is manifested in at least two of the following areas: cognition, affectivity, interpersonal functioning and impulse control; and

(c)   leads to clinically significant distress or impairment in social, occupational or other important areas of functioning; and

(d)   the pattern is not a consequence of a mental illness. (pp.31–2)

The following Recommendation reframed section 8(1)(c) relating to 'the risk to a person's health or safety or to the protection of the public' to include the ability to commit those who may suffer 'significant deterioration of physical or mental condition' to an inpatient service. This was a welcome addition to the criteria for civil commitment, for it recognised the necessity of balancing treatment needs with the protection of members of the community, and it was compatible with Mental Health Review Board practice. The amended section of the Mental Health Act 1986 therefore became:

> A person may be admitted to and detained in an approved mental health service as an involuntary patient...only if –

> (b) because of the person's mental illness, the person should be admitted and detained for treatment as an involuntary patient for his or her health or safety (whether to prevent a deterioration in the person's physical or mental condition or otherwise) or for the protection of members of the public.

The four other criteria are additional to this clause; that is, there must also be evidence of the appearance of mental illness; the need for and availability of, treatment; the inability to otherwise consent; and an indication that a less restrictive alternative is inappropriate.

Although the final amendments to the legislation did not include the proposed definition of personality disorder, treatment services were broadened in two important respects; they should provide 'treatment *and care* to people with a mental *disorder', and have a primary concern for those having a mental illness*, defined in clinical terms [my emphases]. Care was taken to consult with representatives of the Royal Australian and New Zealand College of Psychiatrists in relation to the definitions of these central terms governing the process of civil commitment, and the preamble noted that the words 'mental disorder' were to be interpreted as including 'mental illness'. There was one further change of significance for forensic care. Section 6A(h) of the amended Act states: 'The prescription of medication should meet the best health needs of the person with a mental disorder and should be given only for therapeutic or diagnostic purposes and never as a punishment or for the convenience of others.' Thus the parameters of treatment are now more explicitly linked to a treatment purpose, and the deterioration criterion takes account of the imminence and possible severity of relapse, as well as the likely disruption such an eventuality would cause (see, in particular, Freckelton 1998 (*Review of RD*) p.425).

It was a conciliatory way out of the impasse, couched within a broader reform agenda, and one undoubtedly owing much to the direction of the newly appointed Professor of Forensic Psychiatry, Professor Paul Mullen. It openly recognised that a few with a history of severe personality disorder were already receiving assistance within the psychiatric hospital system, some undoubtedly depending on a diagnosis of dual disability enabling the civil criteria to be met. Had the broad definition of personality disorder in *DSM-IV* been included, it may have had the capacity to draw a significant number of fractious inmates from the prison system into the mental health system; but the more limiting definition of those with a severe personality disorder, *both needing and amenable to the treatment offered*, was a more focused way of deploying mental health services for some of the mentally *disordered*. It recognised the need of a small group, who might otherwise be excluded from direct care, such as those experiencing a severe depression in the context of a personality disorder, rather than a traditional mental illness.

Further support for this directional shift came from a contemporaneous report, based on a consultancy undertaken on behalf of the Psychiatric Services Branch of Health and Community Services (*Service Options for Clients with Severe or Borderline Personality Disorders*, December 1994). This carefully outlined the department's experience with this subgroup of personality-disordered clients and recognised their difficulties. Submissions from consumers were included, with many echoing the views Garry had sought in vain to convey publicly; that is, 'a mix' of psychotic patients with the personality disordered is likely to be anti-therapeutic for both groups of clients; efforts to control behaviour, such as the use of seclusion, are often interpreted as punishment; meaningful rewards or enforceable contracts are difficult to implement; and self-harm, often viewed as manipulation, may reach dangerous levels if ignored. Other comments referred to a disturbing lack of continuity of care with some staff appearing to be judgmental or critical. Because the personality disordered exhibit marked behavioural disturbances, some considered the medical model to disparage their problems by casting them in a moral framework. As one commented, she would expect a medical orientation to focus on 'seriousness' and 'blamelessness', but a diagnosis of personality disorder elicits value judgments in a medical/biological guise with reference to terms, such as 'manipulation', 'attention seeking', 'acting out' and 'dysfunctional relationships'. Surprisingly, some preferred a major mental disorder diagnosis, because its pariah status is less evident (*Service Options for Clients with Severe or Borderline Personality Disorders*, Health and Community Services, December 1994, pp.103–11). Overall, it was an interesting consumer response reinforcing the difficulty of separating the clinical symptoms attaching to antisocial personality disorder from judgments about amoral behaviour, despite the frequent professional transmutations and impression of increased precision in the historical shifts from 'manie sans délire', to moral insanity, psychopathy and sociopathy. Even the more careful attention given to the diagnostic criteria in *DSM-III-R* had done little to assuage this problem because of its emphasis on enduring personality traits and lifestyle rather than mental state symptoms.

On the basis of the submissions made and consultation with clinicians, the Psychiatric Services Division moved a step closer to identifying treatment models and the characteristics of successful service provision for this group of clients. It concluded that the interpretation of key concepts in the Mental Health Act 1986 should be amended to include the short-term detention of those with personality disorders at risk of suicide or significant self harm (*Service Options for Clients with Severe or Borderline Personality Disorders*, 1994, p.70). As a consequence, the Mental Health (Amendment) Bill was introduced into Parliament in October 1995 with section 12A allowing for the continued detention of those who do not satisfy the criteria of the Act regarding mental *illness*, but who have a mental *disorder* likely to lead to self-injury without the provision of available treatment. Clearly this section is intended as a funnelling process to be activated only in tightly controlled circumstances. The procedure enables the Authorised Psychiatrist of a hospital to apply to the Chief Psychiatrist for the continued detention and treatment of a person who 'appears to have a mental disorder' and who, on the basis of past history, is likely to cause further serious physical harm. This application must be determined within seven days, thus avoiding the unjustified detention in the absence of a decision, as had regrettably plagued the hearings of the Community Protection Act. A committee, constituted by the Chief Psychiatrist and two other qualified psychiatrists, must determine the applications and detention is reviewable at three-monthly intervals. Theoretically, it would be possible, although extremely unlikely, for extensions to continue indefinitely, provided that treatment was justifiable. However, as with the judicial reluctance to use the new sentencing option for serious violent offenders, psychiatrists have been cautious and section 12A is yet to be applied, although it could conceivably have been used for Garry David, had it then been available. He could have been retained in the psychiatric system without the need for special legislation and without incurring the unjustifiable delays attributed to unwieldy legislation.

Section 12A is perhaps the most direct outcome of the Garry David experience and is intended to be limited in application, applying only to the continued detention in a psychiatric facility of those who, if unsupervised, would otherwise continue self-mutilatory behaviour. Thus, although psychiatrists had strenuously opposed being held responsible for the treatment of the personality disordered, a limited niche has been created for some of the more difficult clients, who might otherwise slip between the gaps of the health and correctional systems. The Psychiatric Services Division has expressed its willingness to foster appropriate treatment programmes and provide specialised facilities, thereby diminishing the force of clinicians' arguments that there is a custodial intent. The legislation guarantees safeguards in the form of treatment availability with a specific definition in the preamble to the Act as to its meaning:

'Treatment', in relation to a mental disorder means things done in the course of the exercise of professional skills to –

(a)   remedy the mental disorder; or

(b)   lessen its ill effects or the pain and suffering which it causes.

The nature of treatment for psychopathy has already been raised in an English Court of Appeal case in which the Mental Health Review Tribunal had discharged a patient whose condition was unlikely to be alleviated or prevented from deteriorating by the inpatient treatment immediately available. The Court considered that the patient's unwillingness to cooperate did not warrant the conclusion that the nursing, general care and medical supervision, which must also be regarded as part of therapy, were unlikely to be effective in the long term. The psychopathic patient was duly discharged, but then readmitted on the new basis that she was mentally ill. (see *R v Canons Park Mental Health Review Tribunal, Ex parte A* [1994] CA, 630).

The commitment to provide a treatment service has been enhanced by the recent establishment of the Victorian Specialist Personality Disorder Service for those with severe or borderline personality disorders. This state-wide initiative provides significant staffing levels for a small group of clients, including an intensive group therapy day programme, a small inpatient unit, supported accommodation, consultation and training to staff across Victoria – including those in the prisons – and a research and evaluation programme. Staff are expected to be 'creative, innovative and flexible' and are invited to utilise a variety of therapeutic techniques and develop new treatments in a multidisciplinary approach. They also offer a broader consultation liaison service for those at risk because of self-harming behaviours. This redefinition of the place of the personality disorders, and resumption of psychiatric responsibility in principle, has occurred without the turmoil associated with Garry David's management, and in the broader context of national and international obligations to the mentally disordered. It starkly contrasts with the antagonism engendered by the crude government intervention of the early 1990s, which had sought to redefine medical knowledge and direct the legal system in pursuit of a political objective. In that instance, the framing of policy to meet the exigencies of a single case was inevitably a reactive, rather than a convincing solution, as the Victoria Coroner concluded in his report:

> The deceased's contribution to his own death must be seen in the context of a health and legal system which traditionally had enormous difficulties in finding workable solutions to managing extreme behavioral problems such as is evidenced by Garry David. The system was clearly struggling to find solutions. Garry David was an individual at the limits of the extremes our society has been required to manage. His death is an indication, in spite of the best

will in the world, of the inability of our resources and known systems to cope with these problems. (*Coronial Report*, 11 August 1993, pp.4–5)

SOME OTHER APPROACHES TO 'DANGEROUS PERSONS'

South Australia has approached the same dilemma of dealing with a person deemed to be dangerous in the Case of AK, a prisoner with a record of seriously assaultative and unpredictable violence, who was considered inappropriate for discharge into the community at the expiry of his sentence. An impasse developed between mental health services and the government, when psychiatrists found him not to fulfil the criteria of mental illness, although his behaviour was clearly disabling. Kable-type legislation was considered, but rejected. Although guardians do not ordinarily have the power to detain a person in a correctional or psychiatric facility, (the proper term under the Mental Health Act 1993 (SA) is 'an approved treatment centre'). in this case the Public Advocate was appointed as guardian by the Guardianship Board with special powers under the Guardianship and Administration Act 1993 (SA) to authorise AK's detention (renewable at six-monthly intervals) in a one-person facility provided by the Minister of Health. Facility in the grounds of a former psychiatric hospital, whose wards have been gazetted as annexes of the local general hospital. The facility itself is contracted to the private correctional service of Group 4. This proved to be a novel and effective solution, which did not depend on political pressure being exerted on either psychiatry or the law. (I am indebted to Dr John Dawes, the former South Australian Public Advocate, for drawing this case, which has so many parallels with that of Garry David, to my attention.)

There is never an easy resolution to the problem posed by that rare person who appears to be unable to reside safely in the community. There are some recent cases, spanning three continents, worthy of particular mention for their attempts to clarify psychiatrists' treatment obligations. The first has engendered a great deal of controversy in England and pertains to a Michael Stone, who was dealt with entirely in a criminal justice context because psychiatrists deemed him to have a history of extreme and essentially untreatable personality disorder. Stone was convicted of two hammer murders and sentenced to 14 years in custody. The fact that he had previously made threats to kill and had unsuccessfully sought admission to a psychiatric hospital led the Chairman of the Commons' Health Select Committee to launch a full-scale inquiry into the adequacy of the mental health system. Two proposals were put forward, the first being antithetical to the treatability requirements of recent Victoria amendments. The first would amend the Mental Health Act 1983 (UK) to detain 'dangerous' psychopaths for an indeterminate period in a mental health facility, even if they are generally considered to be untreatable. As with the legislation in Victoria, the English counterpart contains a provision that civil commitment can only be used where 'treatment is likely to alleviate or prevent a deterioration of the condition'. The second proposal focuses on the establishment of a specialist unit to detain those suffering from severe personality disorders. This would create a new category of detainees, those 'dangerous' severely personality disordered, who are neither prisoners nor psychiatric patients, with the assessment being made on the grounds of their likely future violence.

Once again, there was an immediate outcry from civil liberties' groups. Rather predictably, the circumstances of the Stone case have also incurred much unfavourable publicity about the perceived inadequacy of the psychiatric profession to protect the community from 'dangerous' individuals. One commentator has described personality disorder in emotive terms as 'the black hole at the heart of psychiatry':

> the label psychiatrists hang round patients' necks when they know something is wrong with them, but they don't know what it is'. And the reason for this is that they don't bother to find out. (*Daily Telegraph* (UK), 25 October 1998)

This case has placed discernible pressure on psychiatrists to re-evaluate their responsibility for those personality-disordered patients who threaten the public. The headlines at the time suggest public disillusionment with both psychiatrists and politicians in their ability to safeguard the community from dangerous offenders as, for example: 'Stone Trial Prompts Mental Health Review' (*Daily Telegraph*, 25 October 1998); 'Disorder that Slips Through Legislation' (*Daily Telegraph,* 24 October 1998); 'Stone Made Death Threats to Nurse Five Days Before Killings' (*Daily Telegraph,* 24 October 1998); 'Forget Psychiatry, Stop Psychopaths' (*Sunday Times,* 25 December 1998); 'Law to End Loophole That Let Stone Kill' (*Sunday Times,* 25 October 1998); 'Psychiatrists Attacked Over the Russell Case'(*Daily Telegraph,* 27 October 1998); '"Ignorant" Straw Under Fire Over Killer' (*Guardian,* 28 October 1998); 'Straw Seeks Powers to Lock Up Psychopaths for Life' (*Observer,* 14 February 1999). The tenor of responses can be seen from the words of Michael Howlett, the Director of the Zito Trust:

> The psychiatric profession is currently divided as to whether this condition is treatable or not. But for any service to say Michael Stone is untreatable is not responsible, given the consequences of not treating him. (*Daily Telegraph* (UK), 26 October 1988)

This is the crux of the dilemma. Society expects psychiatrists to have the ability to foresee the actions of patients and use treatment as a method of control, whereas the clinical task is less concerned with this broader social purpose and focuses on mental health needs. The tension implicit in balancing community interests and clinical responsibilities has been brought to the fore with the recent UK White

Paper *Reforming the Mental Health Act* (UK December 2000). The Government has made it clear that their primary interest is with public safety and risk management strategies, and this has given rise to the delineation of separate category of dangerous persons, now known as DSPDs. In Managing Dangerous People with Severe Personality Disorder (DSPDs), it is proposed to extend civil and criminal powers of detention and intensive monitoring, even allowing a court to give a discretionary life sentence to a person posing a risk of serious harm to others, if this is appropriate to protect the public and care and treatment is not indicated (section 4.10 *Reforming the Health Act, Part 2 'High Risk Patients'*).

It is worth noting that whilst 'dangerousness' retains a centrality in mental health legislation across jurisdictions, it is not intrinsic to any diagnostic category. Control and treatment are different bedfellows indicative of separate state duties – the provision of care for the vulnerable and the implementation of coercive action to ensure community protection. Psychiatrists are often expected to satisfy these competing obligations and become susceptible to scorn for any seeming failure, especially in those high-profile cases arousing public fear. Their own clinical mode is overly restrictive from the perspective of the ordinary person and, as Rosenman aptly points out, 'an austerely scientific diagnosis excludes so many people from treatment that it would be publicly unacceptable' (Rosenman 1998, p.788). This is not to discount the fact that the goals of community protection and therapy do, in fact, mesh on many occasions, but it is the personality disordered who most clearly highlight the gulf between the psychiatrist's social and therapeutic obligations and raise ethical issues about a division of loyalties (see also Murray 1986; Toulmin 1986).

A second high-profile case which has added to the perception that psychiatrists are resisting a social obligation to contain 'dangerous persons', is that of John Lewthwaite in New South Wales. This brief account has been constructed from the wealth of material sent by the Legal Aid Commission of New South Wales and personal knowledge of the case, which has recently been the subject of investigation by the New South Wales Ombudsman.

Lewthwaite had been in custody since 1974 after conviction for the murder of a five-year old girl, whom he stabbed after failing to subject her young brother to his homosexual fantasies. There were many incidents of antisocial behaviour in his childhood, but as adolescence approached, it was his sexual behaviour and sadistic fantasies which began to draw attention. In prison he was largely cooperative and soon acknowledged his homosexual identity. Although eligible for parole since 1994, these applications were refused on five occasions, despite strong psychiatric opinion that he might safely be released under strict parole conditions.

Whilst it is understandable that any government must exercise caution in meeting its responsibilities for community protection, the detention of this man from the age of 19 to 45 years, contrary to prevailing professional opinion, would seem to have been marked by the same obstructionism featuring so strongly in the Garry David case. In New South Wales it was reinforced by publicly linking the malleable notion of 'dangerousness' with paedophilia, thereby highlighting the way in which fantasy plays a role in the labelling of certain violent sexual offenders. Politicians were swayed by the spirited lobbying of vocal community members persuaded of the link between a sex murder and dangerousness, and professional opinions became inconsequential to the case. Even confidence in Parole Board decisions was questioned when, in June 1999, the State Government challenged that body's decision to release Lewthwaite, albeit with an unprecedented regime of strict supervision for three years. These conditions attest to the Parole Board's awareness of the unpopularity of its decision, both in government circles and owing to the public's perception of Lewthwaite's entrenched dangerousness. The proposed restrictions included:

(a)   a return to custody for any misdemeanor within the three-year period;

(b)   daily, and then weekly, reporting to his case officer;

(c)   bi-monthly visits by Parole Board staff and regular phone monitoring;

(d)   monthly progress reports and an annual psychiatric examination;

(e)   a ban from going within 10 kilometres of the murder scene;

(f)   a ban on contact with anyone under the age of 16 years;

(g)   regular urine tests and the possibility that he should consent to blood tests for alcohol or other drugs;

(h)   a prohibition from changing address without permission; and (ix) a prohibition from travelling 'any considerable distance' from home without breaching reporting conditions (as reported in the *Daily Telegraph*, 10 June 1999).

The State Government suggested that it might pursue the rare course of appealing to the New South Wales Court of Criminal Appeal. Nonetheless, within a week of this announcement, Lewthwaite was released from his 25 years custody. Public reaction was immediate and intense, leading the New South Wales Corrective Minister to denounce the 'vigilante, mob mentality' (*The Age*, 24 June 1999) and move Lewthwaite from his initial accommodation to a secret location. Although ordinary legal processes ultimately prevailed for this dangerous offender, the pressures from the media, the public and the government on both psychiatry and the law were overt and sustained.

The third case, that of *Kansas v Hendricks* in the US Supreme Court, is important for its ramifications for preventive detention of the mentally disordered and for reviving, yet again, the use of civil jurisdiction powers for those deemed to be dangerous. It tested the power of the state to commit Leroy Hendricks, who had a long history of convictions for paedophilic offences, to a psychiatric institution on the grounds of his likely future dangerousness. The Kansas Sexually Violent Predator Act 1994 was introduced to couple 'mental abnormality' or 'personality disorder' with dangerousness and effectively forge a new path for preventive detention, which could ultimately embrace other than those simply known for their sexual proclivities. It overrode the existing Kansas mental health code, which had been amended in 1981 explicitly to exclude antisocial personality disorder as a condition satisfying the 'severe mental disorder' criterion of civil commitment. The American Psychiatric Association in its *amicus curiae* brief held that this new legislation was consigning psychiatry to a punitive role, because it deemed the presence or absence of 'mental illness' to be irrelevant. However, the well-respected Menninger Foundation joined with community interest groups to contend that the state did have a duty to use its civil commitment powers to detain dangerous sexual offenders, *independent of whether the person's dangerousness is due to a treatable condition*. The Court upheld the validity of this new state power by suggesting that public interest concerns are forging a place for some of the personality disordered within a framework of preventive detention and that this will encourage psychiatrists to reappraise their function in relation to this group (see Felthous and Gunn 1997, pp.429–31).

These various examples have been introduced to place the case of Garry David in the broader perspective of the 'untreatable' mentally disordered, who are also considered to be dangerous. They indicate that it is a problem unlikely to go away, but will remain as part of the ongoing border dispute between psychiatry and the law, and no form of resolution in the current state of knowledge can fully satisfy the scientific or jurisprudential principles involved. It would seem that striking the balance between the duty to protect the community and the duty to safeguard the rights of individuals is as much a problem for governments as it is for medical and legal professions.

CONCLUSION

I initially posed the question: *Why was Garry David chosen as the epitome of the dangerous individual?* The answer is that there was a timely coalescence of factors rather than any clear demonstration of his special propensity for dangerousness. In brief, the most salient of these were:

- an unusual period of public concern about violent actions committed by unstable individuals, which followed the Queen Street and Hoddle Street massacres;

- the Government's need to reaffirm its support for the Victoria Police after the aborted attempt to introduce an external complaints system;

- the enhanced possibility of a psychiatric alliance with government interests in view of the bureaucratic changes and economic resources vested in the forensic sector;

- the dissemination of press detail about Garry's propensity to disfigure grotesquely his own body, an action which then symbolised his likely violence and need to be excluded.

These factors emanated from different sources and any one would have been an insufficient trigger for the events which followed but, in concert, they set in train a process of exclusion which affronted many lawyers with its erosion of legal principles and equally affronted psychiatrists with governmental interference in their decision making.

I have set out to explore the relational interdependence of domination and resistance displayed in the tension which Garry perceived to be oscillating between the exercise of power and the possibility of his freedom. In doing so, I have desisted from exploring the various meanings that freedom holds and simply used it in the general sense of release from custody. However, this issue does raise some interesting themes worthy of a separate study. Freedom is an inescapable part of the exercise of power in Foucauldian terms and involved very different connotations for all the participants in this case, ranging from a moral awareness, to self-capacity, to an ability to act without obvious constraints. There were many contradictions in the way it presented. Garry himself seemed to be assailed by a paralysing ambivalence and was unable to accept what he simplistically asserted would be the 'freedom' for which he was fighting. He rejected the gains he made and did not understand that his freedom was part of his power play with others, yet it was fundamentally amoral in requiring subjection and humiliation (see also Dumm 1998; Rose 1999).

A further theme I have explored is the exercise of power through disciplinary mechanisms, which in this instance did not suppress autonomy, but actually transformed its object into an adversary. Power and surveillance over human beings cannot be complete even in the face of custodial imperatives and restrictive legislation, nor can they be exercised in an enforced way through the combined forces of punishment and therapy, because the struggle for autonomy is ever-present and gives rise to resistance. Thus, to depict the Garry David case as a failure for either psychiatry or the prison would be a political over-simplification of the human forces involved in the struggle and would ignore some of the positive lessons emerging from the multilayered discourse. Contradictions implicit in the forensic arena were exposed and issues crystallised in a way which had not happened previously, so that the impact of correctional goals on therapeutic interventions within a prison setting were made overt. The legacy for Victoria is that any seeming rigidity of the binary division between badness and madness has weakened. The recent amendment to mental health legislation recognises that *distress* in the form of self-harm as a consequence of a mental disorder (rather than illness) is a legitimate psychiatric responsibility, but 'dangerousness' *per se* must remain situated within the realm of criminality. The addition of preventive detention to sentencing options reflects the current law and order focus, but the lessons derived from Garry David ensure that it must be applied prospectively, rather than retrospectively.

Although these changes may not be entirely palatable for the disciplines of psychiatry or law to accommodate, they are a political response to the two fundamental duties of the state. In that tenuous area between madness and badness and between freedom and restraint, these duties are not fully compatible, and the pendulum must always swing in favour of one or the other in any specific instance. Nonetheless, it is imperative for any society to ascertain the reasons for policy shifts, especially when these appear to undermine civil rights. The containment of those perceived to be dangerous has historically been understood as a legitimate exercise of governance, but it must be approached cautiously without compromising the principles of either the legal or psychiatric profession, as happened in the case of Garry David.

Bibliography

REFERENCES

American Psychiatric Association (1987) *Diagnostic and Statistical Manual of Mental Disorders.* 3rd edition revised. Washington: American Psychiatric Association Press.

American Psychiatric Association (1994) *Diagnostic and Statistical Manual of Mental Disorders.* 4th edition. Washington: American Psychiatric Association Press.

Armstrong, D. (1987) 'Bodies of Knowledge: Foucault and the Problem of Human Anatomy.' In G. Scambler (ed) *Sociological Theory and Medical Sociology.* London: Tavistock.

Attorney-General's Department (1988) *Sentencing: Report of the Victorian Sentencing Committee.* Melbourne: VGP.

Australian Health Ministers' Advisory Council National Mental Health Working Group (March 1995) *Model Mental Health Legislation.* Canberra: Australian Government Publishing Service.

Australian Health Ministers' Conference Mental Health (March 1991) *Statement of Rights and Responsibilities.* Canberra: Australian Government Publishing Service.

Australian Health Ministers (April 1992) *National Mental Health Policy and Plan.* Canberra: Australian Government Publishing Service.

Babcock, B.A. (1978) *The Reversible World: Symbolic Inversion in Art and Society.* Ithaca and London: Cornell University Press.

Bakhtin, M.M. (1968) *Rabelais and His World* (trans. H. Iwolsky). Cambridge, MA: MIT Press.

Barrett, R.J. (1996) *The Psychiatric Team and the Social Definition of Schizophrenia: An Anthropologist's Study of Person and Illness.* Cambridge: Cambridge University Press.

Bartholomew, A.A. (1986) *Psychiatry, the Criminal Law and Corrections: An Exercise in Sciolism.* Bundalong, Vic: Wileman Publications.

Berlin, I. (1967) 'Does Political Theory Still Exist?' In P. Laslett and W. Runciman (eds) *Philosophy, Politics and Society.* Second Series. Oxford: Basil Blackwell.

Borsody, A. and Van Groningen, J. (1990) 'A Reply – Madness or Badness?' *Legal Service Bulletin 15,* 3, 116–117.

Bostock, J.A. (1968) *The Dawn of Australian Psychiatry: An Account of the Measures Taken for the Care of Mental Invalids from the Time of the First Fleet, 1788 to the Year 1850.* Glebe, NSW: Australian Publishing Co.

Bourdieu, P. (1977) 'Symbolic Power' (trans. C. Wringe). In D. Gleeson (ed) *Identity and Structure: Issues in the Sociology of Education.* Driffield: Nafferton Books.

Brothers, C.J. (1961) *Early Victorian Psychiatry 1835–1905.* Melbourne: Australian Government Printer.

Brown, M. and Pratt, J. (eds) (2000) *Dangerous Offenders: Punishment and Social Order.* London and New York: Routledge.

Bryson, J. (1986) *Evil Angels.* Ringwood, Victoria: Penguin.

Burchell, G., Gordon, C., and Miller, P.B. (eds) (1991) *The Foucault Effect: Studies in Governmentality.* Hempstead: Harvester Wheatsheaf.

Burns, C. (1962) *The Tait Case.* Melbourne: Melbourne University Press.

Busfield, J. (1986) *Managing Madness: Changing Ideas and Practice.* London: Hutchinson.

Campbell, I.G. (1988) *Mental Disorder and Criminal Law in Australia and New Zealand.* Sydney: Butterworths.

Castel, R. (1975) 'The Doctors and Judges.' In M. Foucault I, *Pierre Rivière, Having Slaughtered My Mother, My Sister, and My Brother: A Case of Parricide in the Nineteenth Century.* New York: Pantheon Books.

Castel, R. (1991) 'From Dangerousness to Risk.' In G. Burchell, C. Gordon and P.B. Miller (eds) *The Foucault Effect: Studies in Governmentality.* Hempstead: Harvester Wheatsheaf.

Cecil, D. (Lord) (1939) *Melbourne: The Young Melbourne and the Story of His Marriage with Caroline Lamb.* London: Constable.

Charlesworth, H. (1991) 'Australia's Accession to the First Optional Protocol to the International Covenant on Civil and Political Rights.' *Melbourne University Law Review 18,* 428–434.

Clarke, M. (1980) *For the Term of His Natural Life.* Blackburn, Vic: Currey O' Neil, The Dominion Press.

Cleckley, H. (1964) *The Mask of Sanity.* St. Louis, MI: C.V. Mosby.

Cloward, R.R., Cressey, D.R., Grosser, G.H., McCleery, R., Ohlin, L.E., Sykes, G. and Messinger, S.L. (1960) *Theoretical Studies in Social Organization of the Prison.* New York: Social Science Research Council.

Coid, J. (1989) 'Psychopathic Disorders.' *Current Opinion in Psychiatry 2,* 750–756.

Comaroff, J. (1982) 'Medicine: Symbol and Ideology.' In P. Wright and A. Treacher (eds) *The Problem of Medical Knowledge: Examining the Social Construction of Medicine.* Edinburgh: University of Edinburgh Press.

Comaroff, J. (1985) *Body of Power, Spirit of Resistance: The Culture and History of a South African People.* Chicago: University of Chicago Press.

Crawford, C. (1994) 'Legalizing Medicine: Early Modern Legal Systems and the Growth of Medico-Legal Knowledge.' In M. Clark and C. Crawford (eds) *Legal Medicine in History.* Cambridge: Cambridge University Press.

Craze, L. (1993) *The Care and Control of the Criminally Insane in New South Wales: 1788 to 1987.* PhD (unpublished). School of Social Work, University of New South Wales.

Craze, L. and Moynihan, P. (1994) 'Violence, Meaning and the Law: Responses to Garry David.' *Australian and New Zealand Journal of Criminology 27,* 1, 30-45.

Damasio, A.R. (1994) *Descartes' Error: Emotion, Reason and the Human Brain.* New York: G.P. Putnam.

Damasio, A.R., Damasio, H. and Christen, Y. (1996) *The Neurobiology of Decision-Making.* Berlin and New York: Springer.

Dershowitz, A.M. (1973) 'Preventive Confinement: A Suggested Framework for Constitutional Analysis.' *Texas Law Review 51,* 7, 1277-1324.

Détienne, M. (1979) *Dionysus Slain* (trans. M. and L. Mueller). Baltimore: Johns Hopkins University Press.

Deutsch, A. (1973) *The Shame of the States.* New York: Arno.

Dews, P. (1987) *Logics of Disintegration: Post-Structuralist Thought and the Claims of Critical Theory.* London and New York: Verso.

Douglas, M. (1966) *Purity and Danger: An Analysis of Concepts of Pollution and Taboo.* London: Routledge and Kegan Paul.

Dumm, T. (1998) *Michel Foucault and the Politics of Freedom.* Thousand Oaks, CA: Sage.

Durkheim, É. (1964) *The Division of Labor in Society* (orig. pub. 1893). New York: Free Press.

Edelman, M. (1971) *Politics as Symbolic Action: Mass Arousal and Quiescence.* New York: Academic Press.

Edelman, M. (1980) 'Law and Psychiatry as Political Symbolism.' *International Journal of Law and Psychiatry 3,* 235–244.

Edelman, M. (1988) *Constructing the Political Spectacle.* Chicago: University of Chicago Press.

Elias, N. (1956) 'Involvement and Detachment.' *British Journal of Sociology 7,* 3, 226–252.

Elias, N. (1991) *The Symbol Theory* (ed. R. Kilminster). London: Sage.

Ellard, J. (1989) 'The History and Present Status of "Moral Insanity".' In J. Ellard (ed. G. Parker) *Some Rules for Killing People: Essays on Madness, Murder and the Mind.* Sydney: Angus and Robertson.

Ellard, J. (1990) 'The Madness of Mental Health Acts.' *Australian and New Zealand Journal of Psychiatry 24,* 167–174.

Ellard, J. (1991) 'Personality Disorder.' *Modern Medicine of Australia,* April, 38–43.

Ennis, B.J. and Litwack, T.R. (1974) 'Psychiatry and the Presumption of Expertise: Flipping Coins in the Courtroom.' *California Law Review 62,* 693–752.

Ericson, R.V., Baranek, P.M. and Chan, J.B.L. (1987) *Visualizing Deviance: A Study of News Organization.* Toronto: Toronto University Press.

Ericson, R.V., Baranek, P.M. and Chan, J.B.L. (1989) *Negotiating Control: A Study of News Sources.* Toronto: Toronto University Press.

Ericson, R.V., Baranek, P.M. and Chan, J.B.L. (1991) *Representing Order: Crime, Law and Justice in the News Media.* Milton Keynes: Open University Press.

Ericson, R.V. (1991) 'Mass Media, Crime, Law and Justice: An Institutional Approach.' *British Journal of Criminology 31,* 3, 219–240.

Fairall, P.A. (1993) 'Violent Offenders and Community Protection in Victoria – the Garry David Experience.' *Criminal Law Journal 17,* 1, 40–54.

Fairall, P.A. (1995) 'Imprisonment Without Conviction in New South Wales: *Kable v Director of Public Prosecutions.' Sydney Law Review 17,* 573–580.

Felthous, A.R. and Gunn, J. (1997) 'Forensic Psychiatry: An Editorial Review.' *Current Opinion in Psychiatry 10,* 429–431.

Floud, J. and Young, W. (1981) *Dangerousness and Criminal Justice.* London: Heinemann.

Fontana, A. (1975) 'The Intermittences of Rationality.' In M. Foucault *I, Pierre Rivière, Having Slaughtered my Mother, my Sister, and my Brother: A Case of Parricide in the Nineteenth Century.* New York: Pantheon Books.

Foucault, M. (1977a) 'Theatrum Philosophicum.' In D.F. Bouchard (ed) *Language, Counter-Memory and Practice.* Ithaca and New York: Cornell University Press.

Foucault, M. (1977b) *Discipline and Punish: The Birth of the Prison.* London: Allen Lane.

Foucault, M. (1978) 'About the Concept of the 'Dangerous Individual' in 19th Century Legal Psychiatry.' *International Journal of Law and Psychiatry 1,* 1–18.

Foucault, M. (1988a) *Politics, Philosophy and Culture: Interviews and Other Writings 1977–1984* (ed. L. Kritzman). New York: Routledge, Chapman and Hall.

Foucault, M. (1988b) 'Truth, Power and Self: An Interview.' In H. Guttman and P. Hutton (eds) *Technologies of the Self.* London: Tavistock.

Fox, R. (1988) 'The Killings of Bobby Veen: The High Court on Proportion in Sentencing.' *Criminal Law Journal 12,* 339–366.

Fox, R. (1993) 'Legislation Comment: Victoria Turns to the Right in Sentencing Reform: The Sentencing (Amendment) Act 1993 (Vic).' *Criminal Law Journal 17,* 393-415.

Freckelton, I. (1998) 'Decision-making about Involuntary Psychiatric Treatment: An Analysis of the Principles behind Victorian Practice.' *Journal of Psychiatry, Psychology and Law 5*, 2, 249–264.

Garfinkel, H. (1956) 'Conditions of Successful Degradation Ceremonies.' *American Journal of Sociology 61*, 420–424.

Garfinkel, H. (1984) *Studies in Ethnomethodology.* Cambridge: Polity Press.

Garland, D. (1990) *Punishment and Modern Society: A Study in Social Theory.* London: Clarendon Press.

Garton, S. (1988) *Medicine and Madness: A Social History of Insanity in New South Wales 1880–1940.* Kensington, NSW: New South Wales University Press.

Girard, R. (1986) *The Scapegoat* (trans. Y. Freccero). Baltimore: Johns Hopkins University Press.

Glaser, W. (1990) 'Morality and Medicine.' *Legal Service Bulletin 15*, 3, 114–116.

Glaser, W. (1994) 'Commentary: Garry David, Psychiatry, and the Discourse of Dangerousness.' *Australian and New Zealand Journal of Criminology 27*, 1, 46–49.

Goffman, E. (1961) *Asylums: Essays on the Social Situation of Mental Patients and Other Inmates.* New York: Anchor Books.

Greig D.N. (1993) 'The Politics of Dangerousness.' In S. Gerull and W. Lucas (eds) *Serious Violent Offenders: Sentencing, Psychiatry and Law Reform.* Canberra: Australian Institute of Criminology.

Greig, D.N. (1997) 'Professions and the Risk Society.' *Psychiatry, Psychology and Law 4*, 2, 231–240.

Gunn, J. (1977) 'Criminal behaviour and mental disorder.' *British Journal of Psychiatry 130*, 317–29.

Gunn, J. (1979) 'The Law and the Mentally Abnormal Offender in England and Wales.' *International Journal of Law and Psychiatry 2*, 199–214.

Gunn, J., Robertson, G., Dell, S. and Way, D. (1978) *Psychiatric Aspects of Imprisonment.* London: Academic Press.

Gusfield, J.R. (1963) *The Symbolic Crusade: Status Politics and the American Temperance Movement.* Urbana: University of Illinois Press.

Gusfield, J.R. (1981) *The Culture of Public Problems: Drinking, Driving and the Symbolic Order.* Chicago and London: The University of Chicago Press.

Gusfield, J.R. (1989) 'Constructing the Ownership of Social Problems: Fun and Profit in the Welfare State.' *Social Problems 36*, 5, 431–441.

Hare, R.D. (1993) *Without Conscience: The Disturbing World of the Psychopaths Among Us.* New York: Simon and Schuster.

Health and Community Services (HCS), Victoria (April 1994) *Victoria's Mental Health Services: The Framework for Service Delivery.* Melbourne: VGPO.

Health and Community Services (HCS), Victoria (August 1994) *Discussion Paper, Victoria's Mental Health Service: Proposed Amendments to the 'Mental Health Act 1986'.* Melbourne: VGPO.

Health and Community Services (HCS), Victoria (December 1994) *Mental Health Services, Service Options for Clients with Severe or Borderline Personality Disorders.*

Health Department of Victoria, Office of Psychiatric Services (October 1986) *New Directions for Psychiatric Services in Victoria.* Melbourne: VGPO.

Human Rights and Equal Opportunity Commission (1993) *Human Rights and Mental Illness: Report of the National Inquiry into the Rights of People with Mental Illness* ('Burdekin Report'). Canberra: Australian Government Publishing Service.

Johnstone, G. (1996) *Medical Concepts and Penal Policy.* London: Cavendish.

Keon-Cohen, B. (1993) 'Can the Victorian Parliament Abolish Fundamental Rights?' In S. Gerull and W. Lucas (eds) *Serious Violent Offenders: Sentencing, Psychiatry and Law Reform*. Canberra: Australian Institute of Criminology.

Kerr, A. and McClelland, H. (eds) (1991) *Concepts of Mental Disorder: A Continuing Debate*. London: Gaskell (Royal College of Psychiatrists).

Kiel, H. (ed) (1992) *Decisions of the Mental Health Review Board Victoria 1987–1991*. Melbourne: MHRB.

Law Reform Commission of Victoria (LRC) (April 1990) *The Concept of Mental Illness in the 'Mental Health Act 1986'*. Report No. 31. Melbourne: VGPO.

Law Reform Commission of Victoria (LRC) (October 1990) *Mental Malfunction and Criminal Responsibility*. Report no. 34. Melbourne: VGPO.

Lewis, C.S. (1953) 'The Humanitarian Theory of Punishment.' *Res Judicatae 5*, 225–237.

Lewis, M. (1988) *Managing Madness: Psychiatry and Society in Australia 1788–1980*. Canberra: Australian Government Publishing Service.

Lombroso, C. (1913) *Crime: Its Causes and Remedies*. Boston: Little Brown.

Lunbeck, E. (1994) *The Psychiatric Persuasion: Knowledge, Gender, and Power in Modern America*. Princeton, NJ: Princeton University Press.

McBarnet, D. (1983) *Conviction: Law, the State and the Construction of Justice*. London: Macmillan.

McCleery, R.H. (1961) 'The Governmental Process and Informal Social Control and Authoritarianism and the Belief System of Incorrigibles.' In D.R. Cressey (ed) *The Prison: Studies in Institutional Organization and Change*. New York: Holt, Rinehart and Winston.

Maines, D.R. (Spring 1993) 'Narrative's Moment and Sociology's Phenomena: Towards a Narrative Sociology.' *Sociological Quarterly 34*, 1, 17–38.

Manning, P. (1987) 'Ironies of Compliance.' In C. Shearing and P. Stenning (eds) *Private Policing*. Beverly Hills: Sage.

Mead, G.H. (1918) 'The Psychology of Punitive Justice.' *American Journal of Sociology 23*, 577–692.

Menninger, K. (1968) *The Crime of Punishment*. New York: Viking Press.

Mental Health Review Board (MHRB), Victoria (1990) *Annual Report*. Melbourne.

Monahan, J. (1983) 'The Prediction of Violent Behavior: Towards a Second Generation of Theory and Policy.' *American Journal of Psychiatry 14*, 1, 10–15.

Monahan, J. and Steadman, H. (eds) (1983) *Mentally Disordered Offenders: Perspectives from Law and Social Science*. New York: Plenum Press.

Moore, S.F. and Myerhoff, B.G. (eds) (1977) *Secular Ritual*. Amsterdam: Van Gorcum.

Moore, M., Estrich, S.R., McGillis, D. and Spelman, W. (1984) *Dangerous Offenders: The Elusive Target of Justice*. Cambridge, Mass: Harvard University Press.

Moynihan, P. (1992) 'The Community Protection Act: Signalling a Crisis in Modernity?' *Socio-Legal Bulletin*, 9–30.

Murray, T.H. (1986) 'Divided Loyalties for Physicians.' *Social Science and Medicine 23*, 827–32.

O'Malley, P. (1998) *Crime and the Risk Society*. Dartmouth: Ashgate.

Page, T. (1992) *Garry David and the Community Protection Act 1990*. LLM (unpublished). Faculty of Law, University of Melbourne.

Parker, N. (1991) 'The Garry David Case.' *Australian and New Zealand Journal of Psychiatry 25*, 371–4.

Parliament of Victoria, Debates (30 May 1985) Mental Health Bill No. 1, Legislative Assembly. Melbourne: VGPO.

Parliament of Victoria, Debates (4 and 10 April 1990) Community Protection Bill, Legislative Assembly. Melbourne: VGPO.

Parliament of Victoria, Debates (11 April 1990) Community Protection Bill, Legislative Council. Melbourne: VGPO.

Parliament of Victoria, Community Development Committee (October 1995) *Inquiry into Persons Detained at the Governor's Pleasure.* Melbourne: VGPO.

Parliament of Victoria, Social Development Committee (May 1990) *Inquiry into Mental Disturbance and Community Safety, Strategies To Deal with Persons with Severe Personality Disorder Who Pose a Threat to Public Safety.* Interim Report. Melbourne: VGPO.

Parliament of Victoria, Social Development Committee (March 1992) *Inquiry into Mental Disturbance and Community Safety, Incorporating a Range of Views on the Draft Community Protection (Violent Offenders) Bill.* Second Report. Melbourne: VGPO.

Parliament of Victoria, Social Development Committee (April 1992) *Inquiry into Mental Disturbance and Community Safety, A Response to the Draft Community Protection (Violent Offenders) Bill.* Third Report. Melbourne: VGPO.

Parliament of Victoria, Social Development Committee (August 1992) *Inquiry into Mental Disturbance and Community Safety.* Final Report. Melbourne: VGPO.

Pick, D. (1989) *Faces of Degeneration: A European Disorder c.1848–c.1918.* Cambridge: Cambridge University Press.

Pinel, P. (1941) 'Traite médico-philosophique sur la manie.' 2nd ed. In G. Zilboorg and G.W. Henry (eds) *A History of Medical Psychology.* New York: Norton.

Pressman, J.D. (1998) *Last Resort: Psychosurgery and the Limits of Medicine.* Cambridge: Cambridge University Press.

Prichard, J.C. (1835) *A Treatise on Insanity and Other Disorders Affecting the Mind.* London: Sherwood, Gilbert and Piper.

Priest, P. (1992) 'Dangerousness: The Law and Policy Concerning the Dangerous.' LLM (unpublished). Faculty of Law, University of Melbourne.

Ramon, S. (1986) 'The Category of Psychopathy: Its Professional and Social Context in Britain.' In P.B. Miller and N. Rose (eds) *The Power of Psychiatry.* Cambridge: Polity Press.

Rees, N. and Fairall, P. (1995) '*Gregory Wayne Kable v The Director of Public Prosecutions for New South Wales:* The Power to Legislate for One.' *High Court Reports 4,* www.bond/edu/au/law/hcr/104rees.htm

Rhodes, L.A. (1991) *Emptying Beds: The Work of an Emergency Psychiatric Unit.* California: University of California Press.

Richardson, G. (1993) *Law, Process and Custody: Prisoners and Patients.* London: Weidenfeld and Nicolson.

Rose, N. (1998) 'Governing Risky Individuals: The Role of Psychiatry in New Regimes of Control.' *Psychiatry, Psychology and Law 5,* 2, 177–95.

Rose, N. (1996) *Inventing Ourselves: Psychology, Power and Personhood.* Cambridge: Cambridge University Press.

Rose, N. (1999) *Powers of Freedom: Reframing Political Thought.* Cambridge: Cambridge University Press.

Rose, N. and Miller, P.B. (1992) 'Political Power Beyond the State: Problematics of Government.' *British Journal of Sociology 43,* 2, 172–205.

Rosenberg, C. (1968) *Trial of the Assassin Guiteau, Psychiatry and Law in the Gilded Age.* Chicago and London: University of Chicago Press.

Rosenman, S. (1998) 'Psychiatrists and Compulsion: A Map of Ethics.' *Australian and New Zealand Journal of Psychiatry 32*, 785–93.

Rothman, D. (1971) *The Discovery of the Asylum: Social Order and Disorder in the New Republic.* Boston: Little, Brown and Co.

Schiffer, M. (1976) 'Mentally Disordered Offenders.' *Osgoode Hall Law Journal 14*, 317–43.

Scull, A. (1993) *The Most Solitary of Afflictions: Madness and Society in Britain, 1700–1900.* New Haven: Yale University Press.

Shah, S.A. (1981) 'Legal and Mental Health System Interactions: Major Developments and Research Needs.' *International Journal of Law and Psychiatry 4*, 3, 219–70.

Shaw, S.H. (1973) 'The Dangerousness of Dangerousness.' *Medicine, Science and Law 13*, 4, 269–71.

Shea, P. (1993) *Psychiatry in Court: The Use of Psychiatric Reports in Court Proceedings.* Sydney: Institute of Criminology Monograph. Series no. 3.

Sim, J. (1990) *Medical Power in Prisons: The Prison Medical Service in England 1774–1989.* Milton Keynes: Open University Press.

Sleffel, L. (1977) *The Law and the Dangerous Criminal: Statutory Attempts at Definition and Control.* Lexington, MA: Heath and Co.

Smith, R. (1981) *Trial by Medicine: Insanity and Responsibility in Victorian Trials.* Edinburgh: Edinburgh University Press.

Stallybrass, P. and White, A. (1986) *The Politics and Poetics of Transgression.* Ithaca, NY: Cornell University Press.

Steadman, H.J., Monahan, J., Robbins, P.C., Appelbaum, P., Grisso, T., Klassen, D., Mulvey, E.P. and Roth, L. (1993) 'From Dangerousness to Risk Assessment: Implications for Appropriate Research Strategies.' In S. Hodgins (ed) *Mental Disorder and Crime.* Newbury Park, CA: Sage.

Steadman, H.J., Silver, E., Monhan, J., Appelbaum, P.S., Robbins, P.C., Mulvey, E.P., Grisso, T., Roth, L.H. and Banks, S. (2000) 'A Classification tree approach to the development of actuarial violence: Risk assessment tools', *Law and Human Behavior 24*, 83–100.

Stone, A. (1984) *Law, Psychiatry and Morality: Essays and Analysis.* Washington, DC: American Psychiatric Press.

Svensson, P. (1993) 'The Case for Due Process in Reviewable Sentences.' In S. Gerull and W. Lucas (eds) *Serious Violent Offenders: Sentencing, Psychiatry and Law Reform.* Canberra: Australian Institute of Criminology.

Sykes, G. (1958) *The Society of Captives: A Study of a Maximum Security Prison.* Princeton: Princeton University Press.

Tolstoy, L. (1966) *Resurrection.* Harmondsworth and Baltimore: Penguin Books.

Toulmin, S. (1986) 'Divided Loyalties and Ambiguous Relationships.' *Social Science and Medicine 23*, 783–87.

Turner, V. (1990) *Drama, Fields and Metaphors: Symbolic Action in Human Society.* Ithaca: Cornell University Press.

United Kingdom, Department of Health (December 2000) *Reforming the Mental Health Act – Part 2 – 'High Risk Patients'.* London: The Stationery Office.

United Nations (1966) *International Covenant on Civil and Political Rights.* New York and Geneva: UN.

United Nations (1975) *Declaration on the Rights of Disabled Persons,* General Assembly Resolution 3447 (XXX of 9 December). New York: UN.

United Nations (1991) *Principles for the Protection of Persons with Mental Illness and for the Improvement of Mental Health Care*, General Assembly Resolution (46/119, 17 December). New York: UN.

Verdun-Jones, S.N. (1989) 'Sentencing the Partly Mad and the Partly Bad: The Case of the Hospital Order in England and Wales.' *International Journal of Law and Psychiatry 12*, 1–27.

Wagner-Pacifici, E. (1986) *The Moro Morality Play: Terrorism as Social Drama.* Chicago and London: University of Chicago Press.

Waller, L. (ed.) (1997) *Brett, Waller and Williams' Criminal Law: Texts and Cases*, 8th ed. Sydney: Butterworths. (Ch. 4).

Watson, S. (1994) 'Malingerers, the "Weakminded" Criminal and the "Moral Imbecile": How the English Prison Medical Officer Became an Expert in Mental Deficiency, 1880–1930.' In M. Clark and C. Crawford (eds) *Legal Medicine in History.* Cambridge: Cambridge University Press.

White, H.V. (1987) *The Content of the Form: Narrative Discourse and Historical Representation.* Baltimore and London: The Johns Hopkins University Press.

Williams, C. R. (1990) 'Psychopathy, Mental Illness and Preventive Detention: Issues Arising from the Garry David Case.' *Monash Law Review 16*, 161–83.

Wood, D. (1990) 'A One-man Dangerous Offender's Statute: The Community Protection Act 1990 (Vic).' *Melbourne University Law Review 17*, 3, 497–505.

Wootton, B. (1980) 'Psychiatry, Ethics and the Criminal Law.' *British Journal of Psychiatry 136*, 525–32.

Zdenkowski, G. (1997) 'Community Protection through Imprisonment without Conviction: Pragmatism versus Justice.' *Australian Journal of Human Rights 3*, 2, 8–52.

COURT AND TRIBUNAL HEARINGS
Relating to Garry David (chronological)

Statement of Reasons – Rulings on Applications Made on 23 January 1990 in the Appeal of Garry Ian Patrick Webb (also known as Garry Ian Patrick David), Mental Health Review Board No. 230190: X01: 300512, 23 January 1990.

Statement of Reasons in the Appeal of Garry Ian Patrick Webb (also known as Garry Ian Patrick David) a Security Patient at Aradale Hospital, Mental Health Review Board No. 230190: X01: 300512, 9 May 1990.

Attorney-General for the State of Victoria v. President and Members of the Mental Health Review Board and Garry David, Supreme Court of Victoria, Young CJ, Crockett J, Southwell J, Appeal Division, 10 May 1990.

Attorney-General for the State of Victoria v. Mental Health Review Board, Administrative Appeals Tribunal, General Division, Smith J, Appeal No. 18016/1990, 15 May 1990.

Attorney-General for the State of Victoria v. Garry Ian David, Supreme Court of Victoria, Fullagar J, No. 7133/1990, 12 June 1990.

Attorney-General for the State of Victoria v. Mental Health Review Board, Administrative Appeals Tribunal, General Division, Smith, J, Appeal No. 18016/1990, 12 July 1990.

Attorney-General for the State of Victoria v. Garry Ian David, Supreme Court of Victoria, Fullagar J, No. 6823/1990, 18 September 1990 ('First Hearing').

Attorney-General for the State of Victoria v. Garry Ian David, Supreme Court of Victoria, Fullagar J, No. 6823/1990, 5 March 1991.

Attorney-General for the State of Victoria v. Garry Ian David, Supreme Court of Victoria, Hedigan J, No. 6823/1990, 15 November 1991, [1992] 2 VR 46 ('Second Hearing').

Garry Ian David v. Attorney-General for the State of Victoria, Supreme Court, Appeal Division, Harper, J, No. 6160/1992, 4 June 1992 ('First Appeal').

Attorney-General for the State of Victoria v. Garry Ian David, Supreme Court of Victoria, Appeal Division, Smith J, No. 6160/1992, 30 October 1992 ('Third Hearing and Second Appeal')

General

B v. The Medical Superintendent of Macquarie Hospital [1987] 10 NSWLR 440.

Barefoot v. Estelle [1983] 103 S.Ct. 3383 (US).

Bolam v. Friern Hospital Management Committee [1957] I WLR 582 (UK).

Brief for the American Psychiatric Association as Amicus Curiae in Support of Leroy Hendricks, to the United States Supreme Court, Kansas v. Hendricks, 1997.

Brief of the Menninger Foundation, The American Alliance for Rights and Responsibilities, Justice for All, The New York Chapter of Parents of Murdered Children Protecting Our Children, People Against Violent Crime, Victims Outreach, Inc., and Texans for Equal Justice as Amici Curiae in Support of Petitions, the United States Supreme Court, Kansas v. Hendricks, 1997.

Brutus v. Cozens [1983] AC 854 (UK).

Chester v. R [1988] 165 CLR 611.

CN v. The Medical Superintendent of Rozelle Hospital (unreported, 4 March 1986).

DW v. JMW [1983] 1 NSWLR 61.

Dr Grigor and the Chief General Manager of the Department of Health v. Mental Health Review Board and DWP [1989] 3 VAR 258.

GNM v. ER [1983] 1 NSWLR 144.

GPG v. ACF [1983] 1 NSWLR 54.

JAH v. The Medical Superintendent of Rozelle Hospital (unreported, 4 March 1986).

Kable v. DPP for NSW [1995] 36 NSWLR 374.

Kable v. DPP for NSW [1996] 138 ALR 577.

Kansas v. Hendricks [1997] 117 S. Ct. 2972 138 L.Ed.2d 501.

Milirrpum v. Nabalco Pty. Ltd. [1971] 17 FLR 141.

Minister of Health v. Royal Midland County's Homes for Incurables: Leamington Spa's General Committee [1954] 1 All ER 1013.

Nixon v. GSA [1976] S.Ct. 2777 (US).

Polyukovich v. The Commonwealth of Australia and Another [1991] 172 CLR 501 F.C. 91/026.

R v. Darrington and McGauley [1980] VR 353.

R v. Darrington and McGauley [1980] 17 ACR 124.

R v. Gooch [1989] 43 ACR 382.

R v. Roadley [1990] 51 ACR 336.

RAP v. AEP [1982] 2 NSWLR 508.

Re PJ (1993) NZ 28/93.

Re RR (1993) NZ 37/93.

R v. Canons Park Mental Health Review Tribunal, Ex parte A [1994] CA 630 (UK).

R v. Chester [1988] 36 ACR 382.

Re AC (1994) NZ 52/94.

Re RT (1995) NZ 38/95.

Re RWL (1994) NZ 75/94.

Report of Investigation into the Death of Garry Ian Patrick David (known as Garry Webb), State Coroner's Office (Vic), Case No. 1849/93, 11 August 1993.

Rouse v. Cameron [1966] 373 F2d 451 (US).

Statement of Reasons in the Review of PT an Involuntary Patient at Mont Park Hospital, Mental Health Review Board Hearing No. 241287: Z25: 586814, 24 December 1987.

Statement of Reasons in the Appeal of AB an Involuntary Patient at Royal Park Hospital, Mental Health Review Board Hearing No. 250388: Z01: 524666, 25 March 1988.

Statement of Reasons in the Appeal of DWP a Security Patient at J Ward, Aradale Hospital, Mental Health Review Board No. 170289: X01: 524645, 10 May 1989.

Statement of Reasons in the Appeal of KMC an Involuntary Patient at Larundel Hospital, Mental Health Review Board Hearing No. 130989: Z26: 588371, 7 November 1989.

Statement of Reasons in the Review of RD an Involuntary Patient at St. Vincent's Hospital, Mental Health Review Board Hearing No. 190397 B45: 525404, 30 April 1997.

Tait v. The Queen [1963] VR 547.

US v. Lyons [1984] 731 F2d 243.

Veen v. R (No. 1) [1979] 143 CLR 458.

Veen v. R (No. 2) [1988] CLR 465 F.C. 88/011.

W v. L [1974] QB 712.

LEGISLATION

Act of Settlement 1701 (Eng).

Bail Act 1977 (Vic).

Bill of Rights 1688 (Eng).

Community Protection Act 1990 (Vic).

Community Protection (Violent Offenders) Bill 1991 (Vic).

Constitution Act 1975 (Vic).

Corrections Act 1986 (Vic).

Crime Control Act 1984 (US).

Crimes Act 1958 (Vic).

Crimes (Mental Impairment and Unfitness to be Tried) Act 1997 (Vic).

Criminal Lunatics Act 1800 (Eng).

Dangerous Lunatics Act 1843 (NSW).

Freedom of Information Act 1980 (Vic).

Guardianship and Administration Board Act 1986 (Vic).

Guardianship and Administration Act 1993 (SA).

Habeas Corpus Act 1856 (UK).

Kansas Sexually Violent Predator Act 1994 (US).

Intellectually Disabled Persons' Services Act 1986 (Vic).

Magna Carta 1215 (Eng).

Mental Health Act 1959 (Vic).

Mental Health Act 1959 (UK).

Mental Health Act 1983 (UK).

Mental Health Act 1986 (Vic).

Mental Health Act 1993 (SA).

Mental Health Bill No.1 1985 (Vic).

Mental Health (Compulsory Assessment and Treatment) Act 1992 (NZ).

Mental Hygiene Act 1958 (Vic).

Parliamentary Committee Act 1968 (Vic) .

Penalties and Sentences Act 1985 (Vic).

Poor Laws 1601 (Eng).

Sentencing Act 1991 (Vic).

Social Welfare Act 1979 (Vic).

War Crimes Amendment Act i1988 (Cth).

FURTHER READING

Appelbaum, P.S. (1984) 'Psychiatric Ethics in the Courtroom.' *Bulletin of the American Academy of Psychiatry and Law 12*, 3, 225–31.

Ashworth, A. and Shapland, J. (1980) 'Psychopaths in the Criminal Process.' *Criminal Law Review*, October, 628–40.

Ashworth, A. and Gostin, L. (1984) 'Mentally Disordered Offenders and the Sentencing Process.' *Criminal Law Review* April, 195–212.

Baker, E. (1993) 'Dangerousness, Rights and Criminal Justice.' *Modern Law Review 56*, 4, 528–47.

Barnes, B. (1988) *The Nature of Power.* Cambridge: Polity Press.

Bell, C. (1992) *Ritual Theory, Ritual Practice.* New York and Oxford: Oxford University Press.

Blackburn, R.R. (1988) 'On Moral Judgments and Personality Disorder: The Myth of the Psychopathic Personality Revisited.' *British Journal of Psychiatry 153*, 505–12.

Blair, R.J.R. (1995) 'Is the Psychopath Morally Insane?' *Personality and Individual Differences 19*, 5, 741–52.

Bland, L. (1984) 'The Case of the Yorkshire Ripper: Mad, Bad, Beast or Male?' In P. Scraton and P. Gordon (eds) *Causes for Concern: Questions of Law and Justice.* Harmondsworth: Penguin.

Bottoms, A.E. (1977) 'Reflections on the Renaissance of Dangerousness.' *Legal Service Bulletin 16*, 2, 70–96.

Burke, K. (1989) *On Symbols and Society.* Chicago: The University of Chicago Press.

Burkitt, L. (1993) 'Overcoming Metaphysics: Elias and Foucault on Power and Freedom.' *Philosophy of the Social Sciences 23*, 1, 50–72.

Butler, J. (1989) 'Foucault and the Paradox of Bodily Inscriptions.' *Journal of Philosophy 86*, 601–07.

Caputo, I. and Yount, M. (eds) (1993) *Foucault and the Critique of Institutions.* Pennsylvania: Pennsylvania State University Press.

Carlen, P. (1986) 'Psychiatry in Prisons: Promises, Practices and Politics.' In P.B. Miller and N. Rose (eds) *The Power of Psychiatry.* Cambridge: Polity Press.

Cohen, S. (1985) *Visions of Social Control: Crime, Punishment and Classification.* Cambridge: Polity Press.

Cook, D. (1993) *The Subject Finds a Voice: Foucault's Turn Towards Subjectivity.* New York: Peter Lang.

Dant, T. (1991) *Knowledge, Ideology and Discourse: A Sociological Perspective.* London and New York: Routledge.

De Certeau, M. (1986) *Heterologies: Discourse on the Other.* Minneapolis: University of Minnesota Press.

Dews, P. (1984) 'Power and Subjectivity in Foucault.' *New Left Review 144,* 72–95.

Donnelly, M. (1992) 'On Foucault's Uses of the Notion "Biopower".' In T.J. Armstrong (ed) *Michel Foucault Philosopher: Essays Translated from the French and German.* New York: Harvester Wheatsheaf.

Duff, A. and Garland, D. (eds) (1994) *A Reader on Punishment.* Oxford: Oxford University Press.

Elliott, C. (1992) 'Diagnosing Blame: Responsibility and the Psychopath.' *Journal of Medicine and Philosophy 17,* 199–214.

Fairall, P.A. and Johnston, P.W. (1987) 'Antisocial Personality Disorder (APD) and the Insanity Defence.' *Criminal Law Journal 11,* 78–95.

Featherstone, M., Hepworth, M. and Turner, B.S. (eds) (1991) *The Body, Social Process and Cultural Theory.* London: Sage.

Fennell, P. (1986) 'Law and Psychiatry: The Legal Construction of the Psychiatric System.' *Journal of Law and Society 13,* 1, 35–65.

Fennell, P. (1996) *Treatment Without Consent: Law, Psychiatry and the Treatment of Mentally Disordered People Since 1845.* London and New York: Routledge.

Foucault, M. (1973) *Madness and Civilization: A History of Insanity in the Age of Reason.* New York: Vintage/Random House.

Foucault, M. (1980) *Power/Knowledge: Selected Interviews and Other Writings 1972–1977.* (ed. C. Gordon). New York: Pantheon.

Foucault, M. (1988) 'Truth, Power and Self: An Interview.' In H. Guttman and P. Hutton (eds) *Technologies of the Self.* London: Tavistock Publications.

Frank, A. (1990) 'Bringing Bodies Back In: A Decade Review'. *Theory, Culture and Society 7,* 131–62.

Frank, M. (1992) 'On Foucault's Concept of Discourse.' In T.J. Armstrong (ed.) *Michel Foucault Philosopher: Essays Translated from the French and German.* New York: Harvester Wheatsheaf.

Fraser, N. (1989) *Unruly Practices.* Minneapolis: University of Minnesota Press.

Freidson, E. (1986) *Professional Powers: A Study in the Institutionalization of Formal Knowledge.* Chicago: University of Chicago Press.

Garland, D. (1986a) 'The Punitive Mentality: Its Socio-historical Development and Decline.' *Contemporary Crises 10,* 305–20.

Garland, D. (1986b) 'Foucault's *Discipline and Punish*: An Exposition and Critique.' *American Bar Foundation Research Journal 4,* 847–80.

Garland, D. (1990) *Punishment and Modern Society: A Study In Social Theory.* London: Clarendon Press.

Gerard, R. (1987) 'The Usefulness of the Medical Model to the Legal System.' *Rutgers Law Review 39,* 277–94.

Girard, R. (1977) *Violence and the Sacred* (trans. P. Gregory). Baltimore: Johns Hopkins University Press

Glaser, W. (1993–4) 'Is Personality Disorder a Mental Illness?: Garry David and the Lessons of History.' *International Journal of Mental Health 22*, 4, 61–70.

Gleb, G. (1991) 'Washington's Sexually Violent Predator Law: The Need to Bar Unreliable Psychiatric Predictions of Dangerousness from Civil Commitment Proceedings.' *University of California Law Review 39*, 213–50.

Good, B.J. (1994) *Medicine, Rationality and Experience: An Anthropological Perspective.* Cambridge: Cambridge University Press.

Goodrich, P. (1987) *Legal Discourse.* London: Macmillan.

Gostin, L. (1984) 'Psychiatric Detention Without Limit of Time: The Broadmoor Cases. In P. Scraton and P. Gordon (eds) *Causes for Concern: Questions of Law and Justice.* Harmondsworth: Penguin.

Grisso, R. and Appelbaum, P.S. (1992) 'Is it Unthinkable to Offer Predictions of Future Violence?' *Law and Human Behavior 16*, 421–33.

Grounds, A.T. (1999) 'Detention of "Psychopathic Disorder" Patients in Special Hospitals: Critical Issues.' In J. Peay (ed) *Criminal Justice and the Mentally Disordered.* Dartmouth: Ashgate.

Gusfield, J.R. and Michalowicz, J. (1984) 'Secular Symbolism: Studies of Ritual, Ceremony, and the Symbolic Order in Modern Life.' *Annual Review of Sociology 10*, 417–35.

Hacking, I. (1986) 'Making Up People.' In T.C. Heller, M. Sosna and D.C. Wellbery (eds) *Reconstructing Individualism: Autonomy, Individuality and the Self in Western Thought.* Stanford, CA: Stanford University Press.

Handsley, E. (1997) 'Do Hard Laws make Bad Cases?: The High Court's decision in *Kable v. DPP* (NSW).' *Federal Law Review 25*, 1, 171–79.

Hunter, K.M. (1991) *Doctors' Stories: The Narrative Structure of Medical Knowledge.* Princeton NJ: Princeton University Press.

Ignatieff, M. (1978) *A Just Measure of Pain: The Penitentiary in the Industrial Revolution 1750–1850.* London: Macmillan.

Ignatieff, M. (1981) 'State, Civil Society and Total Institutions.' In M. Tonry and N. Morris (eds) *Crime and Justice: An Annual Review of Research,* vol. 3. Chicago: University of Chicago Press.

Ingleby, D. (1985) 'Professionals as Socialisers: The "Psy Complex".' In S. Spitzer and A. Scull (eds) *Research in Law, Deviance and Social Control: A Research Annual* Vol. 7. London: JAI Press.

Ivison, D. (1998) 'The Disciplinary Moment: Foucault, Law and the Reinscription of Rights.' In J. Moss (ed.) *The Later Foucault: Politics and Philosophy.* London: Sage.

Jones, C. and Porter, R. (eds) (1994) *Reassessing Foucault: Power, Medicine and the Body.* London and New York: Routledge.

Kennedy, R. (1996) 'The Dangerous Individual and the Social Body.' In P. Cheah, D. Fraser and J. Grbich (eds) *Thinking Through the Body of the Law.* St. Leonards, NSW: Allen and Unwin.

Krips, H. (1990) 'Power and Resistance.' *Philisophy and Social Science 20*, 170–82.

Moore, M. (1984) *Law and Psychiatry: Rethinking the Relationship.* Cambridge: Cambridge University Press.

Palmer, J. and Pearce, F. (1983) 'Legal Discourse and State Power: Foucault and the Juridical Relation.' *International Journal of the Sociology of Law 11*, 361–83.

Patton, P. (1998) 'Foucault's Subject of Power.' In J. Moss (ed) *The Later Foucault: Politics and Philosophy.* London: Sage.

Peay, J. (1982) ' "Dangerous" – Ascription or Description?' In P. Feldman (ed) *Developments in the Study of Criminal Behaviour, Vol. 2: Violence.* New York: John Wiley.

Petrunik, M. (1966) 'Defective, Delinquent and Habitual Criminal Offender Statutes: Required Constitutional Safeguards.' *Rutgers Law Review 20*, 756–88.

Phelan, P. (1993) *The Politics of Performance.* New York: Routledge and Kegan Paul.

Potter, J. (1996) *Representing Reality: Discourse, Rhetoric and Social Construction.* London: Sage.

Pratt, J. (1997) *Governing the Dangerous: Dangerousness, Law and Social Change.* Sydney: Federation Press.

Prins, H. (1981) 'Dangerous People or Dangerous Situations?: Some Implications for Assessment and Management.' *Medicine, Science and Law 21* 125–33.

Prins, H. (1990) 'Mental Abnormality and Criminality – An Uncertain Relationship.' *Medicine, Science and Law 30*, 2–24.

Prins, H. (1995) 'What Price the Concept of Psychopathic Disorder?' *Medicine, Science and Law 35*, 4, 307–15.

Racevskis, K. (1980) 'The Discourse of Michel Foucault: The Case of an Absent and Forgettable Subject.' *Humanities in Society 3*, 44–54.

Richardson, G. (1993) *Law, Process and Custody: Prisoners and Patients.* London: Weidenfeld and Nicolson.

Rose, N. (1985) 'Calculable Minds and Manageable Individuals.' *History of the Human Sciences 9*, 2, 1–23.

Rose, N. (1998) 'Governing Risky Individuals: The Role of Psychiatry in New Regimes of Control.' *Psychiatry, Psychology and Law 5*, 2, 177–95.

Rosenman, S. (1994) 'Mental Health Law: An Idea whose Time has Passed.' *Australian and New Zealand Journal of Psychiatry 28*, 4, 560–565.

Schattenburg, P. (1981) 'Social Control Functions of Mass Media Depictions of Crime.' *Sociological Inquiry 51*, 71–77.

Shah, S.A. (1978) 'Dangerousness: A Paradigm for Exploring Some Issues in Law and Psychology.' *American Psychologist*, March, 224–38.

Shah, S.A. (1989) 'Mental Disorder and the Criminal Justice System: Some Overarching Issues.' *International Journal of Law and Psychiatry 12*, 3.

Simon, R.J. (1977) 'Civil Commitment, Burden of Proof and Dangerous Acts: A Comparison of the Perspective of Judges and Psychiatrists.' *Journal of Psychiatry and Law 5*, 4, 571–94.

Steadman, J.J. (1973) 'Some Evidence on the Inadequacy of the Concept and Determination of Dangerousness in Law and Psychiatry.' *Journal of Psychiatry and Law 1*, 4, 409–26.

Steedman, P.H. (1992) 'On the Relations Between Seeing, Interpreting and Knowing.' In E. Steier (ed) *Research and Reflexivity.* London: Sage.

Steinert, H. (1980) 'The development of "discipline" according to Michel Foucault: Discourse Analysis vs. Social History'. *Crime and Social Justice 20*, 83–98.

Still, A. and Velody, I. (eds) (1992) *Rewriting the History of Madness: Studies in Foucault's 'Histoire de la folie'.* London: Routledge and Kegan Paul.

Swanson, M., Bland, R. and Newman, R. (1994) 'Antisocial Personality Disorders.' *Acta Psychiatrica Scandinavica 89* (supplement 276), 63–70.

Tomasic, R. (1991) 'Preventive Detention and the High Court.' *Australian Law Journal 55*, 5, 259–66.

Treacher, A. and Baruch, G. (1981) 'Towards a Critical History of the Psychiatric Profession.' In D. Ingleby (ed) *Critical Psychiatry.* Harmondsworth: Penguin.

Turkel, G. (1990) 'Michel Foucault: Law, Power and Knowledge.' *Journal of Law and Society 17*, 2, 170–93.

Tyrer, P. (1988) 'What's Wrong with DSM-III Personality Disorders?' *Journal of Personality Disorders 2*, 4, 281–91.

Turner, B.S. (1987) *Medical Power and Social Knowledge.* London: Sage.

Turner, B.S. (1996) *The Body and Society: Explorations in Social Theory,* (2nd edn). London: Sage.

Von Hirsch, A. (1992) 'Incapacitation.' In A. von Hirsch and A. Ashworth (eds) *Principled Sentencing.* Edinburgh: Edinburgh University Press.

Walker, N. (1983) 'Predicting People.' In J.W. Hinton (ed.) *Dangerousness: Problems of Assessment and Prediction.* London: Allen and Unwin.

Walker, N. (1994) 'Dangerousness and Mental Disorder.' In A.P. Griffiths (ed.) *Philosophy, Psychology and Psychiatry.* Cambridge: Press Syndicate.

Walker, N. (1996) *Dangerous People.* London: Blackstone Press Ltd.

Webb-Pullman, J. (1994) 'Violence, Dangerousness and Mental Illness.' *Law Institute Journal 68*, 12, 1166–68.

Webster, C., Dickens, B. and Addario, S. (1985) *Constructing Dangerousness: Scientific, Legal and Policy Implications.* Toronto: Centre of Criminology, University of Toronto.

Weingart, P. (1977) 'The Scientific Power Elite – A Chimera: The De-Institutionalization and Politicization of Science.' In E. Mendelsohn, P. Weingart and R. Whitley (eds) *The Social Production of Scientific Knowledge.* Dordrecht and Boston: D. Reidel.

Wexler, D.B. (1992) 'Putting Mental Health into Mental Health Law: Therapeutic Jurisprudence.' *Law and Human Behavior 16*, 1, 27–38.

Wexler, D.B. (1993) 'Justice, Mental Health, and Therapeutic Jurisprudence.' *Cleveland State Law Review 40*, 517–26.

Wood, D. (1988) 'Dangerous Offenders and the Morality of Protective Sentencing.' *Criminal Law Review 77*, 424–33.

Wood, D. (1989) 'Dangerous Offenders and Civil Detention.' *Criminal Law Journal 13*, 5, 324–29.

Young, A. (1978) 'Mode of Production of Medical Knowledge.' *Medical Anthropology 2*, 1, 97–122.

Young, A. (1981) 'The Creation of Medical Knowledge: Some Problems of Interpretation.' *Social Science and Medicine, Part B Medical Anthropology 15*, 3, 379–86.

Zalewski, R. (1992) 'Preventive Detention: Justified or Justice Denied?' *Law Institute Journal* November, 1008–011.

Subject Index

AB test 125, 142
Adams, Michael 113, 134, 141, 143, 157, 178–80, 183, 187, 189, 192–4, 197, 200, 223
Administrative Appeals Tribunal 90, 118, 124, 143, 152, 155–8
Adult Parole Board of Victoria 21, 41, 78, 96, 149, 168, 182–3, 185, 187
asylums, history of 20–1, 112
attainder, bills of *see* legal system
Attorney-General and Department 59, 81, 86–7, 94–5, 100, 102, 105, 113, 116, 119, 122, 143–7, 153–8, 241, 246, 250–1, 255
    see also Kennan, Hon. Jim

bail 71, 94–5, 98, 142, 157–8, 161, 180, 241
Barclay, Dr William 148
Bartholomew, Dr. Allen 72–3, 176, 184, 186
Berkeley, Hartog 80–1, 94–5, 106, 113–5, 119, 121, 138, 146, 153, 155
biological factors 15, 108–9
Blueprint for Urban Warfare 45–6, 214, 236–7
body, the *see* theoretical perspectives
Bolam test 90
Brutus v Cozens (UK) case 126

Chief Psychiatrist 79, 81, 84, 95, 105, 129, 133, 158, 185, 258
civil commitment see Mental Health Act 1986 (Vic)
Community Protection Act 1990 (Vic) 14, 22. 35–7, 41, 97, 105–6. 154, 156–164, 174–203, 216, 223, 228, 240–3, 246, 249–53, 258
Community Protection Bill 1990 (Vic) 95–106
    see also dangerousness, preventive detention
    see also dangerousness, preventive detention
Community Protection (Violent Offenders) Bill 1991 (Vic) 167–8, 243
confidentiality 101, 136, 186–8, 242
Corrections Act 1986 (Vic) 28, 31, 80–3, 97, 157, 193–4, 199, 247
Crabb, Hon. Stephen 86–8, 227

Crime Control Act 1984 (US) 110
Crimes Act 1958 (Vic) 86–7, 98, 153
Crimes Compensation Tribunal (Vic) 68
criminal responsibility 108, 124
Crockett, Justice William 155, 162, 178, 192

Dangerous Lunatics Act 1843 (NSW) 21
dangerousness
    clinical 18, 23–4, 177
    community fears 15–17, 74, 101
    definition 17–18
    folk beliefs 15, 17, 74, 218, 223, 240, 246
    legal response 16, 20, 179–80, 249–62
    medical response 17–8, 73
    persons 13–7, 37, 73
    prediction 22, 96, 169, 175, 177, 241. 251, 253
    proof and rebuttal 96, 98, 163, 174, 177, 183, 206, 241
    risk assessment 18
    see also Community Protection Act 1990, preventive detention, violence

David, Garry 13, 41–4
    breaches of parole 42–3
    certification 49–52, 55, 57, 63–4, 67, 71, 74, 78–80, 88–93, 129–9
    costs 47, 120, 156–7
    counselling 92
    court appearances 43, 158
    custodial levels 157
    dangerousness, opinions of 13–4, 51, 176–7
    death 8, 32. 202, 209, 216, 229, 245, 248–9, 253, 259
    disruptive behaviour 43–9, 58, 64–5, 68, 126, 162, 189–92, 195–6
    employment 43
    family members 40–2, 53
    files *see* records and record-keeping
    institutional movements 42, 45, 54–6, 64, 66–7, 73, 79, 195
    liberty, views about 13, 53, 76, 78–9, 87, 118, 129, 132, 182, 189, 212, 217, 219, 243, 250, 265
    offence history 42–3
    poems 204, 209–14
    remand in custody 86, 181–2
    self-mutilation 13, 37, 47–9, 53, 58, 67
    self-perception 36, 203, 206, 216, 236
    sentence 42–4, 78, 82, 155, 183

Author Index